ARCO

POSTAL CLERK AND CARRIER

E.P. Steinberg

Maywood Public Library
121 South 5th Avenue
Maywood IL 60153
Macmillan • USA

Nineteenth Edition

Macmillan General Reference
A Prentice Hall Macmillan Company
15 Columbus Circle
New York, NY 10023

An Arco Book
MACMILLAN is a registered trademark of Macmillan, Inc.
ARCO is a registered trademark of Prentice-Hall, Inc.

Library of Congress Cataloging-in-Publication Data

Steinberg, Eve P.
    Postal clerk and carrier / E.P. Steinberg.—19th ed.
    p.   cm.
    Rev. ed. of: Post office clerk-carrier. 18th ed. © 1994.
    At head of title: Arco
    "An Arco book"—T.p. verso.
    ISBN 0–02–860023–1
    1. Postal service—United States—Employees.   2. Postal service—
United States—Letter carriers.   3. Postal service—United States—
Examinations, questions, etc.   I. Steinberg, Eve P.   Post office
clerk-carrier.   II. Arco Publishing.   III. Title.
HE6499.S75   1995
383'.145'076—dc20   94—27912
                                        CIP

Manufactured in the United States of America

10 9 8 7 6 5 4 3 2 1

Introduction—How to Use This Book   1
Working for the Post Office   3

How To Apply   11

Part I — Preliminary Exam
Before You Take the Preliminary Exam   23
Preliminary Model Exam   29

Part II — Test Strategies
How to Answer Address Checking Questions   63
How to Answer Memory for Addresses Questions   73

How to Answer Number Series Questions 90

How to Answer Following Oral Instructions Questions 98

Part III — Model Exams

Second Model Exam 119

Third Model Exam 155

Fourth Model Exam 191

Fifth Model Exam 227

Final Model Exam 263

Progress Charts 295

Introduction— How to Use This Book

The Postal Service examination for Carriers, Clerks, Mail Handlers, and Processors may be the most important exam you ever take. It can be your ticket to a rewarding career that offers good pay, excellent working conditions, and a secure future. The very features that make a postal career appealing to you, though, make it appealing to many others too, and often hundreds of applicants compete for a single job opening. The only way to get the job you seek is to earn the highest possible score on the postal exam. That's where this book can help. If you follow its advice and take advantage of the training and practice it offers, you will be well prepared to earn high scores on the postal exam and a spot near the top of the list of eligibles for jobs with the postal service.

Ideally, you should start your preparation two or three months before the exam. That gives you plenty of time to devise and perfect a method of learning the memory scheme that works best for you and to complete all of the model exams. If you begin early enough, you will be able to leave a week between model exams so that your memory of one sorting scheme does not interfere with your memorizing of another scheme. No matter how much time you have, start *now*. Work your way through the entire book, and give it all the time and attention you possibly can.

Read the first two chapters. The first describes the jobs filled through this exam and presents the many advantages of working for the postal service. It gives you the encouragement you need to do your very best. The second tells you how to apply for a job with the postal service and gives you an overview of the exam you will have to take.

Next, take the preliminary exam to discover where you stand at this moment. Carefully read through the short introduction, "Before You Take the Preliminary Exam," and follow the procedure spelled out there. Then tear out the answer sheet and get to work. Each model exam in this book, including the preliminary exam, provides a page for calculating your scores on that exam and for plotting your scores on a self-evaluation chart. Do not be discouraged by low scores on the preliminary exam. You will have plenty of opportunities to improve your scores with the instruction and practice that follow. At the back of the book, you will find a set of progress charts. As their name implies, these charts are for charting your own progress as you proceed from the preliminary exam, learn from the instructional chapters, and gain valuable practice working the model exams. You should see improvement in your scores as you master techniques for answering the postal exam questions.

Be sure you understand the techniques taught by the instructional chapters before you take the model exams. It may be worthwhile to return to these chapters between exams and just before the actual exam to refresh yourself on ways to improve your scores.

Leaving ample time between them, take the remaining model exams just the way you took the preliminary exam. Time yourself accurately and score yourself honestly. Analyze your errors so that you can try to avoid making the same mistakes in the future. Learn from the explanations, especially those in the number series part. Chart your progress as you move through the model exams. Gain every bit of practice possible by completing all questions you were unable to answer within time limits.

By the time you have completed this book, you should be well prepared for your postal exam. These few final suggestions should help you do your best on the big day:

- Get a good night's sleep.
- Get up in time to eat breakfast and do whatever you have to do to ensure that you are fully alert.
- Dress comfortably.
- Allow yourself plenty of time to get to the exam.

1

- Remember to bring your admission card, identification that has your picture or your signature, your completed sample answer sheet, and two sharpened pencils with good erasers.
- Also, be sure to wear a watch. You will need it when answering number series questions; there may not be a clock in the testing room.
- Follow the directions of the test administrator. If you don't understand what you are to do, *ask questions*.
- Take a deep breath, relax, and resolve to do your best. Your preparation and practice should pay off in high scores on the exam.

Working for the Post Office

The United States Postal Service is an independent agency of the Federal Government. As such, employees of the Postal Service are federal employees who enjoy the benefits offered by the government. These benefits include an automatic raise at least once a year, regular cost-of-living adjustments, liberal paid vacation and sick leave, life insurance, hospitalization, and the opportunity to join a credit union. At the same time, the operation of the Postal Service is businesslike and independent of politics. A postal worker's job is secure even though presidential administrations may change. An examination system is used to fill vacancies. The examination system provides opportunities for those who are able and motivated to enter the Postal Service and to move within it.

Since postal employment is so popular, entry is very competitive. In most areas a postal exam is administered only once every three years. The resulting list is used to fill vacancies as they occur in the next three years. An individual who has been employed by the Postal Service for at least a year may ask to take the exam for any position and, if properly qualified, may fill a vacancy ahead of a person whose name is on the regular list. (The supervisor may or may not grant the request to take a special exam to fill a vacancy, but most supervisors readily grant such permission to employees with good performance records who have served an adequate period in their current positions.) It is even possible to change careers within the Postal Service. A custodian, for instance, might take a city carrier exam; a stenographer might choose to become a letter sorting machine operator; or a mail handler might take an exam to enter personnel work. If the exam for the precise position that you want will not be administered for some time, it might be worthwhile to take the exam for another position in the hopes of entering the Postal Service and then moving from within.

Salaries, hours, and some other working conditions as well are subject to frequent change. The postal workers have a very effective union that bargains for them and gains increasingly better conditions. At the time of your employment, you should make your own inquiry as to salary, hours, and other conditions as they apply to you. Job descriptions and requirements are less subject to change. In the next few pages we quote job descriptions as provided by the government.

Postal Clerk

Duties of the Job

People are most familiar with the window clerk who sits behind the counter in post office lobbies selling stamps or accepting parcel post. However, the majority of postal clerks are distribution clerks who sort incoming and outgoing mail in workrooms. Only in a small post office does a clerk do both kinds of work.

When mail arrives at the post office it is dumped on long tables where distribution clerks and mail handlers separate it into groups of letters, parcel post, and magazines and newspapers. Clerks feed letters into stamp-canceling machines and cancel the rest by hand. The mail is then taken to other sections of the post office to be sorted by destination. Clerks first separate the mail into primary destination categories: mail for the local area, for each nearby state, for groups of distant states, and for some of the largest cities.

This primary distribution is followed by one or more secondary distributions. For example, local mail is combined with mail coming in from other cities and is sorted according to street and number. In post offices with electronic mail-sorting machines, clerks simply push a button, corresponding to the letter's destination, and the letter drops into the proper slot.

The clerks at post office windows provide a variety of services in addition to selling stamps and money orders. They weigh packages to determine postage and check to see if their size, shape, and condition are satisfactory for mailing. Clerks also register and insure mail and answer questions about postage rates, mailing restrictions, and other postal matters. Occasionally they may help a customer file a claim for a damaged package. In large post offices a window clerk may provide only one or two of these services and be called a registry, stamp, or money order clerk.

Working Conditions

Working conditions of clerks differ according to the specific work assignments and the amount and kind of labor-saving machinery in the post office. In small post offices clerks must carry heavy mail sacks from one part of the building to another and sort the mail by hand. In large post offices, chutes and conveyors move the mail, and much of the sorting is done by machine. In either case, clerks are on their feet most of the time, reaching for sacks of mail, placing packages and bundles into sacks while sorting, and walking around the workroom.

Distribution clerks may become bored with the routine of sorting mail unless they enjoy trying to improve their speed and accuracy. They also may have to work at night, because most large post offices process mail around the clock.

A window clerk, on the other hand, has a greater variety of duties, has frequent contact with the public, generally has a less strenuous job, and never has to work a night shift.

New clerks are trained on the job. Most clerks begin with simple tasks to learn regional groupings of states, cities, and ZIP codes. To help clerks learn these groups, many post offices offer classroom instruction. A good memory, good coordination, and the ability to read rapidly and accurately are important.

Distribution clerks work closely with other clerks, frequently under the tension and strain of meeting mailing deadlines. Window clerks must be tactful when dealing with the public, especially when answering questions or receiving complaints.

City Carrier ✓

Duties of the Job

Most city carriers travel planned routes delivering and collecting mail. Carriers start work at the post office early in the morning, where they spend a few hours arranging their mail for delivery, readdressing letters to be forwarded, and taking care of other details.

A carrier typically covers the route on foot, toting a heavy load of mail in a satchel or pushing it in a cart. In outlying suburban areas where houses are far apart, a car or small truck is sometimes needed to deliver mail. Residential carriers cover their routes only once a day, but carriers assigned a business district may make two trips or more. Deliveries are made house to house except in large buildings, such as apartment houses, that have all the mailboxes on the first floor.

In addition to making deliveries, carriers collect c.o.d. fees and obtain signed receipts for registered and sometimes for insured mail. If a customer is not home, the carrier leaves a notice that tells where special mail is being held. Carriers also pick up letters to be mailed.

After completing their routes, carriers return to the post office with mail gathered from street collection boxes and homes. They may separate letters and parcels so that stamps can be canceled easily, and they turn in the receipts and money collected during the day.

Many carriers have more specialized duties than those just described. Some deliver only parcel post. Others collect mail from street boxes and office mail chutes.

Working Conditions

Most carriers begin work early in the morning, in some cases as early as 6 A.M., if they have routes in a business district. Carriers spend most of their time outdoors in all kinds of weather, walking from house to house with their heavy mailbags. Even those who drive must walk when making deliveries and must lift heavy sacks of parcel post when loading their vehicles.

The job, however, has its advantages. Carriers who begin work early in the morning are through by early afternoon. They are also free to work at their own pace as long as they cover their routes within a certain period of time. Moreover, full-time postal employees have more job security than workers in most other industries.

Applicants must have a driver's license and pass a road test if the job involves driving. They also must pass a physical examination and may be asked to show that they can lift and handle mail sacks weighing up to 70 pounds. Applicants who have had health conditions that might interfere with work must have a special review to determine their eligibility.

Distribution Clerk, Machine (Letter-Sorting Machine Operator)

Duties of the Job

Distribution clerks work indoors. Often clerks must handle sacks of mail weighing as much as 70 pounds. They sort mail and distribute it by using a complicated scheme that must be memorized. Machine distribution clerks must learn computer codes for the automatic routing of mail. Clerks may be on their feet all day. They also have to stretch, reach, and throw mail. The work of the distribution clerk is more routine than that of other postal clerks; however, the starting salary is higher. Distribution clerks begin at postal pay level 6 while other clerks and carriers begin at level 5. Increasing automation within the postal service has made the job of the distribution clerk quite secure.

Although the amount of mail post offices handle is expected to grow as both the population and the number of businesses grow, modernization of post offices and installation of new equipment will increase the amount of mail each clerk can handle. For example, machines that semiautomatically mark destination codes on envelopes are now being tested. These codes can be read by computer-controlled letter-sorting machines, which automatically drop each letter into the proper slot for its destination. With this system, clerks read addresses only once, at the time they are coded, instead of several times, as they now do. Eventually this equipment will be installed in all large post offices.

Applicants must be physically able to perform the duties described. Any physical condition that causes the applicant to be a hazard to him/herself or to others will be a disqualification for appointment.

The distant vision for clerk positions must test at least 20/30 (Snellen) in one eye (glasses are permitted). Some distribution clerk positions may be filled by the hearing impaired.

A physical examination is required before appointment.

Flat Sorting Machine Operator

Duties of the Job

The work of the flat sorting machine operator is very similar to that of the letter sorting machine operator except that the flat sorting machine operator works with large, bulky packages. Greater physical strength and stamina are required in this position. The postal pay level at entry is level 6; with ever-increasing automation and mechanization of post offices, job security is virtually assured.

Mail Handler

Duties of the Job

The mail handler loads, unloads, and moves bulk mail, and performs duties incidental to the movement and processing of mail. Duties may include separation of mail sacks, facing letter mail, canceling stamps on parcel post; operating canceling machines, addressographs, and mimeographs; operating a fork-lift truck; rewrapping parcels, etc.

Strength and Stamina Test

A physical examination is required before appointment. Persons who have had an arm, leg, or foot amputated should not apply.

When eligibles are within reach for appointment, they are required to pass a test of strength and stamina. In this test they are required to lift, shoulder, and carry two 70-pound sacks 15 feet—one at a time—and load them on a hand truck. They are required to push the truck to an area containing some 40-, 50-, and 60-pound sacks. They are required to load the sacks onto the truck. They next have to unload the truck and return the truck to its original location. Eligibles are notified when and where to report for the test of strength and stamina.

Persons with certain physical conditions are not permitted to take the test of strength and stamina without prior approval of a physician. These physical conditions include hernia or rupture, back trouble, heart trouble, pregnancy, or any other condition that makes it dangerous to the eligible to lift and carry 70-pound weights. Persons with these physical conditions are given special instructions at the time they are notified to report for the strength and stamina test.

An eligible being considered for an appointment who fails to qualify on the strength and stamina test is not tested again in the same group of hires. If the eligible fails the test a second time, his or her eligibility for the position of mail handler is canceled.

Mail Processor

Duties of the Job

A mail processor performs such tasks as:

1. Operating mail-processing equipment, including bar code sorters and optical bar code readers;
2. Acting as minor trouble-shooter for the equipment;
3. Collating and bundling processed mail and transferring it from one work area to another;
4. Hand-processing mail that cannot be handled by the machines;
5. Loading mail into bins and onto trucks;
6. Other related tasks.

Physical requirements for mail processors are not as stringent as those for mail handlers because the work is not as strenuous. Since the demands of the work are less, mail processors enter at postal pay level 3 rather than at the level 4 of mail handlers.

Mark-up Clerk, Automated

Duties of the Job

The mark-up clerk, automated, operates an electro-mechanical machine to process mail that is classified as "undeliverable as addressed." In doing this, the mark-up clerk operates the keyboard of a computer terminal to enter and extract data to several databases including change of address, mailer's database, and address-correction file. The mark-up clerk must select the correct program and operating mode for each application, must affix labels to mail either manually or with mechanical devices, and must prepare forms for address-correction services. Other duties may include distribution of processed markups to appropriate separations for further handling, operation of a photocopy machine, and other job-related tasks in support of primary duties.

Qualification Requirements

An applicant for a mark-up clerk position must have had either six months of clerical or office-machine-operating experience or have completed high school or have had a full academic year (36 weeks) of business school. The record of experience and training must show ability to use reference materials and manuals; ability to perform effectively under pressure; ability to operate any office equipment appropriate to the position; ability to work with others; and ability to read, understand, and apply certain regulations and procedures commonly used in processing mail undeliverable as addressed.

For appointment, a mark-up clerk must be 18 years old, or 16 years old if a high school graduate. An applicant who will reach his or her eighteenth birthday within two years from the date of the exam may participate. A mark-up clerk must be able to read, without strain, printed material the size of typewritten characters and must have 20/40 (Snellen) vision in one eye. Glasses are permitted. In addition, the applicant must pass a computer administered alpha-numeric typing test. Candidates with high scores on the competitive exam and with the requisite experience are called to the alpha-numeric typing test individually as openings occur and hiring is likely. The exam is administered on a personal computer with its numeric keyboard disabled so that the candidate must use only the main keyboard. The postal service does not distribute sample questions for this exam, Exam 715, but the instructions at the test site are very clear, and ample time is allowed for preparation. The alpha-numeric typing test is not a competitive test. The candidate needs only to pass to qualify.

Rural Carrier

Duties of the Job

The work of the rural carrier combines the work of the window clerk and the letter carrier but also has special characteristics of its own. The rural carrier's day begins with sorting and loading the mail for delivery on his or her own route. Then comes a day's drive, which may be over unpaved roads and rough terrain. The rural carrier does most deliveries and pickups of outgoing mail from the car. Occasionally, however, bulky packages must be delivered directly to the homeowner's door. Since rural postal patrons may be far from the nearest post office, the rural carrier sells stamps, weighs and charges for packages to be mailed, and performs most other services performed by window clerks in post offices. At the end of the day, the rural carrier returns to the post office with outgoing mail and money collected in various transactions. The rural carrier must be able to account for the stamps, postcards, and other supplies with which he or she left in the morning and must "balance the books" each day.

A rural carrier enjoys a great deal of independence. No supervisor looks over his or her shoulder. On the other hand, there is no supervisor to turn to for advice on how to handle a new situation that may come up.

Since the rural carrier's job requires driving, the minimum age for a rural carrier is 18. The rural carrier must have a valid driver's license, good eyesight, and the ability to hear ordinary conversation (glasses and hearing aid are permitted). In addition, the rural carrier must demonstrate physical stamina and ability to withstand the rigors of the job.

Where the Jobs Are

The Postal Service operates more than 41,000 installations. Most are post offices, but some serve special purposes such as handling payroll records or supplying equipment.

Although every community receives mail service, employment is concentrated in large metropolitan areas. Post offices in cities such as New York, Chicago, and Los Angeles employ a great number of workers because they not only process huge amounts of mail for their own populations but they also serve as mail processing points for the smaller communities that surround them. These large city post offices have sophisticated machines for sorting the mail. In these post offices, distribution clerks who have qualified as machine operators quickly scan addresses and send letters on their way automatically by pushing the proper button. These clerks must be able to read addresses quickly and accurately, must be able to memorize codes and sorting schemes, and must demonstrate machine aptitude by their performance on the Number Series part of the exam.

Training, Other Qualifications, and Advancement

An applicant for a Postal Service job must pass an examination and meet minimum age requirements. Generally, the minimum age is 18 years, but a high school graduate may begin work at 16 years if the job is not hazardous and does not require use of a motor vehicle. Many Postal Service jobs do not require formal education or special training. Applicants for these jobs are hired on the basis of their examination scores.

Applicants should apply at the post office where they wish to work and take the entrance examination for the job they want. Examinations for most jobs include a written test. A physical examination, drug test, and psychological interview are required as well. Applicants for jobs that require strength and stamina are sometimes given a special test. For example, mail handlers must be able to lift mail sacks weighing up to 70 pounds. The names of applicants who pass the examinations are placed on a list in the order of their scores. Separate eligibility lists are maintained for each post office. Five extra points are added to the score of an honorably discharged veteran and 10 extra points to the score of a veteran wounded in combat or disabled. Disabled veterans who have a compensable, service-connected disability of 10 percent or more are placed at the top of the eligibility list. When a job opens, the appointing officer chooses one of the top three applicants. Others are left on the list so that they can be considered for future openings.

New employees are trained either on the job by supervisors and other experienced employees or in local training centers. Training ranges from a few days to several months, depending on the job. For example, mail handlers and mechanics' helpers can learn their jobs in a relatively short time. Postal inspectors, on the other hand, need months of training.

Advancement opportunities are available for most postal workers because there is a managment commitment to provide career development. Also, employees can get preferred assignments, such as the day shift or a more desirable delivery route, as their seniority increases. When an opening occurs, employees may submit written requests, called "bids," for assignment to the vacancy. The bidder who meets the qualifications and has the most seniority gets the job.

In addition, postal workers can advance to better paying positions by learning new skills. Training programs are available for low-skilled workers who wish to become technicians or mechanics.

Applicants for supervisory jobs must pass an examination. Additional requirements for promotion may include training or education, a satisfactory work record, and appropriate personal characteristics such as leadership ability. If the leading candidates are equally qualified, length of service also is considered.

Although opportunities for promotion to supervisory positions in smaller post offices are limited, workers may apply for vacancies in a larger post office and thus increase their chances.

Earnings and Working Conditions

Postal Service employees are paid under several separate pay schedules depending upon the duties of the job and the knowledge, experience, or skill required. For example, there are separate schedules for production workers such as clerks and mail handlers, for rural carriers, for postal managers, and for postal executives. In all pay schedules, except that of executives, employees receive periodic "step" increases up to a specified maximum if their job performance is satisfactory.

The conditions that follow are subject to collective bargaining and may well be different by the time you are employed by the Postal Service.

Full-time employees work an eight-hour day, five days a week. Both full-time and part-time employees who work more than eight hours a day or 40 hours a week receive overtime pay of one and one-half times their hourly rates. In addition, pay is higher for those on the night shift.

Postal employees earn 13 days of annual leave (vacation) during each of their first three years of service, including prior Federal civilian and military service; 20 days each year for 3 to 15 years of service; and 26 days after 15 years. In addition, they earn 13 days of paid sick leave a year regardless of length of service.

Other benefits include retirement and survivorship annuities, free group life insurance, and optional participation in health insurance programs supported in part by the Postal Service.

Most post office buildings are clean and well-lighted, but some of the older ones are not. The Postal Service is in the process of replacing and remodeling its outmoded buildings, and conditions are expected to improve.

Most postal workers are members of unions and are covered by a national agreement between the Postal Service and the unions.

For a detailed description of many more Postal Service jobs, how to qualify for them, sample questions, and model exams for practice, purchase Arco's *Postal Exams Handbook*.

How to Apply

Ask for an application card at your local post office. The card is bright yellow and in two sections joined at a perforation. Do NOT separate the two sections. The section on the left is called the Application Card, that on the right the Admission Card. Instructions for filling out both sections are printed on the back of the card. Follow these directions precisely, and carefully fill out both sections of the card. Hand in or mail the completed application as instructed.

The application and admission card look like this:

(Front)   **(Back)**

APPLICATION CARD		Instructions to Applicants

APPLICATION CARD

Name (Last, First, Middle Initials)

Address (House/Apt. No. & Street)

City, State, ZIP Code

Birthdate (Month, Date, Year) | **Do Not Write in This Space**

Telephone Number | Today's Date

Title of Examination

Post Office Applied for

PS Form 2479-A, April 1983

Instructions to Applicants

Furnish all the information requested on these cards. The attached card will be returned to you with sample questions and necessary instructions, including the time and place of the written test.

TYPEWRITE OR PRINT IN INK. DO NOT SEPARATE THESE CARDS. FOLD ONLY AT PERFORATION.

Mail or Take This Form—Both Parts—to The Postmaster the Post Office Where You Wish to Be Employed.

PS Form 2479-A, April 1983 (Reverse)

P U.S. G.P.O. 1983-655-793

(We have had to separate the sections to fit the book page. You must not separate the sections.)

(Front)

ADMISSION CARD

Title of Examination | Social Security No. | Do Not Write In Thi s Space

Date of Birth | Today's Date | Post Office Applied For

If you have performed active duty in the Armed Forces of the United States and were separated under honorable conditions indicate periods of service

From (Mo., Day, Yr.)_____to (Mo., Day, Yr.)_____
DO YOU CLAIM VETERAN PREFERENCE?   NO   YES   IF YES, BASED ON
(1) Active duty in the Armed Forces of the U.S. during World War I or the period December 7, 1941, through July 1, 1955 (2) More than 180 consecutive days of active duty (other than for training) in the Armed Forces of the U.S. any part of which occurred between Jan. 31, 1955 and Oct. 14, 1976, or (3) Award of a campaign badge or service medal Your status as (1) a disabled veteran or a veteran who was awarded the purple heart for wounds or injuries received in action, (2) a veteran's widow who has not remarried, (3) the wife of an ex serviceman who has a service connected disability which disqualifies him for civil service appointment, or (4) the widowed, divorced or separated mother of an ex-service son or daughter who died in action or who is totally and permanently disabled

Print or Type Your Name and Address | Name (First, Middle, Last)

Address (House, Apt. No. & Street)

City, State, ZIP Code (ZIP Code must be included)

This card will be returned to you. Bring it, along with personal identification bearing your picture or description, with you when you report for the test. ID's will be checked, and a fingerprint or signature specimen may be required.

(Back)

Final Eligibility in This Examination is Subject to Suitability Determination

The collection of information on this form is authorized by 39 U.S.C. 401.1001; completion of this form is voluntary. This information will be used to determine qualification, suitability, and availability of applicants for USPS employment, and may be disclosed to relevant Federal Agencies regarding eligibility and suitability for employment, law enforcement activities when there is an indication of a potential violation of law, in connection with private relief legislation (to Office of Management and Budget/) to a congressional office at your request, to a labor organization as required by the nlra, and where pertinent, in a legal proceeding to which the Postal Service is a party. If this information is not provided, you may not receive full consideration for a position.

Disclosure by you of your Social Security Nmber (SSN) is mandatory to obtain the wervices, benefits, or processes that you are seeking. Solicitation of the SSN by the United States Postal Service is authorized under provisions of Executive Order 9397, dated november 22, 1943. The information gathered through the use of the number will be used only as necessary in authorized personnel administration processes.

Applicant	Fingerprint
Make no marks on this side of the card unless so instructed by examiner.	
Signature of Applicant	

Political Recommendations Prohibited

The law (39 U.S. Code 1002) prohibits political and certain other recommendations for appointments, promotions, assignments, transfers, or designations of persons in the Postal Service. Statements relating solely to character and residence are permitted, but every other kind of statement or recommendation is prohibited unless it either is requested by the Postal Service and consists solely of an evaluation of the work performance, ability, aptitude, and general qualifications of an individual or is requested by a Government representative investigating the individual's loyalty, suitability, and character. Anyone who requests or solicits a prohibited statement or recommendation is subject to disqualification from employment and anyone in the Postal Service who accepts such a statement may be suspended or removed from office.

PS Form 2479-B, April 1983 (Reverse)

Have You Answered All Questions on the Reverse of This Form?

11

You will be notified by mail when the examination date, time, and place are set. You will receive instructions as to where and when to report for the exam. You will also receive the admission card portion of the application card and a sample answer sheet. Be sure to bring the admission card and completed sample answer sheet with you when you report for the exam. Along with the admission card and exam information, you will receive sample questions such as these:

Sample Questions: Postal Exams

After many years of administering a different postal examination for each individual job title or for a small cluster of job titles, the Postal Service has determined that it is more efficient and equally effective to administer the same exam for large groups of postal occupations that require related skills and abilities.

Accordingly, the same examination is now administered for the following job titles:

> Clerk-Carrier
> Mail Handler
> Mail Processor
> Distribution Clerk, Machine
> Mark-up Clerk
> Flat Sorting Machine Operator
> Rural Carrier

The following are official test instructions and official sample questions distributed by the Postal Service to candidates for all of these jobs.

Test Instructions

During the test session, it will be your responsibility to pay close attention to what the examiner has to say and to follow all instructions. One of the purposes of the test is to see how quickly and accurately you can work. Therefore, each part of the test will be carefully timed. You will not START until you are told to do so. Also, when you are told to STOP, you must immediately STOP answering the questions. When you are told to work on a particular part of the examination, regardless of which part, you are to work on that part ONLY. If you finish a part before time is called, you may review your answers for that part, but you will not go on or back to any other part. Failure to follow ANY directions given to you by the examiner may be grounds for disqualification. Instructions read by the examiner are intended to ensure that each applicant has the same fair and objective opportunity to compete in the examination.

The following questions are like the ones that will be on the test. Study these carefully. This will give you practice with the different kinds of questions and show you how to mark your answers.

Part A: Address Checking

In this part of the test, you will have to decide whether two addresses are alike or different. If the two addresses are exactly *Alike* in every way, darken circle A for the question. If the two addresses are *Different* in any way, darken circle D for the question.

Mark your answers to these sample questions on the Sample Answer Grid at the right.

1. ...2134 S 20th St   2134 S 20th St

Sample Answer Grid

Since the two addresses are exactly alike, mark A for question 1 on the Sample Answer Grid.

2. ...4608 N Warnock St   4806 N Warnock St

3. ...1202 W Girard Dr   1202 W Girard Rd

4. ...Chappaqua NY 10514   Chappaqua NY 10514

5. ...2207 Markland Ave   2207 Markham Ave

The correct answers to questions 2 to 5 are: 2D, 3D, 4A, and 5D.

Your score on Part A of the actual test will be based on the number of wrong answers as well as on the number of right answers. Part A is scored as right answers minus wrong answers. Random guessing should not help your score. For the Part A test, you will have six minutes to answer as many of the 95 questions as you can. It will be to your advantage to work as quickly and as accurately as possible. You will not be expected to be able to answer all the questions in the time allowed.

Part B: Memory for Addresses

In this part of the test, you will have to memorize the locations (A, B, C, D, or E) of 25 addresses shown in five boxes, like those below. For example, "Sardis" is in Box C, "6800–6999 Table" is in Box B, etc. (The addresses in the actual test will be different.)

A	B	C	D	E
4700–5599 Table	6800–6999 Table	5600–6499 Table	6500–6799 Table	4400–4699 Table
Lismore	Kelford	Joel	Tatum	Ruskin
5600–6499 West	6500–6799 West	6800–6999 West	4400–4699 West	4700–5599 West
Hesper	Musella	Sardis	Porter	Nathan
4400–4699 Blake	5600–6499 Blake	6500–6799 Blake	4700–5599 Blake	6800–6999 Blake

Study the locations of the addresses for five minutes. As you study, silently repeat these to yourself. Then cover the boxes and try to answer the questions below. Mark your answers for each question by darkening the circle as was done for questions 1 and 2.

1. Musella   5. 4400–4699 Blake   9. 6500–6799 Blake   13. Porter
2. 4700–5599 Blake 6. Hesper   10. Joel   14. 6800–6999 Blake
3. 4700–5599 Table 7. Kelford   11. 4400–4699 Blake
4. Tatum   8. Nathan   12. 6500–6799 West

Sample Answer Grid

The correct answers for questions 3 to 14 are: 3A, 4D, 5A, 6A, 7B, 8E, 9C, 10C, 11A, 12B, 13D, and 14E. During the examination, you will have three practice exercises to help you memorize the location of addresses shown in five boxes. After the practice exercises, the actual test will be given. Part B is scored as right answers minus one-fourth of the wrong answers. Random guessing should not help your score.

But, if you can eliminate one or more alternatives, it is to your advantage to guess. For the Part B test, you will have five minutes to answer as many of the 88 questions as you can. It will be to your advantage to work as quickly and as accurately as you can. You will not be expected to be able to answer all the questions in the time allowed.

Part C: Number Series

For each *Number Series* question there is at the left a series of numbers that follow some definite order and at the right five sets of two numbers each. You are to look at the numbers in the series at the left and find out what order they follow. Then decide what the next two numbers in that series would be if the same order were continued.

1. 1 2 3 4 5 6 7 ....(A) 1 2   (B) 5 6   (C) 8 9   (D) 4 5   (E) 7 8

The numbers in this series are increasing by 1. If the series were continued for two more numbers, it would read: 1 2 3 4 5 6 7 8 9. Therefore the correct answer is 8 and 9 and you should have darkened C for question 1.

2. 15 14 13 12 11 10 9 ......(A) 2 1   (B) 17 16   (C) 8 9   (D) 8 7   (E) 9 8

The numbers in this series are decreasing by 1. If the series were continued for two more numbers, it would read: 15 14 13 12 11 10 9 8 7. Therefore the correct answer is 8 and 7 and you should have darkened D for question 2.

3. 20 20 21 21 22 22 23 ....(A) 23 23   (B) 23 24   (C) 19 19   (D) 22 23   (E) 21 22

Each number in this series is repeated and then increased by 1. If the series were continued for two more numbers, it would read: 20 20 21 21 22 22 23 23 24. Therefore the correct answer is 23 and 24 and you should have darkened B for question 3.

4. 17 3 17 4 17 5 17 ....(A) 6 17   (B) 6 7   (C) 17 6   (D) 5 6   (E) 17 7

This series is the number 17 separated by numbers increasing by 1, beginning with the number 3. If the series were continued for two more numbers, it would read: 17 3 17 4 17 5 17 6 17. Therefore the correct answer is 6 and 17 and you should have darkened A for question 4.

5. 1 2 4 5 7 8 10 ....(A) 11 12   (B) 12 14   (C) 10 13   (D) 12 13   (E) 11 13

	Sample Answer Grid			
1 Ⓐ Ⓑ Ⓒ Ⓓ Ⓔ	3 Ⓐ Ⓑ Ⓒ Ⓓ Ⓔ	4 Ⓐ Ⓑ Ⓒ Ⓓ Ⓔ	5 Ⓐ Ⓑ Ⓒ Ⓓ Ⓔ	
2 Ⓐ Ⓑ Ⓒ Ⓓ Ⓔ				

The numbers in this series are increasing first by 1 (plus 1) and then by 2 (plus 2). If the series were continued for two more numbers, it would read: 1 2 4 5 7 8 10 (plus 1) <u>11</u> and (plus 2) <u>13</u>. Therefore the correct answer is 11 and 13 and you should have darkened E for question 5.

Now read and work sample questions 6 through 10 and mark your answers on the Sample Answer Grid.

6. 21 21 20 20 19 19 18 ....(A) 18 18   (B) 18 17   (C) 17 18   (D) 17 17   (E) 18 19

7. 1 22 1 23 1 24 1 ....(A) 26 1   (B) 25 26   (C) 25 1   (D) 1 26   (E) 1 25

8. 1 20 3 19 5 18 7 ....(A) 8 9   (B) 8 17   (C) 17 10   (D) 17 9   (E) 9 18

9. 4 7 10 13 16 19 22 ....(A) 23 26   (B) 25 27   (C) 25 26   (D) 25 28   (E) 24 27

10. 30 2 28 4 26 6 24 ....(A) 23 9   (B) 26 8   (C) 8 9   (D) 26 22   (E) 8 22

Sample Answer Grid			
6 Ⓐ Ⓑ Ⓒ Ⓓ Ⓔ	8 Ⓐ Ⓑ Ⓒ Ⓓ Ⓔ	9 Ⓐ Ⓑ Ⓒ Ⓓ Ⓔ	10 Ⓐ Ⓑ Ⓒ Ⓓ Ⓔ
7 Ⓐ Ⓑ Ⓒ Ⓓ Ⓔ			

The correct answers to sample questions 6 to 10 are: 6B, 7C, 8D, 9D, and 10E. Explanations follow.

6. Each number in the series repeats itself and then decreases by 1 or minus 1; <u>21</u> (repeat) <u>21</u> (minus 1) <u>20</u> (repeat) <u>20</u> (minus 1) <u>19</u> (repeat) <u>19</u> (minus 1) <u>18</u> (repeat) <u>?</u> (minus 1) <u>?</u>

7. The number 1 is separated by numbers that begin with 22 and increase by 1; <u>1</u> <u>22</u> <u>1</u> (increase 22 by 1) <u>23</u> <u>1</u> (increase 23 by 1) <u>24</u> <u>1</u> (increase 24 by 1) <u>?</u>

8. This is best explained by two alternating series—one series starts with 1 and increases by 2 or plus 2; the other series starts with 20 and decreases by 1 or minus 1.

$$\begin{array}{ccccccccc} 1 & ^\wedge & 3 & ^\wedge & 5 & ^\wedge & 7 & ^\wedge & ? \\ & 20 & & 19 & & 18 & & ? & \end{array}$$

9. This series of numbers increases by 3 (plus 3) beginning with the first number—<u>4</u> <u>7</u> <u>10</u> <u>13</u> <u>16</u> <u>19</u> <u>22</u> <u>?</u> <u>?</u>

10. Look for two alternating series —one series starts with 30 and decreases by 2 (minus 2); the other series starts with 2 and increases by 2 (plus 2).

Now try questions 11 to 15.

11. 5 6 20 7 8 19 9 ....(A) 10 18   (B) 18 17   (C) 10 17   (D) 18 19   (E) 10 11

12. 4 6 9 11 14 16 19 ....(A) 21 24   (B) 22 25   (C) 20 22   (D) 21 23   (E) 22 24

13. 8 8 1 10 10 3 12 ....(A) 13 13   (B) 12 5   (C) 12 4   (D) 13 5   (E) 4 12

14. 10 12 50 15 17 50 20 ....(A) 50 21   (B) 21 50   (C) 50 22   (D) 22 50   (E) 22 24

15. 20 21 23 24 27 28 32 33 38 39.(A) 45 46 (B) 45 52 (C) 44 45 (D) 44 49 (E) 40 46

Sample Answer Grid			
11 Ⓐ Ⓑ Ⓒ Ⓓ Ⓔ	13 Ⓐ Ⓑ Ⓒ Ⓓ Ⓔ	14 Ⓐ Ⓑ Ⓒ Ⓓ Ⓔ	15 Ⓐ Ⓑ Ⓒ Ⓓ Ⓔ
12 Ⓐ Ⓑ Ⓒ Ⓓ Ⓔ			

The correct answers to the sample questions above are: 11A, 12A, 13B, 14D, and 15A.

It will be to your advantage to answer every question in Part C that you can, since your score on this part of the test will be based on the number of questions that you answer correctly. Answer first those questions that are easiest for you. For the Part C test, you will have 20 minutes to answer as many of the 24 questions as you can.

Part D: Following Oral Instructions

In this part of the test, you will be told to follow directions by writing in a test booklet and then on an answer sheet. The test booklet will have lines of material like the following five samples:

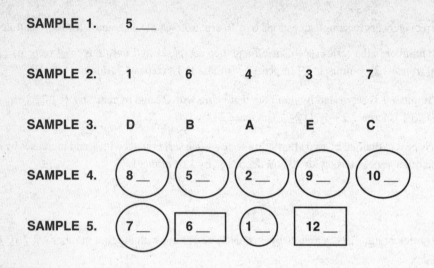

SAMPLE 1.   5 ___

SAMPLE 2.   1   6   4   3   7

SAMPLE 3.   D   B   A   E   C

SAMPLE 4.   8 __   5 __   2 __   9 __   10 __

SAMPLE 5.   7 __   6 __   1 __   12 __

To practice this part of the test, tear out the page of instructions to be read. Then have somebody read the instructions to you while you follow them. When he or she tells you to darken the space on the Sample Answer Grid, use the one on this page.

Your score for Part D will be based on the number of questions that you answer correctly. Therefore, if you are not sure of an answer, it will be to your advantage to guess. Part D will take about 25 minutes.

	Sample Answer Grid				
1 Ⓐ Ⓑ Ⓒ Ⓓ Ⓔ		5 Ⓐ Ⓑ Ⓒ Ⓓ Ⓔ		9 Ⓐ Ⓑ Ⓒ Ⓓ Ⓔ	
2 Ⓐ Ⓑ Ⓒ Ⓓ Ⓔ		6 Ⓐ Ⓑ Ⓒ Ⓓ Ⓔ		10 Ⓐ Ⓑ Ⓒ Ⓓ Ⓔ	
3 Ⓐ Ⓑ Ⓒ Ⓓ Ⓔ		7 Ⓐ Ⓑ Ⓒ Ⓓ Ⓔ		11 Ⓐ Ⓑ Ⓒ Ⓓ Ⓔ	
4 Ⓐ Ⓑ Ⓒ Ⓓ Ⓔ		8 Ⓐ Ⓑ Ⓒ Ⓓ Ⓔ		12 Ⓐ Ⓑ Ⓒ Ⓓ Ⓔ	

Instructions to be read for Part D. (**The words in parentheses should NOT be read aloud.**)

You are to follow the instructions that I shall read to you. I cannot repeat them.

Look at the samples. Sample 1 has a number and a line beside it. On the line write A as in ace. (**Pause 2 seconds.**) Now, on the Sample Answer Grid, find number 5 (**pause 2 seconds**) and darken the letter you just wrote on the line. (**Pause 2 seconds.**)

Look at Sample 2. (**Pause slightly.**) Draw a line under the third number. (**Pause 2 seconds.**) Now look on the Sample Answer Grid, find the number under which you just drew a line, and darken B as in boy. (**Pause 5 seconds.**)

Look at the letters in Sample 3. (**Pause slightly.**) Draw a line under the third letter in the line. (**Pause 2 seconds.**) Now, on your Sample Answer Grid, find number 9 (**pause 2 seconds**) and darken the letter under which you drew a line. (**Pause 5 seconds.**)

Look at the five circles in Sample 4. (**Pause slightly.**) Each circle has a number and a line in it. Write D as in dog on the line in the last circle. (**Pause 2 seconds.**) Now, on the Sample Answer Grid, darken the number-letter combination that is in the circle you just wrote in. (**Pause 5 seconds.**)

Look at Sample 5. (**Pause slightly.**) There are two circles and two boxes of different sizes with numbers in them. (**Pause slightly.**) If 4 is more than 2 and if 5 is less than 3, write A as in ace in the smaller circle. (**Pause slightly.**) Otherwise write C as in car in the larger box. (**Pause 2 seconds.**) Now, on the Sample Answer Grid, darken the number-letter combination in the box or circle in which you just wrote. (**Pause 5 seconds.**)

Now look at the Sample Answer Grid. (**Pause slightly.**) You should have darkened 4B, 5A, 9A, 10D, and 12C on the Sample Answer Grid. (**If the person preparing to take the examination made any mistakes, try to help him or her see why he or she made wrong marks.**)

TEAR HERE

On Examination Day

On the examination day assigned to you, allow the test itself to be the main attraction of the day. Do not squeeze it in between other activities. Arrive rested, relaxed, and on time. In fact, plan to arrive a little bit early. Leave plenty of time for traffic tie-ups or other complications that might upset you and interfere with your test performance. Be sure to bring your yellow admission ticket, identification, completed sample answer sheet, and two sharpened #2 pencils. Check to be certain that the erasers erase completely.

In the test room the examiner will hand out forms for you to fill out. He or she will give you the instructions that you must follow in taking the examination and in filling out the answer grids. Time limits and timing signals will be explained. If you do not understand any of the examiner's instructions, ASK QUESTIONS. Make sure that you know exactly what to do.

During the testing session you will answer both sample questions and actual test questions. You will see the answers to the sample questions. You will not be given the answers to the actual test questions, even after the test is over.

At the examination, you must follow instructions exactly. Fill in the grids on the forms carefully and accurately. Filling in the wrong grid may lead to loss of veterans' credits to which you may be entitled or to an incorrect address for your test results. Do not begin until you are told to begin. Stop as soon as the examiner tells you to stop. Do not turn pages until you are told to. Do not go back to parts you have already completed. Any infraction of the rules is considered cheating. If you cheat, your test paper will not be scored, and you will not be eligible for appointment.

Using the Answer Sheet

The answer sheet for your postal exam is machine scored. You cannot give any explanations to the machine, so you must fill out the answer sheet clearly and correctly.

1. Blacken your answer space firmly and completely. ● is the only correct way to mark the answer sheet. ◖, ⊗, ⊘, and ∅ are all unacceptable. The machine might not read them at all.
2. Mark only one answer for each question. If you mark more than one answer you will be considered wrong even if one of the answers is correct.
3. If you change your mind, you must erase your mark. Attempting to cross out an incorrect answer like this ✿ will not work. You must erase any incorrect answer completely. An incomplete erasure might be read as a second answer.
4. All of your answering should be in the form of blackened spaces. The machine cannot read English. Do not write any notes in the margins.
5. MOST IMPORTANT: Answer each question in the right place. Question 1 must be answered in space 1; question 52 in space 52. If you should skip an answer space and mark a series of answers in the wrong places, you must erase all those answers and do the questions over, marking your answers in the proper places. You cannot afford to use the limited time in this way. Therefore, as you answer *each* question, look at its number and check that you are marking your answer in the space with the same number
6. You may be wondering whether or not it is wise to guess when you are not sure of an answer, or whether it is better to skip a question when you are not certain of the answer. On the Address Checking part there is no reason to skip questions or to guess. Simply answer every question, in order, as quickly and accurately as you can. In the Memory for Addresses part, you must choose for yourself whether to skip questions or to guess. A correct answer gives you one point; a skipped

space gives you nothing at all, but costs you nothing except the chance of getting the answer right; a wrong answer costs you one-fourth of a point. If you are really stumped, you may skip a question. BUT you must then remember to skip its answer space as well. Both the Number Series part and Following Oral Instructions are scored "rights only." On these parts there is no penalty for a wrong answer, so no harm can be caused by guessing wrong. For these parts be certain to mark an answer for every question. A lucky guess can earn you an extra point, and you have nothing to lose.

How the Exam Is Scored

When the exam is over, the examiner will collect test booklets and answer sheets. The answer sheets will be sent to the National Test Administration Center in Merrifield, Virginia, where a machine will scan your answers and mark them as right or wrong. Then your raw score will be calculated according to the system described above.

Your raw score is not your final score. The Postal Service takes the raw scores, combines them according to a formula of its own, and converts them to a scaled score, on a scale of 1 to 100. The entire process of conversion from raw to scaled score is confidential information. The score you receive is not your number right, is not your raw score, and is not a percent. The score you receive is a *scaled score*. Before reporting any scaled scores, the Postal Service adds any veterans' service points or any other advantages to which the applicant might be entitled. Veterans' service points are added only to passing scaled scores of 70 or more. A failing score cannot be brought to passing level by veterans' points. The score earned plus veterans' service points results in the final scaled score that finds its place onto the eligibility list.

A total scaled score of 70 is a passing score. The names of all persons with scaled scores of 70 or more are placed on the list sent to the local post office. Those names are placed on the list in order, with the highest score at the top of the list. Hiring then takes place from the top of the list as vacancies occur.

The scoring process may take six or ten weeks or even longer. Be patient. If you pass the exam, you will receive notice of your scaled score. As the hiring process nears your number, you will be notified to appear for the remaining steps of the hiring process: drug testing, psychological interview, physical performance tests according to the requirements of the position, and, for Mark-up Clerk candidates, the alpha-numeric typing test. Applicants who fail the exam are not told their scores. They are simply notified that they have failed and will not be considered for postal employment.

ONE

Preliminary Exam

Before You Take the Preliminary Exam

The purpose of the Preliminary Exam is to start you in your studies for your postal exam and to establish a base upon which you can build. The preliminary exam will give you an idea of the demands of the exam, of how well you can meet them now, and of how far you need to go. By starting out with a full-length exam, you see from the beginning how many questions you must answer and how quickly you must work to score high on this exam.

Directions for Taking the Preliminary Exam

- Arrange for a friend or family member to read oral instructions for Part D. If you are unable to find a reader, skip ahead to Part II of this book and read the chapter entitled "How to Answer Following Oral Instructions Questions." Prepare a tape according to the suggestions in that chapter.
- Choose a work space that is quiet and well-lit.
- Clear the desk or tabletop of all clutter.
- Bring a stopwatch or kitchen timer and two or three number-two pencils with good erasers to your work area. While the pencils should have plenty of exposed lead, you will find that you fill in answer circles more quickly if the pencils are not razor sharp. The little circles on the answer sheet must be completely filled in, and the fewer strokes needed to fill them the faster you work. Scribble a bit to dull the points now. At the actual exam, you will dull the points as you fill out the grids before the exam begins.
- Tear out the answer sheets for the preliminary exam and place them on the desk or table beside your book, to the right if you are right-handed, to the left if you are left-handed.
- Read page 29 and answer the Address Checking sample questions. Then set the timer and begin work on Part A.
- Stop as soon as time is up and draw a line on your answer sheet at your stopping place. You want an accurate measure of how many questions you were able to answer correctly within the time limit. However, you may go back and get extra practice later on by answering the remaining questions without including them in your score.
- Proceed through the entire exam in this manner. First answer the sample questions for the part just as you will at the exam site; then set the timer and answer as many questions as possible within the time limit. Mark your stopping place on the answer sheet and move on.

Directions for Scoring Your Exam

- When you have completed the entire preliminary exam, check your answers against the correct answer key on pages 53–60. Circle all wrong answers in red so that you can easily locate them when you analyze your errors.
- Calculate your raw score for each part of the exam as instructed on the score sheet on page 28.
- Check to see where your scores fall on the self-evaluation chart on page 28. Plot your scores on the progress chart on page 295.

- Now analyze your errors and begin to learn from them. You may be able to identify a pattern of errors in address checking and in following oral instructions. And you may be able to begin developing expertise at number series as you study the explanations.

After you have completed the preliminary exam and have analyzed your results, you should have a good idea of where you stand and of how much you need to do to prepare for the exam. Plan to spend many hours with the four instructional chapters in Part II. Each will give you valuable help with answering the four distinct question types. Absorb all the information. Follow through with the drills and exercises. Do not jump ahead to the full-length model exams until you have really prepared. Then go on and develop skill and speed with the model exams.

Preliminary Model Exam
Answer Sheet

Part A—Address Checking

1. Ⓐ Ⓓ	20. Ⓐ Ⓓ	39. Ⓐ Ⓓ	58. Ⓐ Ⓓ	77. Ⓐ Ⓓ
2. Ⓐ Ⓓ	21. Ⓐ Ⓓ	40. Ⓐ Ⓓ	59. Ⓐ Ⓓ	78. Ⓐ Ⓓ
3. Ⓐ Ⓓ	22. Ⓐ Ⓓ	41. Ⓐ Ⓓ	60. Ⓐ Ⓓ	79. Ⓐ Ⓓ
4. Ⓐ Ⓓ	23. Ⓐ Ⓓ	42. Ⓐ Ⓓ	61. Ⓐ Ⓓ	80. Ⓐ Ⓓ
5. Ⓐ Ⓓ	24. Ⓐ Ⓓ	43. Ⓐ Ⓓ	62. Ⓐ Ⓓ	81. Ⓐ Ⓓ
6. Ⓐ Ⓓ	25. Ⓐ Ⓓ	44. Ⓐ Ⓓ	63. Ⓐ Ⓓ	82. Ⓐ Ⓓ
7. Ⓐ Ⓓ	26. Ⓐ Ⓓ	45. Ⓐ Ⓓ	64. Ⓐ Ⓓ	83. Ⓐ Ⓓ
8. Ⓐ Ⓓ	27. Ⓐ Ⓓ	46. Ⓐ Ⓓ	65. Ⓐ Ⓓ	84. Ⓐ Ⓓ
9. Ⓐ Ⓓ	28. Ⓐ Ⓓ	47. Ⓐ Ⓓ	66. Ⓐ Ⓓ	85. Ⓐ Ⓓ
10. Ⓐ Ⓓ	29. Ⓐ Ⓓ	48. Ⓐ Ⓓ	67. Ⓐ Ⓓ	86. Ⓐ Ⓓ
11. Ⓐ Ⓓ	30. Ⓐ Ⓓ	49. Ⓐ Ⓓ	68. Ⓐ Ⓓ	87. Ⓐ Ⓓ
12. Ⓐ Ⓓ	31. Ⓐ Ⓓ	50. Ⓐ Ⓓ	69. Ⓐ Ⓓ	88. Ⓐ Ⓓ
13. Ⓐ Ⓓ	32. Ⓐ Ⓓ	51. Ⓐ Ⓓ	70. Ⓐ Ⓓ	89. Ⓐ Ⓓ
14. Ⓐ Ⓓ	33. Ⓐ Ⓓ	52. Ⓐ Ⓓ	71. Ⓐ Ⓓ	90. Ⓐ Ⓓ
15. Ⓐ Ⓓ	34. Ⓐ Ⓓ	53. Ⓐ Ⓓ	72. Ⓐ Ⓓ	91. Ⓐ Ⓓ
16. Ⓐ Ⓓ	35. Ⓐ Ⓓ	54. Ⓐ Ⓓ	73. Ⓐ Ⓓ	92. Ⓐ Ⓓ
17. Ⓐ Ⓓ	36. Ⓐ Ⓓ	55. Ⓐ Ⓓ	74. Ⓐ Ⓓ	93. Ⓐ Ⓓ
18. Ⓐ Ⓓ	37. Ⓐ Ⓓ	56. Ⓐ Ⓓ	75. Ⓐ Ⓓ	94. Ⓐ Ⓓ
19. Ⓐ Ⓓ	38. Ⓐ Ⓓ	57. Ⓐ Ⓓ	76. Ⓐ Ⓓ	95. Ⓐ Ⓓ

Part B —Memory For Addresses

1 Ⓐ Ⓑ Ⓒ Ⓓ Ⓔ   23 Ⓐ Ⓑ Ⓒ Ⓓ Ⓔ   45 Ⓐ Ⓑ Ⓒ Ⓓ Ⓔ   67 Ⓐ Ⓑ Ⓒ Ⓓ Ⓔ

2 Ⓐ Ⓑ Ⓒ Ⓓ Ⓔ   24 Ⓐ Ⓑ Ⓒ Ⓓ Ⓔ   46 Ⓐ Ⓑ Ⓒ Ⓓ Ⓔ   68 Ⓐ Ⓑ Ⓒ Ⓓ Ⓔ

3 Ⓐ Ⓑ Ⓒ Ⓓ Ⓔ   25 Ⓐ Ⓑ Ⓒ Ⓓ Ⓔ   47 Ⓐ Ⓑ Ⓒ Ⓓ Ⓔ   69 Ⓐ Ⓑ Ⓒ Ⓓ Ⓔ

4 Ⓐ Ⓑ Ⓒ Ⓓ Ⓔ   26 Ⓐ Ⓑ Ⓒ Ⓓ Ⓔ   48 Ⓐ Ⓑ Ⓒ Ⓓ Ⓔ   70 Ⓐ Ⓑ Ⓒ Ⓓ Ⓔ

5 Ⓐ Ⓑ Ⓒ Ⓓ Ⓔ   27 Ⓐ Ⓑ Ⓒ Ⓓ Ⓔ   49 Ⓐ Ⓑ Ⓒ Ⓓ Ⓔ   71 Ⓐ Ⓑ Ⓒ Ⓓ Ⓔ

6 Ⓐ Ⓑ Ⓒ Ⓓ Ⓔ   28 Ⓐ Ⓑ Ⓒ Ⓓ Ⓔ   50 Ⓐ Ⓑ Ⓒ Ⓓ Ⓔ   72 Ⓐ Ⓑ Ⓒ Ⓓ Ⓔ

7 Ⓐ Ⓑ Ⓒ Ⓓ Ⓔ   29 Ⓐ Ⓑ Ⓒ Ⓓ Ⓔ   51 Ⓐ Ⓑ Ⓒ Ⓓ Ⓔ   73 Ⓐ Ⓑ Ⓒ Ⓓ Ⓔ

8 Ⓐ Ⓑ Ⓒ Ⓓ Ⓔ   30 Ⓐ Ⓑ Ⓒ Ⓓ Ⓔ   52 Ⓐ Ⓑ Ⓒ Ⓓ Ⓔ   74 Ⓐ Ⓑ Ⓒ Ⓓ Ⓔ

9 Ⓐ Ⓑ Ⓒ Ⓓ Ⓔ   31 Ⓐ Ⓑ Ⓒ Ⓓ Ⓔ   53 Ⓐ Ⓑ Ⓒ Ⓓ Ⓔ   75 Ⓐ Ⓑ Ⓒ Ⓓ Ⓔ

10 Ⓐ Ⓑ Ⓒ Ⓓ Ⓔ   32 Ⓐ Ⓑ Ⓒ Ⓓ Ⓔ   54 Ⓐ Ⓑ Ⓒ Ⓓ Ⓔ   76 Ⓐ Ⓑ Ⓒ Ⓓ Ⓔ

11 Ⓐ Ⓑ Ⓒ Ⓓ Ⓔ   33 Ⓐ Ⓑ Ⓒ Ⓓ Ⓔ   55 Ⓐ Ⓑ Ⓒ Ⓓ Ⓔ   77 Ⓐ Ⓑ Ⓒ Ⓓ Ⓔ

12 Ⓐ Ⓑ Ⓒ Ⓓ Ⓔ   34 Ⓐ Ⓑ Ⓒ Ⓓ Ⓔ   56 Ⓐ Ⓑ Ⓒ Ⓓ Ⓔ   78 Ⓐ Ⓑ Ⓒ Ⓓ Ⓔ

13 Ⓐ Ⓑ Ⓒ Ⓓ Ⓔ   35 Ⓐ Ⓑ Ⓒ Ⓓ Ⓔ   57 Ⓐ Ⓑ Ⓒ Ⓓ Ⓔ   79 Ⓐ Ⓑ Ⓒ Ⓓ Ⓔ

14 Ⓐ Ⓑ Ⓒ Ⓓ Ⓔ   36 Ⓐ Ⓑ Ⓒ Ⓓ Ⓔ   58 Ⓐ Ⓑ Ⓒ Ⓓ Ⓔ   80 Ⓐ Ⓑ Ⓒ Ⓓ Ⓔ

15 Ⓐ Ⓑ Ⓒ Ⓓ Ⓔ   37 Ⓐ Ⓑ Ⓒ Ⓓ Ⓔ   59 Ⓐ Ⓑ Ⓒ Ⓓ Ⓔ   81 Ⓐ Ⓑ Ⓒ Ⓓ Ⓔ

16 Ⓐ Ⓑ Ⓒ Ⓓ Ⓔ   38 Ⓐ Ⓑ Ⓒ Ⓓ Ⓔ   60 Ⓐ Ⓑ Ⓒ Ⓓ Ⓔ   82 Ⓐ Ⓑ Ⓒ Ⓓ Ⓔ

17 Ⓐ Ⓑ Ⓒ Ⓓ Ⓔ   39 Ⓐ Ⓑ Ⓒ Ⓓ Ⓔ   61 Ⓐ Ⓑ Ⓒ Ⓓ Ⓔ   83 Ⓐ Ⓑ Ⓒ Ⓓ Ⓔ

18 Ⓐ Ⓑ Ⓒ Ⓓ Ⓔ   40 Ⓐ Ⓑ Ⓒ Ⓓ Ⓔ   62 Ⓐ Ⓑ Ⓒ Ⓓ Ⓔ   84 Ⓐ Ⓑ Ⓒ Ⓓ Ⓔ

19 Ⓐ Ⓑ Ⓒ Ⓓ Ⓔ   41 Ⓐ Ⓑ Ⓒ Ⓓ Ⓔ   63 Ⓐ Ⓑ Ⓒ Ⓓ Ⓔ   85 Ⓐ Ⓑ Ⓒ Ⓓ Ⓔ

20 Ⓐ Ⓑ Ⓒ Ⓓ Ⓔ   42 Ⓐ Ⓑ Ⓒ Ⓓ Ⓔ   64 Ⓐ Ⓑ Ⓒ Ⓓ Ⓔ   86 Ⓐ Ⓑ Ⓒ Ⓓ Ⓔ

21 Ⓐ Ⓑ Ⓒ Ⓓ Ⓔ   43 Ⓐ Ⓑ Ⓒ Ⓓ Ⓔ   65 Ⓐ Ⓑ Ⓒ Ⓓ Ⓔ   87 Ⓐ Ⓑ Ⓒ Ⓓ Ⓔ

22 Ⓐ Ⓑ Ⓒ Ⓓ Ⓔ   44 Ⓐ Ⓑ Ⓒ Ⓓ Ⓔ   66 Ⓐ Ⓑ Ⓒ Ⓓ Ⓔ   88 Ⓐ Ⓑ Ⓒ Ⓓ Ⓔ

Part C—Number Series

1. Ⓐ Ⓑ Ⓒ Ⓓ Ⓔ   7. Ⓐ Ⓑ Ⓒ Ⓓ Ⓔ   13. Ⓐ Ⓑ Ⓒ Ⓓ Ⓔ   19. Ⓐ Ⓑ Ⓒ Ⓓ Ⓔ

2. Ⓐ Ⓑ Ⓒ Ⓓ Ⓔ   8. Ⓐ Ⓑ Ⓒ Ⓓ Ⓔ   14. Ⓐ Ⓑ Ⓒ Ⓓ Ⓔ   20. Ⓐ Ⓑ Ⓒ Ⓓ Ⓔ

3. Ⓐ Ⓑ Ⓒ Ⓓ Ⓔ   9. Ⓐ Ⓑ Ⓒ Ⓓ Ⓔ   15. Ⓐ Ⓑ Ⓒ Ⓓ Ⓔ   21. Ⓐ Ⓑ Ⓒ Ⓓ Ⓔ

4. Ⓐ Ⓑ Ⓒ Ⓓ Ⓔ   10. Ⓐ Ⓑ Ⓒ Ⓓ Ⓔ   16. Ⓐ Ⓑ Ⓒ Ⓓ Ⓔ   22. Ⓐ Ⓑ Ⓒ Ⓓ Ⓔ

5. Ⓐ Ⓑ Ⓒ Ⓓ Ⓔ   11. Ⓐ Ⓑ Ⓒ Ⓓ Ⓔ   17. Ⓐ Ⓑ Ⓒ Ⓓ Ⓔ   23. Ⓐ Ⓑ Ⓒ Ⓓ Ⓔ

6. Ⓐ Ⓑ Ⓒ Ⓓ Ⓔ   12. Ⓐ Ⓑ Ⓒ Ⓓ Ⓔ   18. Ⓐ Ⓑ Ⓒ Ⓓ Ⓔ   24. Ⓐ Ⓑ Ⓒ Ⓓ Ⓔ

Part D—Following Oral Instructions

1 Ⓐ Ⓑ Ⓒ Ⓓ Ⓔ   23 Ⓐ Ⓑ Ⓒ Ⓓ Ⓔ   45 Ⓐ Ⓑ Ⓒ Ⓓ Ⓔ   67 Ⓐ Ⓑ Ⓒ Ⓓ Ⓔ

2 Ⓐ Ⓑ Ⓒ Ⓓ Ⓔ   24 Ⓐ Ⓑ Ⓒ Ⓓ Ⓔ   46 Ⓐ Ⓑ Ⓒ Ⓓ Ⓔ   68 Ⓐ Ⓑ Ⓒ Ⓓ Ⓔ

3 Ⓐ Ⓑ Ⓒ Ⓓ Ⓔ   25 Ⓐ Ⓑ Ⓒ Ⓓ Ⓔ   47 Ⓐ Ⓑ Ⓒ Ⓓ Ⓔ   69 Ⓐ Ⓑ Ⓒ Ⓓ Ⓔ

4 Ⓐ Ⓑ Ⓒ Ⓓ Ⓔ   26 Ⓐ Ⓑ Ⓒ Ⓓ Ⓔ   48 Ⓐ Ⓑ Ⓒ Ⓓ Ⓔ   70 Ⓐ Ⓑ Ⓒ Ⓓ Ⓔ

5 Ⓐ Ⓑ Ⓒ Ⓓ Ⓔ   27 Ⓐ Ⓑ Ⓒ Ⓓ Ⓔ   49 Ⓐ Ⓑ Ⓒ Ⓓ Ⓔ   71 Ⓐ Ⓑ Ⓒ Ⓓ Ⓔ

6 Ⓐ Ⓑ Ⓒ Ⓓ Ⓔ   28 Ⓐ Ⓑ Ⓒ Ⓓ Ⓔ   50 Ⓐ Ⓑ Ⓒ Ⓓ Ⓔ   72 Ⓐ Ⓑ Ⓒ Ⓓ Ⓔ

7 Ⓐ Ⓑ Ⓒ Ⓓ Ⓔ   29 Ⓐ Ⓑ Ⓒ Ⓓ Ⓔ   51 Ⓐ Ⓑ Ⓒ Ⓓ Ⓔ   73 Ⓐ Ⓑ Ⓒ Ⓓ Ⓔ

8 Ⓐ Ⓑ Ⓒ Ⓓ Ⓔ   30 Ⓐ Ⓑ Ⓒ Ⓓ Ⓔ   52 Ⓐ Ⓑ Ⓒ Ⓓ Ⓔ   74 Ⓐ Ⓑ Ⓒ Ⓓ Ⓔ

9 Ⓐ Ⓑ Ⓒ Ⓓ Ⓔ   31 Ⓐ Ⓑ Ⓒ Ⓓ Ⓔ   53 Ⓐ Ⓑ Ⓒ Ⓓ Ⓔ   75 Ⓐ Ⓑ Ⓒ Ⓓ Ⓔ

10 Ⓐ Ⓑ Ⓒ Ⓓ Ⓔ   32 Ⓐ Ⓑ Ⓒ Ⓓ Ⓔ   54 Ⓐ Ⓑ Ⓒ Ⓓ Ⓔ   76 Ⓐ Ⓑ Ⓒ Ⓓ Ⓔ

11 Ⓐ Ⓑ Ⓒ Ⓓ Ⓔ   33 Ⓐ Ⓑ Ⓒ Ⓓ Ⓔ   55 Ⓐ Ⓑ Ⓒ Ⓓ Ⓔ   77 Ⓐ Ⓑ Ⓒ Ⓓ Ⓔ

12 Ⓐ Ⓑ Ⓒ Ⓓ Ⓔ   34 Ⓐ Ⓑ Ⓒ Ⓓ Ⓔ   56 Ⓐ Ⓑ Ⓒ Ⓓ Ⓔ   78 Ⓐ Ⓑ Ⓒ Ⓓ Ⓔ

13 Ⓐ Ⓑ Ⓒ Ⓓ Ⓔ   35 Ⓐ Ⓑ Ⓒ Ⓓ Ⓔ   57 Ⓐ Ⓑ Ⓒ Ⓓ Ⓔ   79 Ⓐ Ⓑ Ⓒ Ⓓ Ⓔ

14 Ⓐ Ⓑ Ⓒ Ⓓ Ⓔ   36 Ⓐ Ⓑ Ⓒ Ⓓ Ⓔ   58 Ⓐ Ⓑ Ⓒ Ⓓ Ⓔ   80 Ⓐ Ⓑ Ⓒ Ⓓ Ⓔ

15 Ⓐ Ⓑ Ⓒ Ⓓ Ⓔ   37 Ⓐ Ⓑ Ⓒ Ⓓ Ⓔ   59 Ⓐ Ⓑ Ⓒ Ⓓ Ⓔ   81 Ⓐ Ⓑ Ⓒ Ⓓ Ⓔ

16 Ⓐ Ⓑ Ⓒ Ⓓ Ⓔ   38 Ⓐ Ⓑ Ⓒ Ⓓ Ⓔ   60 Ⓐ Ⓑ Ⓒ Ⓓ Ⓔ   82 Ⓐ Ⓑ Ⓒ Ⓓ Ⓔ

17 Ⓐ Ⓑ Ⓒ Ⓓ Ⓔ   39 Ⓐ Ⓑ Ⓒ Ⓓ Ⓔ   61 Ⓐ Ⓑ Ⓒ Ⓓ Ⓔ   83 Ⓐ Ⓑ Ⓒ Ⓓ Ⓔ

18 Ⓐ Ⓑ Ⓒ Ⓓ Ⓔ   40 Ⓐ Ⓑ Ⓒ Ⓓ Ⓔ   62 Ⓐ Ⓑ Ⓒ Ⓓ Ⓔ   84 Ⓐ Ⓑ Ⓒ Ⓓ Ⓔ

19 Ⓐ Ⓑ Ⓒ Ⓓ Ⓔ   41 Ⓐ Ⓑ Ⓒ Ⓓ Ⓔ   63 Ⓐ Ⓑ Ⓒ Ⓓ Ⓔ   85 Ⓐ Ⓑ Ⓒ Ⓓ Ⓔ

20 Ⓐ Ⓑ Ⓒ Ⓓ Ⓔ   42 Ⓐ Ⓑ Ⓒ Ⓓ Ⓔ   64 Ⓐ Ⓑ Ⓒ Ⓓ Ⓔ   86 Ⓐ Ⓑ Ⓒ Ⓓ Ⓔ

21 Ⓐ Ⓑ Ⓒ Ⓓ Ⓔ   43 Ⓐ Ⓑ Ⓒ Ⓓ Ⓔ   65 Ⓐ Ⓑ Ⓒ Ⓓ Ⓔ   87 Ⓐ Ⓑ Ⓒ Ⓓ Ⓔ

22 Ⓐ Ⓑ Ⓒ Ⓓ Ⓔ   44 Ⓐ Ⓑ Ⓒ Ⓓ Ⓔ   66 Ⓐ Ⓑ Ⓒ Ⓓ Ⓔ   88 Ⓐ Ⓑ Ⓒ Ⓓ Ⓔ

TEAR HERE

SCORE SHEET

ADDRESS CHECKING: Your score on the Address Checking part is based upon the number of questions you answered correctly minus the number of questions you answered incorrectly. To determine your score, subtract the number of wrong answers from the number of correct answers.

Number Right — Number Wrong = Raw Score

_____ — _____ = _____

MEMORY FOR ADDRESSES: Your score on the Memory for Addresses part is based upon the number of questions you answered correctly minus one-fourth of the questions you answered incorrectly (number wrong divided by 4). Calculate this now: Number Wrong ÷ 4 = .

Number Right — Number Wrong ÷ 4 = Raw Score

_____ — _____ = _____

NUMBER SERIES: Your score on the Number Series part is based only on the number of questions you answered correctly. Wrong answers do not count against you.

Number Right = Raw Score

_____ = _____

FOLLOWING ORAL INSTRUCTIONS: Your score on the Following Oral Instructions part is based only upon the number of questions you marked correctly on the answer sheet. The worksheet is not scored, and wrong answers on the answer sheet do not count against you.

Number Right = Raw Score

_____ _____

TOTAL SCORE: To find your total raw score, add together the raw scores for each section of the exam.

Address Checking Score _____
\+
Memory for Addresses Score _____
\+
Number Series Score _____
\+
Following Oral Instructions Score _____
=
Total Raw Score _____

Self Evaluation Chart

Calculate your raw score for each test as shown above. Then check to see where your score falls on the scale from Poor to Excellent. Lightly shade in the boxes in which your scores fall.

Part	Excellent	Good	Average	Fair	Poor
Address Checking	80–95	65–79	50–64	35–49	1–34
Memory for Addresses	75–88	60–74	45–59	30–44	1–29
Number Series	21–24	18–20	14–17	11–13	1–10
Following Oral Instructions	27–31	23–26	19–22	14–18	1–13

Preliminary Model Exam

Part A—Address Checking

Sample Questions

You will be allowed three minutes to read the directions and answer the five sample questions that follow. On the actual test, however, you will have only six minutes to answer 95 questions, so see how quickly you can compare addresses and still get the correct answer.

DIRECTIONS: Each question consists of two addresses. If the two addresses are alike in EVERY *way, mark A on your answer sheet. If the two addresses are* different in ANY *way, mark D on your answer sheet.*

1 ...3380 Federal Street		3380 S Federal Street
2 ...1618 Highland Way		1816 Highland Way
3 ...Greenvale NY 11548		Greenvale NY 11548
4 ...Ft. Collins CO 80523		Ft. Collings CO 80523
5 ...7214 NW 83rd St		7214 NW 83rd St

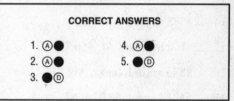

```
SAMPLE ANSWER SHEET

1. Ⓐ Ⓓ        4. Ⓐ Ⓓ
2. Ⓐ Ⓓ        5. Ⓐ Ⓓ
3. Ⓐ Ⓓ
```

```
CORRECT ANSWERS

1. Ⓐ ●        4. Ⓐ ●
2. Ⓐ ●        5. ● Ⓓ
3. ● Ⓓ
```

29

Address Checking

Time: 6 Minutes. 95 Questions.

DIRECTIONS: For each question, compare the address in the left column with the address in the right column. If the two addresses are ALIKE IN EVERY WAY, blacken space A on your answer sheet. If the two addresses are DIFFERENT IN ANY WAY, blacken space D on your answer sheet. Correct answers for this test are on page 53.

1	...197 Wonderview Dr NW	197 Wonderview Dr NW
2	...243 S Capistrano Ave	234 S Capistrano Ave
3.	...4300 Las Pillas Rd	4300 Las Pillas Rd
4	...5551 N Ramara Ave	5551 N Ramara St
5	...Walden Col 80480	Waldon Col 80480
6	...2200 E Dunnington St	2200 E Dowington St
7	...2700 Helena Way	2700 Helena Way
8	...3968 S Zeno Ave	3968 S Zemo Ave
9	...14011 Costilla Ave NE	14011 Costilla Ave SE
10	...1899 N Dearborn Dr	1899 N Dearborn Dr
11	...8911 Scranton Way	8911 Scranton Way
12	...365 Liverpool St	356 Liverpool St
13	...1397 Lewiston Pl	1297 Lewiston Pl
14	...4588 Crystal Way	4588 Crystal Rd
15	...Muscle Shoals AL 35660	Muscle Shoals AL 35660
16	...988 Larkin Johnson Ave SE	988 Larkin Johnson Ave SE
17	...5501 Greenville Blvd NE	5501 Greenview Blvd NE
18	...7133 N Baranmor Pky	7133 N Baranmor Pky
19	...10500 Montana Rd	10500 Montana Rd
20	...4769 E Kalispell Dr	4769 E Kalispell Cir
21	...Daytona Beach Fla 32016	Daytona Beach FL 32016
22	...2227 W 94th Ave	2272 W 94th Ave
23	...6399 E Ponce De Leon St	6399 E Ponce De Leon Ct
24	...20800 N Rainbow Pl	20800 N Rainbow Pl
25	...Sasser GA 31785	Sasser GA 31785
26	...Washington D C 20018	Washington D C 20013
27	...6500 Milwaukee NE	6500 Milwaukee SE
28	...1300 Strasburg Dr	1300 Strasburg Dr
29	...Burnettsville IN 47926	Bornettsville IN 47926

30	...1594 S Frontage St	1594 S Frontage Ave
31	...37099 Oliphant Ln	37909 Oliphant Ln
32	...2248 Avonsdale Cir NW	2248 Avonsdale Cir NE
33	...1733 Norlander Dr SE	1733 Norlander Dr SW
34	...15469 W Oxalida Dr	15469 W Oxalido Dr
35	...4192 E Commonwealth Ave	4192 E Commonwealth Ave
36	...Kingsfield Maine 04947	Kingsfield Maine 04947
37	...246 East Ramsdell Rd	246 East Ramsdale Rd
38	...8456 Vina Del Maro Blvd	8456 Vina Del Maro Blvd
39	...6688 N 26th Street	6888 N 26th Street
40	...1477 Woodrow Wilson Blvd	1477 Woodrow Wilson Blvd
41	...3724 S 18th Ave	3724 S 18th Ave
42	...11454 S Lake Maggiore Blvd	11454 S Lake Maggiore Blvd
43	...4832 N Bougainnvilla Ave	4832 N Bougainnvillia Ave
44	...3713 Coffee Pot Riviera	3773 Coffee Pot Riviera
45	...2800 S Freemont Ter	2800 S Freemond Ter
46	...3654 S Urbane Dr	3654 S Urbane Cir
47	...1408 Oklahoma Ave NE	1408 Oklahoma Ave NE
48	...6201 Meadowland Ln	6201 Meadowlawn Ln
49	...5799 S Augusta Ln	15799 S Augusta Ln
50	...5115 Winchester Rd	5115 Westchester Rd
51	...4611 N Kendall Pl	4611 N Kendall Pl
52	...17045 Dormieone Cir	17045 Dormieone Cir
53	...3349 Palma Del Mar Blvd	3346 Palma Del Mar Blvd
54	...13211 E 182nd Ave	12311 E 182nd Ave
55	...Evansville WY 82636	Evansville WI 82636
56	...6198 N Albritton Rd	6198 N Albretton Rd
57	...11230 Twinflower Cir	11230 Twintower Cir
58	...6191 Lockett Station Rd	6191 Lockett Station Rd
59	...1587 Vanderbilt Dr N	1587 Vanderbilt Dr S
60	...Ontarioville IL 60103	Ontarioville IL 60103
61	...4204 Bridgeton Ave	4204 Bridgeton Ave
62	...31215 N Emerald Dr	31215 N Emerald Cir
63	...4601 N Peniman Ave	4601 N Peniman Ave

64	...3782 SE Verrazanna Bay	3782 SE Verrazana Bay
65	...2766 N Thunderbird Ct	2766 N Thunderbird Ct
66	...2166 N Elmorado Ct	2166 N Eldorado Ct
67	...10538 Innsbruck Ln	1058 Innsbruck Ln
68	...888 Lonesome Rd	8888 Lonesome Rd
69	...4023 N Brainbridge Ave	4023 N Brainbridge Ave
70	...3000 E Roberta Rd	30000 E Roberta Rd
71	...Quenemo KS 66528	Quenemo KS 66528
72	...13845 Donahoo St	13345 Donahoo St
73	...10466 Gertrude NE	10466 Gertrude NE
74	...2733 N 105th Ave	2733 S 105th Ave
75	...3100 N Wyandotte Cir	3100 N Wyandotte Ave
76	...11796 Summittcrest Dr	11769 Summittcrest Dr
77	...Viburnum Miss 65566	Viburnom Miss 65566
78	...9334 Kindleberger Rd	9334 Kindleberger Road
79	...4801 Armourdale Pky	8401 Armourdale Pky
80	...9392 Northrup Ave	9392 Northrop Ave
81	...11736 Rottinghaus Rd	11736 Rottinghaus Rd
82	...3878 Flammang Dr	3878 Flammang Dr
83	...2101 Johnstontown Way	2101 Johnsontown Way
84	...1177 Ghentwoodrow St	1177 Ghentwoodrow Ct
85	...888 Onadaga Ct	888 Onadaga Ct
86	...3205 N Rastetter Ave	3205 N Rastetter Ave
87	...1144 Yellowsands Dr NE	1144 Yellowsands Dr NW
88	...3197 Clerkenwell Ct	3197 Clerkenwell Ct
89	...3021 Pemaquid Way	3210 Pemaquid Way
90	...1398 Angelina Rd	1398 Angelino Rd
91	...4331 NW Zoeller Ave	4881 NW Zoeller Ave
92	...1805 Jeassamine Ln	1805 Jassamine Ln
93	...14411 Bellemeade Ave	14411 Bellemeade Ave
94	...Noquochoke MA 02790	Noguochoke MA 02790
95	...11601 Hagamann Cir	11601 Hagamann Ct

END OF ADDRESS CHECKING

Part B—Memory for Addresses

Sample Questions

The sample questions for this part are based upon the addresses in the five boxes below. Your task is to mark on your answer sheet the letter of the box in which each address belongs. You will have five minutes now to study the locations of the addresses. Then cover the boxes and try to mark the location of the sample questions. You may look back at the boxes if you cannot yet mark the address locations from memory.

The exam itself provides three practice sessions before the question set that really counts. Practice I and Practice III supply you with the boxes and permit you to refer to them if necessary. Practice II and the Memory for Addresses test itself do not permit you to look at the boxes. The test itself is based on memory.

A	B	C	D	E
8300–8699 Ball Meadow 9800–9999 Wren Denim 8200–8299 Slug	9100–9799 Ball Swing 8700–9099 Wren Vapor 9800–9999 Slug	9800–9999 Ball Winter 8300–8699 Wren Artisan 8700–9099 Slug	8200–8299 Ball Checker 9100–9799 Wren Zenith 8300–8699 Slug	8700–9099 Ball Ford 8200–8299 Wren Hammock 9100–9799 Slug

1. 8700–9099 Wren

2. 9100–9799 Slug

3. Denim

4. 9800–9999 Ball

5. Checker

6. Hammock

7. 9800–9999 Slug

8. 8300–8699 Ball

9. 8200–8299 Wren

10. Vapor

11. 8700–9099 Slug

12. Artisan

13. 8200–8299 Ball

14. 9100–9799 Wren

SAMPLE ANSWER SHEET

1. (A) (B) (C) (D) (E)
2. (A) (B) (C) (D) (E)
3. (A) (B) (C) (D) (E)
4. (A) (B) (C) (D) (E)
5. (A) (B) (C) (D) (E)
6. (A) (B) (C) (D) (E)
7. (A) (B) (C) (D) (E)
8. (A) (B) (C) (D) (E)
9. (A) (B) (C) (D) (E)
10. (A) (B) (C) (D) (E)
11. (A) (B) (C) (D) (E)
12. (A) (B) (C) (D) (E)
13. (A) (B) (C) (D) (E)
14. (A) (B) (C) (D) (E)

CORRECT ANSWERS

1. (A) ● (C) (D) (E)
2. (A) (B) (C) (D) ●
3. ● (B) (C) (D) (E)
4. (A) (B) ● (D) (E)
5. (A) (B) (C) ● (E)
6. (A) (B) (C) (D) ●
7. (A) ● (C) (D) (E)
8. ● (B) (C) (D) (E)
9. (A) (B) (C) (D) ●
10. (A) ● (C) (D) (E)
11. (A) (B) ● (D) (E)
12. (A) (B) ● (D) (E)
13. (A) (B) (C) ● (E)
14. (A) (B) (C) ● (E)

Practice for Memory for Addresses

DIRECTIONS: The five boxes below are labeled A, B, C, D, and E. In each box are three sets of number spans with names and two names that are not associated with numbers. In the next THREE MINUTES, you must try to memorize the box location of each name and number span. The position of a name or number span within its box is not important. You need only remember the letter of the box in which the item is to be found. You will use these names and numbers to answer three sets of practice questions that are NOT scored and one actual test that is scored. Correct answers are on pages 54 and 55.

A	B	C	D	E
8300–8699 Ball	9100–9799 Ball	9800–9999 Ball	8200–8299 Ball	8700–9099 Ball
Meadow	Swing	Winter	Checker	Ford
9800–9999 Wren	8700–9099 Wren	8300–8699 Wren	9100–9799 Wren	8200–8299 Wren
Denim	Vapor	Artisan	Zenith	Hammock
8200–8299 Slug	9800–9999 Slug	8700–9099 Slug	8300–8699 Slug	9100–9799 Slug

Practice I

DIRECTIONS: Use the next THREE MINUTES to mark on the answer sheet at the end of Practice I the letter of the box in which each item that follows is to be found. Try to mark each item without looking back at the boxes. If, however, you get stuck, you may refer to the boxes during this practice exercise. If you find that you must look at the boxes, try to memorize as you do so. This test is for practice only. It will not be scored.

1. 9100–9799 Wren
2. 8700–9099 Slug
3. Winter
4. 8700–9099 Ball
5. 9800–9999 Wren
6. 9800–9999 Slug
7. 8700–9099 Wren
8. Meadow
9. Vapor
10. 9100–9799 Ball
11. 9100–9799 Slug
12. 8700–9099 Wren
13. 9800–9999 Ball
14. 8200–8299 Wren
15. Checker
16. Hammock
17. 8300–8699 Ball
18. 9100–9799 Wren
19. 8300–8699 Slug

20. 8700–9099 Wren
21. 8200–8299 Slug
22. Ford
23. Denim
24. 9800–9999 Wren
25. 9100–9799 Ball
26. Artisan
27. 8700–9099 Ball
28. 8200–8299 Ball
29. 8200–8299 Wren
30. Zenith
31. Vapor
32. Meadow
33. 8700–9099 Slug
34. 9800–9999 Slug
35. 9800–9999 Wren
36. Winter
37. Swing
38. 9100–9799 Slug

39. 9800–9999 Ball
40. 8300–9699 Wren
41. 8300–8699 Ball
42. Swing
43. Zenith
44. 9100–9799 Slug
45. 8700–9099 Ball
46. Checker
47. 8300–8699 Wren
48. Vapor
49. 8200–8299 Slug
50. 9800–9999 Wren
51. 9100–9799 Wren
52. Artisan
53. Swing
54. Hammock
55. 8300–8699 Slug
56. 8300–8699 Ball
57. 9800–9999 Ball

58. 8700–9099 Slug
59. Meadow
60. Denim
61. 9100–9799 Ball
62. 8200–8299 Ball
63. Ford
64. 9100–9799 Slug
65. 9800–9999 Slug
66. Winter
67. Zenith
68. 8700–9099 Wren

69. 8200–8299 Wren
70. Checker
71. 8700–9099 Ball
72. 8300–8699 Slug
73. 9100–9799 Wren
74. 9800–9999 Ball
75. Meadow
76. 8700–9099 Wren
77. 8300–8699 Ball
78. 9100–9799 Slug
79. Hammock

80. Vapor
81. 9800–9999 Slug
82. 8200–8299 Wren
83. Artisan
84. Swing
85. 9800–9999 Ball
86. 9100–9799 Wren
87. 8200–8299 Slug
88. 8700–9099 Ball

Practice I Answer Sheet (2)

1 Ⓐ Ⓑ Ⓒ Ⓓ Ⓔ	23 Ⓐ Ⓑ Ⓒ Ⓓ Ⓔ	45 Ⓐ Ⓑ Ⓒ Ⓓ Ⓔ	67 Ⓐ Ⓑ Ⓒ Ⓓ Ⓔ
2 Ⓐ Ⓑ Ⓒ Ⓓ Ⓔ	24 Ⓐ Ⓑ Ⓒ Ⓓ Ⓔ	46 Ⓐ Ⓑ Ⓒ Ⓓ Ⓔ	68 Ⓐ Ⓑ Ⓒ Ⓓ Ⓔ
3 Ⓐ Ⓑ Ⓒ Ⓓ Ⓔ	25 Ⓐ Ⓑ Ⓒ Ⓓ Ⓔ	47 Ⓐ Ⓑ Ⓒ Ⓓ Ⓔ	69 Ⓐ Ⓑ Ⓒ Ⓓ Ⓔ
4 Ⓐ Ⓑ Ⓒ Ⓓ Ⓔ	26 Ⓐ Ⓑ Ⓒ Ⓓ Ⓔ	48 Ⓐ Ⓑ Ⓒ Ⓓ Ⓔ	70 Ⓐ Ⓑ Ⓒ Ⓓ Ⓔ
5 Ⓐ Ⓑ Ⓒ Ⓓ Ⓔ	27 Ⓐ Ⓑ Ⓒ Ⓓ Ⓔ	49 Ⓐ Ⓑ Ⓒ Ⓓ Ⓔ	71 Ⓐ Ⓑ Ⓒ Ⓓ Ⓔ
6 Ⓐ Ⓑ Ⓒ Ⓓ Ⓔ	28 Ⓐ Ⓑ Ⓒ Ⓓ Ⓔ	50 Ⓐ Ⓑ Ⓒ Ⓓ Ⓔ	72 Ⓐ Ⓑ Ⓒ Ⓓ Ⓔ
7 Ⓐ Ⓑ Ⓒ Ⓓ Ⓔ	29 Ⓐ Ⓑ Ⓒ Ⓓ Ⓔ	51 Ⓐ Ⓑ Ⓒ Ⓓ Ⓔ	73 Ⓐ Ⓑ Ⓒ Ⓓ Ⓔ
8 Ⓐ Ⓑ Ⓒ Ⓓ Ⓔ	30 Ⓐ Ⓑ Ⓒ Ⓓ Ⓔ	52 Ⓐ Ⓑ Ⓒ Ⓓ Ⓔ	74 Ⓐ Ⓑ Ⓒ Ⓓ Ⓔ
9 Ⓐ Ⓑ Ⓒ Ⓓ Ⓔ	31 Ⓐ Ⓑ Ⓒ Ⓓ Ⓔ	53 Ⓐ Ⓑ Ⓒ Ⓓ Ⓔ	75 Ⓐ Ⓑ Ⓒ Ⓓ Ⓔ
10 Ⓐ Ⓑ Ⓒ Ⓓ Ⓔ	32 Ⓐ Ⓑ Ⓒ Ⓓ Ⓔ	54 Ⓐ Ⓑ Ⓒ Ⓓ Ⓔ	76 Ⓐ Ⓑ Ⓒ Ⓓ Ⓔ
11 Ⓐ Ⓑ Ⓒ Ⓓ Ⓔ	33 Ⓐ Ⓑ Ⓒ Ⓓ Ⓔ	55 Ⓐ Ⓑ Ⓒ Ⓓ Ⓔ	77 Ⓐ Ⓑ Ⓒ Ⓓ Ⓔ
12 Ⓐ Ⓑ Ⓒ Ⓓ Ⓔ	34 Ⓐ Ⓑ Ⓒ Ⓓ Ⓔ	56 Ⓐ Ⓑ Ⓒ Ⓓ Ⓔ	78 Ⓐ Ⓑ Ⓒ Ⓓ Ⓔ
13 Ⓐ Ⓑ Ⓒ Ⓓ Ⓔ	35 Ⓐ Ⓑ Ⓒ Ⓓ Ⓔ	57 Ⓐ Ⓑ Ⓒ Ⓓ Ⓔ	79 Ⓐ Ⓑ Ⓒ Ⓓ Ⓔ
14 Ⓐ Ⓑ Ⓒ Ⓓ Ⓔ	36 Ⓐ Ⓑ Ⓒ Ⓓ Ⓔ	58 Ⓐ Ⓑ Ⓒ Ⓓ Ⓔ	80 Ⓐ Ⓑ Ⓒ Ⓓ Ⓔ
15 Ⓐ Ⓑ Ⓒ Ⓓ Ⓔ	37 Ⓐ Ⓑ Ⓒ Ⓓ Ⓔ	59 Ⓐ Ⓑ Ⓒ Ⓓ Ⓔ	81 Ⓐ Ⓑ Ⓒ Ⓓ Ⓔ
16 Ⓐ Ⓑ Ⓒ Ⓓ Ⓔ	38 Ⓐ Ⓑ Ⓒ Ⓓ Ⓔ	60 Ⓐ Ⓑ Ⓒ Ⓓ Ⓔ	82 Ⓐ Ⓑ Ⓒ Ⓓ Ⓔ
17 Ⓐ Ⓑ Ⓒ Ⓓ Ⓔ	39 Ⓐ Ⓑ Ⓒ Ⓓ Ⓔ	61 Ⓐ Ⓑ Ⓒ Ⓓ Ⓔ	83 Ⓐ Ⓑ Ⓒ Ⓓ Ⓔ
18 Ⓐ Ⓑ Ⓒ Ⓓ Ⓔ	40 Ⓐ Ⓑ Ⓒ Ⓓ Ⓔ	62 Ⓐ Ⓑ Ⓒ Ⓓ Ⓔ	84 Ⓐ Ⓑ Ⓒ Ⓓ Ⓔ
19 Ⓐ Ⓑ Ⓒ Ⓓ Ⓔ	41 Ⓐ Ⓑ Ⓒ Ⓓ Ⓔ	63 Ⓐ Ⓑ Ⓒ Ⓓ Ⓔ	85 Ⓐ Ⓑ Ⓒ Ⓓ Ⓔ
20 Ⓐ Ⓑ Ⓒ Ⓓ Ⓔ	42 Ⓐ Ⓑ Ⓒ Ⓓ Ⓔ	64 Ⓐ Ⓑ Ⓒ Ⓓ Ⓔ	86 Ⓐ Ⓑ Ⓒ Ⓓ Ⓔ
21 Ⓐ Ⓑ Ⓒ Ⓓ Ⓔ	43 Ⓐ Ⓑ Ⓒ Ⓓ Ⓔ	65 Ⓐ Ⓑ Ⓒ Ⓓ Ⓔ	87 Ⓐ Ⓑ Ⓒ Ⓓ Ⓔ
22 Ⓐ Ⓑ Ⓒ Ⓓ Ⓔ	44 Ⓐ Ⓑ Ⓒ Ⓓ Ⓔ	66 Ⓐ Ⓑ Ⓒ Ⓓ Ⓔ	88 Ⓐ Ⓑ Ⓒ Ⓓ Ⓔ

Practice II

DIRECTIONS: The next 88 questions constitute another practice exercise. Mark your answers on the Practice II answer sheet. Again, the time limit is THREE MINUTES. This time, however, you must NOT look at the boxes while answering the questions. You must rely on your memory in marking the box location of each item. This practice test will not be scored.

1. 8200–8299 Ball
2. 8300–8699 Wren
3. 9800–9999 Slug
4. Hammock
5. Meadow
6. 8700–9099 Ball
7. 8700–9099 Slug
8. 9800–9999 Wren
9. Zenith
10. Swing
11. 8200–8299 Wren
12. 8200–8299 Slug
13. 8300–8699 Slug
14. 9100–9799 Ball
15. Ford
16. Checker
17. Artisan
18. 8300–8699 Ball
19. 8700–9099 Wren
20. 9800–9999 Wren
21. Vapor
22. Meadow
23. 8200–8299 Ball
24. Winter
25. Ford
26. 8300–8699 Ball
27. 8700–9099 Wren
28. 8700–9099 Slug
29. Zenith
30. Checker
31. 8700–9099 Ball
32. 9100–9799 Wren
33. 9800–9999 Slug
34. 8200–8299 Slug
35. Denim
36. Winter
37. Hammock
38. 9100–9799 Slug
39. 9100–9799 Ball
40. 9800–9999 Ball
41. Artisan
42. Meadow
43. 9800–9999 Wren
44. 8300–8699 Wren
45. 8300–8699 Slug
46. 8300–8699 Ball
47. Swing
48. Vapor
49. 9800–9999 Ball
50. 9100–9799 Wren
51. 9100–9799 Slug
52. 8700–9099 Wren
53. 8300–8699 Ball
54. Swing
55. Zenith
56. Hammock
57. Denim
58. 8700–9099 Ball
59. 8300–8699 Slug
60. 9800–9999 Slug
61. 9800–9999 Wren
62. 8700–9099 Slug
63. Meadow
64. 8200–8299 Ball
65. 9100–9799 Ball
66. Ford
67. 8200–8299 Wren
68. 8300–8699 Wren
69. 8300–8699 Slug
70. Checker
71. Artisan
72. 8700–9099 Wren
73. 8200–8299 Slug
74. 8700–9099 Slug
75. Winter
76. Vapor
77. 8300–8699 Ball
78. 8700–9099 Ball
79. 8700–9099 Slug
80. Vapor
81. Swing
82. 9800–9999 Wren
83. 9800–9999 Ball
84. 8300–8699 Wren
85. 8300–8699 Ball
86. 8300–8699 Slug
87. Hammock
88. Denim

Practice II Answer Sheet

1 Ⓐ Ⓑ Ⓒ Ⓓ Ⓔ	23 Ⓐ Ⓑ Ⓒ Ⓓ Ⓔ	45 Ⓐ Ⓑ Ⓒ Ⓓ Ⓔ	67 Ⓐ Ⓑ Ⓒ Ⓓ Ⓔ
2 Ⓐ Ⓑ Ⓒ Ⓓ Ⓔ	24 Ⓐ Ⓑ Ⓒ Ⓓ Ⓔ	46 Ⓐ Ⓑ Ⓒ Ⓓ Ⓔ	68 Ⓐ Ⓑ Ⓒ Ⓓ Ⓔ
3 Ⓐ Ⓑ Ⓒ Ⓓ Ⓔ	25 Ⓐ Ⓑ Ⓒ Ⓓ Ⓔ	47 Ⓐ Ⓑ Ⓒ Ⓓ Ⓔ	69 Ⓐ Ⓑ Ⓒ Ⓓ Ⓔ
4 Ⓐ Ⓑ Ⓒ Ⓓ Ⓔ	26 Ⓐ Ⓑ Ⓒ Ⓓ Ⓔ	48 Ⓐ Ⓑ Ⓒ Ⓓ Ⓔ	70 Ⓐ Ⓑ Ⓒ Ⓓ Ⓔ
5 Ⓐ Ⓑ Ⓒ Ⓓ Ⓔ	27 Ⓐ Ⓑ Ⓒ Ⓓ Ⓔ	49 Ⓐ Ⓑ Ⓒ Ⓓ Ⓔ	71 Ⓐ Ⓑ Ⓒ Ⓓ Ⓔ
6 Ⓐ Ⓑ Ⓒ Ⓓ Ⓔ	28 Ⓐ Ⓑ Ⓒ Ⓓ Ⓔ	50 Ⓐ Ⓑ Ⓒ Ⓓ Ⓔ	72 Ⓐ Ⓑ Ⓒ Ⓓ Ⓔ
7 Ⓐ Ⓑ Ⓒ Ⓓ Ⓔ	29 Ⓐ Ⓑ Ⓒ Ⓓ Ⓔ	51 Ⓐ Ⓑ Ⓒ Ⓓ Ⓔ	73 Ⓐ Ⓑ Ⓒ Ⓓ Ⓔ
8 Ⓐ Ⓑ Ⓒ Ⓓ Ⓔ	30 Ⓐ Ⓑ Ⓒ Ⓓ Ⓔ	52 Ⓐ Ⓑ Ⓒ Ⓓ Ⓔ	74 Ⓐ Ⓑ Ⓒ Ⓓ Ⓔ
9 Ⓐ Ⓑ Ⓒ Ⓓ Ⓔ	31 Ⓐ Ⓑ Ⓒ Ⓓ Ⓔ	53 Ⓐ Ⓑ Ⓒ Ⓓ Ⓔ	75 Ⓐ Ⓑ Ⓒ Ⓓ Ⓔ
10 Ⓐ Ⓑ Ⓒ Ⓓ Ⓔ	32 Ⓐ Ⓑ Ⓒ Ⓓ Ⓔ	54 Ⓐ Ⓑ Ⓒ Ⓓ Ⓔ	76 Ⓐ Ⓑ Ⓒ Ⓓ Ⓔ
11 Ⓐ Ⓑ Ⓒ Ⓓ Ⓔ	33 Ⓐ Ⓑ Ⓒ Ⓓ Ⓔ	55 Ⓐ Ⓑ Ⓒ Ⓓ Ⓔ	77 Ⓐ Ⓑ Ⓒ Ⓓ Ⓔ
12 Ⓐ Ⓑ Ⓒ Ⓓ Ⓔ	34 Ⓐ Ⓑ Ⓒ Ⓓ Ⓔ	56 Ⓐ Ⓑ Ⓒ Ⓓ Ⓔ	78 Ⓐ Ⓑ Ⓒ Ⓓ Ⓔ
13 Ⓐ Ⓑ Ⓒ Ⓓ Ⓔ	35 Ⓐ Ⓑ Ⓒ Ⓓ Ⓔ	57 Ⓐ Ⓑ Ⓒ Ⓓ Ⓔ	79 Ⓐ Ⓑ Ⓒ Ⓓ Ⓔ
14 Ⓐ Ⓑ Ⓒ Ⓓ Ⓔ	36 Ⓐ Ⓑ Ⓒ Ⓓ Ⓔ	58 Ⓐ Ⓑ Ⓒ Ⓓ Ⓔ	80 Ⓐ Ⓑ Ⓒ Ⓓ Ⓔ
15 Ⓐ Ⓑ Ⓒ Ⓓ Ⓔ	37 Ⓐ Ⓑ Ⓒ Ⓓ Ⓔ	59 Ⓐ Ⓑ Ⓒ Ⓓ Ⓔ	81 Ⓐ Ⓑ Ⓒ Ⓓ Ⓔ
16 Ⓐ Ⓑ Ⓒ Ⓓ Ⓔ	38 Ⓐ Ⓑ Ⓒ Ⓓ Ⓔ	60 Ⓐ Ⓑ Ⓒ Ⓓ Ⓔ	82 Ⓐ Ⓑ Ⓒ Ⓓ Ⓔ
17 Ⓐ Ⓑ Ⓒ Ⓓ Ⓔ	39 Ⓐ Ⓑ Ⓒ Ⓓ Ⓔ	61 Ⓐ Ⓑ Ⓒ Ⓓ Ⓔ	83 Ⓐ Ⓑ Ⓒ Ⓓ Ⓔ
18 Ⓐ Ⓑ Ⓒ Ⓓ Ⓔ	40 Ⓐ Ⓑ Ⓒ Ⓓ Ⓔ	62 Ⓐ Ⓑ Ⓒ Ⓓ Ⓔ	84 Ⓐ Ⓑ Ⓒ Ⓓ Ⓔ
19 Ⓐ Ⓑ Ⓒ Ⓓ Ⓔ	41 Ⓐ Ⓑ Ⓒ Ⓓ Ⓔ	63 Ⓐ Ⓑ Ⓒ Ⓓ Ⓔ	85 Ⓐ Ⓑ Ⓒ Ⓓ Ⓔ
20 Ⓐ Ⓑ Ⓒ Ⓓ Ⓔ	42 Ⓐ Ⓑ Ⓒ Ⓓ Ⓔ	64 Ⓐ Ⓑ Ⓒ Ⓓ Ⓔ	86 Ⓐ Ⓑ Ⓒ Ⓓ Ⓔ
21 Ⓐ Ⓑ Ⓒ Ⓓ Ⓔ	43 Ⓐ Ⓑ Ⓒ Ⓓ Ⓔ	65 Ⓐ Ⓑ Ⓒ Ⓓ Ⓔ	87 Ⓐ Ⓑ Ⓒ Ⓓ Ⓔ
22 Ⓐ Ⓑ Ⓒ Ⓓ Ⓔ	44 Ⓐ Ⓑ Ⓒ Ⓓ Ⓔ	66 Ⓐ Ⓑ Ⓒ Ⓓ Ⓔ	88 Ⓐ Ⓑ Ⓒ Ⓓ Ⓔ

Practice III

DIRECTIONS: *The names and addresses are repeated for you in the boxes below. Each name and each number span is in the same box in which you found it in the original set. You will now be allowed FIVE MINUTES to study the locations again. Do your best to memorize the letter of the box in which each item is located. This is your last chance to see the boxes.*

A	B	C	D	E
8300–8699 Ball	9100–9799 Ball	9800–9999 Ball	8200–8299 Ball	8700–9099 Ball
Meadow	Swing	Winter	Checker	Ford
9800–9999 Wren	8700–9099 Wren	8300–8699 Wren	9100–9799 Wren	8200–8299 Wren
Denim	Vapor	Artisan	Zenith	Hammock
8200–8299 Slug	9800–9999 Slug	8700–9099 Slug	8300–8699 Slug	9100–9799 Slug

DIRECTIONS: *This is your last practice test. Mark the location of each of the 88 items on the Practice III answer sheet. You will have FIVE MINUTES to answer these questions. Do NOT look back at the boxes. This practice test will not be scored.*

1. 8200–8299 Ball
2. 9100–9799 Wren
3. 8300–8699 Slug
4. 8700–9099 Wren
5. Denim
6. Ford
7. 8300–8699 Ball
8. 9100–9799 Slug
9. 8200–8299 Slug
10. Meadow
11. Zenith
12. 8700–9099 Slug
13. 9800–9999 Ball
14. 9100–9799 Ball
15. 8700–9099 Wren
16. 9100–9799 Slug
17. 9100–9799 Ball
18. 9100–9799 Wren
19. Artisan
20. Vapor
21. 8300–8699 Wren
22. Meadow

23. 9800–9999 Slug
24. 8700–9099 Wren
25. 8700–9099 Ball
26. Winter
27. Denim
28. 8200–8299 Ball
29. 8300–8699 Slug
30. Hammock
31. Ford
32. 8300–8699 Ball
33. 8700–9099 Wren
34. 8700–9099 Slug
35. Meadow
36. Vapor
37. 8700–9099 Ball
38. 9100–9799 Wren
39. 9800–9999 Ball
40. 9800–9999 Slug
41. Hammock
42. Winter
43. Swing
44. 9100–9799 Ball

45. 9100–9799 Slug
46. 8300–8699 Wren
47. 8200–8299 Wren
48. Ford
49. Zenith
50. 8200–8299 Slug
51. 8300–8699 Slug
52. Denim
53. 8200–8299 Ball
54. 9800–9999 Wren
55. Artisan
56. Checker
57. 9100–9799 Slug
58. 9100–9799 Ball
59. 8200–8299 Wren
60. 8300–8699 Wren
61. 9800–9999 Ball
62. 8200–8299 Wren
63. 8200–8299 Slug
64. 8700–9099 Wren
65. Hammock
66. Zenith

67. 9100–9799 Ball	75. 8300–8699 Slug	83. Swing
68. 9800–9999 Slug	76. Checker	84. Artisan
69. 8300–8699 Ball	77. Winter	85. Ford
70. 8300–8699 Wren	78. Vapor	86. 9800–9999 Ball
71. Denim	79. 9100–9799 Slug	87. 8200–8299 Wren
72. Meadow	80. 9100–9799 Wren	88. 8300–8699 Ball
73. 9800–9999 Wren	81. 8700–9099 Ball	
74. 8200–8299 Ball	82. 8700–9099 Slug	

Practice III Answer Sheet

1 Ⓐ Ⓑ Ⓒ Ⓓ Ⓔ	23 Ⓐ Ⓑ Ⓒ Ⓓ Ⓔ	45 Ⓐ Ⓑ Ⓒ Ⓓ Ⓔ	67 Ⓐ Ⓑ Ⓒ Ⓓ Ⓔ
2 Ⓐ Ⓑ Ⓒ Ⓓ Ⓔ	24 Ⓐ Ⓑ Ⓒ Ⓓ Ⓔ	46 Ⓐ Ⓑ Ⓒ Ⓓ Ⓔ	68 Ⓐ Ⓑ Ⓒ Ⓓ Ⓔ
3 Ⓐ Ⓑ Ⓒ Ⓓ Ⓔ	25 Ⓐ Ⓑ Ⓒ Ⓓ Ⓔ	47 Ⓐ Ⓑ Ⓒ Ⓓ Ⓔ	69 Ⓐ Ⓑ Ⓒ Ⓓ Ⓔ
4 Ⓐ Ⓑ Ⓒ Ⓓ Ⓔ	26 Ⓐ Ⓑ Ⓒ Ⓓ Ⓔ	48 Ⓐ Ⓑ Ⓒ Ⓓ Ⓔ	70 Ⓐ Ⓑ Ⓒ Ⓓ Ⓔ
5 Ⓐ Ⓑ Ⓒ Ⓓ Ⓔ	27 Ⓐ Ⓑ Ⓒ Ⓓ Ⓔ	49 Ⓐ Ⓑ Ⓒ Ⓓ Ⓔ	71 Ⓐ Ⓑ Ⓒ Ⓓ Ⓔ
6 Ⓐ Ⓑ Ⓒ Ⓓ Ⓔ	28 Ⓐ Ⓑ Ⓒ Ⓓ Ⓔ	50 Ⓐ Ⓑ Ⓒ Ⓓ Ⓔ	72 Ⓐ Ⓑ Ⓒ Ⓓ Ⓔ
7 Ⓐ Ⓑ Ⓒ Ⓓ Ⓔ	29 Ⓐ Ⓑ Ⓒ Ⓓ Ⓔ	51 Ⓐ Ⓑ Ⓒ Ⓓ Ⓔ	73 Ⓐ Ⓑ Ⓒ Ⓓ Ⓔ
8 Ⓐ Ⓑ Ⓒ Ⓓ Ⓔ	30 Ⓐ Ⓑ Ⓒ Ⓓ Ⓔ	52 Ⓐ Ⓑ Ⓒ Ⓓ Ⓔ	74 Ⓐ Ⓑ Ⓒ Ⓓ Ⓔ
9 Ⓐ Ⓑ Ⓒ Ⓓ Ⓔ	31 Ⓐ Ⓑ Ⓒ Ⓓ Ⓔ	53 Ⓐ Ⓑ Ⓒ Ⓓ Ⓔ	75 Ⓐ Ⓑ Ⓒ Ⓓ Ⓔ
10 Ⓐ Ⓑ Ⓒ Ⓓ Ⓔ	32 Ⓐ Ⓑ Ⓒ Ⓓ Ⓔ	54 Ⓐ Ⓑ Ⓒ Ⓓ Ⓔ	76 Ⓐ Ⓑ Ⓒ Ⓓ Ⓔ
11 Ⓐ Ⓑ Ⓒ Ⓓ Ⓔ	33 Ⓐ Ⓑ Ⓒ Ⓓ Ⓔ	55 Ⓐ Ⓑ Ⓒ Ⓓ Ⓔ	77 Ⓐ Ⓑ Ⓒ Ⓓ Ⓔ
12 Ⓐ Ⓑ Ⓒ Ⓓ Ⓔ	34 Ⓐ Ⓑ Ⓒ Ⓓ Ⓔ	56 Ⓐ Ⓑ Ⓒ Ⓓ Ⓔ	78 Ⓐ Ⓑ Ⓒ Ⓓ Ⓔ
13 Ⓐ Ⓑ Ⓒ Ⓓ Ⓔ	35 Ⓐ Ⓑ Ⓒ Ⓓ Ⓔ	57 Ⓐ Ⓑ Ⓒ Ⓓ Ⓔ	79 Ⓐ Ⓑ Ⓒ Ⓓ Ⓔ
14 Ⓐ Ⓑ Ⓒ Ⓓ Ⓔ	36 Ⓐ Ⓑ Ⓒ Ⓓ Ⓔ	58 Ⓐ Ⓑ Ⓒ Ⓓ Ⓔ	80 Ⓐ Ⓑ Ⓒ Ⓓ Ⓔ
15 Ⓐ Ⓑ Ⓒ Ⓓ Ⓔ	37 Ⓐ Ⓑ Ⓒ Ⓓ Ⓔ	59 Ⓐ Ⓑ Ⓒ Ⓓ Ⓔ	81 Ⓐ Ⓑ Ⓒ Ⓓ Ⓔ
16 Ⓐ Ⓑ Ⓒ Ⓓ Ⓔ	38 Ⓐ Ⓑ Ⓒ Ⓓ Ⓔ	60 Ⓐ Ⓑ Ⓒ Ⓓ Ⓔ	82 Ⓐ Ⓑ Ⓒ Ⓓ Ⓔ
17 Ⓐ Ⓑ Ⓒ Ⓓ Ⓔ	39 Ⓐ Ⓑ Ⓒ Ⓓ Ⓔ	61 Ⓐ Ⓑ Ⓒ Ⓓ Ⓔ	83 Ⓐ Ⓑ Ⓒ Ⓓ Ⓔ
18 Ⓐ Ⓑ Ⓒ Ⓓ Ⓔ	40 Ⓐ Ⓑ Ⓒ Ⓓ Ⓔ	62 Ⓐ Ⓑ Ⓒ Ⓓ Ⓔ	84 Ⓐ Ⓑ Ⓒ Ⓓ Ⓔ
19 Ⓐ Ⓑ Ⓒ Ⓓ Ⓔ	41 Ⓐ Ⓑ Ⓒ Ⓓ Ⓔ	63 Ⓐ Ⓑ Ⓒ Ⓓ Ⓔ	85 Ⓐ Ⓑ Ⓒ Ⓓ Ⓔ
20 Ⓐ Ⓑ Ⓒ Ⓓ Ⓔ	42 Ⓐ Ⓑ Ⓒ Ⓓ Ⓔ	64 Ⓐ Ⓑ Ⓒ Ⓓ Ⓔ	86 Ⓐ Ⓑ Ⓒ Ⓓ Ⓔ
21 Ⓐ Ⓑ Ⓒ Ⓓ Ⓔ	43 Ⓐ Ⓑ Ⓒ Ⓓ Ⓔ	65 Ⓐ Ⓑ Ⓒ Ⓓ Ⓔ	87 Ⓐ Ⓑ Ⓒ Ⓓ Ⓔ
22 Ⓐ Ⓑ Ⓒ Ⓓ Ⓔ	44 Ⓐ Ⓑ Ⓒ Ⓓ Ⓔ	66 Ⓐ Ⓑ Ⓒ Ⓓ Ⓔ	88 Ⓐ Ⓑ Ⓒ Ⓓ Ⓔ

Memory for Addresses

Time: 5 Minutes. 88 Questions.

DIRECTIONS: Mark your answers on the answer sheet in the section headed "MEMORY FOR ADDRESSES." This test will be scored. You are NOT permitted to look at the boxes. Work from memory, as quickly and as accurately as you can. Correct answers are on page 55.

1. 9800–9999 Wren
2. 9100–9799 Ball
3. Meadow
4. Hammock
5. 9100–9799 Slug
6. 8200–8299 Ball
7. 9800–9999 Slug
8. Zenith
9. Vapor
10. 8200–8299 Wren
11. 8300–8699 Wren
12. 9800–9999 Ball
13. 8300–8699 Slug
14. Ford
15. Artisan
16. Denim
17. 9800–9999 Slug
18. 8200–8299 Slug
19. 8700–9099 Wren
20. 9100–9799 Wren
21. Checker
22. Swing
23. 8300–8699 Slug
24. Winter
25. 9100–9799 Ball
26. 8700–9099 Wren
27. 9100–9799 Slug
28. 8300–8699 Wren
29. Artisan
30. Ford
31. 8300–8699 Ball
32. 8700–9099 Ball
33. 9100–9799 Wren
34. Denim
35. Checker
36. 8200–8299 Slug
37. 8700–9099 Slug
38. 8200–8299 Wren
39. Zenith
40. Hammock
41. 8200–8299 Ball
42. Swing
43. 9800–9999 Slug
44. 9800–9999 Ball
45. Vapor
46. 8700–9099 Ball
47. 9100–9799 Wren
48. 8700–9099 Slug
49. 8700–9099 Wren
50. 8300–8699 Ball
51. Winter
52. Hammock
53. Meadow
54. 8200–8299 Slug
55. 8300–8699 Wren
56. 9100–9799 Slug
57. Denim
58. Swing
59. Ford
60. 9100–9799 Ball
61. 8200–8299 Ball
62. 9100–9799 Wren
63. Checker
64. 9800–9999 Slug
65. 8200–8299 Wren
66. 8300–8699 Slug
67. Vapor
68. Zenith
69. 9800–9999 Ball
70. 9800–9999 Wren
71. Artisan
72. 8200–8299 Ball
73. 8300–8699 Slug
74. 9100–9799 Ball
75. Vapor
76. Meadow
77. 8200–8299 Wren
78. 8700–9099 Slug
79. 9100–9799 Ball
80. Swing
81. Artisan
82. 9800–9999 Wren
83. Hammock
84. 8300–8699 Wren
85. 8300–8699 Ball
86. 9100–9799 Slug
87. Checker
88. Ford

END OF MEMORY FOR ADDRESSES

Part C—Number Series

Sample Questions

The following sample questions show you the type of question that will be used in Part C. You will have three minutes to answer the sample questions below and to study the explanations.

DIRECTIONS: Each number series question consists of a series of numbers that follows some definite order. The numbers progress from left to right according to some rule. One pair of numbers to the right of the series comprises the next two numbers in the series. Study each series to try to find a pattern to the series and to figure out the rule that governs the progression. Choose the answer pair that continues the series according to the pattern established and mark its letter on your answer sheet.

1. 21 21 19 17 17 15 13 .....(A) 11 11 (B) 13 11 (C) 11 9 (D) 9 7 (E) 13 13

   The pattern of this series is: repeat the number, then subtract 2 and subtract 2 again; repeat the number, then subtract 2 and subtract 2 again and so on. Following the pattern, the series should continue with (**B**) 13 11 and then go on 9 9 7 5 5 3 1 1.

2. 23 22 20 19 16 15 11 .....(A) 6 5 (B) 10 9 (C) 6 1 (D) 10 6 (E) 10 5

   If you write in the changes between the numbers of the series, you can see that the pattern being established is: –1, –2, –1, –3, –1, –4, –1, –5... Fitting the pattern to the remaining numbers, it is apparent that (**E**) is the answer because 11 – 1 = 10 and 10 – 5 = 5.

3. 5 6 8 9 11 12 14 ....(A) 15 16 (B) 16 17 (C) 15 17 (D) 16 18 (E) 17 19

   The pattern here is: +1, +2; +1, +2; +1, +2 and so on. The answer is (**C**) because 14 + 1 = 15 and 15 + 2 = 17.

4. 7 10 8 13 16 8 19 ....(A) 22 8 (B) 8 22 (C) 20 21 (D) 22 25 (E) 8 25

   Marking the changes between numbers is not sufficient for solving this series. You first must notice that the number <u>8</u> is repeated after each two numbers. If you disregard the 8's, you can see that the series is increasing by a factor of + 3. With this information, you can choose (**A**) as the correct answer because 19 + 3 = 22, and the two numbers, <u>19</u> and <u>22</u>, are then followed by <u>8</u>.

5. 1 35 2 34 3 33 4 ....(A) 4 5 (B) 32 31 (C) 32 5 (D) 5 32 (E) 31 6

   This series is, in reality, two alternating series. One series, beginning with <u>1</u>, increases at the rate of + 1. The other series alternates with the first. It begins with <u>35</u> and decreases by – 1. The answer is (**C**) because the next number in the decreasing series is <u>32</u> and the next number in the increasing series is <u>5</u>.

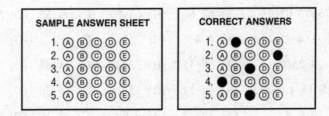

Number Series

Time: 20 Minutes. 24 Questions.

DIRECTIONS: Each number series question consists of a series of numbers that follows some definite order. The numbers progress from left to right according to some rule. One pair of numbers to the right of the series comprises the next two numbers in the series. Study each series to try to find a pattern to the series and to figure out the rule that governs the progression. Choose the answer pair that continues the series according to the pattern established and mark its letter on your answer sheet. Correct answers are on page 55.

1. 8 9 10 8 9 10 8 ....(A) 8 9   (B) 9 10   (C) 9 8   (D) 10 8   (E) 8 10

2. 3 4 4 3 5 5 3 ....(A) 3 3   (B) 6 3   (C) 3 6   (D) 6 6   (E) 6 7

3. 7 7 3 7 7 4 7 ....(A) 7 7   (B) 7 8   (C) 5 7   (D) 8 7   (E) 7 5

4. 18 18 19 20 20 21 22 .....(A) 22 23   (B) 23 24   (C) 23 23   (D) 22 22   (E) 21 22

5. 2 6 10 3 7 11 4 ....(A) 12 16   (B) 5 9   (C) 8 5   (D) 12 5   (E) 8 12

6. 11 8 15 12 19 16 23 ....(A) 27 20   (B) 24 20   (C) 27 24   (D) 20 24   (E) 20 27

7. 16 8 15 9 14 10 13 ....(A) 12 11   (B) 13 12   (C) 11 13   (D) 11 12   (E) 11 14

8. 4 5 13 6 7 12 8 ....(A) 9 11   (B) 13 9   (C) 9 13   (D) 11 9   (E) 11 10

9. 19 24 20 25 21 26 22 .....(A) 18 27   (B) 22 24   (C) 23 29   (D) 27 23   (E) 28 32

10. 25 25 22 22 19 19 16 .....(A) 18 18   (B) 16 16   (C) 16 13   (D) 15 15   (E) 15 13

11. 1 1 2 3 5 8 13 ....(A) 21 29   (B) 21 34   (C) 18 27   (D) 21 27   (E) 24 32

12. 1 3 2 4 3 5 4 ....(A) 6 5   (B) 5 6   (C) 3 1   (D) 3 5   (E) 4 3

13. 1 2 2 3 3 3 4 ....(A) 4 5   (B) 5 5   (C) 3 5   (D) 4 4   (E) 4 3

14. 9 17 24 30 35 39 42 ....(A) 43 44   (B) 44 46   (C) 44 45   (D) 45 49   (E) 46 50

15. 1 4 9 16 25 36 49 ....(A) 56 64   (B) 60 65   (C) 62 75   (D) 64 80   (E) 64 81

16. 8 12 17 24 28 33 40 ....(A) 47 53   (B) 45 50   (C) 43 49   (D) 48 54   (E) 44 49

17. 28 31 34 37 40 43 46 .....(A) 49 52   (B) 47 49   (C) 50 54   (D) 49 53   (E) 51 55

18. 17 17 24 24 31 31 38 .....(A) 38 39   (B) 38 17   (C) 38 45   (D) 38 44   (E) 39 50

19. 3 12 6 24 12 48 24 ....(A) 96 48   (B) 56 23   (C) 64 12   (D) 52 36   (E) 64 48

20. 87 83 79 75 71 67 63 .....(A) 62 61   (B) 63 59   (C) 60 56   (D) 59 55   (E) 59 54

21. 10 2 8 2 6 2 4 ....(A) 4 4   (B) 2 2   (C) 3 3   (D) 4 2   (E) 5 2

22. 8 9 11 14 18 23 29 ....(A) 35 45   (B) 32 33   (C) 38 48   (D) 34 40   (E) 36 44

23. 11 14 12 15 13 16 14 ......(A) 14 17   (B) 15 16   (C) 16 20   (D) 17 15   (E) 18 13

24. 14 2 12 4 10 6 8 ....(A) 10 12   (B) 6 8   (C) 12 10   (D) 8 6   (E) 10 14

END OF NUMBER SERIES

Part D—Following Oral Instructions

Directions and Sample Questions

LISTENING TO INSTRUCTIONS: When you are ready to try these sample questions, give the following instructions to a friend and have the friend read them aloud to you at the rate of 80 words per minute. Do not read them to yourself. Your friend will need a watch with a second hand. Listen carefully and do exactly what your friend tells you to do with the worksheet and answer sheet. Your friend will tell you some things to do with each item on the worksheet. After each set of instructions, your friend will give you time to mark your answer by darkening a circle on the sample answer sheet. Since B and D sound very much alike, your friend will say "B as in baker" when he or she means B and "D as in dog" when he or she means D.

Before proceeding further, tear out the worksheet on page 45. Then hand this book to your friend.

TO THE PERSON WHO IS TO READ THE INSTRUCTIONS: The instructions are to be read at the rate of 80 words per minute. Do not read aloud the material that is in parentheses. Do not repeat any instructions.

Read Aloud to the Candidate

Look at line 1 on the worksheet. (Pause slightly.) Write a D as in dog in the fourth box. (Pause 2 seconds.) Now, on your answer sheet, find the number in that box and darken space D as in dog for that number. (Pause 5 seconds.)

Look at line 2. The number in each circle is the number of employees in a post office. In the circle holding the largest number of employees, write a B as in baker. (Pause 2 seconds.) Now, on your answer sheet, darken the space for the number-letter combination that is in the circle you just wrote in. (Pause 5 seconds.)

Look at line 3 on the worksheet. (Pause slightly.) Write the letter C on the blank next to the right-hand number. (Pause 2 seconds.) Now, on your answer sheet, find the number beside which you just wrote and darken space C. (Pause 5 seconds.)

Look at line 3 again. (Pause slightly.) Write the letter B as in baker on the blank next to the left-hand number. (Pause 2 seconds.) Now, on your answer sheet, find the number beside which you just wrote and darken space B as in baker. (Pause 5 seconds.)

Look at line 4 on your worksheet. (Pause slightly.) Draw a line under every "X" in the line. (Pause 5 seconds.) Count the number of lines that you have drawn, divide by 2, and write that number at the end of the line. (Pause 5 seconds.) Now, on your answer sheet, find that number and darken space C for that number. (Pause 5 seconds.)

Sample Worksheet

DIRECTIONS: Listening carefully to each set of instructions, mark each item on this worksheet as directed. Then complete each question by marking the sample answer sheet below as directed. For each answer you will darken the answer for a number-letter combination. Should you fall behind and miss an instruction, don't become excited. Let that one go and listen for the next one. If, when you start to darken a space for a number, you find that you have already darkened another space for that number, either erase the first mark and darken the space for the new combination or let the first mark stay and do not darken a space for the new combination. Write with a pencil that has a clean eraser. When you finish, you should have no more than one space darkened for each number.

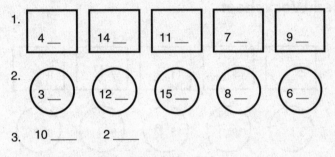

1. 4 __ 14 __ 11 __ 7 __ 9 __

2. 3 __ 12 __ 15 __ 8 __ 6 __

3. 10 ____ 2 ____

4. X O X X X X O O X O X O X X O X

```
SAMPLE ANSWER SHEET

1. Ⓐ Ⓑ Ⓒ Ⓓ Ⓔ      6. Ⓐ Ⓑ Ⓒ Ⓓ Ⓔ     11. Ⓐ Ⓑ Ⓒ Ⓓ Ⓔ
2. Ⓐ Ⓑ Ⓒ Ⓓ Ⓔ      7. Ⓐ Ⓑ Ⓒ Ⓓ Ⓔ     12. Ⓐ Ⓑ Ⓒ Ⓓ Ⓔ
3. Ⓐ Ⓑ Ⓒ Ⓓ Ⓔ      8. Ⓐ Ⓑ Ⓒ Ⓓ Ⓔ     13. Ⓐ Ⓑ Ⓒ Ⓓ Ⓔ
4. Ⓐ Ⓑ Ⓒ Ⓓ Ⓔ      9. Ⓐ Ⓑ Ⓒ Ⓓ Ⓔ     14. Ⓐ Ⓑ Ⓒ Ⓓ Ⓔ
5. Ⓐ Ⓑ Ⓒ Ⓓ Ⓔ     10. Ⓐ Ⓑ Ⓒ Ⓓ Ⓔ     15. Ⓐ Ⓑ Ⓒ Ⓓ Ⓔ
```

TEAR HERE

CORRECT ANSWERS TO SAMPLE QUESTIONS

1. Ⓐ Ⓑ Ⓒ Ⓓ Ⓔ   6. Ⓐ Ⓑ Ⓒ Ⓓ Ⓔ   11. Ⓐ Ⓑ Ⓒ Ⓓ Ⓔ
2. Ⓐ Ⓑ ● Ⓓ Ⓔ   7. Ⓐ Ⓑ Ⓒ ● Ⓔ   12. Ⓐ Ⓑ Ⓒ Ⓓ Ⓔ
3. Ⓐ Ⓑ Ⓒ Ⓓ Ⓔ   8. Ⓐ Ⓑ Ⓒ Ⓓ Ⓔ   13. Ⓐ Ⓑ Ⓒ Ⓓ Ⓔ
4. Ⓐ Ⓑ Ⓒ Ⓓ Ⓔ   9. Ⓐ Ⓑ Ⓒ Ⓓ Ⓔ   14. Ⓐ Ⓑ Ⓒ Ⓓ Ⓔ
5. Ⓐ Ⓑ ● Ⓓ Ⓔ   10. Ⓐ ● Ⓒ Ⓓ Ⓔ   15. Ⓐ ● Ⓒ Ⓓ Ⓔ

Correctly Filled Worksheet

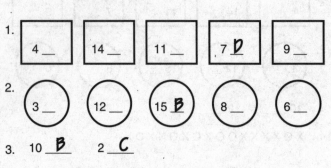

1. | 4 __ | 14 __ | 11 __ | 7 *D* | 9 __ |

2. (3 __) (12 __) (15 *B*) (8 __) (6 __)

3. 10 __*B*__   2 __*C*__

4. X̲O̲X̲X̲X̲X̲OOX̲O̲X̲O̲X̲OX̲X̲OX̲ *5*

Following Oral Instructions

Time: 25 Minutes.

Listening to Instructions

DIRECTIONS: When you are ready to try this test of the Model Exam, give the following instructions to a friend and have the friend read them aloud to you at the rate of 80 words per minute. Do NOT read them to yourself. Your friend will need a watch with a second hand. Listen carefully and do exactly what your friend tells you to do with the worksheet and with the answer sheet. Your friend will tell you some things to do with each item on the worksheet. After each set of instructions, your friend will give you time to mark your answer by darkening a circle on the answer sheet. Since B and D sound very much alike, your friend will say "B as in baker" when he or she means B and "D as in dog" when he or she means D.

> **Before proceeding further, tear out the worksheet on page 51. Then hand this book to your friend.**

TO THE PERSON WHO IS TO READ THE INSTRUCTIONS: The instructions are to be read at the rate of 80 words per minute. Do not read aloud the material that is in parentheses. Once you have begun the test itself, do not repeat any instructions. The next three paragraphs consist of approximately 120 words. Read these three paragraphs aloud to the candidate in about one and one-half minutes. You may reread these paragraphs as often as necessary to establish an 80-words-per-minute reading speed.

Read Aloud to the Candidate

On the job you will have to listen to directions and then do what you have been told to do. In this test, I will read instructions to you. Try to understand them as I read them; I cannot repeat them. Once we begin, you may not ask any questions until the end of the test.

On the job you won't have to deal with pictures, numbers, and letters like those in the test, but you will have to listen to instructions and follow them. We are using this test to see how well you can follow instructions.

You are to mark your test booklet according to the instructions that I'll read to you. After each set of instructions, I'll give you time to record your answers on the separate answer sheet.

The actual test begins now.

Look at line 1 on the worksheet. (Pause slightly.) Draw a line under the fourth number in the line. (Pause 2 seconds.) Now, on your answer sheet, find the number under which you just drew the line and darken space A for that number. (Pause 5 seconds.)

Look at the letters in line 2 on the worksheet. (Pause slightly.) Draw a line under the fifth letter in the line. Now, on your answer sheet, find number 59 (pause 2 seconds) and darken the space for the letter under which you drew a line. (Pause 5 seconds.)

Look at the letters in line 2 on the worksheet again. (Pause slightly.) Now draw two lines under the third letter in the line. (Pause 2 seconds.) Now, on your answer sheet, find number 65 (pause 2 seconds) and darken the space for the letter under which you drew two lines. (Pause 5 seconds.)

Look at line 3 on the worksheet. (Pause slightly.) Write an E in the last box. (Pause 2 seconds.) Now, on your answer sheet, find the number in that box and darken space E for that number. (Pause 5 seconds.)

Now look at line 3 again. (Pause slightly.) Write an A in the first box. (Pause 2 seconds.) Now, on your answer sheet, find the number in that box and darken space A for that number. (Pause 5 seconds.)

Look at line 4. The number in each circle is the number of packages in a mail sack. In the circle for the sack holding the largest number of packages, write a B as in baker. (Pause 2 seconds.) Now, on your answer sheet, darken the space for the number-letter combination that is in the circle you just wrote in. (Pause 5 seconds.)

Look at line 4 again. In the circle for the sack holding the smallest number of packages, write an E. (Pause 2 seconds.) Now, on your answer sheet, darken the space for the number-letter combination that is in the circle you just wrote in. (Pause 5 seconds.)

Look at the drawings on line 5 on the worksheet. The four boxes are trucks for carrying mail. (Pause slightly.) The truck with the highest number is to be loaded first. Write B as in baker on the line beside the highest number. (Pause 2 seconds.) Now, on your answer sheet, darken the space for the number-letter combination that is in the box you just wrote in. (Pause 5 seconds.)

Look at line 6 on the worksheet. (Pause slightly.) Next to the middle number write the letter D as in dog. (Pause 2 seconds.) Now, on your answer sheet, find the space for the number beside which you wrote and darken space D as in dog. (Pause 5 seconds.)

Look at the five circles in line 7 on the worksheet. Write B as in baker on the blank in the second circle. (Pause 2 seconds.) Now, on your answer sheet, darken the space for the number-letter combination that is in the circle you just wrote in. (Pause 5 seconds.)

Now take the worksheet again and write C on the blank in the third circle on line 7. (Pause 2 seconds.) Now, on your answer sheet, darken the space for the number-letter combination that is in the circle you just wrote in. (Pause 5 seconds.)

Now look at line 8 on the worksheet. (Pause slightly.) Write an A on the line next to the right-hand number. (Pause 2 seconds.) Now, on your answer sheet, find the space for the number beside which you wrote and darken box A. (Pause 5 seconds.)

Look at line 9 on the worksheet. (Pause slightly.) Draw a line under every number that is more than 60 but less than 70. (Pause 12 seconds.) Now, on your answer sheet, for each number that you drew a line under, darken space C. (Pause 25 seconds.)

Look at line 10 on the worksheet. (Pause slightly.) Draw a line under every number that is more than 5 and less than 15. (Pause 10 seconds.) Now, on your answer sheet, for each number that you drew a line under, darken space D as in dog. (Pause 25 seconds.)

Look at line 11 on the worksheet. (Pause slightly.) In each circle there is a time when the mail must leave. In the circle for the latest time, write on the line the last two figures of the time. (Pause 5 seconds.) Now, on your answer sheet, darken the space for the number-letter combination that is in the circle you just wrote in. (Pause 5 seconds.)

Look at the five boxes in line 12 on your worksheet. (Pause slightly.) If 6 is less than 3, put an E in the fourth box. (Pause slightly.) If 6 is not less than 3, put a B as in baker in the first box. (Pause 10 seconds.) Now, on your answer sheet, darken the space for the number-letter combination that is in the box you just wrote in. (Pause 5 seconds.)

Now look at line 13 on the worksheet. (Pause slightly.) There are five circles. Each circle has a letter. (Pause slightly.) In the second circle, write the answer to this question: Which of the following numbers is smallest: 72, 51, 88, 71, 58? (Pause 10 seconds.) Now, on your answer sheet, darken the space for the number-letter combination that is in the circle you just wrote in. (Pause 5 seconds.) In the third circle on the same line, write 28. (Pause 2 seconds.) Now, on your answer sheet, darken the space for the number-letter combination that is in the circle you just wrote in. (Pause 5 seconds.) In the fourth circle do nothing. In the fifth circle write the answer to this question: How many months are there in a year? (Pause 5 seconds.) Now, on your answer sheet, darken the space for the number-letter combination that is in the circle you just wrote in. (Pause 5 seconds.)

Look at line 14 on your worksheet. (Pause slightly.) There are two circles and two boxes of different sizes with numbers in them. (Pause slightly.) If 2 is smaller than 4 and if 7 is less than 3, write A in the larger circle. (Pause slightly.) Otherwise write B as in baker in the smaller box. (Pause 10 seconds.) Now, on your answer sheet, darken the space for the number-letter combination in the box or circle in which you just wrote. (Pause 5 seconds.)

Look at the boxes and words in line 15 on the worksheet. (Pause slightly.) Write the second letter of the first word in the third box. (Pause 5 seconds.) Write the first letter of the second word in the first box. (Pause 5 seconds.) Write the first letter of the third word in the second box. (Pause 5 seconds.) Now, on your answer sheet, darken the spaces for the number-letter combinations that are in the three boxes you just wrote in. (Pause 15 seconds.)

Look at line 16 on the worksheet. (Pause slightly.) Draw a line under every "O" in the line. (Pause 5 seconds.) Count the number of lines that you have drawn, subtract 2, and write that number at the end of the line. (Pause 5 seconds.) Now, on your answer sheet, find that number and darken space D as in dog for that number. (Pause 5 seconds.)

Look at line 17 on the worksheet. (Pause slightly.) If the number in the left-hand circle is smaller than the number in the right-hand circle, add 2 to the number in the left-hand circle, and change the number in that circle to this number. (Pause 8 seconds.) Then write B as in baker next to the new number. (Pause slightly.) Next, write E beside the number in the smaller box. (Pause 3 seconds.) Then, on your answer sheet, darken the spaces for the number-letter combinations that are in the box and circle you just wrote in. (Pause 5 seconds.)

Look at line 18 on the worksheet. (Pause slightly.) If in a year October comes before September, write A in the box with the smallest number. (Pause slightly.) If it does not, write C in the box with the largest number. (Pause 10 seconds.) Now, on your answer sheet, darken the space for the number-letter combination that is in the box you just wrote in. (Pause 5 seconds.)

Look at line 19 on the worksheet. (Pause slightly.) On the line beside the second letter, write the highest of these numbers: 12, 56, 42, 39, 8. (Pause 2 seconds.) Now, on your answer sheet, darken the space of the number-letter combination you just wrote. (Pause 5 seconds.)

Following Oral Instructions

Worksheet

DIRECTIONS: Listening carefully to each set of instructions, mark each item on this worksheet as directed. Then complete each question by marking the answer sheet as directed. For each answer you will darken the answer for a number-letter combination. Should you fall behind and miss an instruction, don't get excited. Let that one go and listen for the next one. If, when you go to darken a space for a number, you find that you have already darkened another space for that number, either erase the first mark and darken the space for the new combination or let the first mark stay and do not darken a space for the new combination. Write with a pencil that has a clean eraser. When you finish, you should have no more than one space darkened for each number. Correct answers are on page 58.

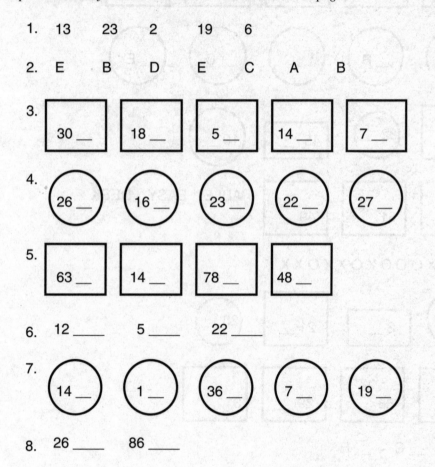

1.   13   23   2   19   6

2.   E   B   D   E   C   A   B

3.   [30 __]   [18 __]   [5 __]   [14 __]   [7 __]

4.   (26 __)   (16 __)   (23 __)   (22 __)   (27 __)

5.   [63 __]   [14 __]   [78 __]   [48 __]

6.   12 ____   5 ____   22 ____

7.   (14 __)   (1 __)   (36 __)   (7 __)   (19 __)

8.   26 ____   86 ____

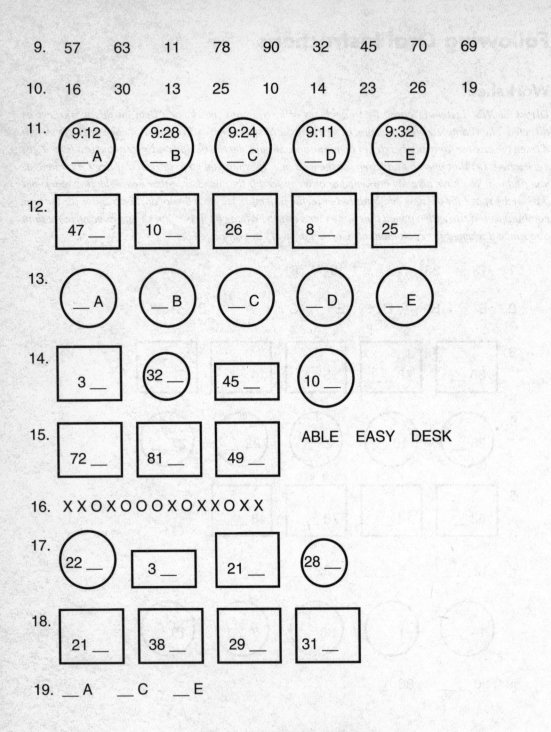

9.   57   63   11   78   90   32   45   70   69

10.   16   30   13   25   10   14   23   26   19

11.   9:12   9:28   9:24   9:11   9:32
       __A   __B   __C   __D   __E

12.   47 __   10 __   26 __   8 __   25 __

13.   __A   __B   __C   __D   __E

14.   3 __   32 __   45 __   10 __

15.   72 __   81 __   49 __   ABLE   EASY   DESK

16.   X X O X O O O X O X X O X X

17.   22 __   3 __   21 __   28 __

18.   21 __   38 __   29 __   31 __

19.   __ A   __ C   __ E

END OF EXAMINATION

Correct Answers for Preliminary Exam

Part A—Address Checking

1. A	13. D	25. A	37. D	49. D	61. A	73. A	85. A
2. D	14. D	26. D	38. A	50. D	62. D	74. D	86. A
3. A	15. A	27. D	39. D	51. A	63. A	75. D	87. D
4. D	16. A	28. A	40. A	52. A	64. D	76. D	88. A
5. D	17. D	29. D	41. A	53. D	65. A	77. D	89. D
6. D	18. A	30. D	42. A	54. D	66. D	78. D	90. D
7. A	19. A	31. D	43. D	55. D	67. D	79. D	91. D
8. D	20. D	32. D	44. D	56. D	68. D	80. D	92. D
9. D	21. D	33. D	45. D	57. D	69. A	81. A	93. A
10. A	22. D	34. D	46. D	58. A	70. D	82. A	94. D
11. A	23. D	35. A	47. A	59. D	71. A	83. D	95. D
12. D	24. A	36. A	48. D	60. A	72. D	84. D	

Analyzing Your Errors

The Address Checking Test of the Preliminary Exam contains 35 addresses that are exactly alike and 60 addresses that are different. The chart below shows what kind of difference occurs in each of the addresses that contains a difference. Check your answers against this chart to see which kind of difference you missed most often. Note also the questions in which you thought you saw a difference but in which there really was none. Becoming aware of your errors will help you to eliminate those errors on future model exams and on the actual exam.

Type of Difference	Question Numbers	Number of Questions You Missed
Difference in NUMBERS	2, 12, 13, 22, 26, 31, 39, 44, 49, 53, 54, 67, 68, 70, 72, 76, 79, 89, 91	
Difference in ABBREVIATIONS	4, 9, 14, 20, 21, 23, 27, 30, 32, 33, 46, 55, 59, 62, 74, 75, 78, 84, 87, 95	
Difference in NAMES	5, 6, 8, 17, 29, 34, 37, 43, 45, 48, 50, 56, 57, 64, 66, 77, 80, 83, 90, 92, 94	
No Difference	1, 3, 7, 10, 11, 15, 16, 18, 19, 24, 25, 28, 35, 36, 38, 40, 41, 42, 47, 51, 52, 58, 60, 61, 63, 65, 69, 71, 73, 81, 82, 85, 86, 88, 93	

Part B—Memory for Addresses

Practice I

1. D	12. B	23. A	34. B	45. E	56. A	67. D	78. E
2. C	13. C	24. A	35. A	46. D	57. C	68. B	79. E
3. C	14. E	25. B	36. C	47. C	58. C	69. E	80. B
4. E	15. D	26. C	37. B	48. B	59. A	70. D	81. B
5. A	16. E	27. E	38. E	49. A	60. A	71. E	82. A
6. B	17. A	28. D	39. C	50. A	61. B	72. D	83. C
7. B	18. D	29. E	40. C	51. D	62. D	73. D	84. B
8. A	19. D	30. D	41. A	52. C	63. E	74. C	85. C
9. B	20. B	31. B	42. B	53. B	64. E	75. A	86. D
10. B	21. A	32. A	43. D	54. E	65. B	76. B	87. A
11. E	22. E	33. C	44. E	55. D	66. C	77. A	88. E

Practice II

1. D	12. A	23. D	34. A	45. D	56. E	67. E	78. E
2. C	13. D	24. C	35. A	46. A	57. A	68. C	79. C
3. B	14. B	25. E	36. C	47. B	58. E	69. D	80. B
4. E	15. E	26. A	37. E	48. B	59. D	70. D	81. B
5. A	16. D	27. B	38. E	49. C	60. B	71. C	82. A
6. E	17. C	28. C	39. B	50. D	61. A	72. B	83. C
7. C	18. A	29. D	40. C	51. E	62. C	73. A	84. C
8. A	19. B	30. D	41. C	52. B	63. E	74. C	85. A
9. D	20. A	31. E	42. A	53. A	64. D	75. C	86. D
10. B	21. B	32. D	43. A	54. B	65. B	76. B	87. E
11. E	22. A	33. B	44. C	55. D	66. E	77. A	88. A

Practice III

1. D	12. C	23. B	34. C	45. E	56. D	67. B	78. B
2. D	13. C	24. B	35. A	46. C	57. E	68. B	79. E
3. D	14. B	25. E	36. B	47. E	58. B	69. A	80. D
4. B	15. B	26. C	37. E	48. E	59. E	70. C	81. E
5. A	16. E	27. A	38. D	49. D	60. C	71. A	82. C
6. E	17. B	28. D	39. C	50. A	61. C	72. A	83. B
7. A	18. D	29. D	40. B	51. D	62. E	73. A	84. C
8. E	19. C	30. E	41. E	52. A	63. A	74. D	85. E
9. A	20. B	31. E	42. C	53. D	64. B	75. D	86. C
10. A	21. C	32. A	43. B	54. A	65. E	76. D	87. E
11. D	22. A	33. B	44. B	55. C	66. D	77. C	88. A

Memory for Addresses

1. A	12. C	23. D	34. A	45. B	56. E	67. B	78. C
2. B	13. D	24. C	35. D	46. E	57. A	68. D	79. B
3. A	14. E	25. B	36. A	47. D	58. B	69. C	80. B
4. E	15. C	26. B	37. C	48. C	59. E	70. A	81. C
5. E	16. A	27. B	38. E	49. B	60. B	71. C	82. A
6. D	17. B	28. C	39. D	50. A	61. D	72. D	83. E
7. B	18. A	29. C	40. E	51. C	62. D	73. D	84. C
8. D	19. B	30. E	41. D	52. E	63. D	74. B	85. A
9. B	20. D	31. A	42. B	53. A	64. B	75. B	86. E
10. E	21. D	32. E	43. B	54. A	65. E	76. A	87. D
11. C	22. B	33. D	44. C	55. C	66. D	77. E	88. E

Part C—Number Series

1. B	4. A	7. D	10. C	13. D	16. E	19. A	22. E
2. D	5. E	8. A	11. B	14. C	17. A	20. D	23. D
3. E	6. E	9. D	12. A	15. E	18. C	21. B	24. D

Explanations

1. **(B)** The series is simply a repetition of the sequence 8 9 10.

2. **(D)** You can feel the rhythm of this series if you read it aloud. Beginning with <u>4</u>, doubled numbers are progressing upwards by + 1, separated by the number <u>3</u>.

3. **(E)** In this series two 7's separate numbers that are increasing by + 1.

4. **(A)** In this series the numbers are increasing by + 1. Every other number is repeated before it increases.

5. **(E)** This series is made up of a number of mini-series. In each mini-series the numbers increase by + 4. After each mini-series of three numbers, a new mini-series begins, each time with a number one higher than the beginning number of the previous mini-series.

6. **(E)** This pattern is not as easy to spot as the ones in the previous questions. If you write in the direction and degree of change between each number, you can see that the rule is –3, +7, –3, +7, and so on.

7. **(D)** This series consists of two alternating series. One series begins with <u>16</u> and decreases by –1. The alternating series begins with <u>8</u> and increases by + 1.

8. **(A)** Again we have alternating series. This time the ascending series consists of two numbers increasing by + 1 before being interrupted by one number of the descending series that is decreasing by –1.

9. **(D)** You may see this series as following the rule: +5, –4, +5, –4…or you may see two alternating series, one beginning with <u>19</u>, the other with <u>24</u>.

10. **(C)** Repeat, –3, repeat, –3, repeat, –3….

11. **(B)** Each number is reached by adding together the two previous numbers. Thus, 1 + 1 = 2; 1+ 2 = 3; 2 + 3 = 5; 5 + 8 = 13; 8 + 13 = 21; 13 + 21 = 34.

12. **(A)** You might see two alternating series increasing by + 1, or you might see a rule: +2, –1, +2, –1.

13. **(D)** In this series, each number appears as often as its name implies: one 1, two 2's, three 3's, four 4's.

14. **(C)** The rule here is: +8, +7, +6, +5, +4, +3, +2.

15. **(E)** The elements of this series are the squares of successive numbers: 1^2, 2^2, 3^2, 4^2, etc.

16. **(E)** The rule is: +4, +5, +7 and repeat +4, +5, +7.

17. **(A)** A simple +3 rule.

18. **(C)** Each number repeats itself, then increases by + 7.

19. **(A)** You might see this as two alternating parallel series. If this is how you see the problem, then you see that in each series, the next number is the previous number multiplied by 2. Another pattern you might see is $\times 4$, $\div 2$, $\times 4$, $\div 2$.

20. **(D)** Here the rule is: – 4.

21. **(B)** Basically the series descends by – 2: 10 8 6 4 2. The number 2 appears between terms of the series.

22. **(E)** The rule is: +1, +2, +3, +4, +5, +6, +7, +8.

23. **(D)** Parallel ascending series alternate or the series follows the rule: +3, –2, +3, –2, +3.

24. **(D)** The first series decreases by –2. The alternating series increases by +2.

Part D—Following Oral Instructions

Correctly Filled Answer Grid

1 Ⓐ ● Ⓒ Ⓓ Ⓔ	23 Ⓐ Ⓑ Ⓒ Ⓓ Ⓔ	45 Ⓐ ● Ⓒ Ⓓ Ⓔ	67 Ⓐ Ⓑ Ⓒ Ⓓ Ⓔ
2 Ⓐ Ⓑ Ⓒ Ⓓ Ⓔ	24 Ⓐ ● Ⓒ Ⓓ Ⓔ	46 Ⓐ Ⓑ Ⓒ Ⓓ Ⓔ	68 Ⓐ Ⓑ Ⓒ Ⓓ Ⓔ
3 Ⓐ Ⓑ Ⓒ Ⓓ ●	25 Ⓐ Ⓑ Ⓒ Ⓓ Ⓔ	47 Ⓐ ● Ⓒ Ⓓ Ⓔ	69 Ⓐ Ⓑ ● Ⓓ Ⓔ
4 Ⓐ Ⓑ Ⓒ ● Ⓔ	26 Ⓐ Ⓑ Ⓒ Ⓓ Ⓔ	48 Ⓐ Ⓑ Ⓒ Ⓓ Ⓔ	70 Ⓐ Ⓑ Ⓒ Ⓓ Ⓔ
5 Ⓐ Ⓑ Ⓒ ● Ⓔ	27 Ⓐ ● Ⓒ Ⓓ Ⓔ	49 Ⓐ ● Ⓒ Ⓓ Ⓔ	71 Ⓐ Ⓑ Ⓒ Ⓓ Ⓔ
6 Ⓐ Ⓑ Ⓒ Ⓓ Ⓔ	28 Ⓐ Ⓑ ● Ⓓ Ⓔ	50 Ⓐ Ⓑ Ⓒ Ⓓ Ⓔ	72 Ⓐ Ⓑ Ⓒ Ⓓ ●
7 Ⓐ Ⓑ Ⓒ Ⓓ ●	29 Ⓐ Ⓑ Ⓒ Ⓓ Ⓔ	51 Ⓐ ● Ⓒ Ⓓ Ⓔ	73 Ⓐ Ⓑ Ⓒ Ⓓ Ⓔ
8 Ⓐ Ⓑ Ⓒ Ⓓ Ⓔ	30 ● Ⓑ Ⓒ Ⓓ Ⓔ	52 Ⓐ Ⓑ Ⓒ Ⓓ Ⓔ	74 Ⓐ Ⓑ Ⓒ Ⓓ Ⓔ
9 Ⓐ Ⓑ Ⓒ Ⓓ Ⓔ	31 Ⓐ Ⓑ Ⓒ Ⓓ Ⓔ	53 Ⓐ Ⓑ Ⓒ Ⓓ Ⓔ	75 Ⓐ Ⓑ Ⓒ Ⓓ Ⓔ
10 Ⓐ Ⓑ Ⓒ ● Ⓔ	32 Ⓐ Ⓑ Ⓒ Ⓓ ●	54 Ⓐ Ⓑ Ⓒ Ⓓ Ⓔ	76 Ⓐ Ⓑ Ⓒ Ⓓ Ⓔ
11 Ⓐ Ⓑ Ⓒ Ⓓ Ⓔ	33 Ⓐ Ⓑ Ⓒ Ⓓ Ⓔ	55 Ⓐ Ⓑ Ⓒ Ⓓ Ⓔ	77 Ⓐ Ⓑ Ⓒ Ⓓ Ⓔ
12 Ⓐ Ⓑ Ⓒ Ⓓ ●	34 Ⓐ Ⓑ Ⓒ Ⓓ Ⓔ	56 Ⓐ Ⓑ ● Ⓓ Ⓔ	78 Ⓐ ● Ⓒ Ⓓ Ⓔ
13 Ⓐ Ⓑ Ⓒ ● Ⓔ	35 Ⓐ Ⓑ Ⓒ Ⓓ Ⓔ	57 Ⓐ Ⓑ Ⓒ Ⓓ Ⓔ	79 Ⓐ Ⓑ Ⓒ Ⓓ Ⓔ
14 Ⓐ Ⓑ Ⓒ ● Ⓔ	36 Ⓐ Ⓑ ● Ⓓ Ⓔ	58 Ⓐ Ⓑ Ⓒ Ⓓ Ⓔ	80 Ⓐ Ⓑ Ⓒ Ⓓ Ⓔ
15 Ⓐ Ⓑ Ⓒ Ⓓ Ⓔ	37 Ⓐ Ⓑ Ⓒ Ⓓ Ⓔ	59 Ⓐ Ⓑ ● Ⓓ Ⓔ	81 Ⓐ Ⓑ Ⓒ ● Ⓔ
16 Ⓐ Ⓑ Ⓒ Ⓓ ●	38 Ⓐ Ⓑ ● Ⓓ Ⓔ	60 Ⓐ Ⓑ Ⓒ Ⓓ Ⓔ	82 Ⓐ Ⓑ Ⓒ Ⓓ Ⓔ
17 Ⓐ Ⓑ Ⓒ Ⓓ Ⓔ	39 Ⓐ Ⓑ Ⓒ Ⓓ Ⓔ	61 Ⓐ Ⓑ Ⓒ Ⓓ Ⓔ	83 Ⓐ Ⓑ Ⓒ Ⓓ Ⓔ
18 Ⓐ Ⓑ Ⓒ Ⓓ Ⓔ	40 Ⓐ Ⓑ Ⓒ Ⓓ Ⓔ	62 Ⓐ Ⓑ Ⓒ Ⓓ Ⓔ	84 Ⓐ Ⓑ Ⓒ Ⓓ Ⓔ
19 ● Ⓑ Ⓒ Ⓓ Ⓔ	41 Ⓐ Ⓑ Ⓒ Ⓓ Ⓔ	63 Ⓐ Ⓑ ● Ⓓ Ⓔ	85 Ⓐ Ⓑ Ⓒ Ⓓ Ⓔ
20 Ⓐ Ⓑ Ⓒ Ⓓ Ⓔ	42 Ⓐ Ⓑ Ⓒ Ⓓ Ⓔ	64 Ⓐ Ⓑ Ⓒ Ⓓ Ⓔ	86 ● Ⓑ Ⓒ Ⓓ Ⓔ
21 Ⓐ Ⓑ Ⓒ Ⓓ Ⓔ	43 Ⓐ Ⓑ Ⓒ Ⓓ Ⓔ	65 Ⓐ Ⓑ Ⓒ ● Ⓔ	87 Ⓐ Ⓑ Ⓒ Ⓓ Ⓔ
22 Ⓐ Ⓑ Ⓒ Ⓓ Ⓔ	44 Ⓐ Ⓑ Ⓒ Ⓓ Ⓔ	66 Ⓐ Ⓑ Ⓒ Ⓓ Ⓔ	88 Ⓐ Ⓑ Ⓒ Ⓓ Ⓔ

Correctly Filled Worksheet

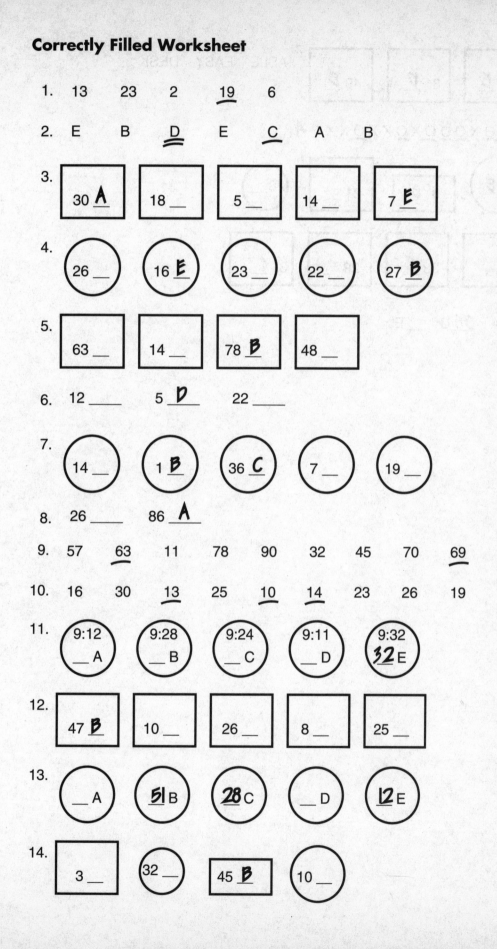

1. 13   23   2   <u>19</u>   6

2. E   B   <u>D</u>   E   <u>C</u>   A   B

3. 30 **A**   18 __   5 __   14 __   7 **E**

4. 26 __   16 **E**   23 __   22 __   27 **B**

5. 63 __   14 __   78 **B**   48 __

6. 12 ___   5 **D**   22 ___

7. 14 __   1 **B**   36 **C**   7 __   19 __

8. 26 ___   86 **A**

9. 57   <u>63</u>   11   78   90   32   45   70   <u>69</u>

10. 16   30   <u>13</u>   25   <u>10</u>   <u>14</u>   23   26   19

11. 9:12 __A   9:28 __B   9:24 __C   9:11 __D   9:32 **32** E

12. 47 **B**   10 __   26 __   8 __   25 __

13. __A   **51** B   **28** C   __D   **12** E

14. 3 __   32 __   45 **B**   10 __

15. [72 _E_] [81 _D_] [49 _B_]   ABLE   EASY   DESK

16. X X <u>O</u> X <u>O</u> <u>O</u> <u>O</u> X <u>O</u> X X <u>O</u> X X   _A_

17. (24 <s>22</s> _B_)   [3 _E_]   [21 __]   (28 __)

18. [21 __]   [38 _C_]   [29 __]   [31 __]

19. __ A   _56_ C   __ E

TWO

Test Strategies

How to Answer Address Checking Questions

The Address Checking Test is not difficult, but it requires great speed and it carries a heavy penalty for inaccuracy. You must learn to spot differences very quickly and to make firm, fast decisions about addresses that are exactly alike. This chapter will help you to develop a system for comparing addresses. Once you have a system, practicing it will help you to build up speed.

The directions make it very clear that if there is *any difference at all* between the two addresses they are to be marked as different. This means that once you spot a difference, mark the answer as D and go immediately to the next question. There is no point in looking at the remainder of an address once you have found a difference. You will be amazed at how much time you can save by not reading the whole of every address.

Read Exactly What You See

The best way to read addresses being compared is to read exactly what you see and to sound out words by syllables. For example:

If you see "St," read "es tee" not "street."

If you see "NH," read "en aitch" not "New Hampshire."

If you see "1035," read "one oh three five" not "one thousand thirty-five."

Read "sassafrass" as "sas-sa-frass."

Psychologists have discovered that the human mind always tries to complete a figure. If you read "Pky" as "Parkway," you will probably read "Pkwy" as "Parkway," and will never notice the difference. Your mind will complete the word without allowing you to focus on the letters. If, however, you read the abbreviation as an abbreviation, you will notice that the two abbreviations are different. If you read "Kansas City MO" as "Kansas City Missouri," you are unlikely to catch the difference with "Kansas City MD." But if you read "Kansas City em oh," you will readily pick up on "Kansas City em dee."

Use Your Hands

Since speed is so important in answering Address Checking questions and since it is so easy to lose your place, you must use both hands during your work on this part. In the hand with which you write, hold your pencil poised at the number on your answer sheet. Run the index finger of your other hand under the addresses being compared. The finger will help you to focus on one line at a time and will help keep your eyes from jumping up or down a line. By holding your place on both question and answer sheet, you are less likely to skip a question or an answer space.

One effective way to tackle Address Checking questions quickly and accurately is to look for differences in only one area at a time. Every address consists of both numbers and words. If you narrow your focus to compare only the numbers or only the words, you are more likely to notice differences and less apt to see what you expect to see rather than what is actually printed on the page.

Look for Differences in Numbers

Look first at the numbers. Read the number in the left column, then skip immediately to the number in the right column. Do the two numbers contain the same number of digits?

A difference of this type should be easy to see. In the questions that follow, blacken A if the two numbers are exactly alike and D if the numbers are different in any way.

Is the Number of Digits the Same?

1. 2003	2003	1. Ⓐ Ⓓ
2. 75864	75864	2. Ⓐ Ⓓ
3. 7300	730	3. Ⓐ Ⓓ
4. 50106	5016	4. Ⓐ Ⓓ
5. 2184	2184	5. Ⓐ Ⓓ

Answers: 1. A   2. A   3. D   4. D   5. A

Did you spot the differences? Train your eye to count digits rapidly.

Is the Order of Digits the Same?

1. 7516	7561	1. Ⓐ Ⓓ
2. 80302	80302	2. Ⓐ Ⓓ
3. 19832	18932	3. Ⓐ Ⓓ
4. 6186	6186	4. Ⓐ Ⓓ
5. 54601	54610	5. Ⓐ Ⓓ

Answers: 1. D   2. A   3. D   4. A   5. D

Did you get these all correct? If not, look again right now. See where you made your mistakes.

Is There a Substitution of One Digit for Another?

1. 16830	16830	1. Ⓐ Ⓓ
2. 94936	94636	2. Ⓐ Ⓓ
3. 3287	3285	3. Ⓐ Ⓓ
4. 54216	54216	4. Ⓐ Ⓓ
5. 32341	33341	5. Ⓐ Ⓓ

Answers: 1. A   2. D   3. D   4. A   5. D

Did you catch all the differences? Were you able to mark A with confidence when there was no difference?

Practice Finding Differences in Numbers

In the following set of practice questions, all differences are in the numbers. Work quickly, focusing only on the numbers. You may find any of the three varieties of differences just described.

#	Address 1	Address 2	Answer
1	...3685 Brite Ave	3865 Brite Ave	1. Ⓐ Ⓓ
2	...Ware MA 08215	Ware MA 08215	2. Ⓐ Ⓓ
3	...4001 Webster Rd	401 Webster Rd	3. Ⓐ Ⓓ
4	...9789 Bell Rd	9786 Bell Rd	4. Ⓐ Ⓓ
5	...Scarsdale NY 10583	Scarsdale NY 10583	5. Ⓐ Ⓓ
6	...1482 Grand Blvd	1482 Grand Blvd	6. Ⓐ Ⓓ
7	...Milwaukee WI 53202	Milwaukee WI 52302	7. Ⓐ Ⓓ
8	...3542 W 48th St	3542 W 84th St	8. Ⓐ Ⓓ
9	...9461 Hansen St	9461 Hansen St	9. Ⓐ Ⓓ
10	...32322 Florence Pkwy	3232 Florence Pkwy	10. Ⓐ Ⓓ
11	...Portland OR 97208	Portland OR 99208	11. Ⓐ Ⓓ
12	...3999 Thompson Dr	3999 Thompson Dr	12. Ⓐ Ⓓ
13	...1672 Sutton Pl	1972 Sutton Pl	13. Ⓐ Ⓓ
14	...Omaha NE 68127	Omaha NE 68127	14. Ⓐ Ⓓ
15	...1473 S 96th St	1743 S 96th St	15. Ⓐ Ⓓ
16	...3425 Geary St	3425 Geary St	16. Ⓐ Ⓓ
17	...Dallas TX 75234	Dallas TX 75234	17. Ⓐ Ⓓ
18	...4094 Horchow Rd	4904 Horchow Rd	18. Ⓐ Ⓓ
19	...San Francisco CA 94108	San Francisco CA 94108	19. Ⓐ Ⓓ
20	...1410 Broadway	141 Broadway	20. Ⓐ Ⓓ
21	...424 Fifth Ave	4240 Fifth Ave	21. Ⓐ Ⓓ
22	...Westport CT 06880	Westport CT 06880	22. Ⓐ Ⓓ
23	...1932 Wilton Rd	1923 Wilton Rd	23. Ⓐ Ⓓ
24	...2052 Victoria Sta	2502 Victoria Sta	24. Ⓐ Ⓓ
25	...1982 Carlton Pl	1982 Carlton Pl	25. Ⓐ Ⓓ

Answers:

1. D	6. A	11. D	16. A	21. D
2. A	7. D	12. A	17. A	22. A
3. D	8. D	13. D	18. D	23. D
4. D	9. A	14. A	19. A	24. D
5. A	10. D	15. D	20. D	25. A

Were you able to focus on the numbers? Were you able to spot the differences quickly? Could you make a rapid decision when there was no difference? If you got any of these questions wrong, look now to see why.

If you find a difference between the two numbers, mark D and go on to the next question. Do not bother to look at the words in any pair of addresses in which you find a difference between the numbers.

If, while concentrating on numbers, you happen to catch a difference in spelling or abbreviations, by all means mark D and go on to the next question. In other words, if you spot *any* difference between the addresses, even while you are looking for a specific type of difference, mark D at once. A system may be useful, but do not stick to it slavishly when an answer is obvious.

Look for Differences in Abbreviations

When you are satisfied that the numbers are alike, and if no other difference has "struck you between the eyes," turn your attention to the abbreviations. Keep alert for differences such as:

Rd	Dr
Wy	Way
NH	NM

In comparing numbers, you began by looking at the numbers in the left column, then moved your eyes to focus on the right column. If you found a difference, you marked D on your answer sheet, moved pencil and hand down one line, and began again with the numbers of the next question. If you found no difference between the numbers, your eyes should have stopped at the right column. Look now at the abbreviations in the right column, then move your eyes to the left column to see if there are any differences. A difference is a difference, left to right or right to left, so do not waste time going back to the left column when you are focusing on the right. Try the next group of practice questions holding your place with pencil and finger and comparing the first question from left to right, the next question from right to left, and so on down the list. Remember to sound out the abbreviations exactly as you see them.

1	...3238 NW 3rd St	3238 NE 3rd St	1. Ⓐ Ⓓ
2	...7865 Harkness Blvd	7865 Harkness Blvd	2. Ⓐ Ⓓ
3	...Seattle WA 98102	Seattle WY 98102	3. Ⓐ Ⓓ
4	...342 Madison Ave	342 Madison St	4. Ⓐ Ⓓ
5	...723 Broadway E	723 Broadway E	5. Ⓐ Ⓓ
6	...4731 W 88th Dr	4731 W 88th Rd	6. Ⓐ Ⓓ
7	...Boiceville NY12412	Boiceville NY 12412	7. Ⓐ Ⓓ
8	...9021 Rodeo Dr	9021 Rodeo Drive	8. Ⓐ Ⓓ
9	...2093 Post St	2093 Post Rd	9. Ⓐ Ⓓ
10	...New Orleans LA 70153	New Orleans LA 70153	10. Ⓐ Ⓓ
11	...5332 SW Bombay St	5332 SW Bombay St	11. Ⓐ Ⓓ
12	...416 Wellington Pkwy	416 Wellington Hwy	12. Ⓐ Ⓓ
13	...2096 Garden Ln	2096 Garden Wy	13. Ⓐ Ⓓ
14	...3220 W Grant Ave	3220 W Grant Ave	14. Ⓐ Ⓓ
15	...Charlotte VT 05445	Charlotte VA 05445	15. Ⓐ Ⓓ

16	...4415 Oriental Blvd	4415 Oriental Blvd	16. (A) (D)
17	...6876 Raffles Rd	6876 Raffles Road	17. (A) (D)
18	...891 S Hotel Hwy	891 E Hotel Hwy	18. (A) (D)
19	...9500 London Br	9500 London Br	19. (A) (D)
20	...24A Motcomb St	24A Motcomb St	20. (A) (D)
21	...801 S Erleigh Ln	801 S Erleigh La	21. (A) (D)
22	...839 Casco St	839 Casco St	22. (A) (D)
23	...Freeport ME 04033	Freeport NE 04033	23. (A) (D)
24	...3535 Island Ave	3535 Island Av	24. (A) (D)
25	...2186 Missouri Ave NE	2186 Missouri Ave NW	25. (A) (D)

Answers:

1. D	6. D	11. A	16. A	21. D
2. A	7. A	12. D	17. D	22. A
3. D	8. D	13. D	18. D	23. D
4. D	9. D	14. A	19. A	24. D
5. A	10. A	15. D	20. A	25. D

Look for Differences in Street or City Names

If, after you have compared the numbers and the abbreviations, you have still not spotted any differences, you must look at the main words of the address. First of all, are the words in the two addresses really the same words?

1.	Brookfield	Brookville	1. (A) (D)
2.	Wayland	Wayland	2. (A) (D)
3.	Ferncliff	Farmcliff	3. (A) (D)
4.	Spring	Springs	4. (A) (D)
5.	New City	New City	5. (A) (D)

Answers:　1. D　2. A　3. D　4. D　5. A

Sound out the words by syllables or spell them out. Is the spelling exactly the same? Are the same letters doubled? Are two letters reversed?

1.	Beech	Beach	1. (A) (D)
2.	Torrington	Torington	2. (A) (D)
3.	Brayton	Brayton	3. (A) (D)
4.	Collegiate	Collegaite	4. (A) (D)
5.	Weston	Wetson	5. (A) (D)

Answers:　1. D　2. D　3. A　4. D　5. D

Practice Finding Differences in Names

Now try some practice questions in which differences may be found between the main words. Remember, you can save precious time by reading one question from the left column to the right column and the next question from the right column to the left.

1	...5254 Shaeffer St	5254 Schaeffer St	1. Ⓐ Ⓓ
2	...8003 Sheraton Wy	8003 Sheraton Wy	2. Ⓐ Ⓓ
3	...1937 Cordelia Terr	1937 Cordelia Terr	3. Ⓐ Ⓓ
4	...392 Kauai Hwy	392 Kauaui Hwy	4. Ⓐ Ⓓ
5	...7500 Preferred Rd	7500 Preffered Rd	5. Ⓐ Ⓓ
6	...Natick MA 01760	Natick MA 01760	6. Ⓐ Ⓓ
7	...727 Stockbridge Rd	727 Stockbridge Rd	7. Ⓐ Ⓓ
8	...294 Friend St	294 Freind St	8. Ⓐ Ⓓ
9	...4550 Munching St	4550 Munchkin St	9. Ⓐ Ⓓ
10	...Gt Barrington MA 01230	Gt Barnington MA 01230	10. Ⓐ Ⓓ
11	...7070 Baltic Wy	7070 Baltic Wy	11. Ⓐ Ⓓ
12	...889 Safari St	889 Seafari St	12. Ⓐ Ⓓ
13	...Irvington NY 10533	Irvington NY 10533	13. Ⓐ Ⓓ
14	...475 Ghirardelli Sq	475 Ghirardelli Sq	14. Ⓐ Ⓓ
15	...Sea Island GA 31561	Sea Inland GA 31561	15. Ⓐ Ⓓ
16	...8486 Massachusetts Tpke	8486 Massachusetts Tpke	16. Ⓐ Ⓓ
17	...6874 Cloister St	6874 Cloister St	17. Ⓐ Ⓓ
18	...292 Westminster MI	292 Westminister MI	18. Ⓐ Ⓓ
19	...Providence RI 02903	Providence RI 02903	19. Ⓐ Ⓓ
20	...Arundel ME 04046	Anurdel ME 04046	20. Ⓐ Ⓓ
21	...1000 Cadiz St	1000 Cadiz St	21. Ⓐ Ⓓ
22	...821 Calphalon Wy	821 Caphalon Wy	22. Ⓐ Ⓓ
23	...Oakland CA 94604	Oakland CA 94604	23. Ⓐ Ⓓ
24	...371 Himalaya St	371 Himalaya St	24. Ⓐ Ⓓ
25	...1053 Columbus Cir	1053 Columbia Cir	25. Ⓐ Ⓓ

Answers:

1. D	6. A	11. A	16. A	21. A
2. A	7. A	12. D	17. A	22. D
3. A	8. D	13. A	18. D	23. A
4. D	9. D	14. A	19. A	24. A
5. D	10. D	15. D	20. D	25. D

Check your answers. Then look at the questions to see where you made your mistakes. If your mistakes fall into any sort of pattern, guard against those errors in the future. If your mistakes seem to be random, then practice and care should help you to improve.

Comparing first the numbers, then the little words and abbreviations, and finally the main words must be done in a flash. If you have gone through this process and have spotted no errors, mark A on your answer sheet and go on to the next question. In order to complete the Address Checking Test, you can allow only *four seconds* for each question. That means you cannot afford to reread a single address. Make your decision based on your first check and go right on.

Keeping these suggestions in mind, try the practice questions that follow. In these questions, you may find differences between numbers, abbreviations, or main words, or you may find no difference at all. Work quickly, but do not time yourself on these practice questions.

Address Checking Practice Exercise

1	...8690 W 134th St	8960 W 134th St	1. Ⓐ Ⓓ
2	...1912 Berkshire Wy	1912 Berkshire Wy	2. Ⓐ Ⓓ
3	...5331 W Professor St	5331 W Proffesor St	3. Ⓐ Ⓓ
4	...Philadelphia PA 19124	Philadelphia PN 19124	4. Ⓐ Ⓓ
5	...7450 Saguenay St	7450 Saguenay St	5. Ⓐ Ⓓ
6	...8650 Christy St	8650 Christey St	6. Ⓐ Ⓓ
7	...Lumberville PA 18933	Lumberville PA 19833	7. Ⓐ Ⓓ
8	...114 Alabama Ave NW	114 Alabama Av NW	8. Ⓐ Ⓓ
9	...1756 Waterford St	1756 Waterville St	9. Ⓐ Ⓓ
10	...2214 Wister Wy	2214 Wister Wy	10. Ⓐ Ⓓ
11	...2974 Repplier Rd	2974 Repplier Dr	11. Ⓐ Ⓓ
12	...Essex CT 06426	Essex CT 06426	12. Ⓐ Ⓓ
13	...7676 N Bourbon St	7616 N Bourbon St	13. Ⓐ Ⓓ
14	...2762 Rosengarten Wy	2762 Rosengarden Wy	14. Ⓐ Ⓓ
15	...239 Windell Ave	239 Windell Ave	15. Ⓐ Ⓓ
16	...4667 Edgeworth Rd	4677 Edgeworth Rd	16. Ⓐ Ⓓ
17	...2661 Kennel St SE	2661 Kennel St SW	17. Ⓐ Ⓓ
18	...Alamo TX 78516	Alamo TX 78516	18. Ⓐ Ⓓ
19	...3709 Columbine St	3709 Columbine St	19. Ⓐ Ⓓ
20	...9699 W 14th St	9699 W 14th Rd	20. Ⓐ Ⓓ
21	...2207 Markland Ave	2207 Markham Ave	21. Ⓐ Ⓓ
22	...Los Angeles CA 90013	Los Angeles CA 90018	22. Ⓐ Ⓓ
23	...4608 N Warnock St	4806 N Warnock St	23. Ⓐ Ⓓ
24	...7718 S Summer St	7718 S Sumner St	24. Ⓐ Ⓓ

25	...New York, NY 10016	New York, NY 10016	25. Ⓐ Ⓓ
26	...4514 Ft Hamilton Pk	4514 Ft Hamilton Pk	26. Ⓐ Ⓓ
27	...5701 Kosciusko St	5701 Koscusko St	27. Ⓐ Ⓓ
28	...5422 Evergreen St	4522 Evergreen St	28. Ⓐ Ⓓ
29	...Gainsville FL 32611	Gainsville FL 32611	29. Ⓐ Ⓓ
30	...5018 Church St	5018 Church Ave	30. Ⓐ Ⓓ
31	...1079 N Blake St	1097 N Blake St	31. Ⓐ Ⓓ
32	...8072 W 20th Rd	8072 W 20th Dr	32. Ⓐ Ⓓ
33	...Onoro ME 04473	Orono ME 04473	33. Ⓐ Ⓓ
34	...2175 Kimbell Rd	2175 Kimball Rd	34. Ⓐ Ⓓ
35	...1243 Mermaid St	1243 Mermaid St	35. Ⓐ Ⓓ
36	...4904 SW 134th St	4904 SW 134th St	36. Ⓐ Ⓓ
37	...1094 Hancock St	1049 Hancock St	37. Ⓐ Ⓓ
38	...Des Moines IA 50311	Des Moines IA 50311	38. Ⓐ Ⓓ
39	...4832 S Rinaldi Rd	4832 S Rinaldo Rd	39. Ⓐ Ⓓ
40	...2015 Dorchester Rd	2015 Dorchester Rd	40. Ⓐ Ⓓ
41	...5216 Woodbine St	5216 Woodburn St	41. Ⓐ Ⓓ
42	...Boulder CO 80302	Boulder CA 80302	42. Ⓐ Ⓓ
43	...4739 N Marion St	479 N Marion St	43. Ⓐ Ⓓ
44	...3720 Nautilus Wy	3720 Nautilus Way	44. Ⓐ Ⓓ
45	...3636 Gramercy Pk	3636 Gramercy Pk	45. Ⓐ Ⓓ
46	...757 Johnson Ave	757 Johnston Ave	46. Ⓐ Ⓓ
47	...3045 Brighton 12th St	3054 Brighton 12th St	47. Ⓐ Ⓓ
48	...237 Ovington Ave	237 Ovington Ave	48. Ⓐ Ⓓ
49	...Kalamazoo MI 49007	Kalamazoo MI 49007	49. Ⓐ Ⓓ
50	...Missoula MT 59812	Missoula MS 59812	50. Ⓐ Ⓓ
51	...Stillwater OK 74704	Stillwater OK 47404	51. Ⓐ Ⓓ
52	...4746 Empire Blvd	4746 Empire Bldg	52. Ⓐ Ⓓ
53	...6321 St Johns Pl	6321 St Johns Pl	53. Ⓐ Ⓓ
54	...2242 Vanderbilt Ave	2242 Vanderbilt Ave	54. Ⓐ Ⓓ
55	...542 Ditmas Blvd	542 Ditmars Blvd	55. Ⓐ Ⓓ
56	...4603 W Argyle Rd	4603 W Argyle Rd	56. Ⓐ Ⓓ
57	...653 Knickerbocker Ave NE	653 Knickerbocker Ave NE	57. Ⓐ Ⓓ
58	...3651 Midwood Terr	3651 Midwood Terr	58. Ⓐ Ⓓ
59	...Chapel Hill NC 27514	Chaple Hill NC 27514	59. Ⓐ Ⓓ
60	...3217 Vernon Pl NW	3217 Vernon Dr NW	60. Ⓐ Ⓓ

61	...1094 Rednor Pkwy	1049 Rednor Pkwy	61. Ⓐ Ⓓ
62	...986 S Doughty Blvd	986 S Douty Blvd	62. Ⓐ Ⓓ
63	...Lincoln NE 68508	Lincoln NE 65808	63. Ⓐ Ⓓ
64	...1517 LaSalle Ave	1517 LaSalle Ave	64. Ⓐ Ⓓ
65	...3857 S Morris St	3857 S Morriss St	65. Ⓐ Ⓓ
66	...6104 Saunders Expy	614 Saunders Expy	66. Ⓐ Ⓓ
67	...2541 Appleton St	2541 Appleton Rd	67. Ⓐ Ⓓ
68	...Washington DC 20052	Washington DC 20052	68. Ⓐ Ⓓ
69	...6439 Kessler Blvd S	6439 Kessler Blvd S	69. Ⓐ Ⓓ
70	...4786 Catalina Dr	4786 Catalana Dr	70. Ⓐ Ⓓ
71	...132 E Hampton Pkwy	1322 E Hampton Pkwy	71. Ⓐ Ⓓ
72	...1066 Goethe Sq S	1066 Geothe Sq S	72. Ⓐ Ⓓ
73	...1118 Jerriman Wy	1218 Jerriman Wy	73. Ⓐ Ⓓ
74	...5798 Gd Central Pkwy	5798 Gd Central Pkwy	74. Ⓐ Ⓓ
75	...Delaware OH 43015	Delaware OK 43015	75. Ⓐ Ⓓ
76	...Corvallis OR 97331	Corvallis OR 97331	76. Ⓐ Ⓓ
77	...4231 Keating Ave N	4231 Keating Av N	77. Ⓐ Ⓓ
78	...5689 Central Pk Pl	5869 Central Pk Pl	78. Ⓐ Ⓓ
79	...1108 Lyndhurst Dr	1108 Lyndhurst Dr	79. Ⓐ Ⓓ
80	...842 Chambers Ct	842 Chamber Ct	80. Ⓐ Ⓓ
81	...Athens OH 45701	Athens GA 45701	81. Ⓐ Ⓓ
82	...Tulsa OK 74171	Tulsa OK 71471	82. Ⓐ Ⓓ
83	...6892 Beech Grove Ave	6892 Beech Grove Ave	83. Ⓐ Ⓓ
84	...2939 E Division St	2939 W Division St	84. Ⓐ Ⓓ
85	...1554 Pitkin Ave	1554 Pitkin Ave	85. Ⓐ Ⓓ
86	...905 St Edwards Plz	950 St Edwards Plz	86. Ⓐ Ⓓ
87	...1906 W 152nd St	1906 W 152nd St	87. Ⓐ Ⓓ
88	...3466 Glenmore Ave	3466 Glenville Ave	88. Ⓐ Ⓓ
89	...Middlebury VT 05753	Middlebery VT 05753	89. Ⓐ Ⓓ
90	...Evanston IL 60201	Evanston IN 60201	90. Ⓐ Ⓓ
91	...9401 W McDonald Ave	9401 W MacDonald Ave	91. Ⓐ Ⓓ
92	...5527 Albermarle Rd	5527 Albermarle Rd	92. Ⓐ Ⓓ
93	...9055 Carter Dr	9055 Carter Rd	93. Ⓐ Ⓓ
94	...Greenvale NY 11548	Greenvale NY 11458	94. Ⓐ Ⓓ
95	...1149 Cherry Gr S	1149 Cherry Gr S	95. Ⓐ Ⓓ

Answers to Practice Exercise

1. D	13. D	25. A	37. D	49. A	61. D	73. D	85. A
2. A	14. D	26. A	38. A	50. D	62. D	74. A	86. D
3. D	15. A	27. D	39. D	51. D	63. D	75. D	87. A
4. D	16. D	28. D	40. A	52. D	64. A	76. A	88. D
5. A	17. D	29. A	41. D	53. A	65. D	77. D	89. D
6. D	18. A	30. D	42. D	54. A	66. D	78. D	90. D
7. D	19. A	31. D	43. D	55. D	67. D	79. A	91. D
8. D	20. D	32. D	44. D	56. A	68. A	80. D	92. A
9. D	21. D	33. D	45. A	57. A	69. A	81. D	93. D
10. A	22. D	34. D	46. D	58. A	70. D	82. D	94. D
11. D	23. D	35. A	47. D	59. D	71. D	83. A	95. A
12. A	24. D	36. A	48. A	60. D	72. D	84. D	

Use the chart below to analyze your errors on the Practice Exercise.

Analyzing Your Errors

Type of Difference	Question Numbers	Number of Questions You Missed
Difference in NUMBERS	1, 7, 13, 16, 22, 23, 28, 31, 37, 43, 47, 51, 61, 63, 66, 71, 73, 78, 82, 86, 94	
Difference in ABBREVIATIONS	4, 8, 11, 17, 20, 30, 32, 42, 44, 50, 52, 60, 67, 75, 77, 81, 84, 90, 93	
Difference in NAMES	3, 6, 9, 14, 21, 24, 27, 33, 34, 39, 41, 46, 55, 59, 62, 65, 70, 72, 80, 88, 89, 91	
No Difference	2, 5, 10, 12, 15, 18, 19, 25, 26, 29, 35, 36, 38, 40, 45, 48, 49, 53, 54, 56, 57, 58, 64, 68, 69, 74, 76, 79, 83, 85, 87, 92, 95	

The Model Exams that follow in the next part will offer you plenty of practice with Address Checking questions. Flip back to this chapter between Model Exams as you work through the book. Reread the chapter the day before your exam for a quick refresher.

REMEMBER: Look first for differences between numbers.

Next, look at the abbreviations and little words.

Read what is written, as it is written.

Finally, sound out or spell out the main words.

When you find any difference, mark D and go immediately to the next question.

If you find no difference, do not linger. Mark A and move right on to the next question.

Do NOT read the whole address as a unit.

How to Answer Memory for Addresses Questions

Memorizing is a special skill, simple for some few people, a chore for most. If you are one of the lucky ones with a good visual memory—that is, if you can look at a page and remember not only what was on the page but how the page looked —you will find this test very easy. You need only picture where on the page each item is located. If, however, you do not have this gift, then the Memory for Addresses Test may appear to be frighteningly difficult. This chapter contains suggestions to help you memorize more efficiently and tips to help you cope with this particular memorizing test.

As you look at the set of boxes on which memory questions are based, your first impression is that you must memorize 10 names and 15 complex number span/name combinations and their locations in five different boxes labeled A, B, C, D, and E. The task is not a simple one, but it is not as overwhelming as it appears at first glance. Let us work together to commit to memory the official sample set of addresses following a step-by-step approach.

A	B	C	D	E
4700–5599 Table	6800–6999 Table	5600–6499 Table	6500–6799 Table	4400–4699 Table
Lismore	Kelford	Joel	Tatum	Ruskin
5600–6499 West	6500–6799 West	6800–6999 West	4400–4699 West	4700–5599 West
Hesper	Musella	Sardis	Porter	Nathan
4400–4699 Blake	5600–6499 Blake	6500–6799 Blake	4700–5599 Blake	6800–6999 Blake

Step One: Take a good look at the five boxes. You will note that in each block there are two single names and three sets of number spans with names. Single names tend to be easier to memorize than number spans connected to names, so concentrate now on only the single names.

A	B	C	D	E
Lismore	Kelford	Joel	Tatum	Ruskin
Hesper	Musella	Sardis	Porter	Nathan

Deciding What to Memorize

Use your imagination to combine the pair of names in any four boxes. Why in only four boxes? Once you have thoroughly memorized the contents of four boxes, any name or number span/name combination that you cannot place automatically may be assigned to the fifth box. If you find all the names equally easy to learn, then eliminate box E. If the names in one particular box give you more trouble than the others, choose that box to skip. When you learn the number span/name combinations, you will skip the same box so that all unknowns can be assigned to the same box when you are answering questions. While all items must be memorized in their correct boxes, the order of the items in the boxes is irrelevant. This means that you can memorize from the top down or from the bottom up. And, you do not need to be consistent in the order in which you memorize the names from one box to the next.

73

In general, the best way to learn which two words belong in the same box is to combine those words in some way that is meaningful to you. With the above names you might choose, for example: HeLI; MucK; JoS; TaP; and RuN. Skip the box in which you find the words most difficult to combine meaningfully. In this set, you would probably choose to skip box C, but the decision is a personal one. You may, of course, choose to memorize all five boxes. The important thing is to memorize the key words from left to right so that the location of each word can be easily recalled under the time pressure of the memory test. If the names suggest different key words to you, you can of course use those. Just remember to learn your boxes from left to right so that you can remember in which box to place each key word and, of course, the two words it represents. All combining of words must be done in your head. You are not permitted to write anything during the memorizing phase.

When you are satisfied that you have learned which names belong in each box, cover the strip of names in boxes and try the questions in this exercise.

1. Sardis

1. Ⓐ Ⓑ Ⓒ Ⓓ Ⓔ

2. Ruskin

2. Ⓐ Ⓑ Ⓒ Ⓓ Ⓔ

3. Lismore

3. Ⓐ Ⓑ Ⓒ Ⓓ Ⓔ

4. Tatum

4. Ⓐ Ⓑ Ⓒ Ⓓ Ⓔ

5. Nathan

5. Ⓐ Ⓑ Ⓒ Ⓓ Ⓔ

6. Porter

6. Ⓐ Ⓑ Ⓒ Ⓓ Ⓔ

7. Hesper

7. Ⓐ Ⓑ Ⓒ Ⓓ Ⓔ

8. Kelford

8. Ⓐ Ⓑ Ⓒ Ⓓ Ⓔ

9. Lismore

9. Ⓐ Ⓑ Ⓒ Ⓓ Ⓔ

10. Musella

10. Ⓐ Ⓑ Ⓒ Ⓓ Ⓔ

11. Nathan

11. Ⓐ Ⓑ Ⓒ Ⓓ Ⓔ

12. Porter

12. Ⓐ Ⓑ Ⓒ Ⓓ Ⓔ

13. Joel

13. Ⓐ Ⓑ Ⓒ Ⓓ Ⓔ

14. Tatum

14. Ⓐ Ⓑ Ⓒ Ⓓ Ⓔ

15. Ruskin

15. Ⓐ Ⓑ Ⓒ Ⓓ Ⓔ

16. Hesper

16. Ⓐ Ⓑ Ⓒ Ⓓ Ⓔ

17. Sardis

17. Ⓐ Ⓑ Ⓒ Ⓓ Ⓔ

18. Nathan

18. Ⓐ Ⓑ Ⓒ Ⓓ Ⓔ

19. Joel

19. Ⓐ Ⓑ Ⓒ Ⓓ Ⓔ

20. Lismore

20. Ⓐ Ⓑ Ⓒ Ⓓ Ⓔ

21. Porter

21. Ⓐ Ⓑ Ⓒ Ⓓ Ⓔ

22. Musella

22. Ⓐ Ⓑ Ⓒ Ⓓ Ⓔ

23. Kelford

23. Ⓐ Ⓑ Ⓒ Ⓓ Ⓔ

24. Ruskin

24. Ⓐ Ⓑ Ⓒ Ⓓ Ⓔ

25. Tatum

25. Ⓐ Ⓑ Ⓒ Ⓓ Ⓔ

Answers:

1. C	2. E	3. A	4. D	5. E	6. D	7. A
8. B	9. A	10. B	11. E	12. D	13. C	14. D
15. E	16. A	17. C	18. E	19. C	20. A	21. D
22. B	23. B	24. E	25. D			

You should have mastered the locations of the ten single names. If you were to take the exam right now, you should score 40 percent. Of course, you need to earn a much higher score. But it has not been difficult to reach this level. You should be building your confidence about your ability to do well with the Memory for Addresses questions.

Step Two: Now, ignoring the single names that you have already memorized, along with their locations, look again at the boxes. Focus on the number spans and the names they go with.

A	B	C	D	E
4700–5599 Table	6800–6999 Table	5600–6499 Table	6500–6799 Table	4400–4699 Table
5600–6499 West	6500–6799 West	6800–6999 West	4400–4699 West	4700–5599 West
4400–4699 Blake	5600–6499 Blake	6500–6799 Blake	4700–5599 Blake	6800–6999 Blake

Looking carefully you will notice that there are just five different number spans. Your first thought may be that this is a plus, that you need only memorize five number spans. Actually, this is what makes the task a difficult one. Each number span is paired with three different names in three different locations, so you must memorize number, name, and location for 12 of the 15 items. As with the single names, you may ignore one box and assign all unmemorized items to it, though you may learn all 15 if you choose.

So the bad news is that you must memorize locations of 12 separate items. Unlike the single names, these items cannot be combined. The good news is that you do not need to memorize number spans. A closer look will show you that the first two digits of each of the five number spans are distinctive. They are 44, 47, 56, 65, and 68. You can mentally disregard the zeros and the numbers at the other end of the span. You cannot cross out extraneous numbers, unfortunately, because you are not permitted even to hold a pencil while memorizing. So, the number span/name combination memory task really looks like this:

A		B		C		D		E	
47	Table	68	Table	56	Table	65	Table	44	Table
56	West	65	West	68	West	44	West	47	West
44	Blake	56	Blake	65	Blake	47	Blake	68	Blake

Step Three: Devise a system for placing a number/name combination into its correct box. Work with one box at a time. Use initials to create a personalized memory scheme. You might, for instance, say to yourself, "47 Table AT, 56 West AW, 44 Blake BA; 68 Table BuT, 65 West BoW, 56 Blake BuB; and so on." Or, you might find it just as easy to commit to memory "47 A Table, 56 A West, 44 A Blake; 68 B Table, 65 B West, 56 B Blake; etc." Or, if the words lend themselves to a different style of combination with the letter of the box, try something like "65 TableD, 44WesteD, 47BlakeD." You do not have to use the same method in each box; you just have to create a system that you can learn quickly and remember without any possible confusion. With these particular names, you might use sound rather than letter for learning which combinations belong in box E, perhaps "44 TableY, 47 WestY, 68 BlakeY."

Learn one box at a time. By learning the contents of one box as a group, you are more likely to remember all contents of that box when faced with 88 items that must rapidly be assigned to their proper boxes. Omit the same box that you omitted when learning the single names. In this way all unknowns can be assigned to the same box. Some combinations may be easier to learn than others, but it would be far too confusing to skip one box for names and another for number/name combinations.

Devise your own system for the sample set now. Learn number/name combinations and their locations to your satisfaction. Then cover the boxes and try the exercise below.

1. 6500–6799 West	1. Ⓐ Ⓑ Ⓒ Ⓓ Ⓔ	14. 6500–6799 West	14. Ⓐ Ⓑ Ⓒ Ⓓ Ⓔ
2. 6800–6999 Blake	2. Ⓐ Ⓑ Ⓒ Ⓓ Ⓔ	15. 4400–4699 Table	15. Ⓐ Ⓑ Ⓒ Ⓓ Ⓔ
3. 4400–4699 West	3. Ⓐ Ⓑ Ⓒ Ⓓ Ⓔ	16. 6800–6999 Blake	16. Ⓐ Ⓑ Ⓒ Ⓓ Ⓔ
4. 5600–6499 Table	4. Ⓐ Ⓑ Ⓒ Ⓓ Ⓔ	17. 5600–6499 Blake	17. Ⓐ Ⓑ Ⓒ Ⓓ Ⓔ
5. 6500–6799 Blake	5. Ⓐ Ⓑ Ⓒ Ⓓ Ⓔ	18. 6800–6999 Table	18. Ⓐ Ⓑ Ⓒ Ⓓ Ⓔ
6. 4700–5599 Table	6. Ⓐ Ⓑ Ⓒ Ⓓ Ⓔ	19. 5600–6499 West	19. Ⓐ Ⓑ Ⓒ Ⓓ Ⓔ
7. 5600–6499 West	7. Ⓐ Ⓑ Ⓒ Ⓓ Ⓔ	20. 5600–6499 Table	20. Ⓐ Ⓑ Ⓒ Ⓓ Ⓔ
8. 4700–5599 Blake	8. Ⓐ Ⓑ Ⓒ Ⓓ Ⓔ	21. 4700–5599 West	21. Ⓐ Ⓑ Ⓒ Ⓓ Ⓔ
9. 6800–6999 Table	9. Ⓐ Ⓑ Ⓒ Ⓓ Ⓔ	22. 6500–6799 Table	22. Ⓐ Ⓑ Ⓒ Ⓓ Ⓔ
10. 6800–6999 West	10. Ⓐ Ⓑ Ⓒ Ⓓ Ⓔ	23. 6500–6799 Blake	23. Ⓐ Ⓑ Ⓒ Ⓓ Ⓔ
11. 4400–4699 Blake	11. Ⓐ Ⓑ Ⓒ Ⓓ Ⓔ	24. 6500–6799 West	24. Ⓐ Ⓑ Ⓒ Ⓓ Ⓔ
12. 4700–5599 Table	12. Ⓐ Ⓑ Ⓒ Ⓓ Ⓔ	25. 6800–6999 Blake	25. Ⓐ Ⓑ Ⓒ Ⓓ Ⓔ
13. 6800–6999 West	13. Ⓐ Ⓑ Ⓒ Ⓓ Ⓔ		

Answers:

1. B	2. E	3. D	4. C	5. C	6. A	7. A
8. D	9. B	10. C	11. A	12. A	13. C	14. B
15. E	16. E	17. B	18. B	19. A	20. C	21. E
22. D	23. C	24. B	25. E			

Now that you have learned to place the separate names and the number span/name combinations into their boxes in two distinct steps, you must put together all that you have memorized and answer questions that combine both sets of information that are contained in the boxes. Try the following exercise right now before you have a chance to forget the systems you devised for memorizing.

1. 4400–4699 West
2. Nathan
3. 4400–4699 Table
4. 6500–6799 Blake
5. 5600–6499 Blake
6. Joel
7. Hesper
8. 4700–5599 Table
9. 6800–6999 West
10. Kelford
11. Musella
12. Ruskin
13. 6500–6799 Table
14. 5600–6499 West
15. 4400–4699 Blake
16. Nathan
17. 6500–6799 Blake
18. 4700–5599 West
19. Tatum
20. 6800–6999 Table
21. 4400–4699 Table
22. Joel
23. 6500–6799 West
24. 6800–6999 West
25. 6800–6999 Blake

1. Ⓐ Ⓑ Ⓒ Ⓓ Ⓔ
2. Ⓐ Ⓑ Ⓒ Ⓓ Ⓔ
3. Ⓐ Ⓑ Ⓒ Ⓓ Ⓔ
4. Ⓐ Ⓑ Ⓒ Ⓓ Ⓔ
5. Ⓐ Ⓑ Ⓒ Ⓓ Ⓔ
6. Ⓐ Ⓑ Ⓒ Ⓓ Ⓔ
7. Ⓐ Ⓑ Ⓒ Ⓓ Ⓔ
8. Ⓐ Ⓑ Ⓒ Ⓓ Ⓔ
9. Ⓐ Ⓑ Ⓒ Ⓓ Ⓔ
10. Ⓐ Ⓑ Ⓒ Ⓓ Ⓔ
11. Ⓐ Ⓑ Ⓒ Ⓓ Ⓔ
12. Ⓐ Ⓑ Ⓒ Ⓓ Ⓔ
13. Ⓐ Ⓑ Ⓒ Ⓓ Ⓔ
14. Ⓐ Ⓑ Ⓒ Ⓓ Ⓔ
15. Ⓐ Ⓑ Ⓒ Ⓓ Ⓔ
16. Ⓐ Ⓑ Ⓒ Ⓓ Ⓔ
17. Ⓐ Ⓑ Ⓒ Ⓓ Ⓔ
18. Ⓐ Ⓑ Ⓒ Ⓓ Ⓔ
19. Ⓐ Ⓑ Ⓒ Ⓓ Ⓔ
20. Ⓐ Ⓑ Ⓒ Ⓓ Ⓔ
21. Ⓐ Ⓑ Ⓒ Ⓓ Ⓔ
22. Ⓐ Ⓑ Ⓒ Ⓓ Ⓔ
23. Ⓐ Ⓑ Ⓒ Ⓓ Ⓔ
24. Ⓐ Ⓑ Ⓒ Ⓓ Ⓔ
25. Ⓐ Ⓑ Ⓒ Ⓓ Ⓔ

26. 5600–6499 Blake
27. Ruskin
28. Sardis
29. 4400–4699 Blake
30. 5600–6499 West
31. Lismore
32. 6500–6799 Table
33. 4700–5599 West
34. Musella
35. 6500–6799 Blake
36. 6800–6999 Table
37. 4700–5599 Table
38. 6800–6999 West
39. Joel
40. Porter
41. Hesper
42. 5600–6499 Table
43. Nathan
44. 4400–4699 West
45. 6500–6799 West
46. Kelford
47. 5600–6499 Blake
48. 6800–6999 Blake
49. 5600–6499 West
50. 6500–6799 Table

26. Ⓐ Ⓑ Ⓒ Ⓓ Ⓔ
27. Ⓐ Ⓑ Ⓒ Ⓓ Ⓔ
28. Ⓐ Ⓑ Ⓒ Ⓓ Ⓔ
29. Ⓐ Ⓑ Ⓒ Ⓓ Ⓔ
30. Ⓐ Ⓑ Ⓒ Ⓓ Ⓔ
31. Ⓐ Ⓑ Ⓒ Ⓓ Ⓔ
32. Ⓐ Ⓑ Ⓒ Ⓓ Ⓔ
33. Ⓐ Ⓑ Ⓒ Ⓓ Ⓔ
34. Ⓐ Ⓑ Ⓒ Ⓓ Ⓔ
35. Ⓐ Ⓑ Ⓒ Ⓓ Ⓔ
36. Ⓐ Ⓑ Ⓒ Ⓓ Ⓔ
37. Ⓐ Ⓑ Ⓒ Ⓓ Ⓔ
38. Ⓐ Ⓑ Ⓒ Ⓓ Ⓔ
39. Ⓐ Ⓑ Ⓒ Ⓓ Ⓔ
40. Ⓐ Ⓑ Ⓒ Ⓓ Ⓔ
41. Ⓐ Ⓑ Ⓒ Ⓓ Ⓔ
42. Ⓐ Ⓑ Ⓒ Ⓓ Ⓔ
43. Ⓐ Ⓑ Ⓒ Ⓓ Ⓔ
44. Ⓐ Ⓑ Ⓒ Ⓓ Ⓔ
45. Ⓐ Ⓑ Ⓒ Ⓓ Ⓔ
46. Ⓐ Ⓑ Ⓒ Ⓓ Ⓔ
47. Ⓐ Ⓑ Ⓒ Ⓓ Ⓔ
48. Ⓐ Ⓑ Ⓒ Ⓓ Ⓔ
49. Ⓐ Ⓑ Ⓒ Ⓓ Ⓔ
50. Ⓐ Ⓑ Ⓒ Ⓓ Ⓔ

Answers:

1. D	2. E	3. E	4. C	5. B	6. C	7. A
8. A	9. C	10. B	11. B	12. E	13. D	14. A
15. A	16. E	17. C	18. E	19. D	20. B	21. E
22. C	23. B	24. C	25. E	26. B	27. E	28. C
29. A	30. A	31. A	32. D	33. E	34. B	35. C
36. B	37. A	38. C	39. C	40. D	41. A	42. C
43. E	44. D	45. B	46. B	47. B	48. E	49. A
50. D						

Now that you have thoroughly learned the locations of the 25 items in the sample questions that are sent to all registrants for this postal exam, you must forget them. The Memory for Addresses items on your actual exam will be different from these and will be different from the items in the practice exercises and the full-length model exams in this book. The items to be memorized on your exam will be new and different from all you have learned before exam day. However, AND THIS IS IMPORTANT, the items on your exam will be the same as the memory items on the short sample set with which you will practice before the memory part of your exam begins. The general procedure at postal exams is to offer a short practice session before each separately timed part of an exam. In this short practice session, the examiner reads through the directions for answering questions with the test-takers. Test-takers have an opportunity to ask questions and to clarify directions for choosing answers and for marking responses. A few minutes are devoted to answering a handful of questions. The boxes that you will see with the pre-test samples in the testing room are the SAME BOXES AND CONTAIN THE SAME ITEMS you will see on the exam. The postal service does not want to trick or confuse you. If you were to use sample moments to memorize location of items in unrelated boxes, this very recent memorizing task would interfere with your performance on the actual exam. Therefore, the postal service introduces you to the same 25 items that you will see and learn when it really counts. What this means to you is that you have a few additional minutes to begin to devise a memorizing plan and to begin memorizing locations of items in the boxes. Use every minute; you'll need all the time you get to memorize thoroughly and answer as many questions as possible.

In the remainder of this chapter, you will find two different sets of items in boxes followed by sets of questions. Do not rush to try these right now. Your memorizing of the items from the sample set is too recent. You will need to allow yourself time to forget old sets and old systems. Go to another chapter of the book now or get involved in another activity altogether. You should not attempt more than one set of memory boxes a day. When you work through the full-length model exams, separate them by a few days. And do not do any practice memory sets for at least a week before you take your postal exam. Review hints, suggestions, and methods, of course, but do not clutter your memory with items and locations or with key words and codes that will interfere with your learning the one set that really matters.

There are two practice exercises in this chapter. Each exercise consists of a set of five boxes and two sets of questions. Begin by devising memory schemes for the names and the number span/name combinations. Memorize to your own satisfaction. Then answer the questions in set 1, referring back to the boxes if necessary. Answer the set 2 questions strictly from memory. As you work through this chapter, do not be concerned about time limits. The time pressure in the actual exam is very real, but in this chapter concentrate on developing your skills. Use the model exams later to work up to speed.

Memory for Addresses Practice Exercise 1

A	B	C	D	E
3200–3499 Peach Gray 3500–3599 Crown Book 2900–3199 Long	1000–2199 Peach Fish 2200–2899 Crown Trace 3200–3499 Long	3500–3599 Peach Arden 3200–3499 Crown Paris 1000–2199 Long	2200–2899 Peach Stewart 2900–3199 Crown Narrows 3500–3599 Long	2900–3199 Peach Hard 1000–2199 Crown Inman 2200–2899 Long

Step One: Zero in on the single names right away. Think of a good combination of each pair of words and write it in directly under the box. Under box A you might write: GraB; under box B, FiT; under box C, PArdon; under box D, StuN or NeSt; under box E, HI. Or you might choose entirely different words and skip any one of these boxes. The important thing is to learn from left to right, that is, from A to E, and to devise words that will lead you to locate immediately a test word in its appropriate box. At the test site you are not permitted to write on your test booklet, but go ahead and write in this first practice exercise.

Step Two: Take your pencil, and cross out from *00* to the end of each number span. Excess numbers can only be distracting. Leave only essential material to be memorized. At this stage of the learning process, your boxes should look like this:

A	B	C	D	E
32~~00–3499~~ Peach Gray 35~~00–3599~~ Crown Book 29~~00–3199~~ Long	10~~00–2199~~ Peach Fish 22~~00–2899~~ Crown Trace 32~~00–3499~~ Long	35~~00–3599~~ Peach Arden 32~~00–3499~~ Crown Paris 10~~00–2199~~ Long	22~~00–2899~~ Peach Stewart 29~~00–3199~~ Crown Narrows 35~~00–3599~~ Long	29~~00–3199~~ Peach Hard 10~~00–2199~~ Crown Inman 22~~00–2899~~ Long
GraB or BoG or other	FiT or other	PArdon or other	StuN or NeSt or other	HI or other

If you choose to skip a box, draw an X right across it so that your eyes do not dwell on any of its contents while you are busy memorizing.

Step Three: Devise a personalized method for remembering the number/name combinations of one box at a time. You do not need to use the same method for each box. If you skipped a box when learning the single names, you MUST skip the SAME box. If you found it easy to learn the locations of all the names, you may still choose to skip the number/name combinations in one of the boxes to lessen the more complex learning task. At step three you are learning four of the five boxes below:

A	B	C	D	E
32 Peach 35 Crown 29 Long	10 Peach 22 Crown 32 Long	35 Peach 32 Crown 10 Long	22 Peach 29 Crown 35 Long	29 Peach 10 Crown 22 Long

Now try the practice exercise. In answering the questions in the first set, you may refer back to the original strip of boxes. Answer the second set strictly from memory. Do not worry about time limits for this practice exercise. When you have completed both sets, check your answers against the key on page 83 to see how well you did.

SET 1

1. 2200–2899 Crown
2. 3500–3599 Long
3. Stewart
4. 3200–3499 Peach
5. 3200–3499 Crown
6. 2200–2899 Peach
7. Inman
8. Gray
9. 3500–3599 Crown
10. 2200–2899 Long
11. 2900–3199 Long
12. Trace
13. Hard
14. Arden
15. 2200–2899 Crown
16. 1000–2199 Crown
17. 1000–2199 Peach
18. Narrows
19. 3200–3499 Long
20. Paris
21. 3500–3599 Long
22. 3500–3599 Peach
23. 2200–2899 Peach
24. Fish
25. Book
26. 2900–3199 Peach
27. 2900–3199 Crown
28. 1000–2199 Long
29. 2200–2899 Crown
30. 3200–3499 Peach

31. Gray
32. Trace
33. Arden
34. 3200–3499 Crown
35. Narrows
36. Hard
37. 2900–3199 Long
38. 2200–2899 Crown
39. 3500–3599 Peach
40. 2900–3199 Crown
41. 2200–2899 Long
42. Inman
43. Stewart
44. Paris
45. 3500–3599 Crown
46. 1000–2199 Peach
47. Fish
48. Book
49. 3200–3499 Long
50. 2200–2899 Peach
51. 3200–3499 Crown
52. 2900–3199 Peach
53. 2200–2899 Long
54. Gray
55. Narrows
56. Hard
57. 3200–3499 Peach
58. 1000–2199 Crown
59. 1000–2199 Long
60. Inman

1. Ⓐ Ⓑ Ⓒ Ⓓ Ⓔ
2. Ⓐ Ⓑ Ⓒ Ⓓ Ⓔ
3. Ⓐ Ⓑ Ⓒ Ⓓ Ⓔ
4. Ⓐ Ⓑ Ⓒ Ⓓ Ⓔ
5. Ⓐ Ⓑ Ⓒ Ⓓ Ⓔ
6. Ⓐ Ⓑ Ⓒ Ⓓ Ⓔ
7. Ⓐ Ⓑ Ⓒ Ⓓ Ⓔ
8. Ⓐ Ⓑ Ⓒ Ⓓ Ⓔ
9. Ⓐ Ⓑ Ⓒ Ⓓ Ⓔ
10. Ⓐ Ⓑ Ⓒ Ⓓ Ⓔ
11. Ⓐ Ⓑ Ⓒ Ⓓ Ⓔ
12. Ⓐ Ⓑ Ⓒ Ⓓ Ⓔ
13. Ⓐ Ⓑ Ⓒ Ⓓ Ⓔ
14. Ⓐ Ⓑ Ⓒ Ⓓ Ⓔ
15. Ⓐ Ⓑ Ⓒ Ⓓ Ⓔ
16. Ⓐ Ⓑ Ⓒ Ⓓ Ⓔ
17. Ⓐ Ⓑ Ⓒ Ⓓ Ⓔ
18. Ⓐ Ⓑ Ⓒ Ⓓ Ⓔ
19. Ⓐ Ⓑ Ⓒ Ⓓ Ⓔ
20. Ⓐ Ⓑ Ⓒ Ⓓ Ⓔ
21. Ⓐ Ⓑ Ⓒ Ⓓ Ⓔ
22. Ⓐ Ⓑ Ⓒ Ⓓ Ⓔ
23. Ⓐ Ⓑ Ⓒ Ⓓ Ⓔ
24. Ⓐ Ⓑ Ⓒ Ⓓ Ⓔ
25. Ⓐ Ⓑ Ⓒ Ⓓ Ⓔ
26. Ⓐ Ⓑ Ⓒ Ⓓ Ⓔ
27. Ⓐ Ⓑ Ⓒ Ⓓ Ⓔ
28. Ⓐ Ⓑ Ⓒ Ⓓ Ⓔ
29. Ⓐ Ⓑ Ⓒ Ⓓ Ⓔ
30. Ⓐ Ⓑ Ⓒ Ⓓ Ⓔ
31. Ⓐ Ⓑ Ⓒ Ⓓ Ⓔ
32. Ⓐ Ⓑ Ⓒ Ⓓ Ⓔ
33. Ⓐ Ⓑ Ⓒ Ⓓ Ⓔ
34. Ⓐ Ⓑ Ⓒ Ⓓ Ⓔ
35. Ⓐ Ⓑ Ⓒ Ⓓ Ⓔ
36. Ⓐ Ⓑ Ⓒ Ⓓ Ⓔ
37. Ⓐ Ⓑ Ⓒ Ⓓ Ⓔ
38. Ⓐ Ⓑ Ⓒ Ⓓ Ⓔ
39. Ⓐ Ⓑ Ⓒ Ⓓ Ⓔ
40. Ⓐ Ⓑ Ⓒ Ⓓ Ⓔ
41. Ⓐ Ⓑ Ⓒ Ⓓ Ⓔ
42. Ⓐ Ⓑ Ⓒ Ⓓ Ⓔ
43. Ⓐ Ⓑ Ⓒ Ⓓ Ⓔ
44. Ⓐ Ⓑ Ⓒ Ⓓ Ⓔ
45. Ⓐ Ⓑ Ⓒ Ⓓ Ⓔ
46. Ⓐ Ⓑ Ⓒ Ⓓ Ⓔ
47. Ⓐ Ⓑ Ⓒ Ⓓ Ⓔ
48. Ⓐ Ⓑ Ⓒ Ⓓ Ⓔ
49. Ⓐ Ⓑ Ⓒ Ⓓ Ⓔ
50. Ⓐ Ⓑ Ⓒ Ⓓ Ⓔ
51. Ⓐ Ⓑ Ⓒ Ⓓ Ⓔ
52. Ⓐ Ⓑ Ⓒ Ⓓ Ⓔ
53. Ⓐ Ⓑ Ⓒ Ⓓ Ⓔ
54. Ⓐ Ⓑ Ⓒ Ⓓ Ⓔ
55. Ⓐ Ⓑ Ⓒ Ⓓ Ⓔ
56. Ⓐ Ⓑ Ⓒ Ⓓ Ⓔ
57. Ⓐ Ⓑ Ⓒ Ⓓ Ⓔ
58. Ⓐ Ⓑ Ⓒ Ⓓ Ⓔ
59. Ⓐ Ⓑ Ⓒ Ⓓ Ⓔ
60. Ⓐ Ⓑ Ⓒ Ⓓ Ⓔ

61. Book

62. 3500–3599 Crown

63. 2900–3199 Crown

64. 3500–3599 Peach

65. 3500–3599 Long

66. Trace

67. Paris

68. 2200–2899 Peach

69. 2900–3199 Long

70. Narrows

71. 2900–3199 Peach

72. 1000–2199 Peach

73. Fish

74. Gray

75. 2200–2899 Long

76. 3500–3599 Peach

77. 2200–2899 Crown

78. Stewart

79. Hard

80. 3500–3599 Crown

81. 2200–2899 Peach

82. Paris

83. 3500–3599 Long

84. 2900–3199 Long

85. Gray

86. 2900–3199 Crown

87. Inman

88. 3500–3599 Peach

61. Ⓐ Ⓑ Ⓒ Ⓓ Ⓔ
62. Ⓐ Ⓑ Ⓒ Ⓓ Ⓔ
63. Ⓐ Ⓑ Ⓒ Ⓓ Ⓔ
64. Ⓐ Ⓑ Ⓒ Ⓓ Ⓔ
65. Ⓐ Ⓑ Ⓒ Ⓓ Ⓔ
66. Ⓐ Ⓑ Ⓒ Ⓓ Ⓔ
67. Ⓐ Ⓑ Ⓒ Ⓓ Ⓔ
68. Ⓐ Ⓑ Ⓒ Ⓓ Ⓔ
69. Ⓐ Ⓑ Ⓒ Ⓓ Ⓔ
70. Ⓐ Ⓑ Ⓒ Ⓓ Ⓔ
71. Ⓐ Ⓑ Ⓒ Ⓓ Ⓔ
72. Ⓐ Ⓑ Ⓒ Ⓓ Ⓔ
73. Ⓐ Ⓑ Ⓒ Ⓓ Ⓔ
74. Ⓐ Ⓑ Ⓒ Ⓓ Ⓔ
75. Ⓐ Ⓑ Ⓒ Ⓓ Ⓔ
76. Ⓐ Ⓑ Ⓒ Ⓓ Ⓔ
77. Ⓐ Ⓑ Ⓒ Ⓓ Ⓔ
78. Ⓐ Ⓑ Ⓒ Ⓓ Ⓔ
79. Ⓐ Ⓑ Ⓒ Ⓓ Ⓔ
80. Ⓐ Ⓑ Ⓒ Ⓓ Ⓔ
81. Ⓐ Ⓑ Ⓒ Ⓓ Ⓔ
82. Ⓐ Ⓑ Ⓒ Ⓓ Ⓔ
83. Ⓐ Ⓑ Ⓒ Ⓓ Ⓔ
84. Ⓐ Ⓑ Ⓒ Ⓓ Ⓔ
85. Ⓐ Ⓑ Ⓒ Ⓓ Ⓔ
86. Ⓐ Ⓑ Ⓒ Ⓓ Ⓔ
87. Ⓐ Ⓑ Ⓒ Ⓓ Ⓔ
88. Ⓐ Ⓑ Ⓒ Ⓓ Ⓔ

SET 2

1. 2200–2899 Long

2. Narrows

3. 3200–3499 Crown

4. Fish

5. 3200–3499 Peach

6. 2900–3199 Long

7. Trace

8. Stewart

9. 2900–3199 Peach

10. 3500–3599 Peach

11. 1000–2199 Long

12. Hard

13. 1000–2199 Crown

14. 3500–3599 Long

15. 1000–2199 Peach

16. Gray

17. Arden

18. 2200–2899 Crown

19. 3200–3499 Crown

20. Paris

21. Book

22. 3500–3599 Crown

23. 3500–3599 Peach

24. Inman

25. 2200–2899 Peach

26. 2900–3199 Long

27. 2900–3199 Peach

28. 3200–3499 Crown

29. Arden

30. Gray

31. 1000–2199 Peach

32. 3500–3599 Long

33. 2200–2899 Long

34. 3500–3599 Peach

35. Trace

36. Stewart

37. Inman

38. 3500–3599 Crown

1. Ⓐ Ⓑ Ⓒ Ⓓ Ⓔ
2. Ⓐ Ⓑ Ⓒ Ⓓ Ⓔ
3. Ⓐ Ⓑ Ⓒ Ⓓ Ⓔ
4. Ⓐ Ⓑ Ⓒ Ⓓ Ⓔ
5. Ⓐ Ⓑ Ⓒ Ⓓ Ⓔ
6. Ⓐ Ⓑ Ⓒ Ⓓ Ⓔ
7. Ⓐ Ⓑ Ⓒ Ⓓ Ⓔ
8. Ⓐ Ⓑ Ⓒ Ⓓ Ⓔ
9. Ⓐ Ⓑ Ⓒ Ⓓ Ⓔ
10. Ⓐ Ⓑ Ⓒ Ⓓ Ⓔ
11. Ⓐ Ⓑ Ⓒ Ⓓ Ⓔ
12. Ⓐ Ⓑ Ⓒ Ⓓ Ⓔ
13. Ⓐ Ⓑ Ⓒ Ⓓ Ⓔ
14. Ⓐ Ⓑ Ⓒ Ⓓ Ⓔ
15. Ⓐ Ⓑ Ⓒ Ⓓ Ⓔ
16. Ⓐ Ⓑ Ⓒ Ⓓ Ⓔ
17. Ⓐ Ⓑ Ⓒ Ⓓ Ⓔ
18. Ⓐ Ⓑ Ⓒ Ⓓ Ⓔ
19. Ⓐ Ⓑ Ⓒ Ⓓ Ⓔ
20. Ⓐ Ⓑ Ⓒ Ⓓ Ⓔ
21. Ⓐ Ⓑ Ⓒ Ⓓ Ⓔ
22. Ⓐ Ⓑ Ⓒ Ⓓ Ⓔ
23. Ⓐ Ⓑ Ⓒ Ⓓ Ⓔ
24. Ⓐ Ⓑ Ⓒ Ⓓ Ⓔ
25. Ⓐ Ⓑ Ⓒ Ⓓ Ⓔ
26. Ⓐ Ⓑ Ⓒ Ⓓ Ⓔ
27. Ⓐ Ⓑ Ⓒ Ⓓ Ⓔ
28. Ⓐ Ⓑ Ⓒ Ⓓ Ⓔ
29. Ⓐ Ⓑ Ⓒ Ⓓ Ⓔ
30. Ⓐ Ⓑ Ⓒ Ⓓ Ⓔ
31. Ⓐ Ⓑ Ⓒ Ⓓ Ⓔ
32. Ⓐ Ⓑ Ⓒ Ⓓ Ⓔ
33. Ⓐ Ⓑ Ⓒ Ⓓ Ⓔ
34. Ⓐ Ⓑ Ⓒ Ⓓ Ⓔ
35. Ⓐ Ⓑ Ⓒ Ⓓ Ⓔ
36. Ⓐ Ⓑ Ⓒ Ⓓ Ⓔ
37. Ⓐ Ⓑ Ⓒ Ⓓ Ⓔ
38. Ⓐ Ⓑ Ⓒ Ⓓ Ⓔ

39. 2900–3199 Crown
40. 2200–2899 Crown
41. 2200–2899 Peach
42. Hard
43. Fish
44. 3500–3599 Long
45. 3200–3499 Crown
46. 3200–3499 Peach
47. 3200–3499 Long
48. Narrows
49. Paris
50. 1000–2199 Peach
51. 2900–3199 Crown
52. 3500–3599 Long
53. 2200–2899 Peach
54. Book
55. Stewart
56. 3500–3599 Crown
57. 2900–3199 Long
58. 1000–2199 Crown
59. 1000–2199 Long
60. Fish
61. Hard
62. 3200–3499 Crown
63. 3200–3499 Long

64. 2200–2899 Long
65. Arden
66. Inman
67. 2900–3199 Peach
68. 1000–2199 Peach
69. 2900–3199 Crown
70. 3500–3599 Crown
71. 2900–3199 Long
72. Paris
73. Book
74. Hard
75. Gray
76. 3200–3499 Long
77. 3200–3499 Peach
78. 1000–2199 Crown
79. 2200–2899 Crown
80. Stewart
81. Fish
82. 2200–2899 Peach
83. 2900–3199 Long
84. 2900–3199 Crown
85. Book
86. Trace
87. 3500–3599 Long
88. 2900–3199 Peach

#	A	B	C	D	E
39.	Ⓐ	Ⓑ	Ⓒ	Ⓓ	Ⓔ
40.	Ⓐ	Ⓑ	Ⓒ	Ⓓ	Ⓔ
41.	Ⓐ	Ⓑ	Ⓒ	Ⓓ	Ⓔ
42.	Ⓐ	Ⓑ	Ⓒ	Ⓓ	Ⓔ
43.	Ⓐ	Ⓑ	Ⓒ	Ⓓ	Ⓔ
44.	Ⓐ	Ⓑ	Ⓒ	Ⓓ	Ⓔ
45.	Ⓐ	Ⓑ	Ⓒ	Ⓓ	Ⓔ
46.	Ⓐ	Ⓑ	Ⓒ	Ⓓ	Ⓔ
47.	Ⓐ	Ⓑ	Ⓒ	Ⓓ	Ⓔ
48.	Ⓐ	Ⓑ	Ⓒ	Ⓓ	Ⓔ
49.	Ⓐ	Ⓑ	Ⓒ	Ⓓ	Ⓔ
50.	Ⓐ	Ⓑ	Ⓒ	Ⓓ	Ⓔ
51.	Ⓐ	Ⓑ	Ⓒ	Ⓓ	Ⓔ
52.	Ⓐ	Ⓑ	Ⓒ	Ⓓ	Ⓔ
53.	Ⓐ	Ⓑ	Ⓒ	Ⓓ	Ⓔ
54.	Ⓐ	Ⓑ	Ⓒ	Ⓓ	Ⓔ
55.	Ⓐ	Ⓑ	Ⓒ	Ⓓ	Ⓔ
56.	Ⓐ	Ⓑ	Ⓒ	Ⓓ	Ⓔ
57.	Ⓐ	Ⓑ	Ⓒ	Ⓓ	Ⓔ
58.	Ⓐ	Ⓑ	Ⓒ	Ⓓ	Ⓔ
59.	Ⓐ	Ⓑ	Ⓒ	Ⓓ	Ⓔ
60.	Ⓐ	Ⓑ	Ⓒ	Ⓓ	Ⓔ
61.	Ⓐ	Ⓑ	Ⓒ	Ⓓ	Ⓔ
62.	Ⓐ	Ⓑ	Ⓒ	Ⓓ	Ⓔ
63.	Ⓐ	Ⓑ	Ⓒ	Ⓓ	Ⓔ
64.	Ⓐ	Ⓑ	Ⓒ	Ⓓ	Ⓔ
65.	Ⓐ	Ⓑ	Ⓒ	Ⓓ	Ⓔ
66.	Ⓐ	Ⓑ	Ⓒ	Ⓓ	Ⓔ
67.	Ⓐ	Ⓑ	Ⓒ	Ⓓ	Ⓔ
68.	Ⓐ	Ⓑ	Ⓒ	Ⓓ	Ⓔ
69.	Ⓐ	Ⓑ	Ⓒ	Ⓓ	Ⓔ
70.	Ⓐ	Ⓑ	Ⓒ	Ⓓ	Ⓔ
71.	Ⓐ	Ⓑ	Ⓒ	Ⓓ	Ⓔ
72.	Ⓐ	Ⓑ	Ⓒ	Ⓓ	Ⓔ
73.	Ⓐ	Ⓑ	Ⓒ	Ⓓ	Ⓔ
74.	Ⓐ	Ⓑ	Ⓒ	Ⓓ	Ⓔ
75.	Ⓐ	Ⓑ	Ⓒ	Ⓓ	Ⓔ
76.	Ⓐ	Ⓑ	Ⓒ	Ⓓ	Ⓔ
77.	Ⓐ	Ⓑ	Ⓒ	Ⓓ	Ⓔ
78.	Ⓐ	Ⓑ	Ⓒ	Ⓓ	Ⓔ
79.	Ⓐ	Ⓑ	Ⓒ	Ⓓ	Ⓔ
80.	Ⓐ	Ⓑ	Ⓒ	Ⓓ	Ⓔ
81.	Ⓐ	Ⓑ	Ⓒ	Ⓓ	Ⓔ
82.	Ⓐ	Ⓑ	Ⓒ	Ⓓ	Ⓔ
83.	Ⓐ	Ⓑ	Ⓒ	Ⓓ	Ⓔ
84.	Ⓐ	Ⓑ	Ⓒ	Ⓓ	Ⓔ
85.	Ⓐ	Ⓑ	Ⓒ	Ⓓ	Ⓔ
86.	Ⓐ	Ⓑ	Ⓒ	Ⓓ	Ⓔ
87.	Ⓐ	Ⓑ	Ⓒ	Ⓓ	Ⓔ
88.	Ⓐ	Ⓑ	Ⓒ	Ⓓ	Ⓔ

Answers to Practice Exercise 1

Set 1

1. B	12. B	23. D	34. C	45. A	56. E	67. C	78. D
2. D	13. E	24. B	35. D	46. B	57. A	68. D	79. E
3. D	14. C	25. A	36. E	47. B	58. E	69. A	80. A
4. A	15. B	26. E	37. A	48. A	59. C	70. D	81. D
5. C	16. E	27. D	38. B	49. B	60. E	71. E	82. C
6. D	17. B	28. C	39. C	50. D	61. A	72. B	83. D
7. E	18. D	29. B	40. D	51. C	62. A	73. B	84. A
8. A	19. B	30. A	41. E	52. E	63. D	74. A	85. A
9. A	20. C	31. A	42. E	53. E	64. C	75. E	86. D
10. E	21. D	32. B	43. D	54. A	65. D	76. C	87. E
11. A	22. C	33. C	44. C	55. D	66. B	77. B	88. C

Set 2

1. E	12. E	23. C	34. C	45. C	56. A	67. E	78. E
2. D	13. E	24. E	35. B	46. A	57. A	68. B	79. B
3. C	14. D	25. D	36. D	47. B	58. E	69. D	80. D
4. B	15. B	26. A	37. E	48. D	59. C	70. A	81. B
5. A	16. A	27. E	38. A	49. C	60. B	71. A	82. D
6. A	17. C	28. C	39. D	50. B	61. E	72. C	83. A
7. B	18. B	29. C	40. B	51. D	62. C	73. A	84. D
8. D	19. C	30. A	41. D	52. D	63. B	74. E	85. A
9. E	20. C	31. B	42. E	53. D	64. E	75. A	86. B
10. C	21. A	32. D	43. B	54. A	65. C	76. B	87. D
11. C	22. A	33. E	44. D	55. D	66. E	77. A	88. E

For this next practice exercise, you are on your own. First, combine the single names in some meaningful way and write your key words under the boxes. Memorize these from left to right so that you not only remember which word is part of each key word but also in which box that word belongs. Then cross out the irrelevant numbers and devise your own method for learning which number/name combinations belong in each box, one box at a time. For the practice exercise take as much time as you need to learn the contents of at least four boxes. When you feel ready, answer the questions in set 1, looking at the boxes if necessary. Mark each answer by blackening the space that contains the letter of the box in which each item is found. When you answer the questions in the second set, do not look at the boxes. Work from memory only. The correct answers appear on page 87.

Memory for Addresses
Practice Exercise 2

A	B	C	D	E
8800–9399 Brick	7000–7599 Brick	7600–8199 Brick	6300–6999 Brick	8200–8799 Brick
Castle	Tower	Light	Flood	Grand
7000–7599 Marsh	6300–6999 Marsh	8200–8799 Marsh	8800–9399 Marsh	7600–8199 Marsh
Peak	Anvil	Dillon	Butter	Oak
7600–8199 Elder	8200–8799 Elder	6300–6999 Elder	7000–7599 Elder	8800–9399 Elder

Set 1

1. 6300–6999 Marsh
2. 7000–7599 Elder
3. 7000–7599 Brick
4. Peak
5. Flood
6. 7600–8199 Elder
7. 8200–8799 Marsh
8. 7600–8199 Marsh
9. Grand
10. Dillon
11. Light
12. 7600–8199 Brick
13. 7600–8199 Elder
14. Anvil
15. 6300–6999 Brick
16. 8800–9399 Marsh
17. 8200–8799 Brick
18. Castle
19. Tower
20. 8200–8799 Elder
21. 8800–8399 Elder
22. Butter
23. 7000–7599 Marsh
24. 8800–9399 Brick
25. Oak
26. 6300–6999 Elder

27. 7000–7599 Brick
28. 7600–8199 Marsh
29. Light
30. Anvil
31. Peak
32. 7600–8199 Elder
33. 7600–8199 Brick
34. 8800–9399 Marsh
35. 7600–8199 Brick
36. Grand
37. Flood
38. 8800–9399 Elder
39. 8200–8799 Brick
40. Tower
41. 8800–9399 Brick
42. 8200–8799 Marsh
43. 6300–6999 Marsh
44. Dillon
45. Castle
46. 7000–7599 Elder
47. 8200–8799 Elder
48. Butter
49. 7000–7599 Marsh
50. Oak
51. 6300–6999 Brick
52. 6300–6999 Elder

1. Ⓐ Ⓑ Ⓒ Ⓓ Ⓔ
2. Ⓐ Ⓑ Ⓒ Ⓓ Ⓔ
3. Ⓐ Ⓑ Ⓒ Ⓓ Ⓔ
4. Ⓐ Ⓑ Ⓒ Ⓓ Ⓔ
5. Ⓐ Ⓑ Ⓒ Ⓓ Ⓔ
6. Ⓐ Ⓑ Ⓒ Ⓓ Ⓔ
7. Ⓐ Ⓑ Ⓒ Ⓓ Ⓔ
8. Ⓐ Ⓑ Ⓒ Ⓓ Ⓔ
9. Ⓐ Ⓑ Ⓒ Ⓓ Ⓔ
10. Ⓐ Ⓑ Ⓒ Ⓓ Ⓔ
11. Ⓐ Ⓑ Ⓒ Ⓓ Ⓔ
12. Ⓐ Ⓑ Ⓒ Ⓓ Ⓔ
13. Ⓐ Ⓑ Ⓒ Ⓓ Ⓔ
14. Ⓐ Ⓑ Ⓒ Ⓓ Ⓔ
15. Ⓐ Ⓑ Ⓒ Ⓓ Ⓔ
16. Ⓐ Ⓑ Ⓒ Ⓓ Ⓔ
17. Ⓐ Ⓑ Ⓒ Ⓓ Ⓔ
18. Ⓐ Ⓑ Ⓒ Ⓓ Ⓔ
19. Ⓐ Ⓑ Ⓒ Ⓓ Ⓔ
20. Ⓐ Ⓑ Ⓒ Ⓓ Ⓔ
21. Ⓐ Ⓑ Ⓒ Ⓓ Ⓔ
22. Ⓐ Ⓑ Ⓒ Ⓓ Ⓔ
23. Ⓐ Ⓑ Ⓒ Ⓓ Ⓔ
24. Ⓐ Ⓑ Ⓒ Ⓓ Ⓔ
25. Ⓐ Ⓑ Ⓒ Ⓓ Ⓔ
26. Ⓐ Ⓑ Ⓒ Ⓓ Ⓔ
27. Ⓐ Ⓑ Ⓒ Ⓓ Ⓔ
28. Ⓐ Ⓑ Ⓒ Ⓓ Ⓔ
29. Ⓐ Ⓑ Ⓒ Ⓓ Ⓔ
30. Ⓐ Ⓑ Ⓒ Ⓓ Ⓔ
31. Ⓐ Ⓑ Ⓒ Ⓓ Ⓔ
32. Ⓐ Ⓑ Ⓒ Ⓓ Ⓔ
33. Ⓐ Ⓑ Ⓒ Ⓓ Ⓔ
34. Ⓐ Ⓑ Ⓒ Ⓓ Ⓔ
35. Ⓐ Ⓑ Ⓒ Ⓓ Ⓔ
36. Ⓐ Ⓑ Ⓒ Ⓓ Ⓔ
37. Ⓐ Ⓑ Ⓒ Ⓓ Ⓔ
38. Ⓐ Ⓑ Ⓒ Ⓓ Ⓔ
39. Ⓐ Ⓑ Ⓒ Ⓓ Ⓔ
40. Ⓐ Ⓑ Ⓒ Ⓓ Ⓔ
41. Ⓐ Ⓑ Ⓒ Ⓓ Ⓔ
42. Ⓐ Ⓑ Ⓒ Ⓓ Ⓔ
43. Ⓐ Ⓑ Ⓒ Ⓓ Ⓔ
44. Ⓐ Ⓑ Ⓒ Ⓓ Ⓔ
45. Ⓐ Ⓑ Ⓒ Ⓓ Ⓔ
46. Ⓐ Ⓑ Ⓒ Ⓓ Ⓔ
47. Ⓐ Ⓑ Ⓒ Ⓓ Ⓔ
48. Ⓐ Ⓑ Ⓒ Ⓓ Ⓔ
49. Ⓐ Ⓑ Ⓒ Ⓓ Ⓔ
50. Ⓐ Ⓑ Ⓒ Ⓓ Ⓔ
51. Ⓐ Ⓑ Ⓒ Ⓓ Ⓔ
52. Ⓐ Ⓑ Ⓒ Ⓓ Ⓔ

53. 8800–9399 Brick

54. 8200–8799 Marsh

55. 8800–8399 Elder

56. Oak

57. Flood

58. Anvil

59. Castle

60. 7600–8199 Elder

61. 6300–6999 Marsh

62. 7600–8199 Brick

63. 6300–6999 Brick

64. 7000–7599 Elder

65. Grand

66. Butter

67. 7600–8199 Marsh

68. 8200–8799 Brick

69. 8800–9399 Marsh

70. 7000–7599 Marsh

71. Dillon

72. Light

73. 8200–8799 Elder

74. 6300–6999 Elder

75. 7000–7599 Brick

76. Peak

77. Tower

78. 7600–8199 Brick

79. 8800–9399 Elder

80. 7000–7599 Marsh

81. 8800–9399 Brick

82. Anvil

83. 6300–6999 Elder

84. Light

85. Grand

86. 8800–9399 Marsh

87. 7000–7599 Brick

88. 7000–7599 Elder

53. Ⓐ Ⓑ Ⓒ Ⓓ Ⓔ
54. Ⓐ Ⓑ Ⓒ Ⓓ Ⓔ
55. Ⓐ Ⓑ Ⓒ Ⓓ Ⓔ
56. Ⓐ Ⓑ Ⓒ Ⓓ Ⓔ
57. Ⓐ Ⓑ Ⓒ Ⓓ Ⓔ
58. Ⓐ Ⓑ Ⓒ Ⓓ Ⓔ
59. Ⓐ Ⓑ Ⓒ Ⓓ Ⓔ
60. Ⓐ Ⓑ Ⓒ Ⓓ Ⓔ
61. Ⓐ Ⓑ Ⓒ Ⓓ Ⓔ
62. Ⓐ Ⓑ Ⓒ Ⓓ Ⓔ
63. Ⓐ Ⓑ Ⓒ Ⓓ Ⓔ
64. Ⓐ Ⓑ Ⓒ Ⓓ Ⓔ
65. Ⓐ Ⓑ Ⓒ Ⓓ Ⓔ
66. Ⓐ Ⓑ Ⓒ Ⓓ Ⓔ
67. Ⓐ Ⓑ Ⓒ Ⓓ Ⓔ
68. Ⓐ Ⓑ Ⓒ Ⓓ Ⓔ
69. Ⓐ Ⓑ Ⓒ Ⓓ Ⓔ
70. Ⓐ Ⓑ Ⓒ Ⓓ Ⓔ
71. Ⓐ Ⓑ Ⓒ Ⓓ Ⓔ
72. Ⓐ Ⓑ Ⓒ Ⓓ Ⓔ
73. Ⓐ Ⓑ Ⓒ Ⓓ Ⓔ
74. Ⓐ Ⓑ Ⓒ Ⓓ Ⓔ
75. Ⓐ Ⓑ Ⓒ Ⓓ Ⓔ
76. Ⓐ Ⓑ Ⓒ Ⓓ Ⓔ
77. Ⓐ Ⓑ Ⓒ Ⓓ Ⓔ
78. Ⓐ Ⓑ Ⓒ Ⓓ Ⓔ
79. Ⓐ Ⓑ Ⓒ Ⓓ Ⓔ
80. Ⓐ Ⓑ Ⓒ Ⓓ Ⓔ
81. Ⓐ Ⓑ Ⓒ Ⓓ Ⓔ
82. Ⓐ Ⓑ Ⓒ Ⓓ Ⓔ
83. Ⓐ Ⓑ Ⓒ Ⓓ Ⓔ
84. Ⓐ Ⓑ Ⓒ Ⓓ Ⓔ
85. Ⓐ Ⓑ Ⓒ Ⓓ Ⓔ
86. Ⓐ Ⓑ Ⓒ Ⓓ Ⓔ
87. Ⓐ Ⓑ Ⓒ Ⓓ Ⓔ
88. Ⓐ Ⓑ Ⓒ Ⓓ Ⓔ

Set 2

1. 8200–8799 Brick

2. Flood

3. 8200–8799 Marsh

4. Anvil

5. 7600–8199 Elder

6. Peak

7. 7000–7599 Brick

8. 6300–6999 Marsh

9. Grand

10. Tower

11. 8800–9399 Brick

12. 7000–7599 Marsh

13. 7600–8199 Marsh

14. 8200–8799 Elder

15. 7000–7599 Elder

16. Oak

17. Castle

18. 7600–8199 Brick

19. 6300–6999 Brick

20. Dillon

21. 6300–6999 Elder

22. 6300–6999 Marsh

23. 8800–9399 Brick

24. 8800–9399 Marsh

25. 8200–8799 Brick

26. Oak

27. Grand

28. 7600–8199 Elder

29. 7000–7599 Elder

30. Light

1. Ⓐ Ⓑ Ⓒ Ⓓ Ⓔ
2. Ⓐ Ⓑ Ⓒ Ⓓ Ⓔ
3. Ⓐ Ⓑ Ⓒ Ⓓ Ⓔ
4. Ⓐ Ⓑ Ⓒ Ⓓ Ⓔ
5. Ⓐ Ⓑ Ⓒ Ⓓ Ⓔ
6. Ⓐ Ⓑ Ⓒ Ⓓ Ⓔ
7. Ⓐ Ⓑ Ⓒ Ⓓ Ⓔ
8. Ⓐ Ⓑ Ⓒ Ⓓ Ⓔ
9. Ⓐ Ⓑ Ⓒ Ⓓ Ⓔ
10. Ⓐ Ⓑ Ⓒ Ⓓ Ⓔ
11. Ⓐ Ⓑ Ⓒ Ⓓ Ⓔ
12. Ⓐ Ⓑ Ⓒ Ⓓ Ⓔ
13. Ⓐ Ⓑ Ⓒ Ⓓ Ⓔ
14. Ⓐ Ⓑ Ⓒ Ⓓ Ⓔ
15. Ⓐ Ⓑ Ⓒ Ⓓ Ⓔ
16. Ⓐ Ⓑ Ⓒ Ⓓ Ⓔ
17. Ⓐ Ⓑ Ⓒ Ⓓ Ⓔ
18. Ⓐ Ⓑ Ⓒ Ⓓ Ⓔ
19. Ⓐ Ⓑ Ⓒ Ⓓ Ⓔ
20. Ⓐ Ⓑ Ⓒ Ⓓ Ⓔ
21. Ⓐ Ⓑ Ⓒ Ⓓ Ⓔ
22. Ⓐ Ⓑ Ⓒ Ⓓ Ⓔ
23. Ⓐ Ⓑ Ⓒ Ⓓ Ⓔ
24. Ⓐ Ⓑ Ⓒ Ⓓ Ⓔ
25. Ⓐ Ⓑ Ⓒ Ⓓ Ⓔ
26. Ⓐ Ⓑ Ⓒ Ⓓ Ⓔ
27. Ⓐ Ⓑ Ⓒ Ⓓ Ⓔ
28. Ⓐ Ⓑ Ⓒ Ⓓ Ⓔ
29. Ⓐ Ⓑ Ⓒ Ⓓ Ⓔ
30. Ⓐ Ⓑ Ⓒ Ⓓ Ⓔ

31. Anvil	60. Butter	
32. Castle	61. 7000–7599 Brick	
33. 7000–7599 Marsh	62. 8200–8799 Marsh	
34. 7600–8199 Brick	63. 7600–8199 Elder	
35. 7000–7599 Brick	64. 8800–9399 Elder	
36. Tower	65. Dillon	
37. Butter	66. Tower	
38. Peak	67. 6300–6999 Brick	
39. 6300–6999 Brick	68. 7600–8199 Brick	
40. 7600–8199 Marsh	69. 7600–8199 Marsh	
41. 8200–8799 Marsh	70. 7000–7599 Marsh	
42. Dillon	71. Flood	
43. Flood	72. Light	
44. 8200–8799 Elder	73. Castle	
45. 8800–9399 Elder	74. 6300–6999 Elder	
46. 7000–7599 Brick	75. 6300–6999 Marsh	
47. 8800–9399 Marsh	76. Peak	
48. Castle	77. 8200–8799 Brick	
49. 6300–6999 Elder	78. 8200–8799 Elder	
50. Light	79. 7000–7599 Brick	
51. 8800–9399 Brick	80. Butter	
52. 6300–6999 Marsh	81. 6300–6999 Brick	
53. 7000–7599 Elder	82. 7000–7599 Elder	
54. 8200–8799 Brick	83. 6300–6999 Marsh	
55. 8200–8799 Elder	84. Dillon	
56. 8800–9399 Marsh	85. Tower	
57. Grand	86. 7600–8199 Marsh	
58. Oak	87. 7600–8199 Brick	
59. Anvil	88. 8200–8799 Elder	

31. Ⓐ Ⓑ Ⓒ Ⓓ Ⓔ
32. Ⓐ Ⓑ Ⓒ Ⓓ Ⓔ
33. Ⓐ Ⓑ Ⓒ Ⓓ Ⓔ
34. Ⓐ Ⓑ Ⓒ Ⓓ Ⓔ
35. Ⓐ Ⓑ Ⓒ Ⓓ Ⓔ
36. Ⓐ Ⓑ Ⓒ Ⓓ Ⓔ
37. Ⓐ Ⓑ Ⓒ Ⓓ Ⓔ
38. Ⓐ Ⓑ Ⓒ Ⓓ Ⓔ
39. Ⓐ Ⓑ Ⓒ Ⓓ Ⓔ
40. Ⓐ Ⓑ Ⓒ Ⓓ Ⓔ
41. Ⓐ Ⓑ Ⓒ Ⓓ Ⓔ
42. Ⓐ Ⓑ Ⓒ Ⓓ Ⓔ
43. Ⓐ Ⓑ Ⓒ Ⓓ Ⓔ
44. Ⓐ Ⓑ Ⓒ Ⓓ Ⓔ
45. Ⓐ Ⓑ Ⓒ Ⓓ Ⓔ
46. Ⓐ Ⓑ Ⓒ Ⓓ Ⓔ
47. Ⓐ Ⓑ Ⓒ Ⓓ Ⓔ
48. Ⓐ Ⓑ Ⓒ Ⓓ Ⓔ
49. Ⓐ Ⓑ Ⓒ Ⓓ Ⓔ
50. Ⓐ Ⓑ Ⓒ Ⓓ Ⓔ
51. Ⓐ Ⓑ Ⓒ Ⓓ Ⓔ
52. Ⓐ Ⓑ Ⓒ Ⓓ Ⓔ
53. Ⓐ Ⓑ Ⓒ Ⓓ Ⓔ
54. Ⓐ Ⓑ Ⓒ Ⓓ Ⓔ
55. Ⓐ Ⓑ Ⓒ Ⓓ Ⓔ
56. Ⓐ Ⓑ Ⓒ Ⓓ Ⓔ
57. Ⓐ Ⓑ Ⓒ Ⓓ Ⓔ
58. Ⓐ Ⓑ Ⓒ Ⓓ Ⓔ
59. Ⓐ Ⓑ Ⓒ Ⓓ Ⓔ
60. Ⓐ Ⓑ Ⓒ Ⓓ Ⓔ
61. Ⓐ Ⓑ Ⓒ Ⓓ Ⓔ
62. Ⓐ Ⓑ Ⓒ Ⓓ Ⓔ
63. Ⓐ Ⓑ Ⓒ Ⓓ Ⓔ
64. Ⓐ Ⓑ Ⓒ Ⓓ Ⓔ
65. Ⓐ Ⓑ Ⓒ Ⓓ Ⓔ
66. Ⓐ Ⓑ Ⓒ Ⓓ Ⓔ
67. Ⓐ Ⓑ Ⓒ Ⓓ Ⓔ
68. Ⓐ Ⓑ Ⓒ Ⓓ Ⓔ
69. Ⓐ Ⓑ Ⓒ Ⓓ Ⓔ
70. Ⓐ Ⓑ Ⓒ Ⓓ Ⓔ
71. Ⓐ Ⓑ Ⓒ Ⓓ Ⓔ
72. Ⓐ Ⓑ Ⓒ Ⓓ Ⓔ
73. Ⓐ Ⓑ Ⓒ Ⓓ Ⓔ
74. Ⓐ Ⓑ Ⓒ Ⓓ Ⓔ
75. Ⓐ Ⓑ Ⓒ Ⓓ Ⓔ
76. Ⓐ Ⓑ Ⓒ Ⓓ Ⓔ
77. Ⓐ Ⓑ Ⓒ Ⓓ Ⓔ
78. Ⓐ Ⓑ Ⓒ Ⓓ Ⓔ
79. Ⓐ Ⓑ Ⓒ Ⓓ Ⓔ
80. Ⓐ Ⓑ Ⓒ Ⓓ Ⓔ
81. Ⓐ Ⓑ Ⓒ Ⓓ Ⓔ
82. Ⓐ Ⓑ Ⓒ Ⓓ Ⓔ
83. Ⓐ Ⓑ Ⓒ Ⓓ Ⓔ
84. Ⓐ Ⓑ Ⓒ Ⓓ Ⓔ
85. Ⓐ Ⓑ Ⓒ Ⓓ Ⓔ
86. Ⓐ Ⓑ Ⓒ Ⓓ Ⓔ
87. Ⓐ Ⓑ Ⓒ Ⓓ Ⓔ
88. Ⓐ Ⓑ Ⓒ Ⓓ Ⓔ

Answers to Practice Exercise 2

Set 1

1. B	12. C	23. A	34. D	45. A	56. E	67. E	78. C
2. D	13. A	24. A	35. C	46. D	57. D	68. E	79. E
3. B	14. B	25. E	36. E	47. B	58. B	69. D	80. A
4. A	15. D	26. C	37. D	48. D	59. A	70. A	81. A
5. D	16. D	27. B	38. E	49. A	60. A	71. C	82. B
6. A	17. E	28. E	39. E	50. E	61. B	72. C	83. C
7. C	18. A	29. C	40. B	51. D	62. C	73. B	84. C
8. E	19. B	30. B	41. A	52. C	63. D	74. C	85. E
9. E	20. B	31. A	42. C	53. A	64. D	75. B	86. D
10. C	21. E	32. A	43. B	54. C	65. E	76. A	87. B
11. C	22. D	33. C	44. C	55. E	66. D	77. B	88. D

Set 2

1. E	12. A	23. A	34. C	45. E	56. D	67. D	78. B
2. D	13. E	24. D	35. B	46. B	57. E	68. C	79. B
3. C	14. B	25. E	36. B	47. D	58. E	69. E	80. D
4. B	15. D	26. E	37. D	48. A	59. B	70. A	81. D
5. A	16. E	27. E	38. A	49. C	60. D	71. D	82. D
6. A	17. A	28. A	39. D	50. C	61. B	72. C	83. B
7. B	18. C	29. D	40. E	51. A	62. C	73. A	84. C
8. B	19. D	30. C	41. C	52. B	63. A	74. C	85. B
9. E	20. C	31. B	42. C	53. D	64. E	75. B	86. E
10. B	21. C	32. A	43. D	54. E	65. C	76. A	87. C
11. A	22. B	33. A	44. B	55. B	66. B	77. E	88. B

With all the training and practice you have now had, you should feel reasonably confident that you can memorize addresses and place them in appropriate boxes. You have begun to develop skill at combining names into key words and then remembering what those key words stand for and where they fit in their boxes. You should also have begun to devise a system for remembering the locations of number/name combinations, especially now that you know that you do not need to be bogged down by long number spans. As you work your way through the model exams in this book, remember all the techniques you have learned and apply them conscientiously so that they become second nature.

You will notice that each model exam provides you with four sets of questions based on one set of address boxes. These four sets are designated "Practice I," "Practice II," "Practice III," and "Memory for Addresses." Practice I and Practice III offer you boxes to look at. Practice II and the Memory for

Addresses test must be answered from memory. Practice I, Practice II and Practice III are answered in the test booklet itself, not on the answer sheet. They are not scored. They do not count. They are strictly opportunities for learning and practice. The Postal Service is not trying to trick you. Only the final set, the Memory for Addresses test, is scored. Your performance on this test is the only one that matters. This means that you need not put full effort into answering as many questions as possible in the practice sets, especially in Practice I. If you have not completed your "system" for learning or feel that you need more memorizing time, you may "borrow" from some of the Practice I answering time. As you search out answers, concentrate on the locations of the items; do not simply rush to answer as many questions as possible. Your performance on the practice tests does not count. When you get to Practice II, you should do your best to answer. This practice session is your opportunity to discover gaps in your mastery of the address locations. Practice III gives you another chance to brush up on locations. Again, concentrate on locations as you search and mark answers; learn from the practice. It is not the number of questions that you answer that is important; what is important is the learning process itself. You can borrow from the testing time without worrying about finishing. On the other hand, if you have the memorizing under control, you can work up speed with the same addresses that you will find on the test itself.

If you were once frightened by the Memory for Addresses part of your postal exam, you should not be frightened any longer. You now know how to memorize the items and their locations. And you know that you have ample time for the learning task. First of all, you should begin planning your memorizing system as soon as you see the boxes with the few sample questions in the testing room. The examiner will go over the questions and method for answering with you. You should listen to instructions just to be certain that nothing has changed. Then, look at the boxes and begin to devise your system as you answer the few sample questions. Then you will have three official minutes to memorize before Practice I and three additional minutes during the time allotted to Practice I, if you need them. You will also have five official memorizing minutes before Practice III and five additional minutes to borrow from Practice III if necessary. This is plenty of time to memorize the items and their locations.

You will have time to memorize the locations of a good many, if not all, of the items, but you may not have time to finish answering the questions. Do not worry. Above all, do not get flustered. Just do your best. The model exams in this book should help you to develop personalized methods and skill in memorizing and should offer you many opportunities to increase your speed. Do not skip over the important practice you will gain by working through all of the model exams. Do them all, but leave enough time between model exams so that your memory of a previous set of boxes does not interfere with the task at hand. Come back to this chapter to brush up whenever necessary. Reread the chapter the day before your exam, but do not do a model exam that day. You want your mind to be a clean slate in order to learn the sorting scheme on your actual postal exam.

With the practice exercises in this chapter, we have encouraged you to write down your word-letter combinations and to cross out unnecessary, distracting numbers. We have also encouraged you to disregard time limits and to work through the exercises. When you get to the remaining full-length model exams, however, you should answer your questions under real testing conditions. This means that you must do all combining of words and all blotting out of extra numbers strictly in your head because you cannot write down anything that will help you. It also means that you should adhere rigidly to time limits: Use only the allotted time to memorize and the allotted time to answer.

It is very easy to lose your place when marking answers in tiny spaces on a separate answer sheet, so we ordinarily advise test takers to answer questions in order rather than risk a string of wrong answers caused by misgridding. This advice does NOT hold for Memory for Addresses, however. You will find that there are some items that you "know cold" and others that you find absolutely impossible to remember. Your time is very limited, and you need as many correct answers as possible, so go ahead and skip around, but be VERY careful to answer each question in the space with the corresponding number. Begin by answering the questions of which you are certain. If you are certain of the placement of all the names, whip through the 88 questions stopping to answer each of the names before you even look at the number spans. Then, go back to the beginning and pick out the number span/name combinations with which you are most comfortable and answer them in turn. If your time has not run out, you can then return to the beginning of the questions and try to conjure up locations of the thus-far-unassigned items, one by one. Skip over items and their answer spaces if you draw a total blank on their locations. Make educated guesses if you are wavering between two or three box locations.

Master this strategy with the model exams in this book. Then use it when you take your exam.

How to Answer Number Series Questions

The Number Series part of your exam is designed to test your aptitude for working with the new generation of sorting, routing, and marking machines that are adding to the speed and efficiency of the modern, mechanized Postal Service. This part of the exam measures your ability to think with numbers and to see the relationship between elements of a series. While this type of task may be new and unfamiliar to you, the actual mathematics of number series questions is not complicated. The problems involve nothing more than simple addition, subtraction, multiplication, and division. What the questions do require of you is concentration. You must be able to see how the numbers in a series are related so that you can supply the next two numbers in that series. You must be flexible enough in your thinking so that if the first pattern you consider for a series turns out to be invalid, you can shift gears and try a different pattern.

There is a system with which to approach number series questions.

Solve at a Glance

First, look hard at the series. The pattern may be obvious to you upon inspection. A series such as: 1 2 3 1 2 3 1 should not require any deep thought. Clearly, the sequence 1 2 3 is repeating itself over and over. The next two numbers in the series must be: 2 3. You might also instantly recognize the pattern of a simple series into which one number periodically intrudes. An example of such a series is: 1 2 15 3 4 15 5 . . . The number 15 appears after each set of two numbers in a simple + 1 series. The next two numbers in this series are 6 and 15. Can you see why?

Here are five series questions that you should be able to answer by inspection. Circle the letter of the next two numbers in each series.

1. 12 10 13 10 14 10 15 ....(A) 15 10 (B) 10 15 (C) 10 16 (D) 10 10 (E) 15 16
2. 20 40 60 20 40 60 20 ....(A) 20 40 (B) 40 60 (C) 60 40 (D) 60 20 (E) 60 40
3. 9 2 9 4 9 6 9 ....(A) 9 9 (B) 9 8 (C) 8 10 (D) 10 8 (E) 8 9
4. 5 8 5 8 5 8 5 ....(A) 8 5 (B) 5 8 (C) 5 5 (D) 5 6 (E) 8 8
5. 10 9 8 7 6 5 4 ....(A) 4 3 (B) 4 2 (C) 3 2 (D) 5 6 (E) 2 1

Answers:

1. (**C**) The series is a simple + 1 series with the number 10 inserted after each step of the series.

2. (**B**) The sequence 20 40 60 repeats itself over and over again.

3. (**E**) This is a simple + 2 series with the number 9 appearing before each member of the series.

4. (**A**) In this series the sequence 5 8 repeats itself.

5. (**C**) You should be able to see that this is a descending series, each number one lower than the one before it. You can call this a – 1 series.

Say It Aloud

Sometimes you may find that your ear is more adept than your eye. You may be able to "hear" a pattern or "feel" a rhythm more easily than you can "see" it. If you cannot immediately spot a pattern, try saying the series softly to yourself. First, read the series through. If that does not help, try accenting the printed numbers and speaking the missing intervening numbers even more softly. Try grouping the numbers within the series into twos or threes. After grouping, try accenting the last number, or the first. If you read aloud: 2 4 6 8 10 12 14, you will hear that the next two numbers are 16 and 18. Likewise, if you see the series: 31 32 33 32 33 34 34, and you group that series: 31 32 33; 32 33 34; 34, you will "feel" the rhythm. The series consists of three-number mini-series. Each mini-series begins with a number one higher that the first number of the previous mini-series. The next two numbers of the series are 35 and 36 to be followed by: 35 36 37.

You may be able to answer the next five series questions by inspection. If you cannot, then try sounding them out.

1. 1 2 5 6 9 10 13 ....(A) 15 17   (B) 14 15   (C) 14 16   (D) 15 16   (E) 14 17

2. 2 3 4 3 4 5 4 ....(A) 4 3   (B) 3 5   (C) 5 6   (D) 3 2   (E) 5 4

3. 10 10 12 14 14 16 18 ....(A) 18 20   (B) 20 20   (C) 20 22   (D) 18 22   (E) 18 18

4. 1 2 3 2 2 3 3 2 3 ....(A) 2 3   (B) 3 2   (C) 3 4   (D) 4 2   (E) 4 3

5. 10 9 8 9 8 7 8 ....(A) 8 7   (B) 7 6   (C) 9 10   (D) 7 8   (E) 8 9

Answers:

1.(**E**) Read aloud (softly): 1   2   5   6   9   10   13

         whisper: 3   4   7   8   11   12

The next number to read aloud is <u>14</u>, to be followed by a whispered <u>15</u>, <u>16</u>, and then aloud again <u>17</u>.

2.(**C**) If you group the numbers into threes and read them aloud, accenting either the first or last number of each group, you should "feel" that each group of three begins and ends with a number one higher than the previous series. Read <u>2</u> 3 4; <u>3</u> 4 5; <u>4</u> 5 6 or 2 3 <u>4</u>; 3 4 <u>5</u>; 4 5 <u>6</u>.

3.(**A**) Once more, group into threes. This time, be certain to accent the third number in each group in order to gain a sense of the rhythm and thereby the pattern of the series: 10 10 1<u>2</u>; 14 14 1<u>6</u>; 18 18 <u>20</u>...

4.(**D**) In this series the rhythm emerges when you accent the first number in each group: <u>1</u> 2 3; <u>2</u> 2 3; <u>3</u> 2 3.

5.(**B**) After you have seen a number of series of this type, you may very well be able to spot the pattern by inspection alone. If not, read aloud, group, and read again.

Mark the Difference

If you cannot see or hear the pattern of a series, the next step to take is marking the degree and direction of change between numbers. Most series progress either + (plus) or − (minus) or a combination of both directions, so first try marking your changes in terms of + and −. If you cannot make sense of a series in terms of + and −, try × (times) and ÷ (divided by). You may mark the changes between numbers right on your exam paper, but be sure to mark the letter of the answer on your answer sheet when you figure it out. Only your answer sheet will be scored. The exam booklet will be collected, but it will not be scored. You do not need to erase markings you make in the exam booklet.

Try this next set of practice questions. If you cannot "see" or "hear" the pattern, mark the differences between the numbers to establish the pattern. Then continue the pattern to determine the next two numbers of the series.

1. 9 10 12 15 19 24 30 ......(A) 35 40   (B) 36 42   (C) 30 36   (D) 30 37   (E) 37 45

2. 35 34 31 30 27 26 23 ....(A) 22 19   (B) 22 20   (C) 23 22   (D) 20 19   (E) 20 17

3. 16 21 19 24 22 27 25 ...(A) 28 30   (B) 30 28   (C) 29 24   (D) 30 27   (E) 26 29

4. 48 44 40 36 32 28 24 ....(A) 22 20   (B) 24 22   (C) 23 22   (D) 20 18   (E) 20 16

5. 20 30 39 47 54 60 65 ....(A) 70 75   (B) 68 70   (C) 69 72   (D) 66 67   (E) 68 71

Answers:

1. **(E)** $9 \,^{+1} 10 \,^{+2} 12 \,^{+3} 15 \,^{+4} 19 \,^{+5} 24 \,^{+6} 30 \,^{+7} 37 \,^{+8} 45$

2. **(A)** $35 \,^{-1} 34 \,^{-3} 31 \,^{-1} 30 \,^{-3} 27 \,^{-1} 26 \,^{-3} 23 \,^{-1} 22 \,^{-3} 19$

3. **(B)** $16 \,^{+5} 21 \,^{-2} 19 \,^{+5} 24 \,^{-2} 22 \,^{+5} 27 \,^{-2} 25 \,^{+5} 30 \,^{-2} 28$

4. **(E)** $48 \,^{-4} 44 \,^{-4} 40 \,^{-4} 36 \,^{-4} 32 \,^{-4} 28 \,^{-4} 24 \,^{-4} 20 \,^{-4} 16$

5. **(C)** $20 \,^{+10} 30 \,^{+9} 39 \,^{+8} 47 \,^{+7} 54 \,^{+6} 60 \,^{+5} 65 \,^{+4} 69 \,^{+3} 72$

Look for Repeated Numbers

Arithmetical series such as the ones above may be interrupted by a particular number that appears periodically or by repetition of numbers according to a certain pattern. For example: 3 6 <u>25</u> 9 12 <u>25</u> 15 18 <u>25</u> ...and <u>50</u> <u>50</u> 35 <u>40</u> <u>40</u> 35 <u>30</u> <u>30</u> 35... In these cases you must search a bit harder to spot both the arithmetic pattern and the pattern of repetition. When choosing your answer you must be alert to the point at which the pattern was interrupted. Do not further repeat a number that has already been repeated; do not forget to repeat before continuing the arithmetical pattern if repetition is called for at this point in the series.

1. 10 13 13 16 16 19 19 ...(A) 19 19   (B) 19 22   (C) 22 22   (D) 22 25   (E) 22 24

2. 2 4 25 8 16 25 32 ....(A) 32 35   (B) 25 64   (C) 48 25   (D) 25 48   (E) 64 25

3. 80 80 75 75 70 70 65 ...(A) 65 60   (B) 65 65   (C) 60 60   (D) 60 55   (E) 55 55

4. 35 35 32 30 30 27 25 ...(A) 22 20   (B) 25 25   (C) 22 22   (D) 25 22   (E) 25 23

5. 76 70 12 65 61 12 58 ...(A) 55 12   (B) 56 12   (C) 12 54   (D) 12 55   (E) 54 51

Answers:

r = repeat; ◯ = extraneous number repeated periodically.

1. **(C)** $10 \,^{+3} 13 \,^{r} 13 \,^{+3} 16 \,^{r} 16 \,^{+3} 19 \,^{r} 19 \,^{+3} 22 \,^{r} 22$

2. **(E)** $2 \,^{\times 2} 4 \,^{\times 2} \,\textcircled{25}\, 8 \,^{\times 2} 16 \,^{\times 2} 25 \quad 32 \,^{\times 2} 64 \,^{\times 2} \,\textcircled{25}\, ... 128 \,^{\times 2}$

3. **(A)** $80 \,^{r} 80 \,^{-5} 75 \,^{r} 75 \,^{-5} 70 \,^{r} 70 \,^{-5} 65 \,^{r} 65 \,^{-5} 60$

4. **(D)** $35 \,^{r} 35 \,^{-3} 32 \,^{-2} 30 \,^{r} 30 \,^{-3} 27 \,^{-2} 25 \,^{r} 25 \,^{-3} 22$

5. **(B)** $76 \,^{-6} 70 \,^{-5} \,\textcircled{12}\, 65 \,^{-4} 61 \,^{-3} \,\textcircled{12}\, 58 \,^{-2} 56 \,^{-1} \,\textcircled{12}\, ... 55$

Look for Alternating Series

If you still cannot determine the pattern of a series by inspection, sounding out, or marking the differences, you may have to shift gears and try a totally new tactic. First, check to see whether the numbers within the series combine to create the following numbers. For instance: 2 0 0 2 1 2 2 2 4, which must be interpreted: $2 \times 0 = 0$; $2 \times 1 = 2$; $2 \times 2 = 4$. The next few numbers of this series would be 2 3 6 2 4 8. Or look for two alternating series. Each of the two series that alternate will follow a pattern, but they may not necessarily follow the same pattern. A series that encompasses two series might look like this: 5 37 10 36 15 35 20. With practice you should be able to solve a series of this variety without diagramming and writing lots of little numbers. Until you get used to alternating series questions, you might work them out this way:

```
     +5       +5        +5              +5          +5
   ⌢        ⌢         ⌢             ⌢          ⌢
5   37   10   36   15   35   20   followed by   34   25   33   30 . . .
   ⌣        ⌣         ⌣           ⌣
     −1       −1        −1              −1
```

The next five questions represent series that are just a little more complicated than the series described earlier in this chapter. Try to figure these out.

1. 38 15 32 17 27 19 23 .....(A) 20 20   (B) 21 26   (C) 20 21   (D) 21 20   (E) 21 25

2. 3 2 5 2 7 2 9 ....(A) 11 13   (B) 9 2   (C) 2 11   (D) 11 2   (E) 2 13

3. 90 83 92 86 94 89 96 .....(A) 92 98   (B) 98 100 (C) 90 99   (D) 98 92   (E) 98 99

4. 80 12 40 17 20 22 10 .....(A) 25 15   (B) 15 25   (C) 24 5   (D) 25 5   (E) 27 5

5. 5 6 20 21 34 35 47 ....(A) 48 49   (B) 48 59   (C) 48 36   (D) 36 48   (E) 48 55

Answers:

```
              −6       −5        −4        −3
            ⌢        ⌢         ⌢        ⌢
1. (D)   38   15   32   17   27   19   23   21   20
              ⌣        ⌣         ⌣
                +2       +2        +2
```

2. **(C)** $3 + 2 = 5 + 2 = 7 + 2 = 9 + 2 = 11$

    or

    $3 \,^{+2}$ ② $5 \,^{+2}$ ② $7 \,^{+2}$ ② $9 \,^{+2}$ ② 11

```
           +2       +2       +2       +2
         ⌢        ⌢        ⌢        ⌢
3. (A)  90   83   92   86   94   89   96   92   98
              ⌣        ⌣        ⌣
                +3       +3       +3
```

```
          ÷2          ÷2       ÷2        ÷2
        ⌢           ⌢        ⌢        ⌢
4. (E)  80   12      40   17   20   22   10      27   5
              ⌣           ⌣            ⌣
                +5          +5          +5
```

```
           +15       +14      +13      +12
         ⌢         ⌢        ⌢        ⌢
5. (B)  5     6    20   21   34   35   47   48   59
                 ⌣        ⌣        ⌣
                   +15      +14      +13
```

In answering the Number Series questions on your exam, be careful and methodical. You are allowed twenty minutes in which to answer twenty-four questions. That should be enough time. Once you have completed this book, you should be skillful enough to handle any kind of number series question.

Number Series Tactics

You may write on the test booklet pages while answering Number Series questions, which is in contrast to Memory for Addresses questions where you were not permitted to write down learning aids. In the Number Series Test you may write notations of the amount of and direction of change directly on the page. You should also write down your starting time at the top of the page, because there is no "2-minute" warning, and no signal is given when time is almost up. If you want to answer every question—as indeed you should since only right answers count and a guess cannot hurt—then you must be aware of the approach of "time's up" so you can finish marking answers. Therefore, when you are told to begin, write down the starting time, add twenty minutes, and write the ending time at the top of the page in the test booklet. Glance at your watch occasionally. Use the last 30 seconds or so to mark answers to all the questions you skipped and to all the questions you did not reach. If you had already eliminated some choices, guess among those remaining. If the answer is a total mystery or if you had not yet looked at the question, make a random guess. If you make all your random guesses the same letter—for example, B— the law of averages will likely make one of them correct.

To summarize:

1. Start by noting and writing the time.
2. Do first the questions that seem easiest for you. The questions are not necessarily arranged in order of difficulty, so answer quickly the questions that require little time and leave yourself extra time for the more difficult questions.

    When you skip a question, put a mark before the question number on the question sheet and SKIP ITS ANSWER SPACE. When you return to a question that you have skipped, be sure to mark its answer in the correct space. The time you spend checking to make sure that question and answer number are alike is time well spent.
3. Follow the procedures outlined in this chapter. First, look for an obvious pattern. Second, sound out the series; if necessary, group the numbers and sound out again. Third, write the direction and amount of change between numbers. If you still have not found the rule, look for two alternating series and for uncommon types of progressions.

    If you do any figuring on the question sheet, be sure to mark the letter of the correct answer on your answer sheet. All answers must be marked on the answer sheet.
4. If none of the answers given fits the rule you have figured out, try again. Try to figure out a rule that makes one of the five answers a correct one.
5. Do not spend too much time on any one question. If a question seems impossible, skip it and come back later. A fresh look will sometimes help you find the answer. If you still cannot figure out the answer, guess. There is no scoring penalty for a wrong answer on this part of your exam, so by all means guess.
6. Keep track of time. Since there is no penalty for a wrong answer, you will want to answer every question. Leave yourself time to go back to the questions you skipped to give them a second look. If you are a slow worker and have not quite finished this part, leave a few seconds to mark random answers for the questions you cannot reach.

Apply everything you have learned as you answer the practice questions that follow. Build up your skill. Do not worry about time as you work on these practice questions. You will have plenty of chance to build up speed in the model exams. All of the questions are explained at the end of the set.

Number Series Practice Exercise

1. Ⓐ Ⓑ Ⓒ Ⓓ Ⓔ	6. Ⓐ Ⓑ Ⓒ Ⓓ Ⓔ	11. Ⓐ Ⓑ Ⓒ Ⓓ Ⓔ	16. Ⓐ Ⓑ Ⓒ Ⓓ Ⓔ	21. Ⓐ Ⓑ Ⓒ Ⓓ Ⓔ
2. Ⓐ Ⓑ Ⓒ Ⓓ Ⓔ	7. Ⓐ Ⓑ Ⓒ Ⓓ Ⓔ	12. Ⓐ Ⓑ Ⓒ Ⓓ Ⓔ	17. Ⓐ Ⓑ Ⓒ Ⓓ Ⓔ	22. Ⓐ Ⓑ Ⓒ Ⓓ Ⓔ
3. Ⓐ Ⓑ Ⓒ Ⓓ Ⓔ	8. Ⓐ Ⓑ Ⓒ Ⓓ Ⓔ	13. Ⓐ Ⓑ Ⓒ Ⓓ Ⓔ	18. Ⓐ Ⓑ Ⓒ Ⓓ Ⓔ	23. Ⓐ Ⓑ Ⓒ Ⓓ Ⓔ
4. Ⓐ Ⓑ Ⓒ Ⓓ Ⓔ	9. Ⓐ Ⓑ Ⓒ Ⓓ Ⓔ	14. Ⓐ Ⓑ Ⓒ Ⓓ Ⓔ	19. Ⓐ Ⓑ Ⓒ Ⓓ Ⓔ	24. Ⓐ Ⓑ Ⓒ Ⓓ Ⓔ
5. Ⓐ Ⓑ Ⓒ Ⓓ Ⓔ	10. Ⓐ Ⓑ Ⓒ Ⓓ Ⓔ	15. Ⓐ Ⓑ Ⓒ Ⓓ Ⓔ	20. Ⓐ Ⓑ Ⓒ Ⓓ Ⓔ	

1. 12 26 15 26 18 26 21 .....(A) 21 24   (B) 24 26   (C) 21 26   (D) 26 24   (E) 26 25

2. 72 67 69 64 66 61 63 .....(A) 58 60   (B) 65 62   (C) 60 58   (D) 65 60   (E) 60 65

3. 81 10 29 81 10 29 81 .....(A) 29 10   (B) 81 29   (C) 10 29   (D) 81 10   (E) 29 81

4. 91 91 90 88 85 81 76 .....(A) 71 66   (B) 70 64   (C) 75 74   (D) 70 65   (E) 70 63

5. 22 44 29 37 36 30 43 .....(A) 50 23   (B) 23 50   (C) 53 40   (D) 40 53   (E) 50 57

6. 0 1 1 0 2 2 0 ....(A) 0 0   (B) 0 3   (C) 3 3   (D) 3 4   (E) 2 3

7. 32 34 36 34 36 38 36 .....(A) 34 32   (B) 36 34   (C) 36 38   (D) 38 40   (E) 38 36

8. 26 36 36 46 46 56 56 .....(A) 66 66   (B) 56 66   (C) 57 57   (D) 46 56   (E) 26 66

9. 64 63 61 58 57 55 52 .....(A) 51 50   (B) 52 49   (C) 50 58   (D) 50 47   (E) 51 49

10. 4 6 8 7 6 8 10 9 8 ....(A) 7 9   (B) 11 12   (C) 12 14   (D) 7 10   (E) 10 12

11. 57 57 52 47 47 42 37 .....(A) 32 32   (B) 37 32   (C) 37 37   (D) 32 27   (E) 27 27

12. 13 26 14 25 16 23 19 .....(A) 20 21   (B) 20 22   (C) 20 23   (D) 20 24   (E) 22 25

13. 15 27 39 51 63 75 87 .....(A) 97 112   (B) 99 111   (C) 88 99   (D) 89 99   (E) 90 99

14. 2 0 2 2 2 4 2 6 2 8 ....(A) 2 2   (B) 2 8   (C) 2 10   (D) 2 12   (E) 2 16

15. 19 18 18 17 17 17 16 .....(A) 16 16   (B) 16 15   (C) 15 15   (D) 15 14   (E) 16 17

16. 55 53 44 51 49 44 47 .....(A) 45 43   (B) 46 45   (C) 46 44   (D) 44 44   (E) 45 44

17. 100 81 64 49 36 25 16 ...(A) 8 4   (B) 8 2   (C) 9 5   (D) 9 4   (E) 9 3

18. 2 2 4 6 8 18 16 ....(A) 32 64   (B) 32 28   (C) 54 32   (D) 32 54   (E) 54 30

19. 47 43 52 48 57 53 62 .....(A) 58 54   (B) 67 58   (C) 71 67   (D) 58 67   (E) 49 58

20. 38 38 53 48 48 63 58 .....(A) 58 58   (B) 58 73   (C) 73 73   (D) 58 68   (E) 73 83

21. 12 14 16 13 15 17 14 .....(A) 17 15   (B) 15 18   (C) 17 19   (D) 15 16   (E) 16 18

22. 30 30 30 37 37 37 30 .....(A) 30 30   (B) 30 37   (C) 37 37   (D) 37 30   (E) 31 31

23. 75 52 69 56 63 59 57 .....(A) 58 62   (B) 55 65   (C) 51 61   (D) 61 51   (E) 63 55

24. 176 88 88 44 44 22 22 ...(A) 22 11   (B) 11 11   (C) 11 10   (D) 11 5   (E) 22 10

Answers to Practice Exercise:

1. D	4. E	7. D	10. E	13. B	16. E	19. D	22. A
2. A	5. B	8. A	11. B	14. C	17. D	20. B	23. D
3. C	6. C	9. E	12. C	15. A	18. C	21. E	24. B

Explanations:

1. **(D)** A + 3 series with the number <u>26</u> between terms.

   12 $^{+3}$ ㉖ 15 $^{+3}$ ㉖ 18 $^{+3}$ ㉖ 21 $^{+3}$ ㉖ 24

2. **(A)** You may read this as a –5, +2 series.

   72 $^{-5}$ 67 $^{+2}$ 69 $^{-5}$ 64 $^{+2}$ 66 $^{-5}$ 61 $^{+2}$ 63 $^{-5}$ 58 $^{+2}$ 60

   or as two alternating –3 series

   $$\overbrace{72 \quad 67}^{-3} \quad \overbrace{69 \quad 64}^{-3} \quad \overbrace{66 \quad 61}^{-3} \quad \overbrace{63 \quad 58}^{-3} \quad 60$$
   $$72 \quad \underbrace{67 \quad 69}_{-3} \quad \underbrace{64 \quad 66}_{-3} \quad \underbrace{61 \quad 63}_{-3} \quad 58 \quad 60$$

3. **(C)** By inspection or grouping, the sequence 81 10 29 repeats itself over and over.

4. **(E)** Write in the numbers for this one.

   91 $^{-0}$ 91 $^{-1}$ 90 $^{-2}$ 88 $^{-3}$ 85 $^{-4}$ 81 $^{-5}$ 76 $^{-6}$ 70 $^{-7}$ 63

5. **(B)** Here we have two distinct alternating series.

   $$\overbrace{22 \quad 44}^{+7} \quad \overbrace{29 \quad 37}^{+7} \quad \overbrace{36 \quad 30}^{+7} \quad \overbrace{43 \quad 23}^{+7} \quad 50$$
   $$22 \quad \underbrace{44 \quad 29}_{-7} \quad \underbrace{37 \quad 36}_{-7} \quad \underbrace{30 \quad 43}_{-7} \quad 23 \quad 50$$

6. **(C)** The digit 0 intervenes after each repeating number of a simple + 1 and repeat series.

   ⓪ 1 ^{r} 1 $^{+1}$ ⓪ 2 ^{r} 2 $^{+1}$ ⓪ 3 ^{r} 3

7. **(D)** Group the numbers into threes. Each succeeding group of three begins with a number two higher than the first number of the preceding group of three. Within each group the pattern is +2, +2.

8. **(A)** The pattern is + 10, repeat the number, +10, repeat the number.

   26 $^{+10}$ 36 ^{r} 36 $^{+10}$ 46 ^{r} 46 $^{+10}$ 56 ^{r} 56 $^{+10}$ 66 ^{r} 66

9. **(E)** The pattern is –1, –2, –3; –1, –2, –3 and so on. If you can't see it, write it in for yourself.

10. **(E)** Here the pattern is +2, +2, –1, –1; +2, +2, –1, –1.

    4 $^{+2}$ 6 $^{+2}$ 8 $^{-1}$ 7 $^{-1}$ 6 $^{+2}$ 8 $^{+2}$ 10 $^{-1}$ 9 $^{-1}$ 8 $^{+2}$ 10 $^{+2}$ 12

    The series that is given to you is a little bit longer than most to better assist you in establishing this extra long pattern.

11. **(B)** This is a –5 pattern with every other term repeated.

    57 ^{r} 57 $^{-5}$ 52 $^{-5}$ 47 ^{r} 47 $^{-5}$ 42 $^{-5}$ 37 ^{r} 37 $^{-5}$ 32

12. **(C)** This series consists of two alternating series.

    $$\overbrace{13 \quad 26}^{+1} \quad \overbrace{14 \quad 25}^{+2} \quad \overbrace{16 \quad 23}^{+3} \quad \overbrace{19 \quad 20}^{+4} \quad 23$$
    $$13 \quad \underbrace{26 \quad 14}_{-1} \quad \underbrace{25 \quad 16}_{-2} \quad \underbrace{23 \quad 19}_{-3} \quad 20 \quad 23$$

13. **(B)** This is a simple +12 series.

14. **(C)** Even with the extra length, you may have trouble with this one. You might have to change your approach a couple of times to figure it out.

    $2^{\times 0}$ 0; $2^{\times 1}$ 2; $2^{\times 2}$ 4; $2^{\times 3}$ 6; $2^{\times 4}$ 8; $2^{\times 5}$ 10

15. **(A)** Each number is repeated one time more than the number before it. 19 appears only once, 18 twice, 17 three times and, if the series were extended beyond the question, 16 would appear four times.

16. **(E)** This is a –2 series with the number 44 appearing after every two numbers of the series. You probably can see this now without writing it out.

17. **(D)** The series consists of the squares of the numbers from two to ten in descending order.

18. **(C)** This is a tricky alternating series question.

    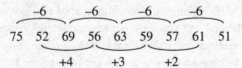

19. **(D)** The progress of this series is –4, +9; –4, +9.

20. **(B)** This series is not really difficult, but you may have to write it out to see it.

    38^{r} 38 $^{+15}$ 53 $^{-5}$ 48 ^{r} 48 $^{+15}$ 63 $^{-5}$ 58 ^{r} 58 $^{+15}$ 73

    You may also see this as two alternating +10 series with the numbers ending in 8 repeated.

21. **(E)** Group into sets of three numbers. Each +2 mini-series begins one step up from the previous mini-series.

22. **(A)** By inspection you can see that this series is nothing more than the number 30 repeated three times and the number 37 repeated three times. Since you have no further clues, you must assume that the series continues with the number 30 repeated three times.

23. **(D)** Here are two alternating series.

    -6   -6   -6   -6
    75 52 69 56 63 59 57 61 51
        +4   +3   +2

24. **(B)** The pattern is ÷2 and repeat the number, ÷2 and repeat the number.

    $176^{\div 2}$ 88^{r} 88 $^{\div 2}$ 44 ^{r} 44 $^{\div 2}$ 22 ^{r} 22 $^{\div 2}$ 11 ^{r} 11

How to Answer Following Oral Instructions Questions

The key to success with Following Oral Instructions questions is total concentration. You must not let your attention wander for even a second. And you must be prepared to follow through instantly on whatever it is you are told to do.

It should go without saying that if you are to listen to and concentrate on the spoken word, you must hear clearly. In the testing room, you will have a short practice session before the actual testing on each part of the exam. This practice session is especially important with Part D: Following Oral Instructions. The practice session gives you an opportunity to get used to the tone of voice, speed, diction, and accent of the reader—live reader or tape. This is also your chance to note the volume of the reader's voice. If you cannot hear clearly, SPEAK UP. Ask to have the volume turned up on the tape or request a change of seat so that you may sit closer to the reader or the loudspeaker. Your score is at stake, and you must hear clearly in order to listen and concentrate. Do not be shy. You are entitled to optimum conditions.

As the name of the test implies, you must "Follow Instructions." This means that you must follow *all* instructions. When the reader says, "Look at line . . . ," you must look at that line immediately. Place your pencil at the beginning of the line and listen. Many of the instructions consist of just one step on the worksheet followed by one step on the answer sheet. Such an instruction might read: "Find the smallest number on line 3 and draw one line under that number. Now, on your answer sheet find the number under which you just drew one line and blacken space C." This is a relatively simple instruction on which to follow through. The moment you hear the word "smallest" you should rivet your attention on line 3 and search out the lowest number. However, you cannot stop listening. You must know what to do with that number. "Draw one line" is uncomplicated. The two-second pause that your reader will take after reading this instruction should be adequate time for you to find the smallest number and to draw one line under it. The second part of the instruction is also uncomplicated, but you must not let your attention wander while your reader is reading it. You must concentrate on which lettered space you are to blacken. You then have five seconds in which to find the number and to blacken the space. A word of caution: You are instructed to look at line 3 on the worksheet and to take certain actions with the numbers, letters, and/or words on that line, but it is most unlikely that you are to mark an answer in space 3 on the answer sheet. If your answer is to be marked in space 3, that is purely coincidental. More likely, the space in which you are to mark your answer is an integral part of the instructions that you are following. Concentrate! Follow instructions. Do not mark your answer in the wrong place. The oral instructions will begin by directing your attention to line 1 of the worksheet and will work straight down the page in numerical order with one or more instructions applying to each line. You will NOT mark your answers in order. The answers that you mark can appear anywhere within the answer spaces for Part D. You will skip around the page, marking answers in the order directed. You will not use all the answer spaces. There are more spaces than answers. Blanks are acceptable, in fact, required. On the other hand, no space should have two answers. If you find yourself filling in two blanks for the same question, one of your answers is wrong.

In our chapter of strategies for answering Address Checking questions, we suggested that a difference from left to right is exactly the same thing as a difference from right to left. In the interest of speed, we recommended that you work in either direction, depending on the second column you had looked at when comparing addresses in the previous question. On the Following Oral Instructions questions, it is important that you work from left to right, just as you read English. Unless specifically instructed otherwise, count from left to right. The "fourth letter" is the fourth letter from the left. The "sixth x" is the sixth x from the left. Of course, if the instructions should refer to the "second circle from the right," you must follow that instruction and do whatever you are told to do to the second circle from the right.

When the instructions get a bit more complicated, you are given more time to follow them. If the instructions tell you to circle each even number between 12 and 25, you will be allowed at least 10 seconds, maybe more, to decide which numbers to circle and then to circle them. As you listen, you must focus on the fact that you are circling only *even* numbers and that these numbers are *between* 12 and 25. Then, after the instructions that tell you what letters to darken, you will be allowed five seconds for *each* combination. Important note: When the instructions speak of the numbers between 12 and 25 they mean only the numbers that fall between these two numbers, not the numbers themselves. Consider the difference between "more than 5" and "5 or more." You must listen *very* carefully.

The most difficult instructions to carry out are ones like these: "If January comes before June and Monday comes after Wednesday, write the letter E in the left-hand box; if not, write the letter A in the right-hand circle." The moment you hear the word "if" your ears should perk up. You will have to make a choice. You must not rush to follow the instructions at the first part of the sentence; you must listen to the whole instruction. Take this type of instruction one step at a time. January comes before June. Part one of the statement is true. Put your pencil in the left-hand box, but do not write until you have heard the other half of the statement. Monday does not come after Wednesday. Part two is false. Since the instructions say "and," they require both parts of the statement to be true. In this statement, one part is false, so you know that you must ignore the directive to write the letter E in the left-hand box. Continue to listen. Listen hard for the instruction that tells you how to proceed if the entire statement is not true. In this case, that instruction is to write the letter A in the right-hand circle. Whenever an instruction begins with "IF," be wary and redouble your concentration. Make no assumptions without listening. The direction need not necessarily read "If . . . and . . . ." It might read "If . . . or. . . .," in which case you would proceed in one way if either part of the statement was true and in the other way if *both* statements were false. Fortunately, only a small number of the questions will be this difficult.

Another instruction you may find difficult to follow is the one that says: "In the first box, write the smallest of these numbers: 52, 41, 13, 29, 60." Since you are permitted to write on the worksheet, you may make markings other than those that you are directed to make. This means that you are permitted to use any means to do well. In this instance, we recommend writing the list of numbers lightly in the margin of the worksheet. You must, of course, remember that it is the *smallest* number that you must write on the *first* line, but you do not have to remember the numbers. You can look at the numbers you have just jotted down and follow through on the instructions. When you have finished with the item, draw a line through the numbers you wrote in the margin. You may find a similar instruction later in the test, and you do not want to confuse yourself with two sets of numbers running into one another.

The worksheet will not be scored; only the answer sheet is scored. You must follow all instructions referring to the worksheet in order to mark the answer sheet correctly. Beyond that, you may use the worksheet to your own benefit, but keep it neat to avoid confusion.

It is very important that you not get flustered or frantic while taking this part of your exam. You must remain calm. If you miss a portion of an instruction try to follow through without it or just let that instruction pass and be ready for the next one. Your reader is not permitted to repeat. Since the Following Oral Instructions Test is marked on the basis of right answers only, one wrong answer here or there or a couple of missed questions will not be likely to rule out your candidacy. Just take a missed instruction in stride and listen hard for the next one. Likewise, if you go to mark a lettered space for a particular number and find that you have already darkened a space for that number, your best bet is probably to leave the mark that is there and wait for the next instruction. You may darken only one space for each number, and the time you spend erasing and changing an answer may cause you to miss the beginning of the next instruction.

In order to develop your skill at listening, concentrating, and following instructions, you must practice filling out worksheets and answer sheets while listening to oral instructions. In the actual testing room, the oral instructions might be read by an examiner standing in the front of the room or might be broadcast over a loudspeaker from a tape recording of the instructions. At home you might have a relative or friend read to you each time you are trying a practice set, or you might have that relative or friend tape record all sets of oral instructions in advance. If you have all the instructions tape recorded in advance, you will not be tied to someone else's schedule. It would be best to have another person make the tape because you will have to adjust to a reading style when taking the actual exam, but if no one is available, you could make your own tape. If you are self-recording, you must record all the model sets at the same time. If you record and then take the test immediately, you may not be taking a true measure of your listening ability. You may find some memory entering in. However, if you record all sets, and then take the tests at some other time, there should be no memory interference for this type of task.

The practice paragraph in the box that follows should take exactly one minute to read. You may want to offer it to your reader for practice. Since this paragraph is not related to any part of the exam, you or your reader can read it over and over to perfect reading speed. If someone else will be reading for you, go over the paragraph to get a feel for how fast the instructions will come at you.

Before a recording session begins, mark the first page of each set of Following Oral Instructions with a sticky paper flag or Post-it™ Note. This will save fumbling around and will ensure that no set is inadvertently omitted. The person making the recording should clearly identify each set of oral instructions by page number and, except for this practice chapter, by model exam number as well. When you take the model exams, you must be certain to use the worksheet that corresponds to the oral instructions. Each worksheet is different and is specific to one set of instructions.

The directions below are the directions to the reader that precede each set of Following Oral Instructions. Whoever will be doing the reading should read these directions now and should practice reading the one-minute practice paragraph aloud a few times to master reading pace and rhythm. If you are planning to take the tests from a prepared tape, this is the time to make the tape.

DIRECTIONS: The words in parentheses should not *be read aloud. They tell you how long you should pause at the various spots. You should time the pauses with a watch with a second hand. The instruction "Pause slightly" means that you should stop long enough to take a breath. You should not repeat any directions.*

One-Minute Practice Paragraph

> **Look at line 20 on your worksheet.** (Pause slightly.) There are two circles and two boxes of different sizes with numbers in them. If 7 is less than 3 and if 2 is smaller than 4, write a C in the larger circle. Otherwise write B as in baker in the smaller box. (Pause 10 seconds.) Now on your answer sheet darken the space for the number-letter combination in the box or circle. (Pause 5 seconds.)

When you are ready to try your skill at this task, you will need the worksheet and answer sheet in front of you. Then, if you are using a live reader, you can hand the book to your reader. If you are working from a tape, switch it to "play" and go to it.

Try the following practice exercise right now. This exercise is set up as if you were in an actual testing situation with a live reader. If you are working with a live reader, read for yourself down to the instruction: *TO THE PERSON WHO IS TO READ THE INSTRUCTIONS.* Then hand the book to your reader. If you are working from taped instructions, read down to *The actual test begins now.* Then tear out the worksheet and answer sheet, close the book, and turn on the tape recorder.

Following Oral Instructions Practice Exercise

Time: 25 Minutes.

Listening to Instructions

DIRECTIONS: When you are ready to try this test of the Model Exam, give the following instructions to a friend and have the friend read them aloud to you at the rate of 80 words per minute. Do NOT read them to yourself. Your friend will need a watch with a second hand. Listen carefully and do exactly what your friend tells you to do with the worksheet and with the answer sheet. Your friend will tell you some things to do with each item on the worksheet. After each set of instructions, your friend will give you time to mark your answer by darkening a circle on the answer sheet. Since B and D sound very much alike, your friend will say "B as in baker" when he or she means B and "D as in dog" when he or she means D.

Before proceeding further, tear out the answer sheet and worksheet on pages 105 and 107 of this test. Then hand this book to your friend.

TO THE PERSON WHO IS TO READ THE INSTRUCTIONS: The instructions are to be read at the rate of 80 words per minute. Do not read aloud the material that is in parentheses. Once you have begun the test itself, do not repeat any instructions. The next three paragraphs consist of approximately 120 words. Read these three paragraphs aloud to the candidate in about one and one-half minutes. You may reread these paragraphs as often as necessary to establish an 80-words-per-minute reading speed.

Read Aloud to the Candidate

On the job you will have to listen to instructions and then do what you have been told to do. In this test, I will read instructions to you. Try to understand them as I read them; I cannot repeat them. Once we begin, you may not ask any questions until the end of the test.

On the job you won't have to deal with pictures, numbers, and letters like those in the test, but you will have to listen to instructions and follow them. We are using this test to see how well you can follow instructions.

You are to mark your worksheet according to the instructions that I'll read to you. After each set of instructions, I'll give you time to record your answers on the separate answer sheet.

The actual test begins now.

Look at line 1 on your worksheet. (Pause slightly.) Circle the seventh letter on line 1. (Pause 5 seconds.) Now, on your answer sheet, find number 83 and for number 83 darken the space for the letter you just circled. (Pause 5 seconds.)

Look at line 2 on your worksheet. (Pause slightly.) Draw a line under all the odd numbers between 12 and 20. (Pause 5 seconds.) Now, on your answer sheet, darken space B as in baker for all the numbers under which you drew a line. (Pause 5 seconds.)

Look at line 2 again. (Pause slightly.) Find the number that is two times another number on line 2 and circle it. (Pause 5 seconds.) Now, on your answer sheet, darken space A for the number you just circled. (Pause 5 seconds.)

Look at line 3 on your worksheet. (Pause slightly.) Write the letter C in the middle box. (Pause 2 seconds.) Now, on your answer sheet, darken the space for the number-letter combination in the figure you just wrote in. (Pause 5 seconds.)

Look at line 3 again. (Pause slightly.) Write the letter D as in dog in the left-hand circle. (Pause 2 seconds.) Now, on your answer sheet, darken the space for the number-letter combination in the figure you just wrote in. (Pause 5 seconds.)

Look at line 4 on your worksheet. (Pause slightly.) If first class mail costs more than bulk rate mail, write the number 22 on the third line; if not, write the number 19 on the fourth line. (Pause 5 seconds.) Now, on your answer sheet, darken the space for the number-letter combination on the line you just wrote on. (Pause 5 seconds.)

Look at line 4 again. (Pause slightly.) Write the number 31 on the second line from the left. (Pause 2 seconds.) Now, on your answer sheet, darken the space for the number-letter combination on the line on which you just wrote. (Pause 5 seconds.)

Look at line 5 on your worksheet. (Pause slightly.) Find the highest number on line 5 and draw a line under the number. (Pause 2 seconds.) Now, on your answer sheet, find the number under which you just drew a line and darken space E for that number. (Pause 5 seconds.)

Look at line 5 again. (Pause slightly.) Find the lowest number on line 5 and draw two lines under the number. (Pause 2 seconds.) Now, on your answer sheet, find the number under which you just drew two lines and darken space A for that number. (Pause 5 seconds.)

Look at line 6 on your worksheet. (Pause slightly.) Write the number 57 in the figure that does not belong on line 6. (Pause 2 seconds.) Now, on your answer sheet, darken the number-letter combination that is in the figure in which you just wrote. (Pause 5 seconds.)

Look at line 7 on your worksheet. (Pause slightly.) Write the second letter of the second word in the first box. (Pause 5 seconds.) Write the fifth letter of the first word in the third box. (Pause 5 seconds.) Write the fourth letter of the second word in the second box. (Pause 5 seconds.) Now, on your answer sheet, darken the number-letter combinations in all three boxes. (Pause 15 seconds.)

Look at line 8 on your worksheet. (Pause slightly.) Count the number of G's on line 8 and divide the number of G's by 2. Write that number at the end of the line. (Pause 5 seconds.) Now, on your answer sheet, darken space D as in dog for the number you wrote at the end of line 8. (Pause 5 seconds.)

Look at line 9 on your worksheet. (Pause slightly.) Write the letter B as in baker in the middle-sized circle. (Pause 2 seconds.) Now, on your answer sheet, darken the space for the number-letter combination in the circle in which you just wrote. (Pause 5 seconds.)

Look at line 10 on your worksheet. (Pause slightly.) The time in each circle represents the last scheduled pickup of the day from a street letter box. Find the circle with the earliest pickup time and write the last two figures of that time on the line in the circle. (Pause 10 seconds.) Now, on your answer sheet, darken the space for the number-letter combination in the circle you just wrote in. (Pause 5 seconds.)

Look at line 10 again. (Pause slightly.) Find the circle with the latest pickup time and write the last two figures of that time on the line in the circle. (Pause 10 seconds.) Now, on your answer sheet, darken the space for the number-letter combination in the circle in which you just wrote. (Pause 5 seconds.)

Look at line 11 on your worksheet. (Pause slightly.) Mail directed for San Francisco and Los Angeles is to be placed in box 37; mail for Milwaukee and Green Bay in box 84; mail for Springfield and Chicago in box 65. Find the box for mail being sent to Green Bay and write the letter A in the box. (Pause 2 seconds.)

Now, on your answer sheet, darken the number-letter combination for the box you just wrote in. (Pause 5 seconds.)

Look at line 11 again. (Pause slightly.) Mr. Green lives in Springfield. Find the box in which to put Mr. Green's mail and write E on the line. (Pause 2 seconds.) Now, on your answer sheet, darken the space for the number-letter combination in the box in which you just wrote. (Pause 5 seconds.)

Look at line 12 on your worksheet. (Pause slightly.) Find the letter on line 12 that is not in the word CREAM and draw a line under the letter. (Pause 2 seconds.) Now, on your answer sheet, find number 38 and darken the space for the letter under which you just drew a line. (Pause 5 seconds.)

Look at line 13 on your worksheet. (Pause slightly.) Write the smallest number in the largest circle. (Pause 2 seconds.) Write the largest number in the left-hand circle. (Pause 2 seconds.) Now, on your answer sheet, darken the number-letter combinations that are in the circles in which you just wrote. (Pause 10 seconds.)

Look at line 14 on your worksheet. (Pause slightly.) If there are 36 inches in a foot, write B as in baker in the first box; if not, write D as in dog in the third box. (Pause 5 seconds.) Now, on your answer sheet, darken the number-letter combination that is in the box in which you just wrote. (Pause 5 seconds.)

Look at line 14 again. (Pause slightly.) Find the box that contains a number in the teens and write B as in baker in that box. (Pause 2 seconds.) Now, on your answer sheet, darken the number-letter combination that is in the box in which you just wrote. (Pause 5 seconds.)

Look at line 15 on your worksheet. (Pause slightly.) Circle the only number on line 15 that is not divisible by 2. (Pause 2 seconds.) Now, on your answer sheet, darken space A for the number you circled. (Pause 5 seconds.)

Look at line 16 on your worksheet. (Pause slightly.) If the number in the circle is greater than the number in the box, write the letter E in the box; if not, write the letter E in the circle. (Pause 5 seconds.) Now, on your answer sheet, darken the number-letter combination that is in the figure in which you just wrote. (Pause 5 seconds.)

Look at line 16 again. (Pause slightly.) If the number in the triangle is smaller than the number in the figure directly to its left, write the letter A in the triangle; if not, write the letter C in the triangle. (Pause 5 seconds.) Now, on your answer sheet, darken the number-letter combination that is in the figure you just wrote in. (Pause 5 seconds.)

Look at line 17 on your worksheet. (Pause slightly.) Count the number of J's on line 17, multiply the number of J's by 5 and write that number at the end of the line. (Pause 5 seconds.) Now, on your answer sheet, find the number you just wrote at the end of the line and darken space C for that number. (Pause 5 seconds.)

Look at line 18 on your worksheet. (Pause slightly.) Draw one line under the number that is at the middle of line 18. (Pause 5 seconds.) Now, on your answer sheet, darken space B as in baker for the number under which you just drew a line. (Pause 5 seconds.)

Look at line 18 again. (Pause slightly.) Draw two lines under each odd number that falls between 35 and 45. (Pause 10 seconds.) Now, on your answer sheet, darken space D as in dog for each number under which you drew two lines. (Pause 5 seconds.)

Look at line 19 on your worksheet. (Pause slightly.) Next to the last letter on line 19, write the first number you hear: 53, 18, 6, 75. (Pause 2 seconds.) Now, on your answer sheet, darken the space for the number-letter combination you just wrote. (Pause 5 seconds.)

Following Oral Instructions Practice Exercise

TEAR HERE

1 Ⓐ Ⓑ Ⓒ Ⓓ Ⓔ	23 Ⓐ Ⓑ Ⓒ Ⓓ Ⓔ	45 Ⓐ Ⓑ Ⓒ Ⓓ Ⓔ	67 Ⓐ Ⓑ Ⓒ Ⓓ Ⓔ
2 Ⓐ Ⓑ Ⓒ Ⓓ Ⓔ	24 Ⓐ Ⓑ Ⓒ Ⓓ Ⓔ	46 Ⓐ Ⓑ Ⓒ Ⓓ Ⓔ	68 Ⓐ Ⓑ Ⓒ Ⓓ Ⓔ
3 Ⓐ Ⓑ Ⓒ Ⓓ Ⓔ	25 Ⓐ Ⓑ Ⓒ Ⓓ Ⓔ	47 Ⓐ Ⓑ Ⓒ Ⓓ Ⓔ	69 Ⓐ Ⓑ Ⓒ Ⓓ Ⓔ
4 Ⓐ Ⓑ Ⓒ Ⓓ Ⓔ	26 Ⓐ Ⓑ Ⓒ Ⓓ Ⓔ	48 Ⓐ Ⓑ Ⓒ Ⓓ Ⓔ	70 Ⓐ Ⓑ Ⓒ Ⓓ Ⓔ
5 Ⓐ Ⓑ Ⓒ Ⓓ Ⓔ	27 Ⓐ Ⓑ Ⓒ Ⓓ Ⓔ	49 Ⓐ Ⓑ Ⓒ Ⓓ Ⓔ	71 Ⓐ Ⓑ Ⓒ Ⓓ Ⓔ
6 Ⓐ Ⓑ Ⓒ Ⓓ Ⓔ	28 Ⓐ Ⓑ Ⓒ Ⓓ Ⓔ	50 Ⓐ Ⓑ Ⓒ Ⓓ Ⓔ	72 Ⓐ Ⓑ Ⓒ Ⓓ Ⓔ
7 Ⓐ Ⓑ Ⓒ Ⓓ Ⓔ	29 Ⓐ Ⓑ Ⓒ Ⓓ Ⓔ	51 Ⓐ Ⓑ Ⓒ Ⓓ Ⓔ	73 Ⓐ Ⓑ Ⓒ Ⓓ Ⓔ
8 Ⓐ Ⓑ Ⓒ Ⓓ Ⓔ	30 Ⓐ Ⓑ Ⓒ Ⓓ Ⓔ	52 Ⓐ Ⓑ Ⓒ Ⓓ Ⓔ	74 Ⓐ Ⓑ Ⓒ Ⓓ Ⓔ
9 Ⓐ Ⓑ Ⓒ Ⓓ Ⓔ	31 Ⓐ Ⓑ Ⓒ Ⓓ Ⓔ	53 Ⓐ Ⓑ Ⓒ Ⓓ Ⓔ	75 Ⓐ Ⓑ Ⓒ Ⓓ Ⓔ
10 Ⓐ Ⓑ Ⓒ Ⓓ Ⓔ	32 Ⓐ Ⓑ Ⓒ Ⓓ Ⓔ	54 Ⓐ Ⓑ Ⓒ Ⓓ Ⓔ	76 Ⓐ Ⓑ Ⓒ Ⓓ Ⓔ
11 Ⓐ Ⓑ Ⓒ Ⓓ Ⓔ	33 Ⓐ Ⓑ Ⓒ Ⓓ Ⓔ	55 Ⓐ Ⓑ Ⓒ Ⓓ Ⓔ	77 Ⓐ Ⓑ Ⓒ Ⓓ Ⓔ
12 Ⓐ Ⓑ Ⓒ Ⓓ Ⓔ	34 Ⓐ Ⓑ Ⓒ Ⓓ Ⓔ	56 Ⓐ Ⓑ Ⓒ Ⓓ Ⓔ	78 Ⓐ Ⓑ Ⓒ Ⓓ Ⓔ
13 Ⓐ Ⓑ Ⓒ Ⓓ Ⓔ	35 Ⓐ Ⓑ Ⓒ Ⓓ Ⓔ	57 Ⓐ Ⓑ Ⓒ Ⓓ Ⓔ	79 Ⓐ Ⓑ Ⓒ Ⓓ Ⓔ
14 Ⓐ Ⓑ Ⓒ Ⓓ Ⓔ	36 Ⓐ Ⓑ Ⓒ Ⓓ Ⓔ	58 Ⓐ Ⓑ Ⓒ Ⓓ Ⓔ	80 Ⓐ Ⓑ Ⓒ Ⓓ Ⓔ
15 Ⓐ Ⓑ Ⓒ Ⓓ Ⓔ	37 Ⓐ Ⓑ Ⓒ Ⓓ Ⓔ	59 Ⓐ Ⓑ Ⓒ Ⓓ Ⓔ	81 Ⓐ Ⓑ Ⓒ Ⓓ Ⓔ
16 Ⓐ Ⓑ Ⓒ Ⓓ Ⓔ	38 Ⓐ Ⓑ Ⓒ Ⓓ Ⓔ	60 Ⓐ Ⓑ Ⓒ Ⓓ Ⓔ	82 Ⓐ Ⓑ Ⓒ Ⓓ Ⓔ
17 Ⓐ Ⓑ Ⓒ Ⓓ Ⓔ	39 Ⓐ Ⓑ Ⓒ Ⓓ Ⓔ	61 Ⓐ Ⓑ Ⓒ Ⓓ Ⓔ	83 Ⓐ Ⓑ Ⓒ Ⓓ Ⓔ
18 Ⓐ Ⓑ Ⓒ Ⓓ Ⓔ	40 Ⓐ Ⓑ Ⓒ Ⓓ Ⓔ	62 Ⓐ Ⓑ Ⓒ Ⓓ Ⓔ	84 Ⓐ Ⓑ Ⓒ Ⓓ Ⓔ
19 Ⓐ Ⓑ Ⓒ Ⓓ Ⓔ	41 Ⓐ Ⓑ Ⓒ Ⓓ Ⓔ	63 Ⓐ Ⓑ Ⓒ Ⓓ Ⓔ	85 Ⓐ Ⓑ Ⓒ Ⓓ Ⓔ
20 Ⓐ Ⓑ Ⓒ Ⓓ Ⓔ	42 Ⓐ Ⓑ Ⓒ Ⓓ Ⓔ	64 Ⓐ Ⓑ Ⓒ Ⓓ Ⓔ	86 Ⓐ Ⓑ Ⓒ Ⓓ Ⓔ
21 Ⓐ Ⓑ Ⓒ Ⓓ Ⓔ	43 Ⓐ Ⓑ Ⓒ Ⓓ Ⓔ	65 Ⓐ Ⓑ Ⓒ Ⓓ Ⓔ	87 Ⓐ Ⓑ Ⓒ Ⓓ Ⓔ
22 Ⓐ Ⓑ Ⓒ Ⓓ Ⓔ	44 Ⓐ Ⓑ Ⓒ Ⓓ Ⓔ	66 Ⓐ Ⓑ Ⓒ Ⓓ Ⓔ	88 Ⓐ Ⓑ Ⓒ Ⓓ Ⓔ

Following Oral Instructions Practice Exercise

Worksheet

DIRECTIONS: Listening carefully to each set of instructions, mark each item on this worksheet as directed. Then complete each question by marking the answer for a number-letter combination. Should you fall behind and miss an instruction, don't become excited. Let that one go and listen for the next one. If when you start to darken a space for a number, you find that you have already darkened another space for that number, either erase the first mark and darken the space for the new combination or let the first mark stay and do not darken a space for the new combination. Write with a pencil that has a clean eraser. When you finish, you should have no more than one space darkened for each number. Correct answers are on page 109.

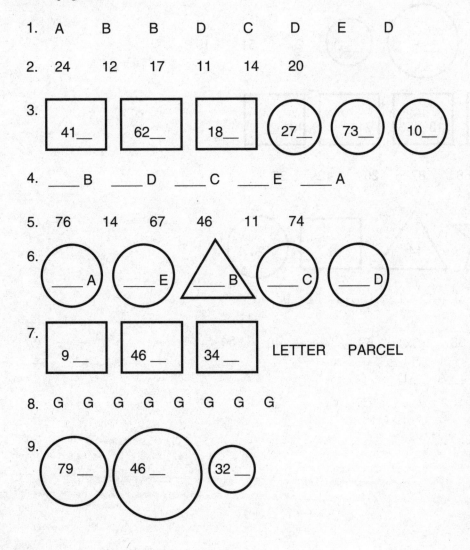

1. A   B   B   D   C   D   E   D

2. 24   12   17   11   14   20

3. 41__   62__   18__   27__   73__   10__

4. ___B   ___D   ___C   ___E   ___A

5. 76   14   67   46   11   74

6. ___A   ___E   ___B   ___C   ___D

7. 9__   46__   34__   LETTER   PARCEL

8. G G G G G G G G

9. 79__   46__   32__

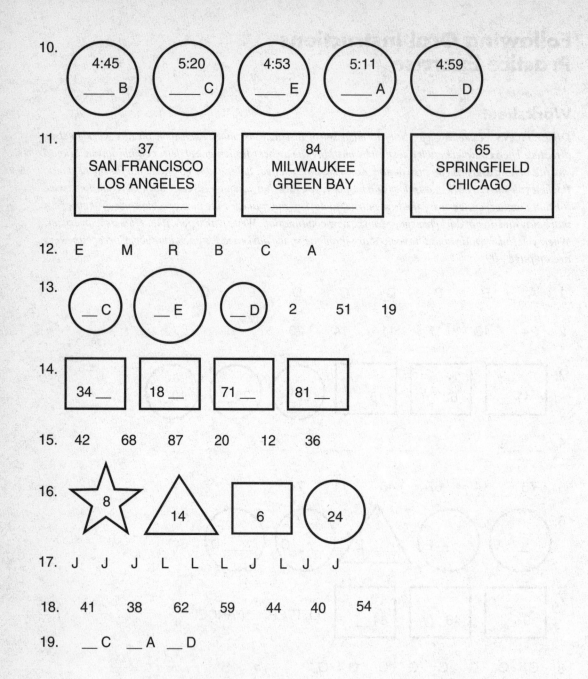

10.

4:45 ___ B   5:20 ___ C   4:53 ___ E   5:11 ___ A   4:59 ___ D

11.

37	84	65
SAN FRANCISCO	MILWAUKEE	SPRINGFIELD
LOS ANGELES	GREEN BAY	CHICAGO
_____	_____	_____

12. E   M   R   B   C   A

13. __ C   __ E   __ D   2   51   19

14. 34 __   18 __   71 __   81 __

15. 42   68   87   20   12   36

16. 8   14   6   24

17. J   J   J   L   L   L   J   L   J   J

18. 41   38   62   59   44   40   54

19. __ C   __ A   __ D

Answers to Practice Exercise

Correctly Filled Answer Grid

1 Ⓐ Ⓑ Ⓒ Ⓓ Ⓔ	23 Ⓐ Ⓑ Ⓒ Ⓓ Ⓔ	45 Ⓐ ● Ⓒ Ⓓ Ⓔ	67 Ⓐ Ⓑ Ⓒ Ⓓ Ⓔ
2 Ⓐ Ⓑ Ⓒ Ⓓ ●	24 ● Ⓑ Ⓒ Ⓓ Ⓔ	46 Ⓐ Ⓑ ● Ⓓ Ⓔ	68 Ⓐ Ⓑ Ⓒ Ⓓ Ⓔ
3 Ⓐ Ⓑ Ⓒ Ⓓ Ⓔ	25 Ⓐ Ⓑ Ⓒ Ⓓ Ⓔ	47 Ⓐ Ⓑ Ⓒ Ⓓ Ⓔ	69 Ⓐ Ⓑ Ⓒ Ⓓ Ⓔ
4 Ⓐ Ⓑ Ⓒ ● Ⓔ	26 Ⓐ Ⓑ Ⓒ Ⓓ Ⓔ	48 Ⓐ Ⓑ Ⓒ Ⓓ Ⓔ	70 Ⓐ Ⓑ Ⓒ Ⓓ Ⓔ
5 Ⓐ Ⓑ Ⓒ Ⓓ Ⓔ	27 Ⓐ Ⓑ Ⓒ ● Ⓔ	49 Ⓐ Ⓑ Ⓒ Ⓓ Ⓔ	71 Ⓐ Ⓑ Ⓒ ● Ⓔ
6 Ⓐ Ⓑ Ⓒ Ⓓ ●	28 Ⓐ Ⓑ Ⓒ Ⓓ Ⓔ	50 Ⓐ Ⓑ Ⓒ Ⓓ Ⓔ	72 Ⓐ Ⓑ Ⓒ Ⓓ Ⓔ
7 Ⓐ Ⓑ Ⓒ Ⓓ Ⓔ	29 Ⓐ Ⓑ Ⓒ Ⓓ Ⓔ	51 Ⓐ Ⓑ ● Ⓓ Ⓔ	73 Ⓐ Ⓑ Ⓒ Ⓓ Ⓔ
8 Ⓐ Ⓑ Ⓒ Ⓓ Ⓔ	30 Ⓐ Ⓑ ● Ⓓ Ⓔ	52 Ⓐ Ⓑ Ⓒ Ⓓ Ⓔ	74 Ⓐ Ⓑ Ⓒ Ⓓ Ⓔ
9 ● Ⓑ Ⓒ Ⓓ Ⓔ	31 Ⓐ Ⓑ Ⓒ ● Ⓔ	53 Ⓐ Ⓑ Ⓒ ● Ⓔ	75 Ⓐ Ⓑ Ⓒ Ⓓ Ⓔ
10 Ⓐ Ⓑ Ⓒ Ⓓ Ⓔ	32 Ⓐ Ⓑ Ⓒ Ⓓ Ⓔ	54 Ⓐ Ⓑ Ⓒ Ⓓ Ⓔ	76 Ⓐ Ⓑ Ⓒ Ⓓ ●
11 ● Ⓑ Ⓒ Ⓓ Ⓔ	33 Ⓐ Ⓑ Ⓒ Ⓓ Ⓔ	55 Ⓐ Ⓑ Ⓒ Ⓓ Ⓔ	77 Ⓐ Ⓑ Ⓒ Ⓓ Ⓔ
12 Ⓐ Ⓑ Ⓒ Ⓓ Ⓔ	34 Ⓐ Ⓑ Ⓒ Ⓓ ●	56 Ⓐ Ⓑ Ⓒ Ⓓ Ⓔ	78 Ⓐ Ⓑ Ⓒ Ⓓ Ⓔ
13 Ⓐ Ⓑ Ⓒ Ⓓ Ⓔ	35 Ⓐ Ⓑ Ⓒ Ⓓ Ⓔ	57 Ⓐ ● Ⓒ Ⓓ Ⓔ	79 Ⓐ ● Ⓒ Ⓓ Ⓔ
14 Ⓐ Ⓑ ● Ⓓ Ⓔ	36 Ⓐ Ⓑ Ⓒ Ⓓ Ⓔ	58 Ⓐ Ⓑ Ⓒ Ⓓ Ⓔ	80 Ⓐ Ⓑ Ⓒ Ⓓ Ⓔ
15 Ⓐ Ⓑ Ⓒ Ⓓ Ⓔ	37 Ⓐ Ⓑ Ⓒ Ⓓ Ⓔ	59 Ⓐ ● Ⓒ Ⓓ Ⓔ	81 Ⓐ Ⓑ Ⓒ Ⓓ Ⓔ
16 Ⓐ Ⓑ Ⓒ Ⓓ Ⓔ	38 Ⓐ ● Ⓒ Ⓓ Ⓔ	60 Ⓐ Ⓑ Ⓒ Ⓓ Ⓔ	82 Ⓐ Ⓑ Ⓒ Ⓓ Ⓔ
17 Ⓐ ● Ⓒ Ⓓ Ⓔ	39 Ⓐ Ⓑ Ⓒ Ⓓ Ⓔ	61 Ⓐ Ⓑ Ⓒ Ⓓ Ⓔ	83 Ⓐ Ⓑ Ⓒ Ⓓ ●
18 Ⓐ ● Ⓒ Ⓓ Ⓔ	40 Ⓐ Ⓑ Ⓒ Ⓓ Ⓔ	62 Ⓐ Ⓑ ● Ⓓ Ⓔ	84 ● Ⓑ Ⓒ Ⓓ Ⓔ
19 Ⓐ Ⓑ Ⓒ Ⓓ Ⓔ	41 Ⓐ Ⓑ Ⓒ ● Ⓔ	63 Ⓐ Ⓑ Ⓒ Ⓓ Ⓔ	85 Ⓐ Ⓑ Ⓒ Ⓓ Ⓔ
20 Ⓐ Ⓑ ● Ⓓ Ⓔ	42 Ⓐ Ⓑ Ⓒ Ⓓ Ⓔ	64 Ⓐ Ⓑ Ⓒ Ⓓ Ⓔ	86 Ⓐ Ⓑ Ⓒ Ⓓ Ⓔ
21 Ⓐ Ⓑ Ⓒ Ⓓ Ⓔ	43 Ⓐ Ⓑ Ⓒ Ⓓ Ⓔ	65 Ⓐ Ⓑ Ⓒ Ⓓ ●	87 ● Ⓑ Ⓒ Ⓓ Ⓔ
22 Ⓐ Ⓑ ● Ⓓ Ⓔ	44 Ⓐ Ⓑ Ⓒ Ⓓ Ⓔ	66 Ⓐ Ⓑ Ⓒ Ⓓ Ⓔ	88 Ⓐ Ⓑ Ⓒ Ⓓ Ⓔ

Correctly Filled Worksheet

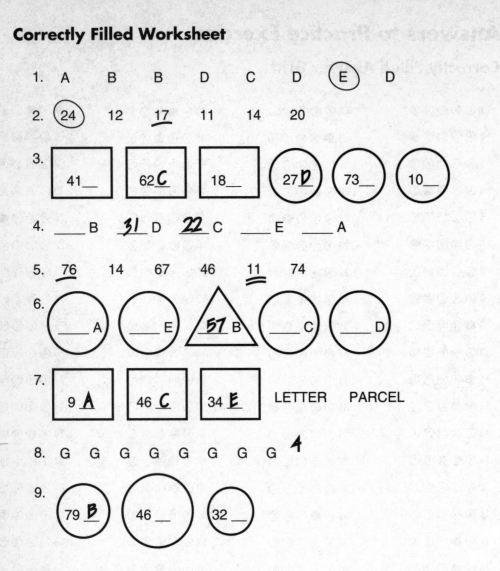

1. A   B   B   D   C   D   (E)   D

2. (24)   12   <u>17</u>   11   14   20

3. [41__]   [62 C]   [18__]   (27 D)   (73__)   (10__)

4. ___ B   <u>31</u> D   **22** C   ___ E   ___ A

5. <u>76</u>   14   67   46   11   74

6. (___ A)   (___ E)   △ <u>57</u> B   (___ C)   (___ D)

7. [9 A]   [46 C]   [34 E]   LETTER   PARCEL

8. G   G   G   G   G   G   G

9. (79 B)   (46 __)   (32 __)

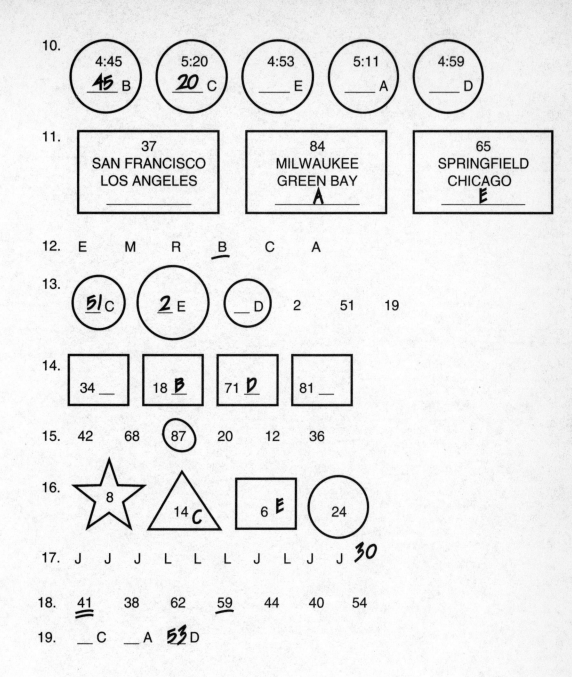

10.

4:45 **45** B   5:20 **20** C   4:53 ___ E   5:11 ___ A   4:59 ___ D

11.

| 37 SAN FRANCISCO LOS ANGELES _____ | 84 MILWAUKEE GREEN BAY **A** | 65 SPRINGFIELD CHICAGO **E** |

12.   E   M   R   <u>B</u>   C   A

13.   **51** C   **2** E   __ D   2   51   19

14.   34 __   18 **B**   71 **D**   81 __

15.   42   68   (87)   20   12   36

16.   8   14 **C**   6 **E**   24

17.   J   J   J   L   L   L   J   L   J   J **30**

18.   <u>41</u>   38   62   <u>59</u>   44   40   54

19.   __ C   __ A   **53** D

THREE

Model Exams

Note: These model exams are not actual exams, but they are patterned very closely on the actual exams in timing, number of questions, level of difficulty, and format of presentation. Practice with these exams will familiarize you with the testing situation and will give you excellent preparation for the real thing.

Second Model Exam
Answer Sheet
Part A—Address Checking

1. Ⓐ Ⓓ	20. Ⓐ Ⓓ	39. Ⓐ Ⓓ	58. Ⓐ Ⓓ	77. Ⓐ Ⓓ
2. Ⓐ Ⓓ	21. Ⓐ Ⓓ	40. Ⓐ Ⓓ	59. Ⓐ Ⓓ	78. Ⓐ Ⓓ
3. Ⓐ Ⓓ	22. Ⓐ Ⓓ	41. Ⓐ Ⓓ	60. Ⓐ Ⓓ	79. Ⓐ Ⓓ
4. Ⓐ Ⓓ	23. Ⓐ Ⓓ	42. Ⓐ Ⓓ	61. Ⓐ Ⓓ	80. Ⓐ Ⓓ
5. Ⓐ Ⓓ	24. Ⓐ Ⓓ	43. Ⓐ Ⓓ	62. Ⓐ Ⓓ	81. Ⓐ Ⓓ
6. Ⓐ Ⓓ	25. Ⓐ Ⓓ	44. Ⓐ Ⓓ	63. Ⓐ Ⓓ	82. Ⓐ Ⓓ
7. Ⓐ Ⓓ	26. Ⓐ Ⓓ	45. Ⓐ Ⓓ	64. Ⓐ Ⓓ	83. Ⓐ Ⓓ
8. Ⓐ Ⓓ	27. Ⓐ Ⓓ	46. Ⓐ Ⓓ	65. Ⓐ Ⓓ	84. Ⓐ Ⓓ
9. Ⓐ Ⓓ	28. Ⓐ Ⓓ	47. Ⓐ Ⓓ	66. Ⓐ Ⓓ	85. Ⓐ Ⓓ
10. Ⓐ Ⓓ	29. Ⓐ Ⓓ	48. Ⓐ Ⓓ	67. Ⓐ Ⓓ	86. Ⓐ Ⓓ
11. Ⓐ Ⓓ	30. Ⓐ Ⓓ	49. Ⓐ Ⓓ	68. Ⓐ Ⓓ	87. Ⓐ Ⓓ
12. Ⓐ Ⓓ	31. Ⓐ Ⓓ	50. Ⓐ Ⓓ	69. Ⓐ Ⓓ	88. Ⓐ Ⓓ
13. Ⓐ Ⓓ	32. Ⓐ Ⓓ	51. Ⓐ Ⓓ	70. Ⓐ Ⓓ	89. Ⓐ Ⓓ
14. Ⓐ Ⓓ	33. Ⓐ Ⓓ	52. Ⓐ Ⓓ	71. Ⓐ Ⓓ	90. Ⓐ Ⓓ
15. Ⓐ Ⓓ	34. Ⓐ Ⓓ	53. Ⓐ Ⓓ	72. Ⓐ Ⓓ	91. Ⓐ Ⓓ
16. Ⓐ Ⓓ	35. Ⓐ Ⓓ	54. Ⓐ Ⓓ	73. Ⓐ Ⓓ	92. Ⓐ Ⓓ
17. Ⓐ Ⓓ	36. Ⓐ Ⓓ	55. Ⓐ Ⓓ	74. Ⓐ Ⓓ	93. Ⓐ Ⓓ
18. Ⓐ Ⓓ	37. Ⓐ Ⓓ	56. Ⓐ Ⓓ	75. Ⓐ Ⓓ	94. Ⓐ Ⓓ
19. Ⓐ Ⓓ	38. Ⓐ Ⓓ	57. Ⓐ Ⓓ	76. Ⓐ Ⓓ	95. Ⓐ Ⓓ

Part B—Memory for Addresses

1 Ⓐ Ⓑ Ⓒ Ⓓ Ⓔ   23 Ⓐ Ⓑ Ⓒ Ⓓ Ⓔ   45 Ⓐ Ⓑ Ⓒ Ⓓ Ⓔ   67 Ⓐ Ⓑ Ⓒ Ⓓ Ⓔ

2 Ⓐ Ⓑ Ⓒ Ⓓ Ⓔ   24 Ⓐ Ⓑ Ⓒ Ⓓ Ⓔ   46 Ⓐ Ⓑ Ⓒ Ⓓ Ⓔ   68 Ⓐ Ⓑ Ⓒ Ⓓ Ⓔ

3 Ⓐ Ⓑ Ⓒ Ⓓ Ⓔ   25 Ⓐ Ⓑ Ⓒ Ⓓ Ⓔ   47 Ⓐ Ⓑ Ⓒ Ⓓ Ⓔ   69 Ⓐ Ⓑ Ⓒ Ⓓ Ⓔ

4 Ⓐ Ⓑ Ⓒ Ⓓ Ⓔ   26 Ⓐ Ⓑ Ⓒ Ⓓ Ⓔ   48 Ⓐ Ⓑ Ⓒ Ⓓ Ⓔ   70 Ⓐ Ⓑ Ⓒ Ⓓ Ⓔ

5 Ⓐ Ⓑ Ⓒ Ⓓ Ⓔ   27 Ⓐ Ⓑ Ⓒ Ⓓ Ⓔ   49 Ⓐ Ⓑ Ⓒ Ⓓ Ⓔ   71 Ⓐ Ⓑ Ⓒ Ⓓ Ⓔ

6 Ⓐ Ⓑ Ⓒ Ⓓ Ⓔ   28 Ⓐ Ⓑ Ⓒ Ⓓ Ⓔ   50 Ⓐ Ⓑ Ⓒ Ⓓ Ⓔ   72 Ⓐ Ⓑ Ⓒ Ⓓ Ⓔ

7 Ⓐ Ⓑ Ⓒ Ⓓ Ⓔ   29 Ⓐ Ⓑ Ⓒ Ⓓ Ⓔ   51 Ⓐ Ⓑ Ⓒ Ⓓ Ⓔ   73 Ⓐ Ⓑ Ⓒ Ⓓ Ⓔ

8 Ⓐ Ⓑ Ⓒ Ⓓ Ⓔ   30 Ⓐ Ⓑ Ⓒ Ⓓ Ⓔ   52 Ⓐ Ⓑ Ⓒ Ⓓ Ⓔ   74 Ⓐ Ⓑ Ⓒ Ⓓ Ⓔ

9 Ⓐ Ⓑ Ⓒ Ⓓ Ⓔ   31 Ⓐ Ⓑ Ⓒ Ⓓ Ⓔ   53 Ⓐ Ⓑ Ⓒ Ⓓ Ⓔ   75 Ⓐ Ⓑ Ⓒ Ⓓ Ⓔ

10 Ⓐ Ⓑ Ⓒ Ⓓ Ⓔ   32 Ⓐ Ⓑ Ⓒ Ⓓ Ⓔ   54 Ⓐ Ⓑ Ⓒ Ⓓ Ⓔ   76 Ⓐ Ⓑ Ⓒ Ⓓ Ⓔ

11 Ⓐ Ⓑ Ⓒ Ⓓ Ⓔ   33 Ⓐ Ⓑ Ⓒ Ⓓ Ⓔ   55 Ⓐ Ⓑ Ⓒ Ⓓ Ⓔ   77 Ⓐ Ⓑ Ⓒ Ⓓ Ⓔ

12 Ⓐ Ⓑ Ⓒ Ⓓ Ⓔ   34 Ⓐ Ⓑ Ⓒ Ⓓ Ⓔ   56 Ⓐ Ⓑ Ⓒ Ⓓ Ⓔ   78 Ⓐ Ⓑ Ⓒ Ⓓ Ⓔ

13 Ⓐ Ⓑ Ⓒ Ⓓ Ⓔ   35 Ⓐ Ⓑ Ⓒ Ⓓ Ⓔ   57 Ⓐ Ⓑ Ⓒ Ⓓ Ⓔ   79 Ⓐ Ⓑ Ⓒ Ⓓ Ⓔ

14 Ⓐ Ⓑ Ⓒ Ⓓ Ⓔ   36 Ⓐ Ⓑ Ⓒ Ⓓ Ⓔ   58 Ⓐ Ⓑ Ⓒ Ⓓ Ⓔ   80 Ⓐ Ⓑ Ⓒ Ⓓ Ⓔ

15 Ⓐ Ⓑ Ⓒ Ⓓ Ⓔ   37 Ⓐ Ⓑ Ⓒ Ⓓ Ⓔ   59 Ⓐ Ⓑ Ⓒ Ⓓ Ⓔ   81 Ⓐ Ⓑ Ⓒ Ⓓ Ⓔ

16 Ⓐ Ⓑ Ⓒ Ⓓ Ⓔ   38 Ⓐ Ⓑ Ⓒ Ⓓ Ⓔ   60 Ⓐ Ⓑ Ⓒ Ⓓ Ⓔ   82 Ⓐ Ⓑ Ⓒ Ⓓ Ⓔ

17 Ⓐ Ⓑ Ⓒ Ⓓ Ⓔ   39 Ⓐ Ⓑ Ⓒ Ⓓ Ⓔ   61 Ⓐ Ⓑ Ⓒ Ⓓ Ⓔ   83 Ⓐ Ⓑ Ⓒ Ⓓ Ⓔ

18 Ⓐ Ⓑ Ⓒ Ⓓ Ⓔ   40 Ⓐ Ⓑ Ⓒ Ⓓ Ⓔ   62 Ⓐ Ⓑ Ⓒ Ⓓ Ⓔ   84 Ⓐ Ⓑ Ⓒ Ⓓ Ⓔ

19 Ⓐ Ⓑ Ⓒ Ⓓ Ⓔ   41 Ⓐ Ⓑ Ⓒ Ⓓ Ⓔ   63 Ⓐ Ⓑ Ⓒ Ⓓ Ⓔ   85 Ⓐ Ⓑ Ⓒ Ⓓ Ⓔ

20 Ⓐ Ⓑ Ⓒ Ⓓ Ⓔ   42 Ⓐ Ⓑ Ⓒ Ⓓ Ⓔ   64 Ⓐ Ⓑ Ⓒ Ⓓ Ⓔ   86 Ⓐ Ⓑ Ⓒ Ⓓ Ⓔ

21 Ⓐ Ⓑ Ⓒ Ⓓ Ⓔ   43 Ⓐ Ⓑ Ⓒ Ⓓ Ⓔ   65 Ⓐ Ⓑ Ⓒ Ⓓ Ⓔ   87 Ⓐ Ⓑ Ⓒ Ⓓ Ⓔ

22 Ⓐ Ⓑ Ⓒ Ⓓ Ⓔ   44 Ⓐ Ⓑ Ⓒ Ⓓ Ⓔ   66 Ⓐ Ⓑ Ⓒ Ⓓ Ⓔ   88 Ⓐ Ⓑ Ⓒ Ⓓ Ⓔ

Part C—Number Series

1. Ⓐ Ⓑ Ⓒ Ⓓ Ⓔ   7. Ⓐ Ⓑ Ⓒ Ⓓ Ⓔ   13. Ⓐ Ⓑ Ⓒ Ⓓ Ⓔ   19. Ⓐ Ⓑ Ⓒ Ⓓ Ⓔ

2. Ⓐ Ⓑ Ⓒ Ⓓ Ⓔ   8. Ⓐ Ⓑ Ⓒ Ⓓ Ⓔ   14. Ⓐ Ⓑ Ⓒ Ⓓ Ⓔ   20. Ⓐ Ⓑ Ⓒ Ⓓ Ⓔ

3. Ⓐ Ⓑ Ⓒ Ⓓ Ⓔ   9. Ⓐ Ⓑ Ⓒ Ⓓ Ⓔ   15. Ⓐ Ⓑ Ⓒ Ⓓ Ⓔ   21. Ⓐ Ⓑ Ⓒ Ⓓ Ⓔ

4. Ⓐ Ⓑ Ⓒ Ⓓ Ⓔ   10. Ⓐ Ⓑ Ⓒ Ⓓ Ⓔ   16. Ⓐ Ⓑ Ⓒ Ⓓ Ⓔ   22. Ⓐ Ⓑ Ⓒ Ⓓ Ⓔ

5. Ⓐ Ⓑ Ⓒ Ⓓ Ⓔ   11. Ⓐ Ⓑ Ⓒ Ⓓ Ⓔ   17. Ⓐ Ⓑ Ⓒ Ⓓ Ⓔ   23. Ⓐ Ⓑ Ⓒ Ⓓ Ⓔ

6. Ⓐ Ⓑ Ⓒ Ⓓ Ⓔ   12. Ⓐ Ⓑ Ⓒ Ⓓ Ⓔ   18. Ⓐ Ⓑ Ⓒ Ⓓ Ⓔ   24. Ⓐ Ⓑ Ⓒ Ⓓ Ⓔ

Part D—Following Oral Instructions

1 Ⓐ Ⓑ Ⓒ Ⓓ Ⓔ 23 Ⓐ Ⓑ Ⓒ Ⓓ Ⓔ 45 Ⓐ Ⓑ Ⓒ Ⓓ Ⓔ 67 Ⓐ Ⓑ Ⓒ Ⓓ Ⓔ

2 Ⓐ Ⓑ Ⓒ Ⓓ Ⓔ 24 Ⓐ Ⓑ Ⓒ Ⓓ Ⓔ 46 Ⓐ Ⓑ Ⓒ Ⓓ Ⓔ 68 Ⓐ Ⓑ Ⓒ Ⓓ Ⓔ

3 Ⓐ Ⓑ Ⓒ Ⓓ Ⓔ 25 Ⓐ Ⓑ Ⓒ Ⓓ Ⓔ 47 Ⓐ Ⓑ Ⓒ Ⓓ Ⓔ 69 Ⓐ Ⓑ Ⓒ Ⓓ Ⓔ

4 Ⓐ Ⓑ Ⓒ Ⓓ Ⓔ 26 Ⓐ Ⓑ Ⓒ Ⓓ Ⓔ 48 Ⓐ Ⓑ Ⓒ Ⓓ Ⓔ 70 Ⓐ Ⓑ Ⓒ Ⓓ Ⓔ

5 Ⓐ Ⓑ Ⓒ Ⓓ Ⓔ 27 Ⓐ Ⓑ Ⓒ Ⓓ Ⓔ 49 Ⓐ Ⓑ Ⓒ Ⓓ Ⓔ 71 Ⓐ Ⓑ Ⓒ Ⓓ Ⓔ

6 Ⓐ Ⓑ Ⓒ Ⓓ Ⓔ 28 Ⓐ Ⓑ Ⓒ Ⓓ Ⓔ 50 Ⓐ Ⓑ Ⓒ Ⓓ Ⓔ 72 Ⓐ Ⓑ Ⓒ Ⓓ Ⓔ

7 Ⓐ Ⓑ Ⓒ Ⓓ Ⓔ 29 Ⓐ Ⓑ Ⓒ Ⓓ Ⓔ 51 Ⓐ Ⓑ Ⓒ Ⓓ Ⓔ 73 Ⓐ Ⓑ Ⓒ Ⓓ Ⓔ

8 Ⓐ Ⓑ Ⓒ Ⓓ Ⓔ 30 Ⓐ Ⓑ Ⓒ Ⓓ Ⓔ 52 Ⓐ Ⓑ Ⓒ Ⓓ Ⓔ 74 Ⓐ Ⓑ Ⓒ Ⓓ Ⓔ

9 Ⓐ Ⓑ Ⓒ Ⓓ Ⓔ 31 Ⓐ Ⓑ Ⓒ Ⓓ Ⓔ 53 Ⓐ Ⓑ Ⓒ Ⓓ Ⓔ 75 Ⓐ Ⓑ Ⓒ Ⓓ Ⓔ

10 Ⓐ Ⓑ Ⓒ Ⓓ Ⓔ 32 Ⓐ Ⓑ Ⓒ Ⓓ Ⓔ 54 Ⓐ Ⓑ Ⓒ Ⓓ Ⓔ 76 Ⓐ Ⓑ Ⓒ Ⓓ Ⓔ

11 Ⓐ Ⓑ Ⓒ Ⓓ Ⓔ 33 Ⓐ Ⓑ Ⓒ Ⓓ Ⓔ 55 Ⓐ Ⓑ Ⓒ Ⓓ Ⓔ 77 Ⓐ Ⓑ Ⓒ Ⓓ Ⓔ

12 Ⓐ Ⓑ Ⓒ Ⓓ Ⓔ 34 Ⓐ Ⓑ Ⓒ Ⓓ Ⓔ 56 Ⓐ Ⓑ Ⓒ Ⓓ Ⓔ 78 Ⓐ Ⓑ Ⓒ Ⓓ Ⓔ

13 Ⓐ Ⓑ Ⓒ Ⓓ Ⓔ 35 Ⓐ Ⓑ Ⓒ Ⓓ Ⓔ 57 Ⓐ Ⓑ Ⓒ Ⓓ Ⓔ 79 Ⓐ Ⓑ Ⓒ Ⓓ Ⓔ

14 Ⓐ Ⓑ Ⓒ Ⓓ Ⓔ 36 Ⓐ Ⓑ Ⓒ Ⓓ Ⓔ 58 Ⓐ Ⓑ Ⓒ Ⓓ Ⓔ 80 Ⓐ Ⓑ Ⓒ Ⓓ Ⓔ

15 Ⓐ Ⓑ Ⓒ Ⓓ Ⓔ 37 Ⓐ Ⓑ Ⓒ Ⓓ Ⓔ 59 Ⓐ Ⓑ Ⓒ Ⓓ Ⓔ 81 Ⓐ Ⓑ Ⓒ Ⓓ Ⓔ

16 Ⓐ Ⓑ Ⓒ Ⓓ Ⓔ 38 Ⓐ Ⓑ Ⓒ Ⓓ Ⓔ 60 Ⓐ Ⓑ Ⓒ Ⓓ Ⓔ 82 Ⓐ Ⓑ Ⓒ Ⓓ Ⓔ

17 Ⓐ Ⓑ Ⓒ Ⓓ Ⓔ 39 Ⓐ Ⓑ Ⓒ Ⓓ Ⓔ 61 Ⓐ Ⓑ Ⓒ Ⓓ Ⓔ 83 Ⓐ Ⓑ Ⓒ Ⓓ Ⓔ

18 Ⓐ Ⓑ Ⓒ Ⓓ Ⓔ 40 Ⓐ Ⓑ Ⓒ Ⓓ Ⓔ 62 Ⓐ Ⓑ Ⓒ Ⓓ Ⓔ 84 Ⓐ Ⓑ Ⓒ Ⓓ Ⓔ

19 Ⓐ Ⓑ Ⓒ Ⓓ Ⓔ 41 Ⓐ Ⓑ Ⓒ Ⓓ Ⓔ 63 Ⓐ Ⓑ Ⓒ Ⓓ Ⓔ 85 Ⓐ Ⓑ Ⓒ Ⓓ Ⓔ

20 Ⓐ Ⓑ Ⓒ Ⓓ Ⓔ 42 Ⓐ Ⓑ Ⓒ Ⓓ Ⓔ 64 Ⓐ Ⓑ Ⓒ Ⓓ Ⓔ 86 Ⓐ Ⓑ Ⓒ Ⓓ Ⓔ

21 Ⓐ Ⓑ Ⓒ Ⓓ Ⓔ 43 Ⓐ Ⓑ Ⓒ Ⓓ Ⓔ 65 Ⓐ Ⓑ Ⓒ Ⓓ Ⓔ 87 Ⓐ Ⓑ Ⓒ Ⓓ Ⓔ

22 Ⓐ Ⓑ Ⓒ Ⓓ Ⓔ 44 Ⓐ Ⓑ Ⓒ Ⓓ Ⓔ 66 Ⓐ Ⓑ Ⓒ Ⓓ Ⓔ 88 Ⓐ Ⓑ Ⓒ Ⓓ Ⓔ

TEAR HERE

SCORE SHEET

ADDRESS CHECKING: Your score on the Address Checking part is based upon the number of questions you answered correctly minus the number of questions you answered incorrectly. To determine your score, subtract the number of wrong answers from the number of correct answers.

Number Right   –   Number Wrong   =   Raw Score

_____   –   _____   =   _____

MEMORY FOR ADDRESSES: Your score on the Memory for Addresses part is based upon the number of questions you answered correctly minus one-fourth of the questions you answered incorrectly (number wrong divided by 4). Calculate this now:

Number wrong ÷ 4 = _____ .

Number Right   –   Number Wrong   ÷   4   =   Raw Score

_____   –   _____   =   _____

NUMBER SERIES: Your score on the Number Series part is based only on the number of questions you answered correctly. Wrong answers do not count against you.

Number Right   =   Raw Score

_____   =   _____

FOLLOWING ORAL INSTRUCTIONS: Your score on the Following Oral Instructions part is based only upon the number of questions you marked correctly on the answer sheet. The worksheet is not scored, and wrong answers on the answer sheet do not count against you.

Number Right   =   Raw Score

_____   =   _____

TOTAL SCORE: To find your total raw score, add together the raw scores for each section of the exam.

Address Checking Score   _____

+

Memory for Addresses Score   _____

+

Number Series Score   _____

+

Following Oral Instructions Score   _____

=

_____

Total Raw Score   _____

Self Evaluation Chart

Calculate your raw score for each test as shown above. Then check to see where your score falls on the scale from Poor to Excellent. Lightly shade in the boxes in which your scores fall.

Part	Excellent	Good	Average	Fair	Poor
Address Checking	80–95	65–79	50–64	35–49	1–34
Memory for Addresses	75–88	60–74	45–59	30–44	1–29
Number Series	21–24	18–20	14–17	11–13	1–10
Following Oral Instructions	27–31	23–26	19–22	14–18	1–13

Second Model Exam

Part A—Address Checking

Sample Questions

You will be allowed three minutes to read the directions and answer the five sample questions that follow. On the actual test, however, you will have only six minutes to answer 95 questions, so see how quickly you can compare addresses and still get the correct answer.

DIRECTIONS: Each question consists of two addresses. If the two addresses are alike in EVERY way, mark A on your answer sheet. If the two addresses are different in ANY way, mark D on your answer sheet.

1 ...4240 SW 146th Rd	4240 NW 146th Rd
2 ...7019 Hutchinson Ave	7019 Hutchinson Ave
3 ...4212 Marsupial Pky	4312 Marsupial Pky
4 ...Boulder CO 80302	Boulder CO 80302
5 ...8364 Barclay Blvd	8364 Barclays Blvd

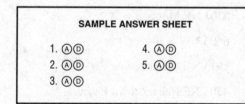

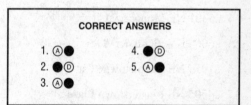

Address Checking

Time: 6 Minutes. 95 Questions.

DIRECTIONS: For each question compare the address in the left column with the address in the right column. If the addresses are ALIKE IN EVERY WAY, blacken space A on your answer sheet. If the two addresses are DIFFERENT IN ANY WAY, blacken space D on your answer sheet. Correct answers for this test are on page 143.

1	...7399 NW Candleworth Dr	7399 NW Candleworth Dr
2	...New Castle AL 35119	New Castle AL 35119
3	...2098 NE Catalpa Ln	2098 NW Catalpa Ln
4	...17001 NE Rappaix Court	17001 NE Rappaix Court
5	...10091 NE Larryvale Rd	10091 NE Larryville Rd
6	...2896 NE Wallaston Way	2896 NE Walleston Way
7	...Timonium MD 21093	Timanium MD 21093
8	...7749 NW Barracuda Cove Ct	7749 NW Barracuda Cove Ct
9	...6099 NW Atterbury Rd	6099 NW Atterbury Dr
10	...2198 NE Springs St	2198 NW Springs St
11	...6089 SE Flintshire Rd	6089 SW Flintshire Rd
12	...13111 SE Throgmorton Ct	13111 SE Throgmorton Ct
13	...Estacada OR 97023	Estacada OK 97023
14	...5301 NE Monocacy Cir	5301 NE Monocacy Ct
15	...6066 NW Schissler Ave	6606 NW Schissler Ave
16	...1915 NE Chapletowne Cir	1915 NE Chapeltowne Cir
17	...4505 NE Reisterstown Plaza	4505 NE Reisterstown Plaza
18	...3399 NW Ivydene Ter	3399 NW Ivydene Trl
19	...8605 Commanche Ave	8605 Commanche Ave
20	...Winnemucca NV 89445	Winnemocca NV 89445
21	...467 SE Chatterleigh Cir	467 SE Chatterleigh Cir
22	...3300 SE Golupski Rd	3300 SE Golpski Rd
23	...4884 NW Farmvale Ave	4884 NW Farmdale Ave
24	...Kalamazoo MI 49009	Kalamazoo MI 49009
25	...11676 SE Harryweiss Rd	11676 SE Harrywise Rd
26	...4395 Auchentoroly Ter	4395 Auchentoroly Ter
27	...11321 NE Pageland Rd	11321 NE Pageland Rd
28	...2488 Jeannett Ave	2488 Jeannett Ave

29 ...1900 Gilford Ter	1900 Gulford Ter
30 ...5177 NE Bridgehampton Dr	5177 NE Bridgehampton Dr
31 ...7333 Martingale Ave	7333 Martingale Ave
32 ...11577 Delagrange Way	11571 Delagrange Way
33 ...13852 NE 68th Ave	13852 NE 86th Ave
34 ...11736 NE Uffington Rd	17736 NE Uffington Rd
35 ...21199 NW Huntington Ave	21199 NW Huntingdon Ave
36 ...Merriweather NY 11548	Merriweather NY 11548
37 ...11001 NE Cedarcrest Rd	11001 NE Cedarchest Rd
38 ...3569 NE Tazewell Rd	3569 NE Tazewell Rd
39 ...5297 Popperdam Creek	5297 Pepperdam Creek
40 ...2288 Dundawan Rd	2288 Dundawan Rd
41 ...17299 Rhuddlan Rd	17299 Rhuddlan Rd
42 ...37719 Underwood Ct	37719 Underwood Cir
43 ...22700 S Strathdale Rd	22700 S Strathdale Rd
44 ...Homeworth OH 44634	Homeworth OH 46434
45 ...3727 NW Ayleshire Rd	3727 NE Ayleshire Rd
46 ...4585 E Englemeade Ave	4585 E Englemeade Ave
47 ...37741 NE Jacqueline Ln	34771 NE Jacqueline Ln
48 ...3800 N Grinnalds Ave	3800 N Grinnalds St
49 ...10990 NE Kennicott Rd	10990 NE Kenningcott Rd
50 ...Vanderpool TX 78885	Vanderpool TX 78885
51 ...11799 NE Brattel Rd	11799 NE Brattle Rd
52 ...2196 Leadenhall Court	2196 Leadenhall Court
53 ...Albuquerque NM 87109	Albuquerque NM 81709
54 ...3789 Featherstone Ln	8789 Featherstone Ln
55 ...18076 Martinque Rd	18076 Martinque Ct
56 ...60111 Debonair Ct	6011 Debonair Ct
57 ...4131 NE Tussock Rd	4131 NE Tussock Road
58 ...299 Susquehanna Ave E	299 Susquehanna Ave W
59 ...53116 NE T Avenue	53116 NE T Avenue
60 ...16917 Saint Elmo Ave	16917 Saint Almo Ave
61 ...10401 Olde Georgetown Rd SE	10401 Old Georgetown Rd SE
62 ...7550 Wisconsin Ave	7550 Wisconsin St

63 ...8054 Aberdeen Rd	8054 Aberdeen Rd
64 ... Wheelersburg KY 41473	Wheelersburg KY 41473
65 ...3138 Edgemere Ave	3138 Edgemore Ave
66 ...11595 Heathcliff Dr	11595 Heathcliff Dr
67 ...13531 N Keutel Rd	13531 N Kratel Rd
68 ...7585 Breezewick Cir	78575 Breezewick Cir
69 ...15530 NE Jimrowe Cir	15530 NE Jimrowe Ct
70 ...2001 Quantico Way	2001 Guantico Way
71 ...8899 Randolph Springs Pl	8899 Rudolph Springs Pl
72 ...4010 Oakleigh Beach Rd	4010 Oakleigh Beach Rd
73 ...3977 Mc Teague Ave	3977 Mc Teague Ave
74 ...13827 N Lavington Pl	13827 N Lavingston Pl
75 ...17390 Youngstown Ave NE	17390 Youngstown Ave SE
76 ...15999 Brookview Ave	15999 Brookview Ave
77 ...12733 NE 88th Ave	1273 NE 88th Ave
78 ...P.O. Box 34001	P.O. Box 34007
79 ...Selinsgrove PA 17870	Selingrove PA 17870
80 ...3425 Chelmareford Trl	3245 Chelmareford Trl
81 ...6080 Knickerbocker Cir	6080 Knickerbocker Dr
82 ...1700 Alconbury Rd	1700 Alconbury Rd
83 ...2620 Winnettka St	2620 Winnettka St
84 ...2367 Essextowne Cir	2367 Essextowne Cir
85 ...3588 Investment Pl	3588 Investment Pl
86 ...11888 Margarette Ave	11888 Margaretta Ave
87 ...4756 Ridervale Rd	4756 Riderview Rd
88 ...16491 Zeppelin Ave	16491 Zepperlin Ave
89 ...10195 Highway 210 N	10195 Highway 201 N
90 ...11811 Vailthorn Ln	11181 Vailthorn Ln
91 ...7299 E 41st St	7299 W 41st St
92 ...P.O. Box 30399	P.O. Box 30399
93 ...4710 Bethesda Ave N	4710 Bethesda Blvd N
94 ...Waynesboro MS 39367	Waynesboro MN 39367
95 ...99 NW M Street	99 NW M Street

END OF ADDRESS CHECKING

Part B—Memory for Addresses

Sample Questions

The sample questions for this part are based upon the addresses in the five boxes below. Your task is to mark on your answer sheet the letter of the box in which each address belongs. You will have five minutes now to study the locations of the addresses. Then cover the boxes and try to mark the location of the sample questions. You may look back at the boxes if you cannot yet mark the address locations from memory.

The exam itself provides three practice sessions before the question set that really counts. Practice I and Practice III supply you with the boxes and permit you to refer to them if necessary. Practice II and the Memory for Addresses Test itself do not permit you to look at the boxes. The test itself is based on memory.

A	B	C	D	E
2500–2999 Mist Forest	3600–3899 Mist Season	1400–1899 Mist Anchor	1900–2499 Mist Cupola	3000–3599 Mist Jester
1400–1899 Tank Tarot	2500–2999 Tank Howard	3600–3899 Tank Bongo	3000–3599 Tank Gibbon	1900–2499 Tank Lattice
3600–3899 Kite	1900–2499 Kite	3000–3599 Kite	2500–2999 Kite	1400–1899 Kite

1. 3000–3599 Kite

2. 1900–2499 Mist

3. Cupola

4. 1400–1899 Kite

5. Howard

6. 1900–2499 Tank

7. 1900–2499 Kite

8. Tarot

9. 2500–2999 Tank

10. 1400–1899 Tank

11. 1400–1899 Mist

12. Jester

13. Lattice

14. 2500–2999 Mist

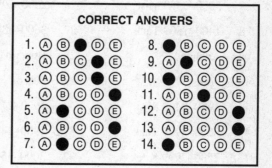

Practice for Memory for Addresses

DIRECTIONS: *The five boxes below are labelled A, B, C, D, and E. In each box are three sets of number spans with names and two names that are not associated with numbers. In the next THREE MINUTES, you must try to memorize the box location of each name and number span. The position of a name or number span within its box is not important. You need only remember the letter of the box in which the item is to be found. You will use these names and numbers to answer three sets of practice questions that are NOT scored and one actual test that is scored. Correct answers are on pages 144 and 145.*

A	B	C	D	E
2500–2999 Mist	3600–3899 Mist	1400–1899 Mist	1900–2499 Mist	3000–3599 Mist
Forest	Season	Anchor	Cupola	Jester
1400–1899 Tank	2500–2999 Tank	3600–3899 Tank	3000–3599 Tank	1900–2499 Tank
Tarot	Howard	Bongo	Gibbon	Lattice
3600–3899 Kite	1900–2499 Kite	3000–3599 Kite	2500–2999 Kite	1400–1899 Kite

Practice I

DIRECTIONS: *Use the next THREE MINUTES to mark on the answer sheet at the end of Practice I the letter of the box in which each item that follows is to be found. Try to mark each item without looking back at the boxes. If, however, you get stuck, you may refer to the boxes during this practice exercise. If you find that you must look at the boxes, try to memorize as you do so. This test is for practice only. It will not be scored.*

1. 2500–2999 Mist
2. 3000–3599 Tank
3. Season
4. Lattice
5. 1400–1899 Kite
6. 3600–3899 Tank
7. 3000–3599 Mist
8. 1400–1899 Tank
9. Anchor
10. Forest
11. 1900–2499 Mist
12. 2500–2999 Tank
13. 2500–2999 Kite
14. Gibbon
15. 3600–3899 Kite
16. 1900–2499 Tank
17. Cupola
18. Bongo
19. 1400–1899 Mist

20. 1900–2499 Tank
21. 3600–3899 Kite
22. 2500–2999 Tank
23. Tarot
24. Jester
25. 3600–3899 Mist
26. 2500–2999 Kite
27. 3600–3899 Tank
28. Howard
29. Season
30. 1900–2499 Kite
31. 1900–2499 Mist
32. 3000–3599 Kite
33. Forest
34. Lattice
35. 1400–1899 Kite
36. 1400–1899 Tank
37. 2500–2999 Mist
38. 3000–3599 Mist

39. Anchor
40. Gibbon
41. 3000–3599 Tank
42. 3600–3899 Mist
43. 3000–3599 Tank
44. 3600–3899 Kite
45. 1900–2499 Tank
46. 2500–2999 Kite
47. Howard
48. Jester
49. 2500–2999 Mist
50. 3600–3899 Kite
51. 1400–1899 Mist
52. 1400–1899 Kite
53. Cupola
54. Bongo
55. Gibbon
56. 2500–2999 Tank
57. 1900–2499 Tank

58. Tarot
59. 1900–2499 Mist
60. 3600–3899 Tank
61. 3000–3599 Mist
62. Forest
63. Anchor
64. Season
65. 1900–2499 Kite
66. 3000–3599 Kite
67. 3600–3899 Mist
68. 1400–1899 Tank

69. 3000–3599 Tank
70. Lattice
71. 3600–3899 Kite
72. 1900–2499 Mist
73. 2500–2999 Tank
74. 3600–3899 Tank
75. 2500–2999 Mist
76. 1400–1899 Kite
77. Bongo
78. Gibbon
79. 3000–3599 Mist

80. 1400–1899 Kite
81. 3600–3899 Tank
82. Tarot
83. Lattice
84. Howard
85. 1900–2499 Mist
86. 1900–2499 Kite
87. 2500–2999 Tank
88. 3600–3899 Mist

Practice I Answer Sheet

1 Ⓐ Ⓑ Ⓒ Ⓓ Ⓔ
2 Ⓐ Ⓑ Ⓒ Ⓓ Ⓔ
3 Ⓐ Ⓑ Ⓒ Ⓓ Ⓔ
4 Ⓐ Ⓑ Ⓒ Ⓓ Ⓔ
5 Ⓐ Ⓑ Ⓒ Ⓓ Ⓔ
6 Ⓐ Ⓑ Ⓒ Ⓓ Ⓔ
7 Ⓐ Ⓑ Ⓒ Ⓓ Ⓔ
8 Ⓐ Ⓑ Ⓒ Ⓓ Ⓔ
9 Ⓐ Ⓑ Ⓒ Ⓓ Ⓔ
10 Ⓐ Ⓑ Ⓒ Ⓓ Ⓔ
11 Ⓐ Ⓑ Ⓒ Ⓓ Ⓔ
12 Ⓐ Ⓑ Ⓒ Ⓓ Ⓔ
13 Ⓐ Ⓑ Ⓒ Ⓓ Ⓔ
14 Ⓐ Ⓑ Ⓒ Ⓓ Ⓔ
15 Ⓐ Ⓑ Ⓒ Ⓓ Ⓔ
16 Ⓐ Ⓑ Ⓒ Ⓓ Ⓔ
17 Ⓐ Ⓑ Ⓒ Ⓓ Ⓔ
18 Ⓐ Ⓑ Ⓒ Ⓓ Ⓔ
19 Ⓐ Ⓑ Ⓒ Ⓓ Ⓔ
20 Ⓐ Ⓑ Ⓒ Ⓓ Ⓔ
21 Ⓐ Ⓑ Ⓒ Ⓓ Ⓔ
22 Ⓐ Ⓑ Ⓒ Ⓓ Ⓔ

23 Ⓐ Ⓑ Ⓒ Ⓓ Ⓔ
24 Ⓐ Ⓑ Ⓒ Ⓓ Ⓔ
25 Ⓐ Ⓑ Ⓒ Ⓓ Ⓔ
26 Ⓐ Ⓑ Ⓒ Ⓓ Ⓔ
27 Ⓐ Ⓑ Ⓒ Ⓓ Ⓔ
28 Ⓐ Ⓑ Ⓒ Ⓓ Ⓔ
29 Ⓐ Ⓑ Ⓒ Ⓓ Ⓔ
30 Ⓐ Ⓑ Ⓒ Ⓓ Ⓔ
31 Ⓐ Ⓑ Ⓒ Ⓓ Ⓔ
32 Ⓐ Ⓑ Ⓒ Ⓓ Ⓔ
33 Ⓐ Ⓑ Ⓒ Ⓓ Ⓔ
34 Ⓐ Ⓑ Ⓒ Ⓓ Ⓔ
35 Ⓐ Ⓑ Ⓒ Ⓓ Ⓔ
36 Ⓐ Ⓑ Ⓒ Ⓓ Ⓔ
37 Ⓐ Ⓑ Ⓒ Ⓓ Ⓔ
38 Ⓐ Ⓑ Ⓒ Ⓓ Ⓔ
39 Ⓐ Ⓑ Ⓒ Ⓓ Ⓔ
40 Ⓐ Ⓑ Ⓒ Ⓓ Ⓔ
41 Ⓐ Ⓑ Ⓒ Ⓓ Ⓔ
42 Ⓐ Ⓑ Ⓒ Ⓓ Ⓔ
43 Ⓐ Ⓑ Ⓒ Ⓓ Ⓔ
44 Ⓐ Ⓑ Ⓒ Ⓓ Ⓔ

45 Ⓐ Ⓑ Ⓒ Ⓓ Ⓔ
46 Ⓐ Ⓑ Ⓒ Ⓓ Ⓔ
47 Ⓐ Ⓑ Ⓒ Ⓓ Ⓔ
48 Ⓐ Ⓑ Ⓒ Ⓓ Ⓔ
49 Ⓐ Ⓑ Ⓒ Ⓓ Ⓔ
50 Ⓐ Ⓑ Ⓒ Ⓓ Ⓔ
51 Ⓐ Ⓑ Ⓒ Ⓓ Ⓔ
52 Ⓐ Ⓑ Ⓒ Ⓓ Ⓔ
53 Ⓐ Ⓑ Ⓒ Ⓓ Ⓔ
54 Ⓐ Ⓑ Ⓒ Ⓓ Ⓔ
55 Ⓐ Ⓑ Ⓒ Ⓓ Ⓔ
56 Ⓐ Ⓑ Ⓒ Ⓓ Ⓔ
57 Ⓐ Ⓑ Ⓒ Ⓓ Ⓔ
58 Ⓐ Ⓑ Ⓒ Ⓓ Ⓔ
59 Ⓐ Ⓑ Ⓒ Ⓓ Ⓔ
60 Ⓐ Ⓑ Ⓒ Ⓓ Ⓔ
61 Ⓐ Ⓑ Ⓒ Ⓓ Ⓔ
62 Ⓐ Ⓑ Ⓒ Ⓓ Ⓔ
63 Ⓐ Ⓑ Ⓒ Ⓓ Ⓔ
64 Ⓐ Ⓑ Ⓒ Ⓓ Ⓔ
65 Ⓐ Ⓑ Ⓒ Ⓓ Ⓔ
66 Ⓐ Ⓑ Ⓒ Ⓓ Ⓔ

67 Ⓐ Ⓑ Ⓒ Ⓓ Ⓔ
68 Ⓐ Ⓑ Ⓒ Ⓓ Ⓔ
69 Ⓐ Ⓑ Ⓒ Ⓓ Ⓔ
70 Ⓐ Ⓑ Ⓒ Ⓓ Ⓔ
71 Ⓐ Ⓑ Ⓒ Ⓓ Ⓔ
72 Ⓐ Ⓑ Ⓒ Ⓓ Ⓔ
73 Ⓐ Ⓑ Ⓒ Ⓓ Ⓔ
74 Ⓐ Ⓑ Ⓒ Ⓓ Ⓔ
75 Ⓐ Ⓑ Ⓒ Ⓓ Ⓔ
76 Ⓐ Ⓑ Ⓒ Ⓓ Ⓔ
77 Ⓐ Ⓑ Ⓒ Ⓓ Ⓔ
78 Ⓐ Ⓑ Ⓒ Ⓓ Ⓔ
79 Ⓐ Ⓑ Ⓒ Ⓓ Ⓔ
80 Ⓐ Ⓑ Ⓒ Ⓓ Ⓔ
81 Ⓐ Ⓑ Ⓒ Ⓓ Ⓔ
82 Ⓐ Ⓑ Ⓒ Ⓓ Ⓔ
83 Ⓐ Ⓑ Ⓒ Ⓓ Ⓔ
84 Ⓐ Ⓑ Ⓒ Ⓓ Ⓔ
85 Ⓐ Ⓑ Ⓒ Ⓓ Ⓔ
86 Ⓐ Ⓑ Ⓒ Ⓓ Ⓔ
87 Ⓐ Ⓑ Ⓒ Ⓓ Ⓔ
88 Ⓐ Ⓑ Ⓒ Ⓓ Ⓔ

Practice II

DIRECTIONS: The next 88 questions constitute another practice exercise. Mark your answers on the Practice II answer sheet. Again, the time limit is THREE MINUTES. This time, however, you must NOT look at the boxes while answering the questions. You must rely on your memory in marking the box location of each item. This practice test will not be scored.

1. 1400–1899 Mist
2. 3000–3599 Kite
3. 1900–2499 Tank
4. 1400–1899 Tank
5. Howard
6. Gibbon
7. 3600–3899 Mist
8. 2500–2999 Kite
9. 1400–1899 Kite
10. Lattice
11. Jester
12. 2500–2999 Mist
13. 3600–3899 Tank
14. 3000–3599 Mist
15. 3000–3599 Tank
16. Cupola
17. Tarot
18. Bongo
19. 1900–2499 Kite
20. 3600–3899 Kite
21. Anchor
22. Season
23. 1900–2499 Mist
24. 2500–2999 Tank
25. Forest
26. 3000–3599 Mist
27. 3000–3599 Tank
28. 3000–3599 Kite
29. Jester
30. Gibbon

31. 2500–2999 Mist
32. 2500–2999 Tank
33. 1400–1899 Mist
34. Tarot
35. Forest
36. Anchor
37. 1400–1899 Kite
38. 3600–3899 Tank
39. 3600–3899 Kite
40. 1900–2499 Mist
41. 1400–1899 Tank
42. Bongo
43. Cupola
44. Season
45. Howard
46. 1900–2499 Tank
47. 1900–2499 Kite
48. 2500–2999 Kite
49. 3600–3899 Mist
50. 3600–3899 Tank
51. 2500–2999 Kite
52. 3000–3599 Mist
53. 3600–3899 Kite
54. Cupola
55. Lattice
56. Season
57. 1400–1899 Mist
58. 3000–3599 Kite
59. Anchor
60. Gibbon

61. 1900–2499 Tank
62. 1400–1899 Tank
63. 2500–2999 Mist
64. 1400–1899 Kite
65. Forest
66. Tarot
67. 1900–2499 Mist
68. 2500–2999 Tank
69. 3000–3599 Tank
70. Jester
71. Howard
72. Bongo
73. 1900–2499 Kite
74. 3600–3899 Tank
75. 1400–1899 Kite
76. 2500–2999 Mist
77. Cupola
78. Season
79. 1900–2499 Kite
80. 1900–2499 Mist
81. 1900–2499 Tank
82. 1400–1899 Tank
83. Lattice
84. Anchor
85. 3600–3899 Mist
86. 2500–2999 Kite
87. 3000–3599 Kite
88. 3000–3599 Mist

Practice II Answer Sheet

1 Ⓐ Ⓑ Ⓒ Ⓓ Ⓔ
2 Ⓐ Ⓑ Ⓒ Ⓓ Ⓔ
3 Ⓐ Ⓑ Ⓒ Ⓓ Ⓔ
4 Ⓐ Ⓑ Ⓒ Ⓓ Ⓔ
5 Ⓐ Ⓑ Ⓒ Ⓓ Ⓔ
6 Ⓐ Ⓑ Ⓒ Ⓓ Ⓔ
7 Ⓐ Ⓑ Ⓒ Ⓓ Ⓔ
8 Ⓐ Ⓑ Ⓒ Ⓓ Ⓔ
9 Ⓐ Ⓑ Ⓒ Ⓓ Ⓔ
10 Ⓐ Ⓑ Ⓒ Ⓓ Ⓔ
11 Ⓐ Ⓑ Ⓒ Ⓓ Ⓔ
12 Ⓐ Ⓑ Ⓒ Ⓓ Ⓔ
13 Ⓐ Ⓑ Ⓒ Ⓓ Ⓔ
14 Ⓐ Ⓑ Ⓒ Ⓓ Ⓔ
15 Ⓐ Ⓑ Ⓒ Ⓓ Ⓔ
16 Ⓐ Ⓑ Ⓒ Ⓓ Ⓔ
17 Ⓐ Ⓑ Ⓒ Ⓓ Ⓔ
18 Ⓐ Ⓑ Ⓒ Ⓓ Ⓔ
19 Ⓐ Ⓑ Ⓒ Ⓓ Ⓔ
20 Ⓐ Ⓑ Ⓒ Ⓓ Ⓔ
21 Ⓐ Ⓑ Ⓒ Ⓓ Ⓔ
22 Ⓐ Ⓑ Ⓒ Ⓓ Ⓔ

23 Ⓐ Ⓑ Ⓒ Ⓓ Ⓔ
24 Ⓐ Ⓑ Ⓒ Ⓓ Ⓔ
25 Ⓐ Ⓑ Ⓒ Ⓓ Ⓔ
26 Ⓐ Ⓑ Ⓒ Ⓓ Ⓔ
27 Ⓐ Ⓑ Ⓒ Ⓓ Ⓔ
28 Ⓐ Ⓑ Ⓒ Ⓓ Ⓔ
29 Ⓐ Ⓑ Ⓒ Ⓓ Ⓔ
30 Ⓐ Ⓑ Ⓒ Ⓓ Ⓔ
31 Ⓐ Ⓑ Ⓒ Ⓓ Ⓔ
32 Ⓐ Ⓑ Ⓒ Ⓓ Ⓔ
33 Ⓐ Ⓑ Ⓒ Ⓓ Ⓔ
34 Ⓐ Ⓑ Ⓒ Ⓓ Ⓔ
35 Ⓐ Ⓑ Ⓒ Ⓓ Ⓔ
36 Ⓐ Ⓑ Ⓒ Ⓓ Ⓔ
37 Ⓐ Ⓑ Ⓒ Ⓓ Ⓔ
38 Ⓐ Ⓑ Ⓒ Ⓓ Ⓔ
39 Ⓐ Ⓑ Ⓒ Ⓓ Ⓔ
40 Ⓐ Ⓑ Ⓒ Ⓓ Ⓔ
41 Ⓐ Ⓑ Ⓒ Ⓓ Ⓔ
42 Ⓐ Ⓑ Ⓒ Ⓓ Ⓔ
43 Ⓐ Ⓑ Ⓒ Ⓓ Ⓔ
44 Ⓐ Ⓑ Ⓒ Ⓓ Ⓔ

45 Ⓐ Ⓑ Ⓒ Ⓓ Ⓔ
46 Ⓐ Ⓑ Ⓒ Ⓓ Ⓔ
47 Ⓐ Ⓑ Ⓒ Ⓓ Ⓔ
48 Ⓐ Ⓑ Ⓒ Ⓓ Ⓔ
49 Ⓐ Ⓑ Ⓒ Ⓓ Ⓔ
50 Ⓐ Ⓑ Ⓒ Ⓓ Ⓔ
51 Ⓐ Ⓑ Ⓒ Ⓓ Ⓔ
52 Ⓐ Ⓑ Ⓒ Ⓓ Ⓔ
53 Ⓐ Ⓑ Ⓒ Ⓓ Ⓔ
54 Ⓐ Ⓑ Ⓒ Ⓓ Ⓔ
55 Ⓐ Ⓑ Ⓒ Ⓓ Ⓔ
56 Ⓐ Ⓑ Ⓒ Ⓓ Ⓔ
57 Ⓐ Ⓑ Ⓒ Ⓓ Ⓔ
58 Ⓐ Ⓑ Ⓒ Ⓓ Ⓔ
59 Ⓐ Ⓑ Ⓒ Ⓓ Ⓔ
60 Ⓐ Ⓑ Ⓒ Ⓓ Ⓔ
61 Ⓐ Ⓑ Ⓒ Ⓓ Ⓔ
62 Ⓐ Ⓑ Ⓒ Ⓓ Ⓔ
63 Ⓐ Ⓑ Ⓒ Ⓓ Ⓔ
64 Ⓐ Ⓑ Ⓒ Ⓓ Ⓔ
65 Ⓐ Ⓑ Ⓒ Ⓓ Ⓔ
66 Ⓐ Ⓑ Ⓒ Ⓓ Ⓔ

67 Ⓐ Ⓑ Ⓒ Ⓓ Ⓔ
68 Ⓐ Ⓑ Ⓒ Ⓓ Ⓔ
69 Ⓐ Ⓑ Ⓒ Ⓓ Ⓔ
70 Ⓐ Ⓑ Ⓒ Ⓓ Ⓔ
71 Ⓐ Ⓑ Ⓒ Ⓓ Ⓔ
72 Ⓐ Ⓑ Ⓒ Ⓓ Ⓔ
73 Ⓐ Ⓑ Ⓒ Ⓓ Ⓔ
74 Ⓐ Ⓑ Ⓒ Ⓓ Ⓔ
75 Ⓐ Ⓑ Ⓒ Ⓓ Ⓔ
76 Ⓐ Ⓑ Ⓒ Ⓓ Ⓔ
77 Ⓐ Ⓑ Ⓒ Ⓓ Ⓔ
78 Ⓐ Ⓑ Ⓒ Ⓓ Ⓔ
79 Ⓐ Ⓑ Ⓒ Ⓓ Ⓔ
80 Ⓐ Ⓑ Ⓒ Ⓓ Ⓔ
81 Ⓐ Ⓑ Ⓒ Ⓓ Ⓔ
82 Ⓐ Ⓑ Ⓒ Ⓓ Ⓔ
83 Ⓐ Ⓑ Ⓒ Ⓓ Ⓔ
84 Ⓐ Ⓑ Ⓒ Ⓓ Ⓔ
85 Ⓐ Ⓑ Ⓒ Ⓓ Ⓔ
86 Ⓐ Ⓑ Ⓒ Ⓓ Ⓔ
87 Ⓐ Ⓑ Ⓒ Ⓓ Ⓔ
88 Ⓐ Ⓑ Ⓒ Ⓓ Ⓔ

Practice III

DIRECTIONS: *The names and addresses are repeated for you in the boxes below. Each name and each number span is in the same box in which you found it in the original set. You will now be allowed FIVE MINUTES to study the locations again. Do your best to memorize the letter of the box in which each item is located. This is your last chance to see the boxes.*

A	B	C	D	E
2500–2999 Mist Forest 1400–1899 Tank Tarot 3600–3899 Kite	3600–3899 Mist Season 2500–2999 Tank Howard 1900–2499 Kite	1400–1899 Mist Anchor 3600–3899 Tank Bongo 3000–3599 Kite	1900–2499 Mist Cupola 3000–3599 Tank Gibbon 2500–2999 Kite	3000–3599 Mist Jester 1900–2499 Tank Lattice 1400–1899 Kite

DIRECTIONS: *This is your last practice test. Mark the location of each of the 88 items on your answer sheet. You will have FIVE MINUTES to answer these questions. Do NOT look back at the boxes. This practice test will not be scored.*

1. 3600–3899 Kite
2. 1400–1899 Mist
3. Season
4. Howard
5. 1900–2499 Tank
6. 1400–1899 Kite
7. 1900–2499 Mist
8. 2500–2999 Tank
9. Gibbon
10. Jester
11. 1400–1899 Tank
12. 3000–3599 Kite
13. 1400–1899 Mist
14. 3000–3599 Tank
15. 2500–2999 Mist
16. 1900–2499 Kite
17. Bongo
18. Anchor
19. 3600–3899 Tank
20. 3600–3899 Mist
21. 2500–2999 Kite
22. 2500–2999 Tank

23. Lattice
24. Cupola
25. Tarot
26. 3000–3599 Kite
27. 3000–3599 Mist
28. 1400–1899 Tank
29. 3000–3599 Mist
30. 3600–3899 Kite
31. 2500–2999 Mist
32. 1400–1899 Kite
33. Season
34. Forest
35. Jester
36. 1400–1899 Tank
37. 1900–2499 Tank
38. 3600–3899 Mist
39. 2500–2999 Kite
40. 2500–2999 Tank
41. Tarot
42. Lattice
43. Bongo
44. Cupola

45. 3600–3899 Tank
46. 3000–3599 Tank
47. 1400–1899 Mist
48. 1900–2499 Kite
49. Gibbon
50. Howard
51. 1900–2499 Mist
52. 3000–3599 Kite
53. Anchor
54. 1900–2499 Tank
55. 2500–2999 Kite
56. 3600–3899 Mist
57. 1400–1899 Tank
58. 2500–2999 Mist
59. 1900–2499 Kite
60. Season
61. Bongo
62. Lattice
63. 2500–2999 Tank
64. 2500–2999 Kite
65. 3600–3899 Tank
66. 3600–3899 Kite

67. Jester
68. Forest
69. 3000–3599 Kite
70. 1900–2499 Tank
71. 3600–3899 Mist
72. 1900–2499 Mist
73. Anchor
74. Cupola

75. 3000–3899 Tank
76. 1400–1899 Mist
77. 1400–1899 Kite
78. Tarot
79. Gibbon
80. 3000–3899 Mist
81. 1400–1899 Tank
82. Howard

83. 3600–3899 Mist
84. 2500–2999 Kite
85. 3600–3899 Kite
86. 2500–2999 Mist
87. Bongo
88. Lattice

Practice III Answer Sheet

1 Ⓐ Ⓑ Ⓒ Ⓓ Ⓔ	23 Ⓐ Ⓑ Ⓒ Ⓓ Ⓔ	45 Ⓐ Ⓑ Ⓒ Ⓓ Ⓔ	67 Ⓐ Ⓑ Ⓒ Ⓓ Ⓔ
2 Ⓐ Ⓑ Ⓒ Ⓓ Ⓔ	24 Ⓐ Ⓑ Ⓒ Ⓓ Ⓔ	46 Ⓐ Ⓑ Ⓒ Ⓓ Ⓔ	68 Ⓐ Ⓑ Ⓒ Ⓓ Ⓔ
3 Ⓐ Ⓑ Ⓒ Ⓓ Ⓔ	25 Ⓐ Ⓑ Ⓒ Ⓓ Ⓔ	47 Ⓐ Ⓑ Ⓒ Ⓓ Ⓔ	69 Ⓐ Ⓑ Ⓒ Ⓓ Ⓔ
4 Ⓐ Ⓑ Ⓒ Ⓓ Ⓔ	26 Ⓐ Ⓑ Ⓒ Ⓓ Ⓔ	48 Ⓐ Ⓑ Ⓒ Ⓓ Ⓔ	70 Ⓐ Ⓑ Ⓒ Ⓓ Ⓔ
5 Ⓐ Ⓑ Ⓒ Ⓓ Ⓔ	27 Ⓐ Ⓑ Ⓒ Ⓓ Ⓔ	49 Ⓐ Ⓑ Ⓒ Ⓓ Ⓔ	71 Ⓐ Ⓑ Ⓒ Ⓓ Ⓔ
6 Ⓐ Ⓑ Ⓒ Ⓓ Ⓔ	28 Ⓐ Ⓑ Ⓒ Ⓓ Ⓔ	50 Ⓐ Ⓑ Ⓒ Ⓓ Ⓔ	72 Ⓐ Ⓑ Ⓒ Ⓓ Ⓔ
7 Ⓐ Ⓑ Ⓒ Ⓓ Ⓔ	29 Ⓐ Ⓑ Ⓒ Ⓓ Ⓔ	51 Ⓐ Ⓑ Ⓒ Ⓓ Ⓔ	73 Ⓐ Ⓑ Ⓒ Ⓓ Ⓔ
8 Ⓐ Ⓑ Ⓒ Ⓓ Ⓔ	30 Ⓐ Ⓑ Ⓒ Ⓓ Ⓔ	52 Ⓐ Ⓑ Ⓒ Ⓓ Ⓔ	74 Ⓐ Ⓑ Ⓒ Ⓓ Ⓔ
9 Ⓐ Ⓑ Ⓒ Ⓓ Ⓔ	31 Ⓐ Ⓑ Ⓒ Ⓓ Ⓔ	53 Ⓐ Ⓑ Ⓒ Ⓓ Ⓔ	75 Ⓐ Ⓑ Ⓒ Ⓓ Ⓔ
10 Ⓐ Ⓑ Ⓒ Ⓓ Ⓔ	32 Ⓐ Ⓑ Ⓒ Ⓓ Ⓔ	54 Ⓐ Ⓑ Ⓒ Ⓓ Ⓔ	76 Ⓐ Ⓑ Ⓒ Ⓓ Ⓔ
11 Ⓐ Ⓑ Ⓒ Ⓓ Ⓔ	33 Ⓐ Ⓑ Ⓒ Ⓓ Ⓔ	55 Ⓐ Ⓑ Ⓒ Ⓓ Ⓔ	77 Ⓐ Ⓑ Ⓒ Ⓓ Ⓔ
12 Ⓐ Ⓑ Ⓒ Ⓓ Ⓔ	34 Ⓐ Ⓑ Ⓒ Ⓓ Ⓔ	56 Ⓐ Ⓑ Ⓒ Ⓓ Ⓔ	78 Ⓐ Ⓑ Ⓒ Ⓓ Ⓔ
13 Ⓐ Ⓑ Ⓒ Ⓓ Ⓔ	35 Ⓐ Ⓑ Ⓒ Ⓓ Ⓔ	57 Ⓐ Ⓑ Ⓒ Ⓓ Ⓔ	79 Ⓐ Ⓑ Ⓒ Ⓓ Ⓔ
14 Ⓐ Ⓑ Ⓒ Ⓓ Ⓔ	36 Ⓐ Ⓑ Ⓒ Ⓓ Ⓔ	58 Ⓐ Ⓑ Ⓒ Ⓓ Ⓔ	80 Ⓐ Ⓑ Ⓒ Ⓓ Ⓔ
15 Ⓐ Ⓑ Ⓒ Ⓓ Ⓔ	37 Ⓐ Ⓑ Ⓒ Ⓓ Ⓔ	59 Ⓐ Ⓑ Ⓒ Ⓓ Ⓔ	81 Ⓐ Ⓑ Ⓒ Ⓓ Ⓔ
16 Ⓐ Ⓑ Ⓒ Ⓓ Ⓔ	38 Ⓐ Ⓑ Ⓒ Ⓓ Ⓔ	60 Ⓐ Ⓑ Ⓒ Ⓓ Ⓔ	82 Ⓐ Ⓑ Ⓒ Ⓓ Ⓔ
17 Ⓐ Ⓑ Ⓒ Ⓓ Ⓔ	39 Ⓐ Ⓑ Ⓒ Ⓓ Ⓔ	61 Ⓐ Ⓑ Ⓒ Ⓓ Ⓔ	83 Ⓐ Ⓑ Ⓒ Ⓓ Ⓔ
18 Ⓐ Ⓑ Ⓒ Ⓓ Ⓔ	40 Ⓐ Ⓑ Ⓒ Ⓓ Ⓔ	62 Ⓐ Ⓑ Ⓒ Ⓓ Ⓔ	84 Ⓐ Ⓑ Ⓒ Ⓓ Ⓔ
19 Ⓐ Ⓑ Ⓒ Ⓓ Ⓔ	41 Ⓐ Ⓑ Ⓒ Ⓓ Ⓔ	63 Ⓐ Ⓑ Ⓒ Ⓓ Ⓔ	85 Ⓐ Ⓑ Ⓒ Ⓓ Ⓔ
20 Ⓐ Ⓑ Ⓒ Ⓓ Ⓔ	42 Ⓐ Ⓑ Ⓒ Ⓓ Ⓔ	64 Ⓐ Ⓑ Ⓒ Ⓓ Ⓔ	86 Ⓐ Ⓑ Ⓒ Ⓓ Ⓔ
21 Ⓐ Ⓑ Ⓒ Ⓓ Ⓔ	43 Ⓐ Ⓑ Ⓒ Ⓓ Ⓔ	65 Ⓐ Ⓑ Ⓒ Ⓓ Ⓔ	87 Ⓐ Ⓑ Ⓒ Ⓓ Ⓔ
22 Ⓐ Ⓑ Ⓒ Ⓓ Ⓔ	44 Ⓐ Ⓑ Ⓒ Ⓓ Ⓔ	66 Ⓐ Ⓑ Ⓒ Ⓓ Ⓔ	88 Ⓐ Ⓑ Ⓒ Ⓓ Ⓔ

Memory for Addresses

Time: 5 Minutes. 88 Questions.

DIRECTIONS: Mark your answers on the answer sheet in the section headed "MEMORY FOR ADDRESSES." This test will be scored. You are NOT permitted to look at the boxes. Work from memory, as quickly and as accurately as you can. Correct answers are on page 145.

1. 3600–3899 Tank
2. 1900–2499 Kite
3. 1900–2499 Mist
4. Bongo
5. Tarot
6. 2500–2999 Mist
7. 1400–1899 Kite
8. 3000–3599 Tank
9. Jester
10. Anchor
11. Forest
12. 1400–1899 Tank
13. 2500–2999 Kite
14. 2500–2999 Tank
15. 3600–3899 Mist
16. 3000–3599 Mist
17. Lattice
18. Forest
19. Gibbon
20. 1900–2499 Tank
21. 1400–1899 Mist
22. 3000–3599 Kite
23. Howard
24. Season
25. Cupola
26. 2500–2999 Kite
27. 1900–2499 Tank
28. 3600–3899 Mist
29. Lattice
30. 1900–2499 Kite

31. 1400–1899 Mist
32. 1400–1899 Tank
33. Tarot
34. Bongo
35. 3000–3599 Tank
36. 3600–3899 Kite
37. 2500–2999 Mist
38. 3000–3599 Mist
39. 3600–3899 Tank
40. Howard
41. Anchor
42. Gibbon
43. 1400–1899 Kite
44. 2500–2999 Tank
45. 3000–3599 Kite
46. Season
47. Anchor
48. 1900–2499 Tank
49. 2500–2999 Kite
50. 1900–2499 Kite
51. 3600–3899 Mist
52. Jester
53. Howard
54. 3600–3899 Kite
55. 2500–2999 Tank
56. 1400–1899 Mist
57. 2500–2999 Mist
58. Tarot
59. Lattice
60. Bongo

61. 1400–1899 Tank
62. 3600–3899 Tank
63. 3000–3599 Kite
64. 3000–3599 Mist
65. Gibbon
66. Forest
67. Cupola
68. 3000–3599 Tank
69. 1400–1899 Kite
70. 1900–2499 Mist
71. 3600–3899 Mist
72. 1900–2499 Mist
73. 3000–3599 Kite
74. Bongo
75. Howard
76. 2500–2999 Mist
77. 1400–1899 Kite
78. 3600–3899 Tank
79. 2500–2999 Tank
80. Anchor
81. Jester
82. 3600–3899 Mist
83. 1900–2499 Mist
84. 1900–2499 Tank
85. Lattice
86. 1900–2499 Kite
87. Tarot
88. 3000–3599 Tank

END OF MEMORY FOR ADDRESSES

Part C—Number Series

Sample Questions

The following sample questions show you the type of question that will be used in Part C. You will have three minutes to answer the sample questions and to study the explanations.

DIRECTIONS: Each number series question consists of a series of numbers that follows some definite order. The numbers progress from left to right according to some rule. One pair of numbers to the right of the series comprises the next two numbers in the series. Study each series to figure out the rule that governs the progression. Choose the answer pair that continues the series according to the pattern established and mark its letter on your answer sheet.

1. 17 20 20 23 23 26 26 ....(A) 26 26   (B) 26 27   (C) 26 29   (D) 29 29 (E) 29 32

In this series, the pattern is: +3, repeat the number, +3, repeat the number, +3, repeat the number. Since <u>26</u> has been repeated, the next number in the series should be <u>29</u>, which should then be repeated. (**D**) is the correct answer.

2. 76 75 73 70 66 61 55 ....(A) 50 41   (B) 54 51   (C) 46 40   (D) 45 35 (E) 48 40

The pattern here is: –1, –2, –3, –4, –5, –6, –7, –8 . . . Continuing the series we see that 55 – 7 = 48– 8 = 40, so (**E**) is the correct answer.

3. 22 26 31 35 40 44 49 ....(A) 53 58   (B) 54 58   (C) 54 59   (D) 53 57 (E) 55 61

Here the pattern is +4, +5, +4, +5, +4, +5 . . . (**A**) is the correct answer because 49 + 4 = 53 + 5 = 58.

4. 12 36 14 33 16 30 18 ....(A) 20 27   (B) 27 20   (C) 20 22   (D) 28 26 (E) 16 14

This series is actually two alternating series. The first series begins with <u>12</u> and ascends at the rate of +2. This series reads: 12 14 16 18 20. The alternating series begins with <u>36</u> and descends at the rate of –3. This series reads: 36 33 30 27. The correct answer is (**B**) because the next number in the total series must be the next number in the descending series, which is <u>27</u>, followed by the next number in the ascending series, <u>20</u>.

5. 4 12 8 12 12 12 16 12 20 ....(A) 16 16   (B) 20 20   (C) 20 24   (D) 24 28
                                                                                    (E) 12 24

This is a difficult series that has been extended to give you more opportunity to spot the pattern. Actually the basic series is a simple +4: 4 8 12 16 20 24. After each number in the basic series, you find the number <u>12</u>. The problem would be easy if it were not for the coincidence of the number <u>12</u> appearing in the series itself. Once you understand the series, you can easily see that (**E**) is the answer.

```
┌─────────────────────────┐   ┌─────────────────────────┐
│  SAMPLE ANSWER SHEET     │   │  CORRECT ANSWERS        │
│                          │   │                         │
│  1. Ⓐ Ⓑ Ⓒ Ⓓ Ⓔ         │   │  1. Ⓐ Ⓑ Ⓒ ● Ⓔ         │
│  2. Ⓐ Ⓑ Ⓒ Ⓓ Ⓔ         │   │  2. Ⓐ Ⓑ Ⓒ Ⓓ ●         │
│  3. Ⓐ Ⓑ Ⓒ Ⓓ Ⓔ         │   │  3. ● Ⓑ Ⓒ Ⓓ Ⓔ         │
│  4. Ⓐ Ⓑ Ⓒ Ⓓ Ⓔ         │   │  4. Ⓐ ● Ⓒ Ⓓ Ⓔ         │
│  5. Ⓐ Ⓑ Ⓒ Ⓓ Ⓔ         │   │  5. Ⓐ Ⓑ Ⓒ Ⓓ ●         │
└─────────────────────────┘   └─────────────────────────┘
```

Number Series

Time: 20 Minutes. 24 Questions.

DIRECTIONS: Each number series question consists of a series of numbers that follows some definite order. The numbers progress from left to right according to some rule. One lettered pair of numbers comprises the next two numbers in the series. Study each series to try to find a pattern to the series and to figure the rule that governs the progression. Choose the answer pair that continues the series according to the pattern established and mark its letter on your answer sheet. Correct answers are on page 145.

1. 10 11 12 10 12 12 10 ....(A) 10 11 (B) 12 10 (C) 11 10 (D) 11 12 (E) 10 12

2. 4 6 7 4 6 7 4 ....(A) 6 7 (B) 4 7 (C) 7 6 (D) 7 4 (E) 6 8

3. 10 10 9 11 11 10 12 ......(A) 13 14 (B) 12 11 (C) 13 13 (D) 12 12 (E) 12 13

4. 3 4 10 5 6 10 7 ....(A) 10 8 (B) 9 8 (C) 8 14 (D) 8 9 (E) 8 10

5. 6 6 7 7 8 8 9 ....(A) 10 11 (B) 10 10 (C) 9 10 (D) 9 9 (E) 10 9

6. 3 8 9 4 9 10 5 ....(A) 6 10 (B) 10 11 (C) 9 10 (D) 11 6 (E) 10 6

7. 2 4 3 6 4 8 5 ....(A) 6 10 (B) 10 7 (C) 10 6 (D) 9 6 (E) 6 7

8. 11 5 9 7 7 9 5 ....(A) 11 3 (B) 7 9 (C) 7 11 (D) 9 7 (E) 3 7

9. 7 16 9 15 11 14 13 ....(A) 12 14 (B) 13 15 (C) 17 15 (D) 15 12 (E) 13 12

10. 40 42 39 44 38 46 37 ....(A) 48 36 (B) 37 46 (C) 36 48 (D) 43 39 (E) 46 40

11. 1 3 6 10 15 21 28 36 ....(A) 40 48 (B) 36 45 (C) 38 52 (D) 45 56 (E) 45 55

12. 1 2 3 3 4 7 5 6 11 7 ....(A) 8 12 (B) 9 15 (C) 8 15 (D) 6 12 (E) 8 7

13. 3 18 4 24 5 30 6 ....(A) 7 40 (B) 7 42 (C) 42 7 (D) 36 7 (E) 40 7

14. 3 3 4 8 10 30 33 132 ....(A) 152 158 (B) 136 680 (C) 165 500 (D) 143 560 (E) 300 900

15. 18 20 22 20 18 20 22 ....(A) 18 20 (B) 20 18 (C) 22 20 (D) 24 20 (E) 18 22

16. 4 8 8 16 16 32 32 ....(A) 32 64 (B) 36 40 (C) 64 64 (D) 64 128 (E) 64 82

17. 1 2 12 3 4 34 5 ....(A) 6 5 (B) 7 12 (C) 5 6 (D) 6 60 (E) 6 56

18. 8 16 24 32 40 48 56 ......(A) 64 72 (B) 60 64 (C) 70 78 (D) 62 70 (E) 64 68

19. 5 15 18 54 57 171 174 ..(A) 176 528 (B) 522 821 (C) 177 531 (D) 522 525 (E) 525 528

20. 25 20 24 21 23 22 22 ....(A) 24 20 (B) 23 21 (C) 23 24 (D) 24 21 (E) 22 23

21. 99 88 77 66 55 44 33 ....(A) 22 11 (B) 33 22 (C) 44 55 (D) 32 22 (E) 30 20

22. 7 5 9 7 11 9 13 ....(A) 9 11 (B) 11 9 (C) 7 11 (D) 9 15 (E) 11 15

23. 47 44 41 38 35 32 29 ....(A) 28 27 (B) 27 24 (C) 26 23 (D) 25 21 (E) 26 22

24. 99 99 99 33 33 33 11 ....(A) 9 7 (B) 22 33 (C) 11 0 (D) 11 33 (E) 11 11

END OF NUMBER SERIES

Part D—Following Oral Instructions

Directions and Sample Questions

LISTENING TO INSTRUCTIONS: When you are ready to try these sample questions, give the following instructions to a friend and have the friend read them aloud to you at the rate of 80 words per minute. Do not read them to yourself. Your friend will need a watch with a second hand. Listen carefully and do exactly what your friend tells you to do with the worksheet and answer sheet. Your friend will tell you some things to do with each item on the worksheet. After each set of instructions, your friend will give you time to mark your answer by darkening a circle on the sample answer sheet. Since B and D sound very much alike, your friend will say "B as in baker" when he or she means B and "D as in dog" when he or she means D.

> **Before proceeding further, tear out the worksheet on page 135. Then hand this book to your friend.**

TO THE PERSON WHO IS TO READ THE INSTRUCTIONS: The instructions are to be read at the rate of 80 words per minute. Do not read aloud the material that is in parentheses. Do not repeat any instructions.

Read Aloud to the Candidate

Look at line 1 on your worksheet. (Pause slightly.) In the fourth box, write the letter A. (Pause 2 seconds.) Now, on your answer sheet, darken the space for the number-letter combination for the box you just wrote in. (Pause 5 seconds.)

Look at line 2 on your worksheet. (Pause slightly.) Circle the only letter that is in the line that is not in the word BEARD. (Pause 5 seconds.) On the answer sheet, find the answer to 9 ÷ 3. (Pause 5 seconds.) Darken the space for the letter you have circled next to the number you have found. (Pause 10 seconds.)

Look at line 3 on your worksheet. (Pause slightly.) Write the first letter of the last word in the third box. (Pause 5 seconds.) Write the last letter of the second word in the first box. (Pause 5 seconds.) Now, on your answer sheet, darken the spaces for the number-letter combinations in the two boxes you just wrote in. (Pause 10 seconds.)

Look at line 4 on your worksheet. (Pause slightly.) Draw a line under every number that is under 12 and even. (Pause 5 seconds.) Now, on your answer sheet, for each number that you drew a line under, darken space A. (Pause 5 seconds.)

Sample Worksheet

DIRECTIONS: Listening carefully to each set of instructions, mark each item on this worksheet as directed. Then complete each question by marking the sample answer sheet below as directed. For each answer you will darken the answer for a number-letter combination. Should you fall behind and miss an instruction, don't become excited. Let that one go and listen for the next one. If, when you start to darken a space for a number, you find that you have already darkened another space for that number, either erase the first mark and darken the space for the new combination or let the first mark stay and do not darken a space for the new combination. Write with a pencil that has a clean eraser. When you finish, you should have no more than one space darkened for each number.

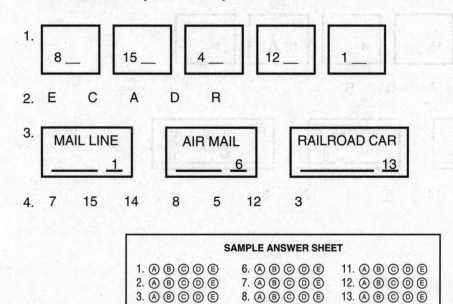

1. | 8 __ | 15 __ | 4 __ | 12 __ | 1 __ |

2. E   C   A   D   R

3. | MAIL LINE _____ 1 | AIR MAIL _____ 6 | RAILROAD CAR _____ 13 |

4. 7   15   14   8   5   12   3

SAMPLE ANSWER SHEET

1. Ⓐ Ⓑ Ⓒ Ⓓ Ⓔ	6. Ⓐ Ⓑ Ⓒ Ⓓ Ⓔ	11. Ⓐ Ⓑ Ⓒ Ⓓ Ⓔ
2. Ⓐ Ⓑ Ⓒ Ⓓ Ⓔ	7. Ⓐ Ⓑ Ⓒ Ⓓ Ⓔ	12. Ⓐ Ⓑ Ⓒ Ⓓ Ⓔ
3. Ⓐ Ⓑ Ⓒ Ⓓ Ⓔ	8. Ⓐ Ⓑ Ⓒ Ⓓ Ⓔ	13. Ⓐ Ⓑ Ⓒ Ⓓ Ⓔ
4. Ⓐ Ⓑ Ⓒ Ⓓ Ⓔ	9. Ⓐ Ⓑ Ⓒ Ⓓ Ⓔ	14. Ⓐ Ⓑ Ⓒ Ⓓ Ⓔ
5. Ⓐ Ⓑ Ⓒ Ⓓ Ⓔ	10. Ⓐ Ⓑ Ⓒ Ⓓ Ⓔ	15. Ⓐ Ⓑ Ⓒ Ⓓ Ⓔ

TEAR HERE

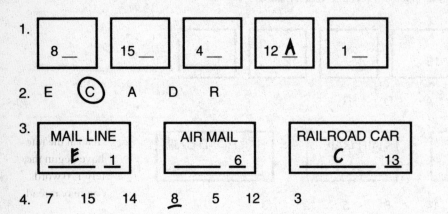

CORRECT ANSWERS TO SAMPLE QUESTIONS

1. Ⓐ Ⓑ Ⓒ Ⓓ ●   6. Ⓐ Ⓑ Ⓒ Ⓓ Ⓔ   11. Ⓐ Ⓑ Ⓒ Ⓓ Ⓔ
2. Ⓐ Ⓑ Ⓒ Ⓓ Ⓔ   7. Ⓐ Ⓑ Ⓒ Ⓓ Ⓔ   12. ● Ⓑ Ⓒ Ⓓ Ⓔ
3. Ⓐ Ⓑ ● Ⓓ Ⓔ   8. ● Ⓑ Ⓒ Ⓓ Ⓔ   13. Ⓐ Ⓑ ● Ⓓ Ⓔ
4. Ⓐ Ⓑ Ⓒ Ⓓ Ⓔ   9. Ⓐ Ⓑ Ⓒ Ⓓ Ⓔ   14. Ⓐ Ⓑ Ⓒ Ⓓ Ⓔ
5. Ⓐ Ⓑ Ⓒ Ⓓ Ⓔ   10. Ⓐ Ⓑ Ⓒ Ⓓ Ⓔ   15. Ⓐ Ⓑ Ⓒ Ⓓ Ⓔ

Correctly Filled Worksheet

1.
| 8 __ | 15 __ | 4 __ | 12 A | 1 __ |

2. E Ⓒ A D R

3.
| MAIL LINE | AIR MAIL | RAILROAD CAR |
| E ____ 1 | ____ 6 | C ____ 13 |

4. 7   15   14   8   5   12   3

Following Oral Instructions

Time: 25 Minutes

Listening to Instructions

DIRECTIONS: When you are ready to try this test of the Model Exam, give the following instructions to a friend and have the friend read them aloud to you at the rate of 80 words per minute. Do NOT read them to yourself. Your friend will need a watch with a second hand. Listen carefully and do exactly what your friend tells you to do with the worksheet and with the answer sheet. Your friend will tell you some things to do with each item on the worksheet. After each set of instructions, your friend will give you time to mark your answer by darkening a circle on the answer sheet. Since B and D sound very much alike, your friend will say "B as in baker" when he or she means B and "D as in dog" when he or she means D.

Before proceeding further, tear out the worksheet on page 141 of this test. Then hand this book to your friend.

TO THE PERSON WHO IS TO READ THE INSTRUCTIONS: The instructions are to be read at the rate of 80 words per minute. Do not read aloud the material that is in parentheses. Once you have begun the test itself, do not repeat any instructions. The next three paragraphs consist of approximately 120 words. Read these three paragraphs aloud to the candidate in about one and one-half minutes. You may reread these paragraphs as often as necessary to establish an 80-words-per-minute reading speed.

Read Aloud to the Candidate

On the job you will have to listen to directions and then do what you have been told to do. In this test, I will read instructions to you. Try to understand them as I read them; I cannot repeat them. Once we begin, you may not ask any questions until the end of the test.

On the job you won't have to deal with pictures, numbers, and letters like those in the test, but you will have to listen to instructions and follow them. We are using this test to see how well you can follow instructions.

You are to mark your test booklet according to the instructions that I'll read to you. After each set of instructions, I'll give you time to record your answers on the separate answer sheet.

The actual test begins now.

Look at line 1 on your worksheet. (Pause slightly.) Next to the left-hand number write the letter E. (Pause 2 seconds.) Now, on your answer sheet, find the space for the number beside which you wrote and darken space E. (Pause 5 seconds.)

Now look at line 2 on your worksheet. (Pause slightly.) There are 5 boxes. Each box has a letter. (Pause slightly.) In the fifth box write the answer to this question: Which of the following numbers is largest: 18, 9, 15, 19, 13? (Pause 5 seconds.) Now, on your answer sheet, darken the space for the number-letter combination that is in the box you just wrote in. (Pause 5 seconds.) In the fourth box on the same line do nothing. In the third box write 5. (Pause 2 seconds.) Now, on your answer sheet, darken the space for the number-letter combination that is in the box you just wrote in. (Pause 5 seconds.) In the second box, write the answer to this question: How many hours are there in a day? (Pause 2 seconds.) Now, on your answer sheet, darken the space for the number-letter combination that is in the box you just wrote in. (Pause 5 seconds.)

Look at line 3 on your worksheet. (Pause slightly.) Draw a line under every number that is more than 50 but less than 85. (Pause 12 seconds.) Now, on your answer sheet, for each number that you drew a line under, darken space D as in dog. (Pause 25 seconds.)

Look at line 4 on your worksheet. (Pause slightly.) Write a B as in baker in the third circle. (Pause 2 seconds.) Now, on your answer sheet, find the number in that circle and darken space B as in baker for that number. (Pause 5 seconds.)

Look at line 4 again. (Pause slightly.) Write C in the first circle. (Pause 2 seconds.) Now, on your answer sheet, find the number in that circle and darken space C for that number. (Pause 5 seconds.)

Look at line 5 on your worksheet. (Pause slightly.) There are two circles and two boxes of different sizes with numbers in them. (Pause slightly.) If 4 is more than 6 and if 9 is less than 7, write D as in dog in the smaller box. (Pause slightly.) Otherwise write A in the larger circle. (Pause 2 seconds.) Now, on your answer sheet, darken the space for the number-letter combination for the box or circle you just wrote in. (Pause 5 seconds.)

Now look at line 6 on your worksheet. (Pause slightly.) Write an E in the second circle. (Pause 2 seconds.) Now, on your answer sheet, find the number in that circle and darken space E for that number. (Pause 5 seconds.)

Now look at line 6 again. (Pause slightly.) Write a B as in baker in the middle circle. (Pause 2 seconds.) Now, on your answer sheet, find the number in that circle and darken space B as in baker for that number. (Pause 5 seconds.)

Look at the numbers on line 7 on your worksheet. (Pause slightly.) Draw a line under the largest number in the line. (Pause 2 seconds.) Now, on your answer sheet, find the number and darken space C for that number. (Pause 5 seconds.)

Now look at line 7 again. (Pause slightly.) Draw a circle around the smallest number in the line. (Pause 2 seconds.) Now, on your answer sheet, find the number that you just drew a circle around and darken space A for that number. (Pause 5 seconds.)

Now look at line 8 on your worksheet. There are 3 boxes with words and letters in them. (Pause slightly.) Each box represents a station in a large city. Station A delivers mail in the Chestnut Street area, Station B delivers mail in Hyde Park, and Station C delivers mail in the Prudential Plaza. Mr. Adams lives in Hyde Park. Write the number 30 on the line inside the box that represents the station that delivers Mr. Adams' mail. (Pause 2 seconds.) Now, on your answer sheet, find number 30 and darken the space for the letter that is in the box you just wrote in. (Pause 5 seconds.)

Now look at line 9 on your worksheet. (Pause slightly.) Write a D as in dog in the third box. (Pause 2 seconds.) Now, on your answer sheet, find the number that is in the box you just wrote in and darken space D as in dog for that number. (Pause 5 seconds.)

Now look at line 10 on your worksheet. (Pause slightly.) Draw a line under all the even numbers in line 10. (Pause 5 seconds.) Find the second number with a line drawn under it. (Pause 2 seconds.) On your answer sheet blacken space C for that number. (Pause 5 seconds.)

Now look at line 11 on your worksheet. (Pause slightly.) Count the number of C's in line 11 and write the number at the end of the line. (Pause 3 seconds.) On your answer sheet blacken the letter E for that number. (Pause 5 seconds.)

Now look at line 12 on your worksheet. (Pause slightly.) The time written in each circle represents the last pickup of the day from a particular street box. Write the last two numbers of the earliest pickup time on the line next to the letter in that circle. (Pause 2 seconds.) Now, on your answer sheet, blacken the space for the number-letter combination in the circle in which you just wrote. (Pause 5 seconds.)

Look at line 12 on the worksheet again. (Pause slightly.) Find the second earliest pickup time and write the last two numbers of the second earliest pickup time on the line next to the letter in that circle. (Pause 2 seconds.) Now, on your answer sheet, blacken the space for the number-letter combination in the circle in which you just wrote. (Pause 5 seconds.)

Look at line 13 on the worksheet. (Pause slightly.) If there are 365 days in a leap year, write the letter B as in baker in the small circle. (Pause 2 seconds.) If not, write the letter A in the triangle. (Pause 2 seconds.) Now, on your answer sheet, blacken the space for the letter-number combination in the figure in which you just wrote. (Pause 5 seconds.)

Look at line 13 again. (Pause slightly.) Write the letter D as in dog in the box with the lower number. (Pause 2 seconds.) Now, on your answer sheet, blacken the space for the number-letter combination in the box in which you just wrote. (Pause 5 seconds.)

Look at line 14 on the worksheet. (Pause slightly.) Draw two lines under all the numbers that are greater than 12 but less than 41. (Pause 8 seconds.) Count the number of numbers under which you drew two lines and blacken the letter B as in baker for that number on your answer sheet. (Pause 10 seconds.) Still on *line 14* on the worksheet (pause slightly) circle all the even numbers. (Pause 2 seconds.) Count all the numbers that you marked in any way and blacken the letter E for that number on your answer sheet. (Pause 10 seconds.)

Look at line 15 on the worksheet. (Pause slightly.) Circle the fourth letter in the line. (Pause 2 seconds.) Add together the number of hours in a day, the number of months in a year, and the number of days in a week. (Pause 10 seconds.) Now, on your answer sheet, blacken the circled letter for that number. (Pause 5 seconds.)

Look at line 16 on the worksheet. (Pause slightly.) Write the first letter of the third word in the second box. (Pause 5 seconds.) On your answer sheet, mark the number-letter combination in the box in which you just wrote. (Pause 5 seconds.) Look again at line 16. (Pause slightly.) Write the third letter of the second word in the first box. (Pause 5 seconds.) On your answer sheet, mark the number-letter combination in the box in which you just wrote. (Pause 5 seconds.) Look once more at line 16. (Pause slightly.) Write the second letter of the second word in the third box. (Pause 5 seconds.) Now, on your answer sheet, mark the number-letter combination in the box in which you just wrote. (Pause 5 seconds.)

Look at line 17 on the worksheet. (Pause slightly.) Draw a wavy line under the middle letter in the line. (Pause 2 seconds.) On your answer sheet, blacken that letter for answer space 36. (Pause 5 seconds.)

Look at line 18 on the worksheet. (Pause slightly.) Count the number of Y's in the line and write the number at the end of the line. (Pause 2 seconds.) Add 27 to that number (pause 2 seconds) and blacken B as in baker for the space that represents the total of 27 plus the number of Y's. (Pause 5 seconds.)

Look at line 19 on the worksheet. (Pause slightly.) In the last box write the answer to this question: Which of the following numbers is smaller than 20: 41, 82, 1, 36? (Pause 2 seconds.) Now, on your answer sheet, darken the space for the number-letter combination in the box you just wrote in. (Pause 5 seconds.)

Following Oral Instructions

Worksheet

DIRECTIONS: Listening carefully to each set of instructions, mark each item on this worksheet as directed. Then complete each question by marking the answer sheet as directed. For each answer you will darken the answer for a number-letter combination. Should you fall behind and miss an instruction, don't become excited. Let that one go and listen for the next one. If, when you start to darken a space for a number, you find that you have already darkened another space for that number, either erase the first mark and darken the space for the new combination or let the first mark stay and do not darken a space for the new combination. Write with a pencil that has a clean eraser. When you finish, you should have no more than one space darkened for each number. Correct answers are on page 147.

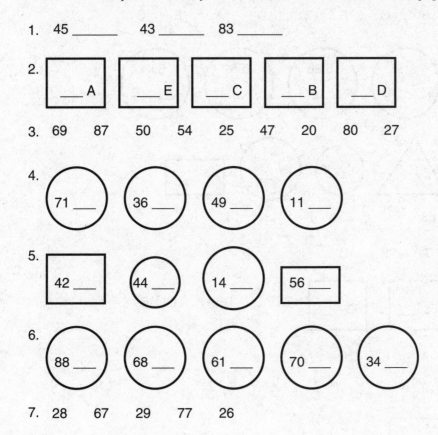

1. 45 _____   43 _____   83 _____

2. ___ A   ___ E   ___ C   ___ B   ___ D

3. 69   87   50   54   25   47   20   80   27

4. 71 ___   36 ___   49 ___   11 ___

5. 42 ___   44 ___   14 ___   56 ___

6. 88 ___   68 ___   61 ___   70 ___   34 ___

7. 28   67   29   77   26

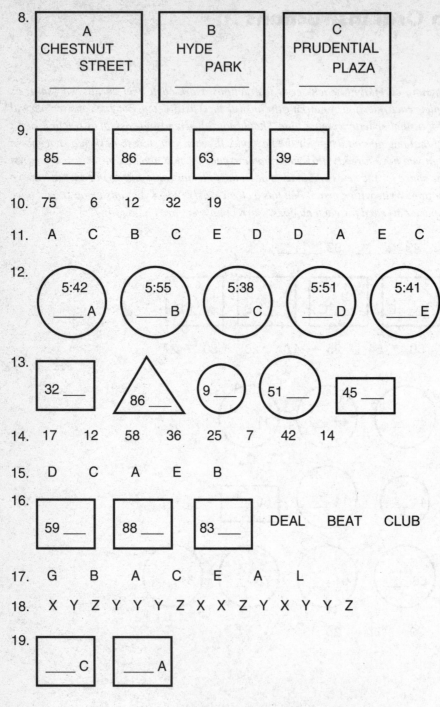

8.

| A CHESTNUT STREET _____ | B HYDE PARK _____ | C PRUDENTIAL PLAZA _____ |

9.

85 ___   86 ___   63 ___   39 ___

10. 75   6   12   32   19

11. A   C   B   C   E   D   D   A   E   C

12.

5:42 ___ A   5:55 ___ B   5:38 ___ C   5:51 ___ D   5:41 ___ E

13.

32 ___   86 ___   9 ___   51 ___   45 ___

14. 17   12   58   36   25   7   42   14

15. D   C   A   E   B

16.

59 ___   88 ___   83 ___   DEAL   BEAT   CLUB

17. G   B   A   C   E   A   L

18. X   Y   Z   Y   Y   Y   Z   X   X   Z   Y   X   Y   Y   Z

19.

___ C   ___ A

END OF EXAMINATION

Correct Answers for Second Model Exam

Part A—Address Checking

1. A	13. D	25. D	37. D	49. D	61. D	73. A	85. A
2. A	14. D	26. A	38. A	50. A	62. D	74. D	86. D
3. D	15. D	27. A	39. D	51. D	63. A	75. D	87. D
4. A	16. D	28. A	40. A	52. A	64. A	76. A	88. D
5. D	17. A	29. D	41. A	53. D	65. D	77. D	89. D
6. D	18. D	30. A	42. D	54. D	66. A	78. D	90. D
7. D	19. A	31. A	43. A	55. D	67. D	79. D	91. D
8. A	20. D	32. D	44. D	56. D	68. D	80. D	92. A
9. D	21. A	33. D	45. D	57. D	69. D	81. D	93. D
10. D	22. D	34. D	46. A	58. D	70. D	82. A	94. D
11. D	23. D	35. D	47. D	59. A	71. D	83. A	95. A
12. A	24. A	36. A	48. D	60. D	72. A	84. A	

Analyzing Your Errors

Type of Difference	Question Numbers	Number of Questions You Missed
Difference in NUMBERS	15, 32, 33, 34, 44, 47, 53, 54, 56, 68, 77, 78, 80, 89, 90	
Difference in ABBREVIATIONS	3, 9, 10, 11, 13, 14, 18, 42, 45, 48, 55, 57, 58, 62, 69, 75, 81, 91, 93, 94	
Difference in NAMES	5, 6, 7, 16, 20, 22, 23, 25, 29, 35, 37, 39, 49, 51, 60, 61, 65, 67, 70, 71, 74, 79, 86, 87, 88	
No Difference	1, 2, 4, 8, 12, 17, 19, 21, 24, 26, 27, 28, 30, 31, 36, 38, 40, 41, 43, 46, 50, 52, 59, 63, 64, 66, 72, 73, 76, 82, 83, 84, 85, 92, 95	

Part B—Memory for Addresses

Practice I

1. A	12. B	23. A	34. E	45. E	56. B	67. B	78. D
2. D	13. D	24. E	35. E	46. D	57. E	68. A	79. E
3. B	14. D	25. B	36. A	47. B	58. A	69. D	80. E
4. E	15. A	26. D	37. A	48. E	59. D	70. E	81. C
5. E	16. E	27. C	38. E	49. A	60. C	71. A	82. A
6. C	17. D	28. B	39. C	50. A	61. E	72. D	83. E
7. E	18. C	29. B	40. D	51. C	62. A	73. B	84. B
8. A	19. C	30. B	41. D	52. E	63. C	74. C	85. D
9. C	20. E	31. D	42. B	53. D	64. B	75. A	86. B
10. A	21. A	32. C	43. D	54. C	65. B	76. E	87. B
11. D	22. B	33. A	44. A	55. D	66. C	77. C	88. B

Practice II

1. C	12. A	23. D	34. A	45. B	56. B	67. D	78. B
2. C	13. C	24. B	35. A	46. E	57. C	68. B	79. B
3. E	14. E	25. A	36. C	47. B	58. C	69. D	80. D
4. A	15. D	26. E	37. E	48. D	59. C	70. E	81. E
5. B	16. D	27. D	38. C	49. B	60. D	71. B	82. A
6. D	17. A	28. C	39. A	50. C	61. E	72. C	83. E
7. B	18. C	29. E	40. D	51. D	62. A	73. B	84. C
8. D	19. B	30. D	41. A	52. E	63. A	74. C	85. B
9. E	20. A	31. A	42. C	53. A	64. E	75. E	86. D
10. E	21. C	32. B	43. D	54. D	65. A	76. A	87. C
11. E	22. B	33. C	44. B	55. E	66. A	77. D	88. E

Practice III

1. A	12. C	23. E	34. A	45. C	56. B	67. E	78. A
2. C	13. C	24. D	35. E	46. D	57. A	68. A	79. D
3. B	14. D	25. A	36. A	47. C	58. A	69. C	80. E
4. B	15. A	26. C	37. E	48. B	59. B	70. E	81. A
5. E	16. B	27. E	38. B	49. D	60. B	71. B	82. B
6. E	17. C	28. A	39. D	50. B	61. C	72. D	83. B
7. D	18. C	29. E	40. B	51. D	62. E	73. C	84. D
8. B	19. C	30. A	41. A	52. C	63. B	74. D	85. A
9. D	20. B	31. A	42. E	53. C	64. D	75. D	86. A
10. E	21. D	32. E	43. C	54. E	65. C	76. C	87. C
11. A	22. B	33. B	44. D	55. D	66. A	77. E	88. E

Memory for Addresses

1. C	12. A	23. B	34. C	45. C	56. C	67. D	78. C
2. B	13. D	24. B	35. D	46. B	57. A	68. D	79. B
3. D	14. B	25. D	36. A	47. C	58. A	69. E	80. C
4. C	15. B	26. D	37. A	48. E	59. E	70. D	81. E
5. A	16. E	27. E	38. E	49. D	60. C	71. B	82. B
6. A	17. E	28. B	39. C	50. B	61. A	72. D	83. D
7. E	18. A	29. E	40. B	51. B	62. C	73. C	84. E
8. D	19. D	30. B	41. C	52. E	63. C	74. C	85. E
9. E	20. E	31. C	42. D	53. B	64. E	75. B	86. B
10. C	21. C	32. A	43. E	54. A	65. D	76. A	87. A
11. A	22. C	33. A	44. B	55. B	66. A	77. E	88. D

Part C—Number Series

1. D	4. E	7. C	10. A	13. D	16. C	19. D	22. E
2. A	5. C	8. A	11. E	14. B	17. E	20. B	23. C
3. B	6. B	9. B	12. C	15. B	18. A	21. A	24. E

Explanations

1. **(D)** The sequence, 10 11 12, repeats itself.

2. **(A)** Another repeating sequence; this one is 4 6 7.

3. **(B)** Two sequences alternate. The first repeats itself, then advances by +1 and repeats again. The alternating sequence proceeds forward one number at a time.

4. **(E)** The sequence consists of numbers proceeding upward from <u>3</u>, with the number 10 intervening between each set of two numbers in the sequence.

5. **(C)** The numbers proceed upward from <u>6</u> by +1, with each number repeating itself.

6. **(B)** One series starts at <u>3</u> and proceeds upward by +1. The alternating series consists of two numbers that ascend according to the following rule: +1, repeat; +1, repeat.

7. **(C)** One series proceeds upward by +1. The alternating series proceeds up by +2.

8. **(A)** The first series begins with <u>11</u> and descends by –2. The alternating series begins with <u>5</u> and ascends by +2.

9. **(B)** There are two alternating series, the first ascending by +2, the other descending one number at a time.

10. **(A)** The first series descends one number at a time while the alternating series ascends at the rate of +2.

11. **(E)** The rule is +2, +3, +4, +5, +6, +7, +8, +9.

12. **(C)** Basically the series ascends 1 2 3 4 5 6 7 8, but there is a twist to this problem. The number which intervenes after each two numbers of the series is the sum of those two numbers. Thus, the series may be read: 1 + 2 = 3; 3 + 4 = 7; 5 + 6 = 11; 7 + 8 = 15.

13. **(D)** Look carefully. This is a × 6 series. 3 × 6 = 18; 4 × 6 = 24; 5 × 6 = 30; 6 × 6 = 36; 7 . . . .

14. **(B)** This one is not easy, but if you wrote out the steps between numbers, you should have come up with: × 1, + 1; × 2, + 2; × 3, + 3; × 4, + 4; × 5 . . . .

15. **(B)** This series is deceptively simple. The sequence 18 20 22 20 is repeated over and over again.

16. **(C)** The series picks up with the second member of a repeat. The pattern is × 2 and repeat, × 2 and repeat . . . .

17. **(E)** There is no mathematical formula for this series. By inspection you may see that two successive numbers are brought together to form a larger number. Thus, 1 2 12; 3 4 34; 5 6 56 . . .

18. **(A)** Straightforward +8.

19. **(D)** The pattern is × 3, + 3; × 3, + 3 . . . .

20. **(B)** There are two alternating series. The first begins with <u>25</u> and descends, one number at a time. The alternating series begins with <u>20</u> and ascends one number at a time.

21. **(A)** A simple descending series of –11.

22. **(E)** You may see this as two alternating series, both ascending in steps of + 2. You might also interpret the series as reading – 2, +4; –2, +4 . . . With either solution you should reach the correct answer.

23. **(C)** The series is a simple – 3 series that begins with an unusual number.

24. **(E)** Repeat, repeat, ÷3, repeat, repeat, ÷3, repeat, repeat, ÷3.

Part D—Following Oral Instructions

Correctly Filled Answer Grid

1 ● Ⓑ Ⓒ Ⓓ Ⓔ   23 Ⓐ Ⓑ Ⓒ Ⓓ Ⓔ   45 Ⓐ Ⓑ Ⓒ Ⓓ ●   67 Ⓐ Ⓑ Ⓒ Ⓓ Ⓔ

2 Ⓐ Ⓑ Ⓒ Ⓓ Ⓔ   24 Ⓐ Ⓑ Ⓒ Ⓓ ●   46 Ⓐ Ⓑ Ⓒ Ⓓ Ⓔ   68 Ⓐ Ⓑ Ⓒ Ⓓ ●

3 Ⓐ Ⓑ Ⓒ Ⓓ ●   25 Ⓐ Ⓑ Ⓒ Ⓓ Ⓔ   47 Ⓐ Ⓑ Ⓒ Ⓓ Ⓔ   69 Ⓐ Ⓑ Ⓒ ● Ⓔ

4 Ⓐ ● Ⓒ Ⓓ Ⓔ   26 ● Ⓑ Ⓒ Ⓓ Ⓔ   48 Ⓐ Ⓑ Ⓒ Ⓓ Ⓔ   70 Ⓐ Ⓑ Ⓒ Ⓓ Ⓔ

5 Ⓐ Ⓑ ● Ⓓ Ⓔ   27 Ⓐ Ⓑ Ⓒ Ⓓ Ⓔ   49 Ⓐ ● Ⓒ Ⓓ Ⓔ   71 Ⓐ Ⓑ ● Ⓓ Ⓔ

6 Ⓐ Ⓑ Ⓒ Ⓓ Ⓔ   28 Ⓐ Ⓑ Ⓒ Ⓓ Ⓔ   50 Ⓐ Ⓑ Ⓒ Ⓓ Ⓔ   72 Ⓐ Ⓑ Ⓒ Ⓓ Ⓔ

7 Ⓐ Ⓑ Ⓒ Ⓓ ●   29 Ⓐ Ⓑ Ⓒ Ⓓ Ⓔ   51 Ⓐ Ⓑ Ⓒ Ⓓ Ⓔ   73 Ⓐ Ⓑ Ⓒ Ⓓ Ⓔ

8 Ⓐ Ⓑ Ⓒ Ⓓ Ⓔ   30 Ⓐ ● Ⓒ Ⓓ Ⓔ   52 Ⓐ Ⓑ Ⓒ Ⓓ Ⓔ   74 Ⓐ Ⓑ Ⓒ Ⓓ Ⓔ

9 Ⓐ Ⓑ Ⓒ Ⓓ Ⓔ   31 Ⓐ Ⓑ Ⓒ Ⓓ Ⓔ   53 Ⓐ Ⓑ Ⓒ Ⓓ Ⓔ   75 Ⓐ Ⓑ Ⓒ Ⓓ Ⓔ

10 Ⓐ Ⓑ Ⓒ Ⓓ Ⓔ   32 Ⓐ Ⓑ Ⓒ ● Ⓔ   54 Ⓐ Ⓑ Ⓒ ● Ⓔ   76 Ⓐ Ⓑ Ⓒ Ⓓ Ⓔ

11 Ⓐ Ⓑ Ⓒ Ⓓ Ⓔ   33 Ⓐ Ⓑ Ⓒ Ⓓ Ⓔ   55 Ⓐ Ⓑ Ⓒ Ⓓ Ⓔ   77 Ⓐ Ⓑ ● Ⓓ Ⓔ

12 Ⓐ Ⓑ ● Ⓓ Ⓔ   34 Ⓐ ● Ⓒ Ⓓ Ⓔ   56 Ⓐ Ⓑ Ⓒ Ⓓ Ⓔ   78 Ⓐ Ⓑ Ⓒ Ⓓ Ⓔ

13 Ⓐ Ⓑ Ⓒ Ⓓ Ⓔ   35 Ⓐ Ⓑ Ⓒ Ⓓ Ⓔ   57 Ⓐ Ⓑ Ⓒ Ⓓ Ⓔ   79 Ⓐ Ⓑ Ⓒ Ⓓ Ⓔ

14 ● Ⓑ Ⓒ Ⓓ Ⓔ   36 Ⓐ Ⓑ ● Ⓓ Ⓔ   58 Ⓐ Ⓑ Ⓒ Ⓓ Ⓔ   80 Ⓐ Ⓑ Ⓒ ● Ⓔ

15 Ⓐ Ⓑ Ⓒ Ⓓ Ⓔ   37 Ⓐ Ⓑ Ⓒ Ⓓ Ⓔ   59 ● Ⓑ Ⓒ Ⓓ Ⓔ   81 Ⓐ Ⓑ Ⓒ Ⓓ Ⓔ

16 Ⓐ Ⓑ Ⓒ Ⓓ Ⓔ   38 Ⓐ Ⓑ ● Ⓓ Ⓔ   60 Ⓐ Ⓑ Ⓒ Ⓓ Ⓔ   82 Ⓐ Ⓑ Ⓒ Ⓓ Ⓔ

17 Ⓐ Ⓑ Ⓒ Ⓓ Ⓔ   39 Ⓐ Ⓑ Ⓒ Ⓓ Ⓔ   61 Ⓐ ● Ⓒ Ⓓ Ⓔ   83 Ⓐ Ⓑ Ⓒ Ⓓ ●

18 Ⓐ Ⓑ Ⓒ Ⓓ Ⓔ   40 Ⓐ Ⓑ Ⓒ Ⓓ Ⓔ   62 Ⓐ Ⓑ Ⓒ Ⓓ Ⓔ   84 Ⓐ Ⓑ Ⓒ Ⓓ Ⓔ

19 Ⓐ Ⓑ Ⓒ ● Ⓔ   41 Ⓐ Ⓑ Ⓒ Ⓓ ●   63 Ⓐ Ⓑ Ⓒ ● Ⓔ   85 Ⓐ Ⓑ Ⓒ Ⓓ Ⓔ

20 Ⓐ Ⓑ Ⓒ Ⓓ Ⓔ   42 Ⓐ Ⓑ Ⓒ Ⓓ Ⓔ   64 Ⓐ Ⓑ Ⓒ Ⓓ Ⓔ   86 ● Ⓑ Ⓒ Ⓓ Ⓔ

21 Ⓐ Ⓑ Ⓒ Ⓓ Ⓔ   43 Ⓐ Ⓑ Ⓒ Ⓓ ●   65 Ⓐ Ⓑ Ⓒ Ⓓ Ⓔ   87 Ⓐ Ⓑ Ⓒ Ⓓ Ⓔ

22 Ⓐ Ⓑ Ⓒ Ⓓ Ⓔ   44 Ⓐ Ⓑ Ⓒ Ⓓ Ⓔ   66 Ⓐ Ⓑ Ⓒ Ⓓ Ⓔ   88 Ⓐ Ⓑ ● Ⓓ Ⓔ

Correctly Filled Worksheet

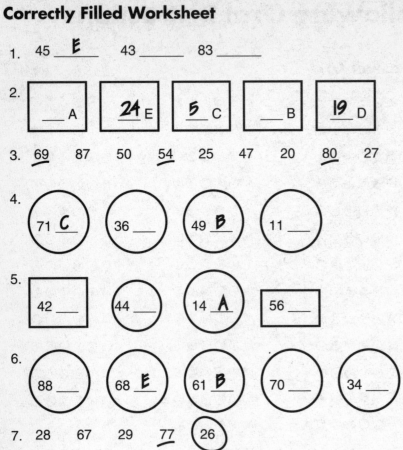

1. 45 __E__   43 _____   83 _____

2.
   | ___ A | **24** E | **5** C | ___ B | **19** D |

3. <u>69</u>   87   50   <u>54</u>   25   47   20   <u>80</u>   27

4. 71 __C__   36 ___   49 __B__   11 ___

5. 42 ___   44 ___   14 __A__   56 ___

6. 88 ___   68 __E__   61 __B__   70 ___   34 ___

7. 28   67   29   <u>77</u>   (26)

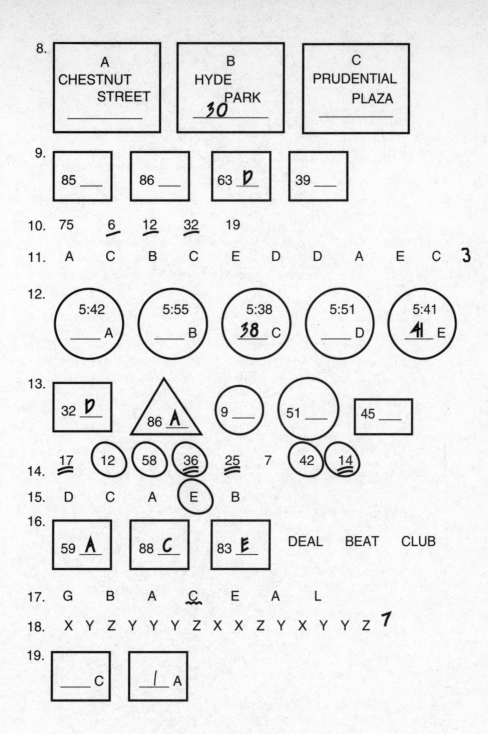

8.

| A CHESTNUT STREET _____ | B HYDE PARK _30_ | C PRUDENTIAL PLAZA _____ |

9.

| 85 ___ | 86 ___ | 63 _D_ | 39 ___ |

10. 75 _6_ _12_ _32_ 19

11. A C B C E D D A E C **3**

12.

5:42 ___ A   5:55 ___ B   5:38 _38_ C   5:51 ___ D   5:41 _41_ E

13.

| 32 _D_ | 86 _A_ | 9 ___ | 51 ___ | 45 ___ |

14. _17_ 12 58 _36_ _25_ 7 42 _14_

15. D   C   A   (E)   B

16.

| 59 _A_ | 88 _C_ | 83 _E_ | DEAL   BEAT   CLUB

17. G B A _C_ E A L

18. X Y Z Y Y Y Z X X Z Y X Y Y Z **7**

19.

| ___ C | _/_ A |

Third Model Exam
Answer Sheet

Part A—Address Checking

1. Ⓐ Ⓓ	20. Ⓐ Ⓓ	39. Ⓐ Ⓓ	58. Ⓐ Ⓓ	77. Ⓐ Ⓓ
2. Ⓐ Ⓓ	21. Ⓐ Ⓓ	40. Ⓐ Ⓓ	59. Ⓐ Ⓓ	78. Ⓐ Ⓓ
3. Ⓐ Ⓓ	22. Ⓐ Ⓓ	41. Ⓐ Ⓓ	60. Ⓐ Ⓓ	79. Ⓐ Ⓓ
4. Ⓐ Ⓓ	23. Ⓐ Ⓓ	42. Ⓐ Ⓓ	61. Ⓐ Ⓓ	80. Ⓐ Ⓓ
5. Ⓐ Ⓓ	24. Ⓐ Ⓓ	43. Ⓐ Ⓓ	62. Ⓐ Ⓓ	81. Ⓐ Ⓓ
6. Ⓐ Ⓓ	25. Ⓐ Ⓓ	44. Ⓐ Ⓓ	63. Ⓐ Ⓓ	82. Ⓐ Ⓓ
7. Ⓐ Ⓓ	26. Ⓐ Ⓓ	45. Ⓐ Ⓓ	64. Ⓐ Ⓓ	83. Ⓐ Ⓓ
8. Ⓐ Ⓓ	27. Ⓐ Ⓓ	46. Ⓐ Ⓓ	65. Ⓐ Ⓓ	84. Ⓐ Ⓓ
9. Ⓐ Ⓓ	28. Ⓐ Ⓓ	47. Ⓐ Ⓓ	66. Ⓐ Ⓓ	85. Ⓐ Ⓓ
10. Ⓐ Ⓓ	29. Ⓐ Ⓓ	48. Ⓐ Ⓓ	67. Ⓐ Ⓓ	86. Ⓐ Ⓓ
11. Ⓐ Ⓓ	30. Ⓐ Ⓓ	49. Ⓐ Ⓓ	68. Ⓐ Ⓓ	87. Ⓐ Ⓓ
12. Ⓐ Ⓓ	31. Ⓐ Ⓓ	50. Ⓐ Ⓓ	69. Ⓐ Ⓓ	88. Ⓐ Ⓓ
13. Ⓐ Ⓓ	32. Ⓐ Ⓓ	51. Ⓐ Ⓓ	70. Ⓐ Ⓓ	89. Ⓐ Ⓓ
14. Ⓐ Ⓓ	33. Ⓐ Ⓓ	52. Ⓐ Ⓓ	71. Ⓐ Ⓓ	90. Ⓐ Ⓓ
15. Ⓐ Ⓓ	34. Ⓐ Ⓓ	53. Ⓐ Ⓓ	72. Ⓐ Ⓓ	91. Ⓐ Ⓓ
16. Ⓐ Ⓓ	35. Ⓐ Ⓓ	54. Ⓐ Ⓓ	73. Ⓐ Ⓓ	92. Ⓐ Ⓓ
17. Ⓐ Ⓓ	36. Ⓐ Ⓓ	55. Ⓐ Ⓓ	74. Ⓐ Ⓓ	93. Ⓐ Ⓓ
18. Ⓐ Ⓓ	37. Ⓐ Ⓓ	56. Ⓐ Ⓓ	75. Ⓐ Ⓓ	94. Ⓐ Ⓓ
19. Ⓐ Ⓓ	38. Ⓐ Ⓓ	57. Ⓐ Ⓓ	76. Ⓐ Ⓓ	95. Ⓐ Ⓓ

TEAR HERE

Part B—Memory for Addresses

1 Ⓐ Ⓑ Ⓒ Ⓓ Ⓔ	23 Ⓐ Ⓑ Ⓒ Ⓓ Ⓔ	45 Ⓐ Ⓑ Ⓒ Ⓓ Ⓔ	67 Ⓐ Ⓑ Ⓒ Ⓓ Ⓔ
2 Ⓐ Ⓑ Ⓒ Ⓓ Ⓔ	24 Ⓐ Ⓑ Ⓒ Ⓓ Ⓔ	46 Ⓐ Ⓑ Ⓒ Ⓓ Ⓔ	68 Ⓐ Ⓑ Ⓒ Ⓓ Ⓔ
3 Ⓐ Ⓑ Ⓒ Ⓓ Ⓔ	25 Ⓐ Ⓑ Ⓒ Ⓓ Ⓔ	47 Ⓐ Ⓑ Ⓒ Ⓓ Ⓔ	69 Ⓐ Ⓑ Ⓒ Ⓓ Ⓔ
4 Ⓐ Ⓑ Ⓒ Ⓓ Ⓔ	26 Ⓐ Ⓑ Ⓒ Ⓓ Ⓔ	48 Ⓐ Ⓑ Ⓒ Ⓓ Ⓔ	70 Ⓐ Ⓑ Ⓒ Ⓓ Ⓔ
5 Ⓐ Ⓑ Ⓒ Ⓓ Ⓔ	27 Ⓐ Ⓑ Ⓒ Ⓓ Ⓔ	49 Ⓐ Ⓑ Ⓒ Ⓓ Ⓔ	71 Ⓐ Ⓑ Ⓒ Ⓓ Ⓔ
6 Ⓐ Ⓑ Ⓒ Ⓓ Ⓔ	28 Ⓐ Ⓑ Ⓒ Ⓓ Ⓔ	50 Ⓐ Ⓑ Ⓒ Ⓓ Ⓔ	72 Ⓐ Ⓑ Ⓒ Ⓓ Ⓔ
7 Ⓐ Ⓑ Ⓒ Ⓓ Ⓔ	29 Ⓐ Ⓑ Ⓒ Ⓓ Ⓔ	51 Ⓐ Ⓑ Ⓒ Ⓓ Ⓔ	73 Ⓐ Ⓑ Ⓒ Ⓓ Ⓔ
8 Ⓐ Ⓑ Ⓒ Ⓓ Ⓔ	30 Ⓐ Ⓑ Ⓒ Ⓓ Ⓔ	52 Ⓐ Ⓑ Ⓒ Ⓓ Ⓔ	74 Ⓐ Ⓑ Ⓒ Ⓓ Ⓔ
9 Ⓐ Ⓑ Ⓒ Ⓓ Ⓔ	31 Ⓐ Ⓑ Ⓒ Ⓓ Ⓔ	53 Ⓐ Ⓑ Ⓒ Ⓓ Ⓔ	75 Ⓐ Ⓑ Ⓒ Ⓓ Ⓔ
10 Ⓐ Ⓑ Ⓒ Ⓓ Ⓔ	32 Ⓐ Ⓑ Ⓒ Ⓓ Ⓔ	54 Ⓐ Ⓑ Ⓒ Ⓓ Ⓔ	76 Ⓐ Ⓑ Ⓒ Ⓓ Ⓔ
11 Ⓐ Ⓑ Ⓒ Ⓓ Ⓔ	33 Ⓐ Ⓑ Ⓒ Ⓓ Ⓔ	55 Ⓐ Ⓑ Ⓒ Ⓓ Ⓔ	77 Ⓐ Ⓑ Ⓒ Ⓓ Ⓔ
12 Ⓐ Ⓑ Ⓒ Ⓓ Ⓔ	34 Ⓐ Ⓑ Ⓒ Ⓓ Ⓔ	56 Ⓐ Ⓑ Ⓒ Ⓓ Ⓔ	78 Ⓐ Ⓑ Ⓒ Ⓓ Ⓔ
13 Ⓐ Ⓑ Ⓒ Ⓓ Ⓔ	35 Ⓐ Ⓑ Ⓒ Ⓓ Ⓔ	57 Ⓐ Ⓑ Ⓒ Ⓓ Ⓔ	79 Ⓐ Ⓑ Ⓒ Ⓓ Ⓔ
14 Ⓐ Ⓑ Ⓒ Ⓓ Ⓔ	36 Ⓐ Ⓑ Ⓒ Ⓓ Ⓔ	58 Ⓐ Ⓑ Ⓒ Ⓓ Ⓔ	80 Ⓐ Ⓑ Ⓒ Ⓓ Ⓔ
15 Ⓐ Ⓑ Ⓒ Ⓓ Ⓔ	37 Ⓐ Ⓑ Ⓒ Ⓓ Ⓔ	59 Ⓐ Ⓑ Ⓒ Ⓓ Ⓔ	81 Ⓐ Ⓑ Ⓒ Ⓓ Ⓔ
16 Ⓐ Ⓑ Ⓒ Ⓓ Ⓔ	38 Ⓐ Ⓑ Ⓒ Ⓓ Ⓔ	60 Ⓐ Ⓑ Ⓒ Ⓓ Ⓔ	82 Ⓐ Ⓑ Ⓒ Ⓓ Ⓔ
17 Ⓐ Ⓑ Ⓒ Ⓓ Ⓔ	39 Ⓐ Ⓑ Ⓒ Ⓓ Ⓔ	61 Ⓐ Ⓑ Ⓒ Ⓓ Ⓔ	83 Ⓐ Ⓑ Ⓒ Ⓓ Ⓔ
18 Ⓐ Ⓑ Ⓒ Ⓓ Ⓔ	40 Ⓐ Ⓑ Ⓒ Ⓓ Ⓔ	62 Ⓐ Ⓑ Ⓒ Ⓓ Ⓔ	84 Ⓐ Ⓑ Ⓒ Ⓓ Ⓔ
19 Ⓐ Ⓑ Ⓒ Ⓓ Ⓔ	41 Ⓐ Ⓑ Ⓒ Ⓓ Ⓔ	63 Ⓐ Ⓑ Ⓒ Ⓓ Ⓔ	85 Ⓐ Ⓑ Ⓒ Ⓓ Ⓔ
20 Ⓐ Ⓑ Ⓒ Ⓓ Ⓔ	42 Ⓐ Ⓑ Ⓒ Ⓓ Ⓔ	64 Ⓐ Ⓑ Ⓒ Ⓓ Ⓔ	86 Ⓐ Ⓑ Ⓒ Ⓓ Ⓔ
21 Ⓐ Ⓑ Ⓒ Ⓓ Ⓔ	43 Ⓐ Ⓑ Ⓒ Ⓓ Ⓔ	65 Ⓐ Ⓑ Ⓒ Ⓓ Ⓔ	87 Ⓐ Ⓑ Ⓒ Ⓓ Ⓔ
22 Ⓐ Ⓑ Ⓒ Ⓓ Ⓔ	44 Ⓐ Ⓑ Ⓒ Ⓓ Ⓔ	66 Ⓐ Ⓑ Ⓒ Ⓓ Ⓔ	88 Ⓐ Ⓑ Ⓒ Ⓓ Ⓔ

Part C—Number Series

1. Ⓐ Ⓑ Ⓒ Ⓓ Ⓔ	7. Ⓐ Ⓑ Ⓒ Ⓓ Ⓔ	13. Ⓐ Ⓑ Ⓒ Ⓓ Ⓔ	19. Ⓐ Ⓑ Ⓒ Ⓓ Ⓔ
2. Ⓐ Ⓑ Ⓒ Ⓓ Ⓔ	8. Ⓐ Ⓑ Ⓒ Ⓓ Ⓔ	14. Ⓐ Ⓑ Ⓒ Ⓓ Ⓔ	20. Ⓐ Ⓑ Ⓒ Ⓓ Ⓔ
3. Ⓐ Ⓑ Ⓒ Ⓓ Ⓔ	9. Ⓐ Ⓑ Ⓒ Ⓓ Ⓔ	15. Ⓐ Ⓑ Ⓒ Ⓓ Ⓔ	21. Ⓐ Ⓑ Ⓒ Ⓓ Ⓔ
4. Ⓐ Ⓑ Ⓒ Ⓓ Ⓔ	10. Ⓐ Ⓑ Ⓒ Ⓓ Ⓔ	16. Ⓐ Ⓑ Ⓒ Ⓓ Ⓔ	22. Ⓐ Ⓑ Ⓒ Ⓓ Ⓔ
5. Ⓐ Ⓑ Ⓒ Ⓓ Ⓔ	11. Ⓐ Ⓑ Ⓒ Ⓓ Ⓔ	17. Ⓐ Ⓑ Ⓒ Ⓓ Ⓔ	23. Ⓐ Ⓑ Ⓒ Ⓓ Ⓔ
6. Ⓐ Ⓑ Ⓒ Ⓓ Ⓔ	12. Ⓐ Ⓑ Ⓒ Ⓓ Ⓔ	18. Ⓐ Ⓑ Ⓒ Ⓓ Ⓔ	24. Ⓐ Ⓑ Ⓒ Ⓓ Ⓔ

Part D—Following Oral Instructions

1 Ⓐ Ⓑ Ⓒ Ⓓ Ⓔ   23 Ⓐ Ⓑ Ⓒ Ⓓ Ⓔ   45 Ⓐ Ⓑ Ⓒ Ⓓ Ⓔ   67 Ⓐ Ⓑ Ⓒ Ⓓ Ⓔ
2 Ⓐ Ⓑ Ⓒ Ⓓ Ⓔ   24 Ⓐ Ⓑ Ⓒ Ⓓ Ⓔ   46 Ⓐ Ⓑ Ⓒ Ⓓ Ⓔ   68 Ⓐ Ⓑ Ⓒ Ⓓ Ⓔ
3 Ⓐ Ⓑ Ⓒ Ⓓ Ⓔ   25 Ⓐ Ⓑ Ⓒ Ⓓ Ⓔ   47 Ⓐ Ⓑ Ⓒ Ⓓ Ⓔ   69 Ⓐ Ⓑ Ⓒ Ⓓ Ⓔ
4 Ⓐ Ⓑ Ⓒ Ⓓ Ⓔ   26 Ⓐ Ⓑ Ⓒ Ⓓ Ⓔ   48 Ⓐ Ⓑ Ⓒ Ⓓ Ⓔ   70 Ⓐ Ⓑ Ⓒ Ⓓ Ⓔ
5 Ⓐ Ⓑ Ⓒ Ⓓ Ⓔ   27 Ⓐ Ⓑ Ⓒ Ⓓ Ⓔ   49 Ⓐ Ⓑ Ⓒ Ⓓ Ⓔ   71 Ⓐ Ⓑ Ⓒ Ⓓ Ⓔ
6 Ⓐ Ⓑ Ⓒ Ⓓ Ⓔ   28 Ⓐ Ⓑ Ⓒ Ⓓ Ⓔ   50 Ⓐ Ⓑ Ⓒ Ⓓ Ⓔ   72 Ⓐ Ⓑ Ⓒ Ⓓ Ⓔ
7 Ⓐ Ⓑ Ⓒ Ⓓ Ⓔ   29 Ⓐ Ⓑ Ⓒ Ⓓ Ⓔ   51 Ⓐ Ⓑ Ⓒ Ⓓ Ⓔ   73 Ⓐ Ⓑ Ⓒ Ⓓ Ⓔ
8 Ⓐ Ⓑ Ⓒ Ⓓ Ⓔ   30 Ⓐ Ⓑ Ⓒ Ⓓ Ⓔ   52 Ⓐ Ⓑ Ⓒ Ⓓ Ⓔ   74 Ⓐ Ⓑ Ⓒ Ⓓ Ⓔ
9 Ⓐ Ⓑ Ⓒ Ⓓ Ⓔ   31 Ⓐ Ⓑ Ⓒ Ⓓ Ⓔ   53 Ⓐ Ⓑ Ⓒ Ⓓ Ⓔ   75 Ⓐ Ⓑ Ⓒ Ⓓ Ⓔ
10 Ⓐ Ⓑ Ⓒ Ⓓ Ⓔ   32 Ⓐ Ⓑ Ⓒ Ⓓ Ⓔ   54 Ⓐ Ⓑ Ⓒ Ⓓ Ⓔ   76 Ⓐ Ⓑ Ⓒ Ⓓ Ⓔ
11 Ⓐ Ⓑ Ⓒ Ⓓ Ⓔ   33 Ⓐ Ⓑ Ⓒ Ⓓ Ⓔ   55 Ⓐ Ⓑ Ⓒ Ⓓ Ⓔ   77 Ⓐ Ⓑ Ⓒ Ⓓ Ⓔ
12 Ⓐ Ⓑ Ⓒ Ⓓ Ⓔ   34 Ⓐ Ⓑ Ⓒ Ⓓ Ⓔ   56 Ⓐ Ⓑ Ⓒ Ⓓ Ⓔ   78 Ⓐ Ⓑ Ⓒ Ⓓ Ⓔ
13 Ⓐ Ⓑ Ⓒ Ⓓ Ⓔ   35 Ⓐ Ⓑ Ⓒ Ⓓ Ⓔ   57 Ⓐ Ⓑ Ⓒ Ⓓ Ⓔ   79 Ⓐ Ⓑ Ⓒ Ⓓ Ⓔ
14 Ⓐ Ⓑ Ⓒ Ⓓ Ⓔ   36 Ⓐ Ⓑ Ⓒ Ⓓ Ⓔ   58 Ⓐ Ⓑ Ⓒ Ⓓ Ⓔ   80 Ⓐ Ⓑ Ⓒ Ⓓ Ⓔ
15 Ⓐ Ⓑ Ⓒ Ⓓ Ⓔ   37 Ⓐ Ⓑ Ⓒ Ⓓ Ⓔ   59 Ⓐ Ⓑ Ⓒ Ⓓ Ⓔ   81 Ⓐ Ⓑ Ⓒ Ⓓ Ⓔ
16 Ⓐ Ⓑ Ⓒ Ⓓ Ⓔ   38 Ⓐ Ⓑ Ⓒ Ⓓ Ⓔ   60 Ⓐ Ⓑ Ⓒ Ⓓ Ⓔ   82 Ⓐ Ⓑ Ⓒ Ⓓ Ⓔ
17 Ⓐ Ⓑ Ⓒ Ⓓ Ⓔ   39 Ⓐ Ⓑ Ⓒ Ⓓ Ⓔ   61 Ⓐ Ⓑ Ⓒ Ⓓ Ⓔ   83 Ⓐ Ⓑ Ⓒ Ⓓ Ⓔ
18 Ⓐ Ⓑ Ⓒ Ⓓ Ⓔ   40 Ⓐ Ⓑ Ⓒ Ⓓ Ⓔ   62 Ⓐ Ⓑ Ⓒ Ⓓ Ⓔ   84 Ⓐ Ⓑ Ⓒ Ⓓ Ⓔ
19 Ⓐ Ⓑ Ⓒ Ⓓ Ⓔ   41 Ⓐ Ⓑ Ⓒ Ⓓ Ⓔ   63 Ⓐ Ⓑ Ⓒ Ⓓ Ⓔ   85 Ⓐ Ⓑ Ⓒ Ⓓ Ⓔ
20 Ⓐ Ⓑ Ⓒ Ⓓ Ⓔ   42 Ⓐ Ⓑ Ⓒ Ⓓ Ⓔ   64 Ⓐ Ⓑ Ⓒ Ⓓ Ⓔ   86 Ⓐ Ⓑ Ⓒ Ⓓ Ⓔ
21 Ⓐ Ⓑ Ⓒ Ⓓ Ⓔ   43 Ⓐ Ⓑ Ⓒ Ⓓ Ⓔ   65 Ⓐ Ⓑ Ⓒ Ⓓ Ⓔ   87 Ⓐ Ⓑ Ⓒ Ⓓ Ⓔ
22 Ⓐ Ⓑ Ⓒ Ⓓ Ⓔ   44 Ⓐ Ⓑ Ⓒ Ⓓ Ⓔ   66 Ⓐ Ⓑ Ⓒ Ⓓ Ⓔ   88 Ⓐ Ⓑ Ⓒ Ⓓ Ⓔ

TEAR HERE

SCORE SHEET

ADDRESS CHECKING: Your score on the Address Checking part is based upon the number of questions you answered correctly minus the number of questions you answered incorrectly. To determine your score, subtract the number of wrong answers from the number of correct answers.

Number Right	–	Number Wrong	=	Raw Score
_____	–	_____	=	_____

MEMORY FOR ADDRESSES: Your score on the Memory for Addresses part is based upon the number of questions you answered correctly minus one-fourth of the questions you answered incorrectly (number wrong divided by 4). Calculate this now:

Number Wrong ÷ 4 = _____ .

Number Right	–	Number Wrong	÷	4	=	Raw Score
_____	–	_____			=	_____

NUMBER SERIES: Your score on the Number Series part is based only on the number of questions you answered correctly. Wrong answers do not count against you.

Number Right	=	Raw Score
_____	=	_____

FOLLOWING ORAL INSTRUCTIONS: Your score on the Following Oral Instructions part is based only upon the number of questions you marked correctly on the answer sheet. The worksheet is not scored, and wrong answers on the answer sheet do not count against you.

Number Right	=	Raw Score
_____	=	_____

TOTAL SCORE: To find your total raw score, add together the raw scores for each section of the exam.

Address Checking Score   _____
+
Memory for Addresses Score   _____
+
Number Series Score   _____
+
Following Oral Instructions Score   _____
=
    _____
Total Raw Score   _____

Self Evaluation Chart

Calculate your raw score for each test as shown above. Then check to see where your score falls on the scale from Poor to Excellent. Lightly shade in the boxes in which your scores fall.

Part	Excellent	Good	Average	Fair	Poor
Address Checking	80–95	65–79	50–64	35–49	1–34
Memory for Addresses	75–88	60–74	45–59	30–44	1–29
Number Series	21–24	18–20	14–17	11–13	1–10
Following Oral Instructions	27–31	23–26	19–22	14–18	1–13

Third Model Exam

Part A—Address Checking

Sample Questions

You will be allowed three minutes to read the directions and answer the five sample questions that follow. On the actual test, however, you will have only six minutes to answer 95 questions, so see how quickly you can compare addresses and still get the correct answer.

DIRECTIONS: Each question consists of two addresses. If the two addresses are alike in EVERY *way, mark A on your answer sheet. If the two addresses are* different in ANY *way, mark D on your answer sheet.*

1 ... 1706 Artillery La   1706 Artillery Ln

2 ... 4464 Baroque Blvd   4644 Baroque Blvd

3 ... Santa Cruz CA 95064   Santa Cruz GA 95064

4 ... 2859 SW 145th Dr   2859 SW 145th Dr

5 ... 1984 Oregon Ave SE   1984 Oregon Ave SE

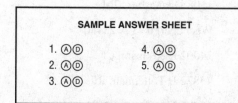

SAMPLE ANSWER SHEET		CORRECT ANSWERS	
1. Ⓐ Ⓓ	4. Ⓐ Ⓓ	1. Ⓐ ●	4. ● Ⓓ
2. Ⓐ Ⓓ	5. Ⓐ Ⓓ	2. Ⓐ ●	5. ● Ⓓ
3. Ⓐ Ⓓ		3. Ⓐ ●	

Address Checking

Time: 6 Minutes. 95 Questions.

*DIRECTIONS: For each question, compare the address in the left column with the address in the right column. If the two addresses are ALIKE IN **EVERY** WAY, blacken space A on your answer sheet. If the two addresses are DIFFERENT IN **ANY** WAY, blacken space D on your answer sheet. Correct answers for this test are on page 179.*

1	12310 Clairmond Pl	12310 Clarimond Pl
2	24038 Johnson Rd	24038 Johnston Rd
3	578 Abraham Kazan Blvd	5788 Abraham Kazan Blvd
4	11390 W Wynnewood Rd	11390 E Wynnewood Rd
5	11000 W 221st St	11000 W 221st St
6	Canadiqua NY 14424	Canadiqua NY 14424
7	13450 Montgomery Park	13450 Montegomery Park
8	16235 Zimbrich Dr	16235 Zimbrench Dr
9	43961 Remmington Ave	43691 Remmington Ave
10	11236 Shorewood Ln	11236 Sherwood Ln
11	16002 Dalewood Gardens	1602 Dalewood Gardens
12	11335 Yarkerdale Dr	11335 Yorkerdale Dr
13	12305 NE Teutonia Ave	12305 NW Teutonia Ave
14	1508 Duanesburg Rd	1508 Duanesburg Rd
15	Wachapregue VA 23480	Wachapergue VA 23480
16	34001 E Atkinson Cir	34001 E Atkinson Ct
17	43872 E Tottenham Rd	43872 E Tottenham Rd
18	13531 Yancey Ave NE	13531 Yancey Ave NW
19	14615 Lost Mountain Trl	14615 Last Mountain Trl
20	11633 N Abingdon Pl	11633 N Abingdon Pl
21	14609 Lakeview Ter	14609 Lakeview Park
22	10001 N Magee Ave	10001 N McGee Ave
23	14617 Quattara Blvd	14716 Quattara Blvd
24	98 North Timberland Rd	98 North Timberland Rd
25	14615 Coca Cola Park	14615 Coca Cola Pky
26	13444 Glenthorne Way	13444 Glenthorne Way
27	16567 Pinnacle Rd	16567 Pinnacel Rd
28	12726 N Montaine Park	12726 S Montaine Park
29	5071 E Trelawne Dr	5071 E Treelawne Dr

30 ...5304 SE Winterroth St	5304 SE Winterroth St
31 ...Emancipation PR 00802	Emancipation PR 00802
32 ...11925 Resolute Cir	11925 Resolute Dr
33 ...31011 Lynchford Park A	31011 Lynchford Park B
34 ...12306 Woolacott Rd	12306 Woolacott St
35 ...31991 Abbottsford Rd	31991 Abbotsford Rd
36 ...14201 W Galbraith Ave	14201 W Galbraith Ave
37 ...11367 Olentangy Ln	11367 Olengtongy Ln
38 ...11235 N Zumstein Ave	11235 N Zomstein Ave
39 ...21003 NE Cronwell Blvd	21003 NE Cromwell Blvd
40 ...11450 S Westonridge Dr	14150 S Westonridge Dr
41 ...22122 Jonguilmeadow Rd	22122 Jonquilmeadow Rd
42 ...4434 N Glenorchard Pl	4434 N Glenorchard Ln
43 ...12087 Neyartnell Pky	12087 Neyartell Pky
44 ...31756 Falconbridge Dr	31756 Falconbridge Dr
45 ...Stambaugh MI 49964	Stanbaugh MI 49964
46 ...16735 Halidonhill Ln	16735 Hanlidonhill Ln
47 ...13299 La Boiteaux Ave	1329 La Boiteaux Ave
48 ...10154 Ottercreek Rd	10154 Ottercreek Rd
49 ...4867 NE Kellerman Ct	4867 NE Kellerman Ct
50 ...16089 Carnation Cir	16089 Carnation Dr
51 ...12196 SE Kensington Pl	12196 SE Kensington Pl
52 ...7800 SE Grantham Way	7800 SE Grantham Way
53 ...10697 Indianbluff Dr	10997 Indianbluff Dr
54 ...2200 Amberacres Rd	2200 Amberacers Rd
55 ...3901 Paulmeadows Dr	3901 Paulmeadows Dr
56 ...4201 Tanagerwoods Ln	4201 Tanagerwoods Ln
57 ...1399 Clarendon Ave NE	1399 Clarendon Ave SE
58 ...6377 Kuenerle Ct NE	6377 Kuenerle Cir NE
59 ...12397 Reicosky Ln NW	12397 Reikosky Ln NW
60 ...4600 Henrietta Ave SE	4600 Henrietta Ave SE
61 ...5263 Tuscarawas W	5263 Tuscarawas W
62 ...3567 Villa Padova Dr NW	3567 Villa Padova Dr NW
63 ...1190 Edinberry Dr SE	1190 Edinbury Dr SE

64 ... 1107 NE Julie Ann Cir	1107 NE Julie Anna Cir
65 ... 11300 South Central Ave	11300 South Center Ave
66 ... 11205 Trenaman Cir	11205 Trenamar Cir
67 ... 2288 Altament Ave	2288 Altament St
68 ... 4056 Sprucewood Ln NW	4056 Sprucewood Ln SW
69 ... Cynthiana OH 45624	Cynthiana OH 45642
70 ... 1257 Zesiger Ave	1257 Zesinger Ave
71 ... 2697 Demington Ave NW	2697 Demington Ave NW
72 ... 3401 East Nimidila Rd	3401 East Nimidila Rd
73 ... 801 Airymeadows Ln	801 Airymeadows Ln
74 ... 1795 NE 24th Avenue	1795 NW 24th Avenue
75 ... PO Box 41001	PO Box 41081
76 ... 11299 Wolverine Ct SE	11929 Wolverine Ct SE
77 ... 1800 Youngdale Ave NW	1800 Youngdale St NW
78 ... 25011 Fulmore Pl NW	25011 Filmore Pl NW
79 ... 5700 Inverness Pky NW	5700 Inverness Pky NW
80 ... 699 Mount Marie Ave SE	699 Mount Maria Ave SE
81 ... 1166 Schwalm Ave SE	1166 Schwalm Ave SE
82 ... 7744 Otterbein Trl	7744 Otterbein Trl
83 ... Fort Steilacoon WA 98494	Fort Stielacoon WA 98494
84 ... 1155 Parkridge Cir NW	1155 Partridge Cir NW
85 ... 3477 Eastbury Ave NE	3477 Eastbury St NE
86 ... 25501 Gambrinus Ct SE	2501 Gambrinus Ct SE
87 ... 11089 Nicklaus St NW	11909 Nicklaus St NW
88 ... 5500 Knollridge Dr NW	5500 Knollridge Cir NW
89 ... 2203 Forestdale Pl SE	2203 Forestdale Pl NE
90 ... 11449 Vaniman Trl	11449 Vaniman Trl
91 ... 9903 Hometown Rd S	9903 Hometown Rd S
92 ... 13468 Ritchie Ave	13486 Ritchie Ave
93 ... Tununak AK 99681	Tununak AR 99681
94 ... 400 Nimishillen Church Rd	400 Nimishollen Church Rd
95 ... 3577 Brunnerdale Ct NW	3577 Brunnerdale St NW

END OF ADDRESS CHECKING

Part B—Memory for Addresses

Sample Questions

The sample questions for this part are based upon the addresses in the five boxes below. Your task is to mark on your answer sheet the letter of the box in which each address belongs. You will have five minutes now to study the locations of the addresses. Then cover the boxes and try to mark the location of the sample questions. You may look back at the boxes if you cannot yet mark the address locations from memory.

The exam itself provides three practice sessions before the question set that really counts. Practice I and Practice III supply you with the boxes and permit you to refer to them if necessary. Practice II and the Memory for Addresses test itself do not permit you to look at the boxes. The test itself is based on memory.

A	B	C	D	E
2300–3499 Club	3500–3999 Club	4000–4299 Club	1200–2199 Club	2200–2299 Club
Unit	Summer	Hopper	Magnet	Carrot
4000–4299 Pine	2200–2299 Pine	1200–2199 Pine	3500–3999 Pine	2300–3499 Pine
Iron	Boulder	Window	Press	Timber
1200–2199 Arch	2300–3499 Arch	3500–3999 Arch	2200–2299 Arch	4000–4299 Arch

1. Summer

2. 2200–2299 Pine

3. 1200–2199 Arch

4. 4000–4299 Club

5. Press

6. Carrot

7. 2200–2299 Arch

8. 2200–2299 Club

9. 4000–4299 Pine

10. 3500–3999 Club

11. Boulder

12. Timber

13. 1200–2199 Pine

14. 2300–3499 Arch

SAMPLE ANSWER SHEET

1. Ⓐ Ⓑ Ⓒ Ⓓ Ⓔ
2. Ⓐ Ⓑ Ⓒ Ⓓ Ⓔ
3. Ⓐ Ⓑ Ⓒ Ⓓ Ⓔ
4. Ⓐ Ⓑ Ⓒ Ⓓ Ⓔ
5. Ⓐ Ⓑ Ⓒ Ⓓ Ⓔ
6. Ⓐ Ⓑ Ⓒ Ⓓ Ⓔ
7. Ⓐ Ⓑ Ⓒ Ⓓ Ⓔ
8. Ⓐ Ⓑ Ⓒ Ⓓ Ⓔ
9. Ⓐ Ⓑ Ⓒ Ⓓ Ⓔ
10. Ⓐ Ⓑ Ⓒ Ⓓ Ⓔ
11. Ⓐ Ⓑ Ⓒ Ⓓ Ⓔ
12. Ⓐ Ⓑ Ⓒ Ⓓ Ⓔ
13. Ⓐ Ⓑ Ⓒ Ⓓ Ⓔ
14. Ⓐ Ⓑ Ⓒ Ⓓ Ⓔ

CORRECT ANSWERS

1. Ⓐ ● Ⓒ Ⓓ Ⓔ
2. Ⓐ ● Ⓒ Ⓓ Ⓔ
3. ● Ⓑ Ⓒ Ⓓ Ⓔ
4. Ⓐ Ⓑ ● Ⓓ Ⓔ
5. Ⓐ Ⓑ Ⓒ ● Ⓔ
6. Ⓐ Ⓑ Ⓒ Ⓓ ●
7. Ⓐ Ⓑ Ⓒ ● Ⓔ
8. Ⓐ Ⓑ Ⓒ Ⓓ ●
9. ● Ⓑ Ⓒ Ⓓ Ⓔ
10. Ⓐ ● Ⓒ Ⓓ Ⓔ
11. Ⓐ ● Ⓒ Ⓓ Ⓔ
12. Ⓐ Ⓑ Ⓒ Ⓓ ●
13. Ⓐ Ⓑ ● Ⓓ Ⓔ
14. Ⓐ ● Ⓒ Ⓓ Ⓔ

Practice for Memory for Addresses

DIRECTIONS: The five boxes below are labelled A, B, C, D, and E. In each box are three sets of number spans with names and two names that are not associated with numbers. In the next THREE MINUTES, you must try to memorize the box location of each name and number span. The position of a name or number span within its box is not important. You need only remember the letter of the box in which the item is to be found. You will use these names and numbers to answer three sets of practice questions that are NOT scored and one actual test that is scored. Correct answers are on pages 180 and 181.

A	B	C	D	E
2300–3499 Club	3500–3999 Club	4000–4299 Club	1200–2199 Club	2200–2299 Club
Unit	Summer	Hopper	Magnet	Carrot
4000–4299 Pine	2200–2299 Pine	1200–2199 Pine	3500–3999 Pine	2300–3499 Pine
Iron	Boulder	Window	Press	Timber
1200–2199 Arch	2300–3499 Arch	3500–3999 Arch	2200–2299 Arch	4000–4299 Arch

Practice I

DIRECTIONS: Use the next THREE MINUTES to mark on the Practice I answer sheet the letter of the box in which each item that follows is to be found. Try to mark each item without looking back at the boxes. If, however, you get stuck, you may refer to the boxes during this practice exercise. If you find that you must look at the boxes, try to memorize as you do so. This test is for practice only. It will not be scored.

1. 3500–3999 Pine	20. Press	39. 3500–3999 Club
2. 2300–3499 Arch	21. 2300–3499 Arch	40. 2200–2299 Club
3. Iron	22. 4000–4299 Pine	41. Timber
4. Timber	23. 4000–4299 Arch	42. Window
5. 4000–4299 Club	24. 3500–3999 Pine	43. 3500–3999 Pine
6. 2300–3299 Pine	25. Magnet	44. 2300–3499 Arch
7. 3500–3999 Arch	26. Boulder	45. 2300–3499 Club
8. 2300–3499 Club	27. Summer	46. 2200–2299 Pine
9. Magnet	28. 4000–4299 Club	47. 3500–3999 Arch
10. Carrot	29. 2300–3499 Club	48. 3500–3999 Pine
11. 2200–2299 Arch	30. 3500–3999 Arch	49. 2200–2299 Club
12. 3500–3999 Club	31. 1200–2199 Arch	50. Magnet
13. 2200–2299 Club	32. Unit	51. Window
14. 4000–4299 Pine	33. Carrot	52. Summer
15. Unit	34. 2200–2299 Pine	53. 4000–4299 Arch
16. Summer	35. 2300–3499 Pine	54. Press
17. 1200–2199 Pine	36. Hopper	55. 1200–2199 Pine
18. 1200–2199 Club	37. Iron	56. Boulder
19. Window	38. 2200–2299 Arch	57. 1200–2199 Arch

58. 4000–4299 Pine

59. 2300–3499 Pine

60. 4000–4299 Club

61. Carrot

62. Timber

63. 1200–2199 Club

64. 3500–3999 Club

65. 2300–3499 Arch

66. Unit

67. Hopper

68. 2200–2299 Arch

69. Iron

70. 1200–2199 Pine

71. 3500–3999 Arch

72. Boulder

73. 2200–2299 Club

74. 1200–2199 Arch

75. Press

76. Carrot

77. 4000–4299 Arch

78. 4000–4299 Pine

79. 2300–3499 Club

80. 3500–3999 Pine

81. Window

82. Hopper

83. Boulder

84. 1200–2199 Pine

85. 1200–2199 Club

86. 2300–3499 Arch

87. Summer

88. Unit

Practice I Answer Sheet

1 Ⓐ Ⓑ Ⓒ Ⓓ Ⓔ
2 Ⓐ Ⓑ Ⓒ Ⓓ Ⓔ
3 Ⓐ Ⓑ Ⓒ Ⓓ Ⓔ
4 Ⓐ Ⓑ Ⓒ Ⓓ Ⓔ
5 Ⓐ Ⓑ Ⓒ Ⓓ Ⓔ
6 Ⓐ Ⓑ Ⓒ Ⓓ Ⓔ
7 Ⓐ Ⓑ Ⓒ Ⓓ Ⓔ
8 Ⓐ Ⓑ Ⓒ Ⓓ Ⓔ
9 Ⓐ Ⓑ Ⓒ Ⓓ Ⓔ
10 Ⓐ Ⓑ Ⓒ Ⓓ Ⓔ
11 Ⓐ Ⓑ Ⓒ Ⓓ Ⓔ
12 Ⓐ Ⓑ Ⓒ Ⓓ Ⓔ
13 Ⓐ Ⓑ Ⓒ Ⓓ Ⓔ
14 Ⓐ Ⓑ Ⓒ Ⓓ Ⓔ
15 Ⓐ Ⓑ Ⓒ Ⓓ Ⓔ
16 Ⓐ Ⓑ Ⓒ Ⓓ Ⓔ
17 Ⓐ Ⓑ Ⓒ Ⓓ Ⓔ
18 Ⓐ Ⓑ Ⓒ Ⓓ Ⓔ
19 Ⓐ Ⓑ Ⓒ Ⓓ Ⓔ
20 Ⓐ Ⓑ Ⓒ Ⓓ Ⓔ
21 Ⓐ Ⓑ Ⓒ Ⓓ Ⓔ
22 Ⓐ Ⓑ Ⓒ Ⓓ Ⓔ

23 Ⓐ Ⓑ Ⓒ Ⓓ Ⓔ
24 Ⓐ Ⓑ Ⓒ Ⓓ Ⓔ
25 Ⓐ Ⓑ Ⓒ Ⓓ Ⓔ
26 Ⓐ Ⓑ Ⓒ Ⓓ Ⓔ
27 Ⓐ Ⓑ Ⓒ Ⓓ Ⓔ
28 Ⓐ Ⓑ Ⓒ Ⓓ Ⓔ
29 Ⓐ Ⓑ Ⓒ Ⓓ Ⓔ
30 Ⓐ Ⓑ Ⓒ Ⓓ Ⓔ
31 Ⓐ Ⓑ Ⓒ Ⓓ Ⓔ
32 Ⓐ Ⓑ Ⓒ Ⓓ Ⓔ
33 Ⓐ Ⓑ Ⓒ Ⓓ Ⓔ
34 Ⓐ Ⓑ Ⓒ Ⓓ Ⓔ
35 Ⓐ Ⓑ Ⓒ Ⓓ Ⓔ
36 Ⓐ Ⓑ Ⓒ Ⓓ Ⓔ
37 Ⓐ Ⓑ Ⓒ Ⓓ Ⓔ
38 Ⓐ Ⓑ Ⓒ Ⓓ Ⓔ
39 Ⓐ Ⓑ Ⓒ Ⓓ Ⓔ
40 Ⓐ Ⓑ Ⓒ Ⓓ Ⓔ
41 Ⓐ Ⓑ Ⓒ Ⓓ Ⓔ
42 Ⓐ Ⓑ Ⓒ Ⓓ Ⓔ
43 Ⓐ Ⓑ Ⓒ Ⓓ Ⓔ
44 Ⓐ Ⓑ Ⓒ Ⓓ Ⓔ

45 Ⓐ Ⓑ Ⓒ Ⓓ Ⓔ
46 Ⓐ Ⓑ Ⓒ Ⓓ Ⓔ
47 Ⓐ Ⓑ Ⓒ Ⓓ Ⓔ
48 Ⓐ Ⓑ Ⓒ Ⓓ Ⓔ
49 Ⓐ Ⓑ Ⓒ Ⓓ Ⓔ
50 Ⓐ Ⓑ Ⓒ Ⓓ Ⓔ
51 Ⓐ Ⓑ Ⓒ Ⓓ Ⓔ
52 Ⓐ Ⓑ Ⓒ Ⓓ Ⓔ
53 Ⓐ Ⓑ Ⓒ Ⓓ Ⓔ
54 Ⓐ Ⓑ Ⓒ Ⓓ Ⓔ
55 Ⓐ Ⓑ Ⓒ Ⓓ Ⓔ
56 Ⓐ Ⓑ Ⓒ Ⓓ Ⓔ
57 Ⓐ Ⓑ Ⓒ Ⓓ Ⓔ
58 Ⓐ Ⓑ Ⓒ Ⓓ Ⓔ
59 Ⓐ Ⓑ Ⓒ Ⓓ Ⓔ
60 Ⓐ Ⓑ Ⓒ Ⓓ Ⓔ
61 Ⓐ Ⓑ Ⓒ Ⓓ Ⓔ
62 Ⓐ Ⓑ Ⓒ Ⓓ Ⓔ
63 Ⓐ Ⓑ Ⓒ Ⓓ Ⓔ
64 Ⓐ Ⓑ Ⓒ Ⓓ Ⓔ
65 Ⓐ Ⓑ Ⓒ Ⓓ Ⓔ
66 Ⓐ Ⓑ Ⓒ Ⓓ Ⓔ

67 Ⓐ Ⓑ Ⓒ Ⓓ Ⓔ
68 Ⓐ Ⓑ Ⓒ Ⓓ Ⓔ
69 Ⓐ Ⓑ Ⓒ Ⓓ Ⓔ
70 Ⓐ Ⓑ Ⓒ Ⓓ Ⓔ
71 Ⓐ Ⓑ Ⓒ Ⓓ Ⓔ
72 Ⓐ Ⓑ Ⓒ Ⓓ Ⓔ
73 Ⓐ Ⓑ Ⓒ Ⓓ Ⓔ
74 Ⓐ Ⓑ Ⓒ Ⓓ Ⓔ
75 Ⓐ Ⓑ Ⓒ Ⓓ Ⓔ
76 Ⓐ Ⓑ Ⓒ Ⓓ Ⓔ
77 Ⓐ Ⓑ Ⓒ Ⓓ Ⓔ
78 Ⓐ Ⓑ Ⓒ Ⓓ Ⓔ
79 Ⓐ Ⓑ Ⓒ Ⓓ Ⓔ
80 Ⓐ Ⓑ Ⓒ Ⓓ Ⓔ
81 Ⓐ Ⓑ Ⓒ Ⓓ Ⓔ
82 Ⓐ Ⓑ Ⓒ Ⓓ Ⓔ
83 Ⓐ Ⓑ Ⓒ Ⓓ Ⓔ
84 Ⓐ Ⓑ Ⓒ Ⓓ Ⓔ
85 Ⓐ Ⓑ Ⓒ Ⓓ Ⓔ
86 Ⓐ Ⓑ Ⓒ Ⓓ Ⓔ
87 Ⓐ Ⓑ Ⓒ Ⓓ Ⓔ
88 Ⓐ Ⓑ Ⓒ Ⓓ Ⓔ

Practice II

DIRECTIONS: The next 88 questions constitute another practice exercise. Mark your answers on the Practice II answer sheet. Again, the time limit is THREE MINUTES. This time, however, you must NOT look at the boxes while answering the questions. You must rely on your memory in marking the box location of each item. This practice test will not be scored.

1. 2300–3499 Pine	31. 4000–4299 Club	61. 4000–4299 Arch
2. 2200–2299 Arch	32. 2300–3499 Club	62. Carrot
3. 3500–3999 Club	33. 4000–4299 Pine	63. Unit
4. 1200–2199 Arch	34. 2300–3499 Arch	64. 3500–3999 Pine
5. Hopper	35. Boulder	65. 2300–3499 Club
6. Carrot	36. Unit	66. 3500–3999 Club
7. 4000–4299 Club	37. Timber	67. Summer
8. 1200–2199 Pine	38. 2200–2299 Pine	68. Boulder
9. 2300–3499 Arch	39. 4000–4299 Arch	69. 1200–2199 Arch
10. Timber	40. 3500–3999 Pine	70. Magnet
11. Boulder	41. Summer	71. Window
12. 4000–4299 Pine	42. Carrot	72. 4000–4299 Club
13. 2200–2299 Club	43. 3500–3999 Arch	73. 3500–3999 Arch
14. 1200–2199 Arch	44. 2200–2299 Club	74. 2200–2299 Club
15. 3500–3999 Pine	45. 3500–3999 Club	75. 4000–4299 Arch
16. Magnet	46. Iron	76. 2300–3499 Club
17. Summer	47. 1200–2199 Club	77. 3500–3999 Pine
18. Unit	48. 4000–4299 Pine	78. 2200–2299 Pine
19. 3500–3999 Arch	49. 2200–2299 Arch	79. Summer
20. 1200–2199 Club	50. Press	80. Hopper
21. 2300–3499 Club	51. Timber	81. 1200–2199 Pine
22. 2200–2299 Pine	52. 2200–2299 Club	82. 1200–2199 Arch
23. Iron	53. 1200–2199 Pine	83. 2200–2299 Club
24. Press	54. 2300–3499 Arch	84. Carrot
25. Window	55. 3500–3999 Arch	85. Iron
26. 1200–2199 Club	56. Hopper	86. Unit
27. 1200–2199 Pine	57. Iron	87. 3500–3999 Club
28. 2200–2299 Arch	58. 4000–4299 Club	88. 2200–2299 Arch
29. Hopper	59. 2200–2299 Pine	
30. Magnet	60. 2300–3499 Pine	

Practice II Answer Sheet

1 Ⓐ Ⓑ Ⓒ Ⓓ Ⓔ	23 Ⓐ Ⓑ Ⓒ Ⓓ Ⓔ	45 Ⓐ Ⓑ Ⓒ Ⓓ Ⓔ	67 Ⓐ Ⓑ Ⓒ Ⓓ Ⓔ
2 Ⓐ Ⓑ Ⓒ Ⓓ Ⓔ	24 Ⓐ Ⓑ Ⓒ Ⓓ Ⓔ	46 Ⓐ Ⓑ Ⓒ Ⓓ Ⓔ	68 Ⓐ Ⓑ Ⓒ Ⓓ Ⓔ
3 Ⓐ Ⓑ Ⓒ Ⓓ Ⓔ	25 Ⓐ Ⓑ Ⓒ Ⓓ Ⓔ	47 Ⓐ Ⓑ Ⓒ Ⓓ Ⓔ	69 Ⓐ Ⓑ Ⓒ Ⓓ Ⓔ
4 Ⓐ Ⓑ Ⓒ Ⓓ Ⓔ	26 Ⓐ Ⓑ Ⓒ Ⓓ Ⓔ	48 Ⓐ Ⓑ Ⓒ Ⓓ Ⓔ	70 Ⓐ Ⓑ Ⓒ Ⓓ Ⓔ
5 Ⓐ Ⓑ Ⓒ Ⓓ Ⓔ	27 Ⓐ Ⓑ Ⓒ Ⓓ Ⓔ	49 Ⓐ Ⓑ Ⓒ Ⓓ Ⓔ	71 Ⓐ Ⓑ Ⓒ Ⓓ Ⓔ
6 Ⓐ Ⓑ Ⓒ Ⓓ Ⓔ	28 Ⓐ Ⓑ Ⓒ Ⓓ Ⓔ	50 Ⓐ Ⓑ Ⓒ Ⓓ Ⓔ	72 Ⓐ Ⓑ Ⓒ Ⓓ Ⓔ
7 Ⓐ Ⓑ Ⓒ Ⓓ Ⓔ	29 Ⓐ Ⓑ Ⓒ Ⓓ Ⓔ	51 Ⓐ Ⓑ Ⓒ Ⓓ Ⓔ	73 Ⓐ Ⓑ Ⓒ Ⓓ Ⓔ
8 Ⓐ Ⓑ Ⓒ Ⓓ Ⓔ	30 Ⓐ Ⓑ Ⓒ Ⓓ Ⓔ	52 Ⓐ Ⓑ Ⓒ Ⓓ Ⓔ	74 Ⓐ Ⓑ Ⓒ Ⓓ Ⓔ
9 Ⓐ Ⓑ Ⓒ Ⓓ Ⓔ	31 Ⓐ Ⓑ Ⓒ Ⓓ Ⓔ	53 Ⓐ Ⓑ Ⓒ Ⓓ Ⓔ	75 Ⓐ Ⓑ Ⓒ Ⓓ Ⓔ
10 Ⓐ Ⓑ Ⓒ Ⓓ Ⓔ	32 Ⓐ Ⓑ Ⓒ Ⓓ Ⓔ	54 Ⓐ Ⓑ Ⓒ Ⓓ Ⓔ	76 Ⓐ Ⓑ Ⓒ Ⓓ Ⓔ
11 Ⓐ Ⓑ Ⓒ Ⓓ Ⓔ	33 Ⓐ Ⓑ Ⓒ Ⓓ Ⓔ	55 Ⓐ Ⓑ Ⓒ Ⓓ Ⓔ	77 Ⓐ Ⓑ Ⓒ Ⓓ Ⓔ
12 Ⓐ Ⓑ Ⓒ Ⓓ Ⓔ	34 Ⓐ Ⓑ Ⓒ Ⓓ Ⓔ	56 Ⓐ Ⓑ Ⓒ Ⓓ Ⓔ	78 Ⓐ Ⓑ Ⓒ Ⓓ Ⓔ
13 Ⓐ Ⓑ Ⓒ Ⓓ Ⓔ	35 Ⓐ Ⓑ Ⓒ Ⓓ Ⓔ	57 Ⓐ Ⓑ Ⓒ Ⓓ Ⓔ	79 Ⓐ Ⓑ Ⓒ Ⓓ Ⓔ
14 Ⓐ Ⓑ Ⓒ Ⓓ Ⓔ	36 Ⓐ Ⓑ Ⓒ Ⓓ Ⓔ	58 Ⓐ Ⓑ Ⓒ Ⓓ Ⓔ	80 Ⓐ Ⓑ Ⓒ Ⓓ Ⓔ
15 Ⓐ Ⓑ Ⓒ Ⓓ Ⓔ	37 Ⓐ Ⓑ Ⓒ Ⓓ Ⓔ	59 Ⓐ Ⓑ Ⓒ Ⓓ Ⓔ	81 Ⓐ Ⓑ Ⓒ Ⓓ Ⓔ
16 Ⓐ Ⓑ Ⓒ Ⓓ Ⓔ	38 Ⓐ Ⓑ Ⓒ Ⓓ Ⓔ	60 Ⓐ Ⓑ Ⓒ Ⓓ Ⓔ	82 Ⓐ Ⓑ Ⓒ Ⓓ Ⓔ
17 Ⓐ Ⓑ Ⓒ Ⓓ Ⓔ	39 Ⓐ Ⓑ Ⓒ Ⓓ Ⓔ	61 Ⓐ Ⓑ Ⓒ Ⓓ Ⓔ	83 Ⓐ Ⓑ Ⓒ Ⓓ Ⓔ
18 Ⓐ Ⓑ Ⓒ Ⓓ Ⓔ	40 Ⓐ Ⓑ Ⓒ Ⓓ Ⓔ	62 Ⓐ Ⓑ Ⓒ Ⓓ Ⓔ	84 Ⓐ Ⓑ Ⓒ Ⓓ Ⓔ
19 Ⓐ Ⓑ Ⓒ Ⓓ Ⓔ	41 Ⓐ Ⓑ Ⓒ Ⓓ Ⓔ	63 Ⓐ Ⓑ Ⓒ Ⓓ Ⓔ	85 Ⓐ Ⓑ Ⓒ Ⓓ Ⓔ
20 Ⓐ Ⓑ Ⓒ Ⓓ Ⓔ	42 Ⓐ Ⓑ Ⓒ Ⓓ Ⓔ	64 Ⓐ Ⓑ Ⓒ Ⓓ Ⓔ	86 Ⓐ Ⓑ Ⓒ Ⓓ Ⓔ
21 Ⓐ Ⓑ Ⓒ Ⓓ Ⓔ	43 Ⓐ Ⓑ Ⓒ Ⓓ Ⓔ	65 Ⓐ Ⓑ Ⓒ Ⓓ Ⓔ	87 Ⓐ Ⓑ Ⓒ Ⓓ Ⓔ
22 Ⓐ Ⓑ Ⓒ Ⓓ Ⓔ	44 Ⓐ Ⓑ Ⓒ Ⓓ Ⓔ	66 Ⓐ Ⓑ Ⓒ Ⓓ Ⓔ	88 Ⓐ Ⓑ Ⓒ Ⓓ Ⓔ

Practice III

DIRECTIONS: *The names and addresses are repeated for you in the boxes below. Each name and each number span is in the same box in which you found it in the original set. You will now be allowed FIVE MINUTES to study the locations again. Do your best to memorize the letter of the box in which each item is located. This is your last chance to see the boxes.*

A	B	C	D	E
2300–3499 Club Unit 4000–4299 Pine Iron 1200–2199 Arch	3500–3999 Club Summer 2200–2299 Pine Boulder 2300–3499 Arch	4000–4299 Club Hopper 1200–2199 Pine Window 3500–3999 Arch	1200–2199 Club Magnet 3500–3999 Pine Press 2200–2299 Arch	2200–2299 Club Carrot 2300–3499 Pine Timber 4000–4299 Arch

DIRECTIONS: *This is your last practice test. Mark the location of each of the 88 items on the Practice III answer sheet. You will have FIVE MINUTES to answer these questions. Do NOT look back at the boxes. This practice test will not be scored.*

1. Summer
2. Window
3. 1200–2199 Club
4. 3500–3999 Arch
5. 4000–4299 Pine
6. 2300–3499 Pine
7. 2200–2299 Arch
8. Unit
9. Carrot
10. Magnet
11. 2300–3499 Club
12. 4000–4299 Club
13. 1200–2199 Arch
14. 2200–2299 Pine
15. Hopper
16. 3500–3999 Club
17. 3500–3999 Pine
18. 2300–3499 Arch
19. Press
20. Boulder
21. 4000–4299 Club
22. 1200–2199 Arch

23. 2300–3499 Pine
24. Iron
25. Timber
26. 4000–4299 Pine
27. 2300–3499 Club
28. 2200–2299 Arch
29. 4000–4299 Arch
30. Summer
31. 1200–2199 Pine
32. 3500–3999 Club
33. 2200–2299 Arch
34. Timber
35. Magnet
36. 2300–3499 Arch
37. 4000–4299 Club
38. 1200–2199 Club
39. Carrot
40. Press
41. 2300–3499 Pine
42. 4000–4299 Pine
43. 3500–3999 Arch
44. 4000–4299 Arch

45. Unit
46. Boulder
47. Hopper
48. 2300–3499 Club
49. 2200–2299 Club
50. 3500–3999 Pine
51. Window
52. Summer
53. 2200–2299 Pine
54. 1200–2199 Arch
55. 2200–2299 Pine
56. Iron
57. 1200–2199 Club
58. 2300–3499 Pine
59. 4000–4299 Club
60. 4000–4299 Pine
61. 3500–3999 Club
62. 2200–2299 Arch
63. 2300–3499 Arch
64. 2200–2299 Pine
65. Boulder
66. Summer

67. 1200–2199 Pine

68. 2200–2299 Club

69. 1200–2199 Arch

70. 4000–4299 Arch

71. Magnet

72. Hopper

73. Carrot

74. 2200–2299 Pine

75. 2300–3499 Pine

76. 2300–3499 Club

77. 4000–4299 Club

78. Timber

79. Press

80. Iron

81. 3500–3999 Arch

82. 3500–3999 Pine

83. 1200–2199 Club

84. Unit

85. Window

86. 1200–2199 Pine

87. 1200–2199 Arch

88. 2200–2299 Club

Practice III Answer Sheet

1 Ⓐ Ⓑ Ⓒ Ⓓ Ⓔ
2 Ⓐ Ⓑ Ⓒ Ⓓ Ⓔ
3 Ⓐ Ⓑ Ⓒ Ⓓ Ⓔ
4 Ⓐ Ⓑ Ⓒ Ⓓ Ⓔ
5 Ⓐ Ⓑ Ⓒ Ⓓ Ⓔ
6 Ⓐ Ⓑ Ⓒ Ⓓ Ⓔ
7 Ⓐ Ⓑ Ⓒ Ⓓ Ⓔ
8 Ⓐ Ⓑ Ⓒ Ⓓ Ⓔ
9 Ⓐ Ⓑ Ⓒ Ⓓ Ⓔ
10 Ⓐ Ⓑ Ⓒ Ⓓ Ⓔ
11 Ⓐ Ⓑ Ⓒ Ⓓ Ⓔ
12 Ⓐ Ⓑ Ⓒ Ⓓ Ⓔ
13 Ⓐ Ⓑ Ⓒ Ⓓ Ⓔ
14 Ⓐ Ⓑ Ⓒ Ⓓ Ⓔ
15 Ⓐ Ⓑ Ⓒ Ⓓ Ⓔ
16 Ⓐ Ⓑ Ⓒ Ⓓ Ⓔ
17 Ⓐ Ⓑ Ⓒ Ⓓ Ⓔ
18 Ⓐ Ⓑ Ⓒ Ⓓ Ⓔ
19 Ⓐ Ⓑ Ⓒ Ⓓ Ⓔ
20 Ⓐ Ⓑ Ⓒ Ⓓ Ⓔ
21 Ⓐ Ⓑ Ⓒ Ⓓ Ⓔ
22 Ⓐ Ⓑ Ⓒ Ⓓ Ⓔ

23 Ⓐ Ⓑ Ⓒ Ⓓ Ⓔ
24 Ⓐ Ⓑ Ⓒ Ⓓ Ⓔ
25 Ⓐ Ⓑ Ⓒ Ⓓ Ⓔ
26 Ⓐ Ⓑ Ⓒ Ⓓ Ⓔ
27 Ⓐ Ⓑ Ⓒ Ⓓ Ⓔ
28 Ⓐ Ⓑ Ⓒ Ⓓ Ⓔ
29 Ⓐ Ⓑ Ⓒ Ⓓ Ⓔ
30 Ⓐ Ⓑ Ⓒ Ⓓ Ⓔ
31 Ⓐ Ⓑ Ⓒ Ⓓ Ⓔ
32 Ⓐ Ⓑ Ⓒ Ⓓ Ⓔ
33 Ⓐ Ⓑ Ⓒ Ⓓ Ⓔ
34 Ⓐ Ⓑ Ⓒ Ⓓ Ⓔ
35 Ⓐ Ⓑ Ⓒ Ⓓ Ⓔ
36 Ⓐ Ⓑ Ⓒ Ⓓ Ⓔ
37 Ⓐ Ⓑ Ⓒ Ⓓ Ⓔ
38 Ⓐ Ⓑ Ⓒ Ⓓ Ⓔ
39 Ⓐ Ⓑ Ⓒ Ⓓ Ⓔ
40 Ⓐ Ⓑ Ⓒ Ⓓ Ⓔ
41 Ⓐ Ⓑ Ⓒ Ⓓ Ⓔ
42 Ⓐ Ⓑ Ⓒ Ⓓ Ⓔ
43 Ⓐ Ⓑ Ⓒ Ⓓ Ⓔ
44 Ⓐ Ⓑ Ⓒ Ⓓ Ⓔ

45 Ⓐ Ⓑ Ⓒ Ⓓ Ⓔ
46 Ⓐ Ⓑ Ⓒ Ⓓ Ⓔ
47 Ⓐ Ⓑ Ⓒ Ⓓ Ⓔ
48 Ⓐ Ⓑ Ⓒ Ⓓ Ⓔ
49 Ⓐ Ⓑ Ⓒ Ⓓ Ⓔ
50 Ⓐ Ⓑ Ⓒ Ⓓ Ⓔ
51 Ⓐ Ⓑ Ⓒ Ⓓ Ⓔ
52 Ⓐ Ⓑ Ⓒ Ⓓ Ⓔ
53 Ⓐ Ⓑ Ⓒ Ⓓ Ⓔ
54 Ⓐ Ⓑ Ⓒ Ⓓ Ⓔ
55 Ⓐ Ⓑ Ⓒ Ⓓ Ⓔ
56 Ⓐ Ⓑ Ⓒ Ⓓ Ⓔ
57 Ⓐ Ⓑ Ⓒ Ⓓ Ⓔ
58 Ⓐ Ⓑ Ⓒ Ⓓ Ⓔ
59 Ⓐ Ⓑ Ⓒ Ⓓ Ⓔ
60 Ⓐ Ⓑ Ⓒ Ⓓ Ⓔ
61 Ⓐ Ⓑ Ⓒ Ⓓ Ⓔ
62 Ⓐ Ⓑ Ⓒ Ⓓ Ⓔ
63 Ⓐ Ⓑ Ⓒ Ⓓ Ⓔ
64 Ⓐ Ⓑ Ⓒ Ⓓ Ⓔ
65 Ⓐ Ⓑ Ⓒ Ⓓ Ⓔ
66 Ⓐ Ⓑ Ⓒ Ⓓ Ⓔ

67 Ⓐ Ⓑ Ⓒ Ⓓ Ⓔ
68 Ⓐ Ⓑ Ⓒ Ⓓ Ⓔ
69 Ⓐ Ⓑ Ⓒ Ⓓ Ⓔ
70 Ⓐ Ⓑ Ⓒ Ⓓ Ⓔ
71 Ⓐ Ⓑ Ⓒ Ⓓ Ⓔ
72 Ⓐ Ⓑ Ⓒ Ⓓ Ⓔ
73 Ⓐ Ⓑ Ⓒ Ⓓ Ⓔ
74 Ⓐ Ⓑ Ⓒ Ⓓ Ⓔ
75 Ⓐ Ⓑ Ⓒ Ⓓ Ⓔ
76 Ⓐ Ⓑ Ⓒ Ⓓ Ⓔ
77 Ⓐ Ⓑ Ⓒ Ⓓ Ⓔ
78 Ⓐ Ⓑ Ⓒ Ⓓ Ⓔ
79 Ⓐ Ⓑ Ⓒ Ⓓ Ⓔ
80 Ⓐ Ⓑ Ⓒ Ⓓ Ⓔ
81 Ⓐ Ⓑ Ⓒ Ⓓ Ⓔ
82 Ⓐ Ⓑ Ⓒ Ⓓ Ⓔ
83 Ⓐ Ⓑ Ⓒ Ⓓ Ⓔ
84 Ⓐ Ⓑ Ⓒ Ⓓ Ⓔ
85 Ⓐ Ⓑ Ⓒ Ⓓ Ⓔ
86 Ⓐ Ⓑ Ⓒ Ⓓ Ⓔ
87 Ⓐ Ⓑ Ⓒ Ⓓ Ⓔ
88 Ⓐ Ⓑ Ⓒ Ⓓ Ⓔ

Memory for Addresses

Time: 5 Minutes. 88 Questions.

DIRECTIONS: Mark your answers on the answer sheet in the section headed "MEMORY FOR ADDRESSES." This test will be scored. You are NOT permitted to look at the boxes. Work from memory, as quickly and as accurately as you can. Correct answers are on page 181.

1. 2300–3499 Club
2. 1200–2199 Pine
3. 4000–4299 Arch
4. 2200–2299 Club
5. 1200–2199 Arch
6. Iron
7. Boulder
8. Magnet
9. 2300–3499 Pine
10. 4000–4299 Pine
11. 3500–3999 Arch
12. 4000–4299 Club
13. Carrot
14. Timber
15. Window
16. 3500–3999 Club
17. 3500–3999 Arch
18. 2300–3499 Arch
19. 3500–3999 Pine
20. Press
21. Unit
22. 4000–4299 Pine
23. 3500–3999 Arch
24. 1200–2199 Club
25. Window
26. Iron
27. 2200–2299 Club
28. 3500–3999 Pine
29. 2300–3499 Arch
30. Summer

31. Timber
32. 1200–2199 Arch
33. 1200–2199 Pine
34. 4000–4299 Club
35. Hopper
36. Carrot
37. 2300–3499 Club
38. 2300–3499 Pine
39. 2200–2299 Pine
40. Unit
41. Magnet
42. 3500–3999 Club
43. 3500–3999 Arch
44. 4000–4299 Arch
45. 4000–4299 Pine
46. 2200–2299 Club
47. Hopper
48. Summer
49. 2300–3499 Arch
50. 1200–2199 Club
51. 2300–3499 Club
52. Window
53. Unit
54. Iron
55. 1200–2199 Pine
56. 2300–3499 Pine
57. 4000–4299 Club
58. 1200–2199 Arch
59. Carrot
60. Timber

61. 2200–2299 Pine
62. 2200–2299 Arch
63. 3500–3999 Club
64. 3500–3999 Pine
65. Boulder
66. Magnet
67. 1200–2199 Pine
68. 2200–2299 Club
69. Press
70. 1200–2199 Arch
71. 4000–4299 Pine
72. 2200–2299 Arch
73. 3500–3999 Club
74. Unit
75. 4000–4299 Arch
76. 2300–3499 Club
77. Window
78. Magnet
79. 1200–2199 Pine
80. 2300–3499 Pine
81. 1200–2199 Club
82. 2300–3499 Arch
83. Hopper
84. Press
85. 2200–2299 Pine
86. 4000–4299 Club
87. 3500–3999 Arch
88. Timber

END OF MEMORY FOR ADDRESSES

Part C—Number Series

Sample Questions

The following sample questions show you the type of question that will be used in Part C. You will have three minutes to answer the sample questions and to study the explanations.

DIRECTIONS: Each number series question consists of a series of numbers that follows some definite order. The numbers progress from left to right according to some rule. One pair of numbers to the right of the series comprises the next two numbers in the series. Study each series to try to find a pattern to the series and to figure out the rule that governs the progression. Choose the answer pair that continues the series according to the pattern established and mark its letter on your answer sheet.

1. 42   40   38   35   32   28   24 .. (A) 20 18 (B) 18 14 (C) 19 14 (D) 20 16   (E) 19   15

   If you write the steps between the numbers, you will find this pattern emerging: –2, –2, –3, –3, –4, –4, ... Since it appears that after each two numbers the number being subtracted increases, it is logical to choose answer (**C**) because 24 – 5 = 19 and 19 – 5 = 14.

2. 2   2   4   2   6   2   8 .... (A) 8 2   (B) 2 8   (C) 2 10   (D) 10 2   (E) 10 12

   The series progresses by a factor of +2; 2 4 6 8 10. After each number of the advancing series, we find the number 2. The answer is, of course, (**C**).

3. 88   88   82   82   76   76   70...(A) 70 70 (B) 70 65 (C) 64 64 (D) 70 64 (E) 64 48

   The pattern in this series is a simple one: repeat the number, –6; repeat the number, –6; and so on. To complete the series, repeat the 70 and subtract 6 to yield 64. The answer is (**D**).

4. 35   46   39   43   43   40   47 . (A) 47 43 (B) 51 40 (C) 43 51 (D) 40 50 (E) 37 51

   This is a more complicated problem. There are really two series that alternate. The first series begins with 35 and ascends by +4; 35 39 43 47 51. The alternating series begins with 46 and descends by –3; 46 43 40 37. The number 43 is not really repeated; the two series simply pass each other at that point. In answering a question of this type, you must be careful to maintain the alternation of series. The answer is (**E**) because 37 continues the descending series and 51 continues the ascending one.

5. 8   10   13   17   22   28   35 .. (A) 43 52 (B) 40 45 (C) 35 42 (D) 42 50 (E) 44 53

   The pattern is: +2, +3, +4, +5, +6, +7. Continue the series with: 35 + 8 = 43 + 9 = 52 to choose (**A**) as the correct answer.

SAMPLE ANSWER SHEET	CORRECT ANSWERS
1. Ⓐ Ⓑ Ⓒ Ⓓ Ⓔ	1. Ⓐ Ⓑ ● Ⓓ Ⓔ
2. Ⓐ Ⓑ Ⓒ Ⓓ Ⓔ	2. Ⓐ Ⓑ ● Ⓓ Ⓔ
3. Ⓐ Ⓑ Ⓒ Ⓓ Ⓔ	3. Ⓐ Ⓑ Ⓒ ● Ⓔ
4. Ⓐ Ⓑ Ⓒ Ⓓ Ⓔ	4. Ⓐ Ⓑ Ⓒ Ⓓ ●
5. Ⓐ Ⓑ Ⓒ Ⓓ Ⓔ	5. ● Ⓑ Ⓒ Ⓓ Ⓔ

Number Series

Time: 20 Minutes. 24 Questions.

DIRECTIONS: Each number series question consists of a series of numbers that follows some definite order. The numbers progress from left to right according to some rule. One lettered pair of numbers to the right of the series comprises the next two numbers in the series. Study each series to try to find a pattern to the series and to figure out the rule that governs the progression. Choose the answer pair that continues the series according to the pattern established and mark its letter on your answer sheet. Correct answers are on page 181.

1. 13 12 8 11 10 8 9.................(A) 8 7   (B) 6 8   (C) 8 6   (D) 8 8   (E) 7 8

2. 13 18 13 17 13 16 13..........(A) 15 13   (B) 13 14   (C) 13 15 (D) 14 15 (E) 15 14

3. 13 13 10 12 12 10 11..........(A) 10 10   (B) 10 9   (C) 11 9   (D) 9 11   (E) 11 10

4. 6 5 4 6 5 4 6...................(A) 4 6   (B) 6 4   (C) 5 4   (D) 5 6   (E) 4 5

5. 10 10 9 8 8 7 6..................(A) 5 5   (B) 5 4   (C) 6 5   (D) 6 4   (E) 5 3

6. 20 16 18 14 16 12 14..........(A) 16 12   (B) 10 12   (C) 16 18 (D) 12 12   (E) 12 10

7. 7 12 8 11 9 10 10................(A) 11 9   (B) 9 8   (C) 9 11   (D) 10 11   (E) 9 10

8. 13 13 12 15 15 14 17..........(A) 17 16   (B) 14 17   (C) 16 19 (D) 19 19   (E) 16 16

9. 65 59 53 51 49 43 37 35....(A) 29 27   (B) 33 29   (C) 27 24 (D) 33 27   (E) 32 25

10. 73 65 65 58 58 52 52..........(A) 52 46   (B) 52 47   (C) 47 47 (D) 46 46   (E) 45 45

11. 6 4 8 5 15 13 26 23............(A) 69 67   (B) 37 33   (C) 29 44   (D) 75 78   (E) 46 49

12. 19 16 21 18 23 20 25..........(A) 30 33   (B) 22 27   (C) 28 22   (D) 22 24   (E) 30 27

13. 35 40 5 45 50 5 55.............(A) 55 5   (B) 60 5   (C) 5 60   (D) 5 55   (E) 60 65

14. 22 20 18 18 16 14 14...........(A) 14 12   (B) 12 12   (C) 14 10 (D) 14 16   (E) 12 10

15. 11 22 23 13 26 27 17..........(A) 7 8   (B) 18 36   (C) 18 8   (D) 7 14   (E) 34 35

16. 9 1 10 1 11 1 12.................(A) 13 14   (B) 13 1   (C) 1 13   (D) 12 1   (E) 12 13

17. 48 10 46 17 44 24 42..........(A) 31 40   (B) 27 28   (C) 40 38 (D) 28 38   (E) 30 40

18. 8 8 17 26 26 35 44.............(A) 53 53   (B) 44 53   (C) 44 44 (D) 45 55   (E) 44 54

19. 71 68 62 59 53 50 44..........(A) 40 32   (B) 38 35   (C) 41 38   (D) 41 35   (E) 41 33

20. 1 7 8 2 7 8 3......................(A) 4 7   (B) 7 8   (C) 4 5   (D) 7 4   (E) 2 8

21. 1 2 2 1 1 2 2......................(A) 1 1   (B) 1 2   (C) 2 1   (D) 2 2   (E) 1 3

22. 14 25 37 48 60 71 83 ....(A) 92 100   (B) 96 110   (C) 89 98   (D) 95 105   (E) 94 106

23. 35 43 45 53 55 63 65..........(A) 65 68   (B) 75 83   (C) 73 75 (D) 65 73   (E) 73 83

24. 3 6 12 12 24 48 48..............(A) 48 96   (B) 96 96   (C) 60 96 (D) 96 192 (E) 60 60

END OF NUMBER SERIES

Part D—Following Oral Instructions

Directions and Sample Questions

LISTENING TO INSTRUCTIONS: When you are ready to try these sample questions, give the following instructions to a friend and have the friend read them aloud to you at the rate of 80 words per minute. Do not read them to yourself. Your friend will need a watch with a second hand. Listen carefully and do exactly what your friend tells you to do with the worksheet and answer sheet. Your friend will tell you some things to do with each item on the worksheet. After each set of instructions, your friend will give you time to mark your answer by darkening a circle on the sample answer sheet. Since B and D sound very much alike, your friend will say "B as in baker" when he or she means B and "D as in dog" when he or she means D.

Before proceeding further, tear out the worksheet on page 171. Then hand this book to your friend.

TO THE PERSON WHO IS TO READ THE INSTRUCTIONS: The instructions are to be read at the rate of 80 words per minute. Do not read aloud the material that is in parentheses. Do not repeat any instructions.

Read Aloud to the Candidate

Look at line 1 on your worksheet. (Pause slightly.) Write a C in the third box. (Pause 2 seconds.) Now, on your answer sheet, find the number in that box and darken space C for that number. (Pause 5 seconds.)

Look at line 2 on your worksheet. (Pause slightly.) The number in each circle is the number of employees in a post office. In the circle for the post office holding more than 10 employees, but less than 15, write the letter E next to the number. (Pause 5 seconds.) Now, on your answer sheet, darken the space for the number-letter combination that is in the circle you just wrote in. (Pause 5 seconds.)

Look at the circles on line 3 of your worksheet. (Pause slightly.) In the second circle, write the answer to this question: Which of the following numbers is smallest: 9, 21, 16, 17, 23? (Pause 5 seconds.) In the third circle, write the answer to this question: How many days are there in a week? (Pause 2 seconds.) Now, on your answer sheet, darken the number-letter combinations that are in the circles you wrote in. (Pause 10 seconds.)

Look at line 4 on your worksheet. (Pause slightly.) Count the number of "O's" in the line. (Pause 5 seconds.) Subtract 2 from the number you have counted, and darken the space for the letter B as in baker on your answer sheet next to that number. (Pause 10 seconds.)

Sample Worksheet

DIRECTIONS: Listening carefully to each set of instructions, mark each item on this worksheet as directed. Then complete each question by marking the sample answer sheet below as directed. For each answer you will darken the answer for a number-letter combination. Should you fall behind and miss an instruction, don't become excited. Let that one go and listen for the next one. If, when you start to darken a space for a number, you find that you have already darkened another space for that number, either erase the first mark and darken the space for the new combination or let the first mark stay and do not darken a space for the new combination. Write with a pencil that has a clean eraser. When you finish, you should have no more than one space darkened for each number.

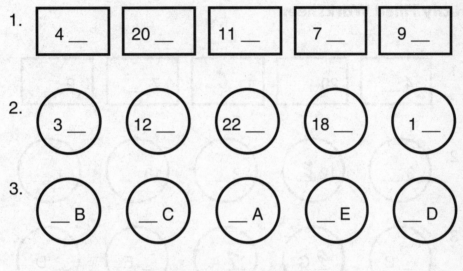

1. | 4 __ | 20 __ | 11 __ | 7 __ | 9 __ |

2. (3 __) (12 __) (22 __) (18 __) (1 __)

3. (__ B) (__ C) (__ A) (__ E) (__ D)

4. X O X X X X O O X O X O X X O X

```
SAMPLE ANSWER SHEET

1. Ⓐ Ⓑ Ⓒ Ⓓ Ⓔ      6. Ⓐ Ⓑ Ⓒ Ⓓ Ⓔ     11. Ⓐ Ⓑ Ⓒ Ⓓ Ⓔ
2. Ⓐ Ⓑ Ⓒ Ⓓ Ⓔ      7. Ⓐ Ⓑ Ⓒ Ⓓ Ⓔ     12. Ⓐ Ⓑ Ⓒ Ⓓ Ⓔ
3. Ⓐ Ⓑ Ⓒ Ⓓ Ⓔ      8. Ⓐ Ⓑ Ⓒ Ⓓ Ⓔ     13. Ⓐ Ⓑ Ⓒ Ⓓ Ⓔ
4. Ⓐ Ⓑ Ⓒ Ⓓ Ⓔ      9. Ⓐ Ⓑ Ⓒ Ⓓ Ⓔ     14. Ⓐ Ⓑ Ⓒ Ⓓ Ⓔ
5. Ⓐ Ⓑ Ⓒ Ⓓ Ⓔ     10. Ⓐ Ⓑ Ⓒ Ⓓ Ⓔ     15. Ⓐ Ⓑ Ⓒ Ⓓ Ⓔ
```

TEAR HERE

CORRECT ANSWERS TO SAMPLE QUESTIONS

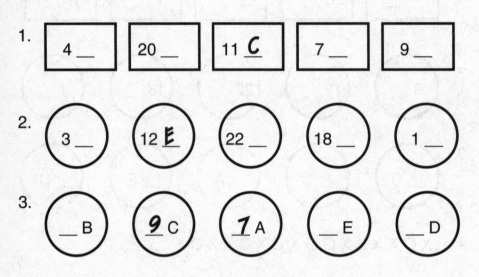

Correctly Filled Worksheet

1. | 4 __ | 20 __ | 11 _C_ | 7 __ | 9 __ |

2. 3 __   12 _E_   22 __   18 __   1 __

3. __B   _9_ C   _7_ A   __E   __D

4. X O X X X X O O X O X O X O X X O X

Following Oral Instructions

Time: 25 Minutes.

Listening to Instructions

DIRECTIONS: When you are ready to try this test of the Model Exam, give the following instructions to a friend and have the friend read them aloud to you at the rate of 80 words per minute. Do NOT read them to yourself. Your friend will need a watch with a second hand. Listen carefully and do exactly what your friend tells you to do with the worksheet and with the answer sheet. Your friend will tell you some things to do with each item on the worksheet. After each set of instructions, your friend will give you time to mark your answer by darkening a circle on the answer sheet. Since B and D sound very much alike, your friend will say "B as in baker" when he or she means B and "D as in dog" when he or she means D.

> Before proceeding further, tear out the worksheet on page 177 of this test. Then hand this book to your friend.

TO THE PERSON WHO IS TO READ THE INSTRUCTIONS: The instructions are to be read at the rate of 80 words per minute. Do not read aloud the material that is in parentheses. Once you have begun the test itself, do not repeat any instructions. The next three paragraphs consist of approximately 120 words. Read these three paragraphs aloud to the candidate in about one and one-half minutes. You may reread these paragraphs as often as necessary to establish an 80-words-per-minute reading speed.

Read Aloud to the Candidate

On the job you will have to listen to instructions and then do what you have been told to do. In this test, I will read instructions to you. Try to understand them as I read them; I cannot repeat them. Once we begin, you may not ask any questions until the end of the test.

On the job you won't have to deal with pictures, numbers, and letters like those in the test, but you will have to listen to instructions and follow them. We are using this test to see how well you can follow instructions.

You are to mark your test booklet according to the instructions that I'll read to you. After each set of instructions, I'll give you time to record your answers on the separate answer sheet.

The actual test begins now.

Look at line 1 on your worksheet. (Pause slightly.) Draw a line under the largest number in the line. (Pause 2 seconds.) Now, on your answer sheet, find the number under which you just drew a line and darken box D as in dog for that number. (Pause 5 seconds.)

Look at line 1 on your worksheet again. (Pause slightly.) Draw two lines under the smallest number in the line. (Pause 2 seconds.) Now, on your answer sheet, find the number under which you just drew two lines and darken box E. (Pause 5 seconds.)

Look at the circles in line 2 on your worksheet. (Pause slightly.) In the second circle, write the answer to this question: How much is 6 plus 4? (Pause 8 seconds.) In the third circle, write the answer to this question: Which of the following numbers is largest: 67, 48, 15, 73, 61? (Pause 5 seconds.) In the fourth circle, write the answer to this question: How many months are there in a year? (Pause 2 seconds.) Now, on your answer sheet, darken the number-letter combinations that are in the circles you wrote in. (Pause 10 seconds.)

Now look at line 3 on your worksheet. (Pause slightly.) Write the letter C on the blank next to the right-hand number. (Pause 2 seconds.) Now, on your answer sheet, find the space for the number beside which you wrote and darken box C. (Pause 5 seconds.)

Now look at line 3 on your worksheet again. (Pause slightly.) Write the letter B as in baker on the blank next to the left-hand number. (Pause 2 seconds.) Now, on your answer sheet, find the space for the number beside which you just wrote and darken box B as in baker. (Pause 5 seconds.)

Look at the boxes and words in line 4 on your worksheet. (Pause slightly.) Write the first letter of the second word in the third box. (Pause 2 seconds.) Write the last letter of the first word in the second box. (Pause 2 seconds.) Write the first letter of the third word in the first box. (Pause 2 seconds.) Now, on your answer sheet, darken the space for the number-letter combinations that are in the three boxes you just wrote in. (Pause 10 seconds.)

Look at the letters on line 5 on your worksheet. (Pause slightly.) Draw a line under the fifth letter in the line. (Pause 2 seconds.) Now, on your answer sheet, find the number 56 (pause 2 seconds) and darken the space for the letter under which you drew a line. (Pause 5 seconds.)

Look at the letters on line 5 on your worksheet again. (Pause slightly.) Draw two lines under the fourth letter in the line. (Pause 2 seconds.) Now, on your answer sheet, find the number 66 (pause 2 seconds) and darken the space for the letter under which you drew two lines. (Pause 5 seconds.)

Look at the drawings on line 6 on your worksheet. (Pause slightly.) The four boxes indicate the number of buildings in four different carrier routes. In the box for the route with the fewest number of buildings, write an A. (Pause 2 seconds.) Now, on your answer sheet, darken the space for the number-letter combination that is in the box you just wrote in. (Pause 5 seconds.)

Now look at line 7 on your worksheet. (Pause slightly.) If fall comes before summer, write the letter B as in baker on the line next to the middle number. (Pause slightly.) Otherwise, write an E on the blank next to the left-hand number. (Pause 5 seconds.) Now, on your answer sheet, darken the space for the number-letter combination that you have just written. (Pause 5 seconds.)

Now look at line 8 on your worksheet. (Pause slightly.) Write a D as in dog in the circle with the lowest number. (Pause 2 seconds.) Now, on your answer sheet, darken the space for the number-letter combination that is in the circle you just wrote in. (Pause 5 seconds.)

Look at the drawings in line 9 on your worksheet. The four boxes are planes for carrying mail. (Pause slightly.) The plane with the highest number is to be loaded first. Write an E in the box with the highest number. (Pause 2 seconds.) Now, on your answer sheet, darken the space for the number-letter combination that is in the box you just wrote in. (Pause 5 seconds.)

Look at line 10 on your worksheet. (Pause slightly.) Draw a line under every number that is more than 35 but less than 55. (Pause 12 seconds.) Now, on your answer sheet, for each number that you drew a line under, darken box A. (Pause 25 seconds.)

Now look at line 10 on your worksheet again. (Pause slightly.) Draw two lines under every number that is more than 55 and less than 80. (Pause 12 seconds.) Now, on your answer sheet, for each number that you drew two lines under, darken box C. (Pause 25 seconds.)

Look at line 11 on your worksheet. (Pause slightly.) Write an E in the last box. (Pause 2 seconds.) Now, on your answer sheet, find the number in that box and darken box E for that number. (Pause 5 seconds.)

Look at line 12 on your worksheet. (Pause slightly.) Draw a line under every "X" in the line. (Pause 5 seconds.) Count the number of lines that you have drawn, add 3, and write that number at the end of the line. (Pause 5 seconds.) Now, on your answer sheet, find that number and darken space E for that number. (Pause 5 seconds.)

Look at line 13 on your worksheet. (Pause slightly.) If the number in the right-hand box is larger than the number in the left-hand circle, add 4 to the number in the left-hand circle, and change the number in the circle to this number. (Pause 8 seconds.) Then, write C next to the new number. (Pause slightly.) Otherwise, write A next to the number in the smaller box. (Pause 3 seconds.) Now, on your answer sheet, darken the space for the number-letter combination that is in the box or circle you just wrote in. (Pause 5 seconds.)

Now look at line 14 on your worksheet. (Pause slightly.) Draw a line under the middle number in the line. (Pause 2 seconds.) Now, on your answer sheet, find the number under which you just drew the line and darken box D as in dog for that number. (Pause 5 seconds.)

Now look at line 15 on your worksheet. (Pause slightly.) Write a B as in baker in the third circle. (Pause 2 seconds.) Now, on your answer sheet, find the number in that circle and darken box B as in baker for that number. (Pause 5 seconds.)

Now look at line 15 again. (Pause slightly.) Write a C in the last circle. (Pause 2 seconds.) Now, on your answer sheet, find the number in that circle and darken box C for that number. (Pause 5 seconds.)

Look at the the drawings on line 16 on your worksheet. The number in each box is the number of employees in a post office. (Pause slightly.) In the box for the post office with the smallest number of employees, write on the line the last two figures of the number of employees. (Pause 5 seconds.) Now, on your answer sheet, darken the space for the number-letter combination that is in the box you just wrote in. (Pause 5 seconds.)

Now look at line 17 on your worksheet. (Pause slightly.) Write an A on the line next to the right-hand number. (Pause 2 seconds.) Now, on your answer sheet find the space for the number next to which you just wrote and darken box A. (Pause 5 seconds.)

Look at line 18 on your worksheet. (Pause slightly.) In the fourth box, write the answer to this question: How many feet are in a yard? (Pause 2 seconds.) Now, on your answer sheet darken the space for the number-letter combination that is in the box you just wrote in. (Pause 5 seconds.)

Look at line 18 again . (Pause slightly.) In the second box, write the number 32. (Pause 2 seconds.) Now, on your answer sheet, find the number-letter combination that is in the box you just wrote in. (Pause 5 seconds.)

Look at line 19 on your worksheet. (Pause slightly.) In the circle with the highest number, write the second letter that I will read to you: <u>B</u> as in baker, <u>D</u> as in dog, <u>A</u> as in apple. (Pause 5 seconds.) Now, on your answer sheet, darken the space for the number-letter combination in the circle you just wrote in. (Pause 5 seconds.)

Following Oral Instructions

Worksheet

DIRECTIONS: *Listening carefully to each set of instructions, mark each item on this worksheet as directed. Then complete each question by marking the answer sheet as directed. For each answer you will darken the answer for a number-letter combination. Should you fall behind and miss an instruction, don't become excited. Let that one go and listen for the next one. If, when you start to darken a space for a number, you find that you have already darkened another space for that number, either erase the first mark and darken the space for the new combination or let the first mark stay and do not darken a space for the new combination. Write with a pencil that has a clean eraser. When you finish, you should have no more than one space darkened for each number. Correct answers are on page 183.*

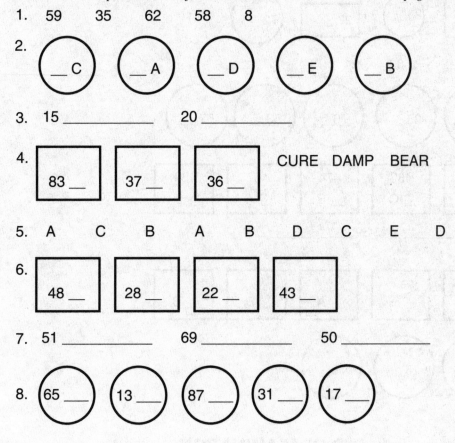

1. 59   35   62   58   8

2. (__C)   (__A)   (__D)   (__E)   (__B)

3. 15 _____   20 _____

4. [83 __]   [37 __]   [36 __]   CURE   DAMP   BEAR

5. A   C   B   A   B   D   C   E   D

6. [48 __]   [28 __]   [22 __]   [43 __]

7. 51 _____   69 _____   50 _____

8. (65 __)   (13 __)   (87 __)   (31 __)   (17 __)

TEAR HERE

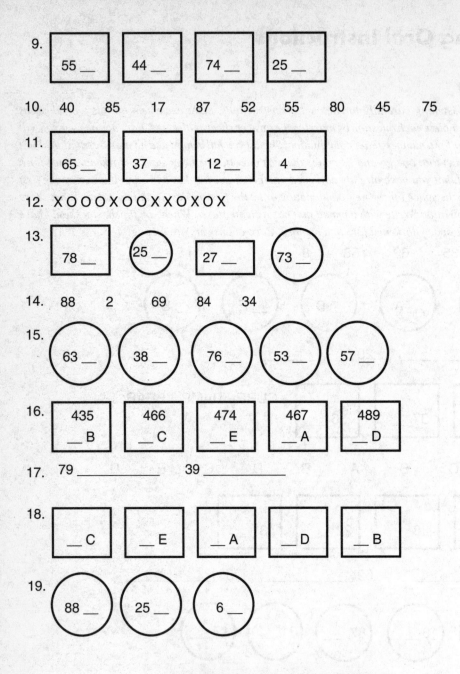

9. | 55 __ | 44 __ | 74 __ | 25 __ |

10. 40   85   17   87   52   55   80   45   75

11. | 65 __ | 37 __ | 12 __ | 4 __ |

12. X O O O X O O X X O X O X

13. | 78 __ | 25 __ | 27 __ | 73 __ |

14. 88   2   69   84   34

15. 63 __   38 __   76 __   53 __   57 __

16. | 435 __ B | 466 __ C | 474 __ E | 467 __ A | 489 __ D |

17. 79 _____   39 _____

18. | __ C | __ E | __ A | __ D | __ B |

19. 88 __   25 __   6 __

END OF EXAMINATION

Correct Answers for Third Model Exam

Part A—Address Checking

1. D	13. D	25. D	37. D	49. A	61. A	73. A	85. D
2. D	14. A	26. A	38. D	50. D	62. A	74. D	86. D
3. D	15. D	27. D	39. D	51. A	63. D	75. D	87. D
4. D	16. D	28. D	40. D	52. A	64. D	76. D	88. D
5. A	17. A	29. D	41. D	53. D	65. D	77. D	89. D
6. A	18. D	30. A	42. D	54. D	66. D	78. D	90. A
7. D	19. D	31. A	43. D	55. A	67. D	79. A	91. A
8. D	20. A	32. D	44. A	56. A	68. D	80. D	92. D
9. D	21. D	33. D	45. D	57. D	69. D	81. A	93. D
10. D	22. D	34. D	46. D	58. D	70. D	82. A	94. D
11. D	23. D	35. D	47. D	59. D	71. A	83. D	95. D
12. D	24. A	36. A	48. A	60. A	72. A	84. D	

Analyzing Your Errors

By now you should be able to analyze your own pattern of errors. Make up a tally sheet by cross-checking your incorrect answers against the correct answers and against the questions themselves. Mark your tally sheet like this: ⦀⦀ ‖ .

Type of Error	Tally	Total Number
Number of addresses that were alike and you incorrectly marked "different"		
Number of addresses that were different and you incorrectly marked "alike"		
Number of addresses in which you missed a difference in NUMBERS		
Number of addresses in which you missed a difference in ABBREVIATIONS		
Number of addresses in which you missed a difference in NAMES		

Part B—Memory for Addresses

Practice I

1. D	12. B	23. E	34. B	45. A	56. B	67. C	78. A
2. B	13. E	24. D	35. E	46. B	57. A	68. D	79. A
3. A	14. A	25. D	36. C	47. C	58. A	69. A	80. D
4. E	15. A	26. B	37. A	48. D	59. E	70. C	81. C
5. C	16. B	27. B	38. D	49. E	60. C	71. C	82. C
6. E	17. C	28. C	39. B	50. D	61. E	72. B	83. B
7. C	18. D	29. A	40. E	51. C	62. E	73. E	84. C
8. A	19. C	30. C	41. E	52. B	63. D	74. A	85. D
9. D	20. D	31. A	42. C	53. E	64. B	75. D	86. B
10. E	21. B	32. A	43. D	54. D	65. B	76. E	87. B
11. D	22. A	33. E	44. B	55. C	66. A	77. E	88. A

Practice II

1. E	12. A	23. A	34. B	45. B	56. C	67. B	78. B
2. D	13. E	24. D	35. B	46. A	57. A	68. B	79. B
3. B	14. A	25. C	36. A	47. D	58. C	69. A	80. C
4. A	15. D	26. D	37. E	48. A	59. B	70. D	81. C
5. C	16. D	27. C	38. B	49. D	60. E	71. C	82. A
6. E	17. B	28. D	39. E	50. D	61. E	72. C	83. E
7. C	18. A	29. C	40. D	51. E	62. E	73. C	84. E
8. C	19. C	30. D	41. B	52. E	63. A	74. E	85. A
9. B	20. D	31. C	42. E	53. C	64. D	75. E	86. A
10. E	21. A	32. A	43. C	54. B	65. A	76. A	87. B
11. B	22. B	33. A	44. E	55. C	66. B	77. D	88. D

Practice III

1. B	12. C	23. E	34. E	45. A	56. A	67. C	78. E
2. C	13. A	24. A	35. D	46. B	57. D	68. E	79. D
3. D	14. B	25. E	36. B	47. C	58. E	69. A	80. A
4. C	15. C	26. A	37. C	48. A	59. C	70. E	81. C
5. A	16. B	27. A	38. D	49. E	60. A	71. D	82. D
6. E	17. D	28. D	39. E	50. D	61. B	72. C	83. D
7. D	18. B	29. E	40. D	51. C	62. D	73. E	84. A
8. A	19. D	30. B	41. E	52. B	63. B	74. B	85. C
9. E	20. B	31. C	42. A	53. B	64. B	75. E	86. C
10. D	21. C	32. B	43. C	54. A	65. B	76. A	87. A
11. A	22. A	33. D	44. E	55. B	66. B	77. C	88. E

Memory for Addresses

1. A	12. C	23. C	34. C	45. A	56. E	67. C	78. D
2. C	13. E	24. D	35. C	46. E	57. C	68. E	79. C
3. E	14. E	25. C	36. E	47. C	58. A	69. D	80. E
4. E	15. C	26. A	37. A	48. B	59. E	70. A	81. D
5. A	16. B	27. E	38. E	49. B	60. E	71. A	82. B
6. A	17. C	28. D	39. B	50. D	61. B	72. D	83. C
7. B	18. B	29. B	40. A	51. A	62. D	73. B	84. D
8. D	19. D	30. B	41. D	52. C	63. B	74. A	85. B
9. E	20. D	31. E	42. B	53. A	64. D	75. E	86. C
10. A	21. A	32. A	43. C	54. A	65. B	76. A	87. C
11. C	22. A	33. C	44. E	55. C	66. D	77. C	88. E

Part C—Number Series

1. D	4. C	7. C	10. C	13. B	16. C	19. D	22. E
2. A	5. C	8. A	11. A	14. E	17. A	20. B	23. C
3. E	6. B	9. D	12. B	15. E	18. B	21. A	24. D

Explanations

1. **(D)** The series descends 13 12 11 10 9 8, with the number 8 appearing between each set of two numbers.

2. **(A)** Again the series descends. This time the number 13 appears between all numbers.

3. **(E)** This time the number repeats itself before descending. The number 10 appears between each set of descending numbers.

4. **(C)** The three-number series repeats itself over and over.

5. **(C)** The series descends. The even numbers repeat.

6. **(B)** Mark the differences between numbers. The pattern that emerges is –4, +2, –4, +2, and so on.

7. **(C)** There are two alternating series. The first series begins with 7 and ascends by +1. The alternating series begins with 12 and descends one number at a time.

8. **(A)** One series, the odd numbers, repeats and ascends by +2. The alternating series, the even numbers, also ascends by +2, but does not repeat.

9. **(D)** The pattern is: –6, –6, –2, –2; –6, –6, –2, –2 . . . .

10. **(C)** The pattern is: –8, repeat the number; –7, repeat the number; –6, repeat the number; –5, repeat the number . . . .

11. **(A)** The pattern is: –2, ×2, –3, ×3; –2, ×2, –3, ×3; –2, ×2, –3, ×3.

12. **(B)** The easiest way to see this is to mark the pattern: –3, +5; –3, +5; and so on. If, however, you see two alternating series both ascending by +2, you will also get the correct answer.

13. **(B)** This is a +5 series with the number 5 appearing after each two numbers in the series.

14. **(E)** The pattern is: –2. –2, repeat the number; –2, –2, repeat the number . . . .

15. **(E)** The pattern is ×2, +1, –10; ×2, +1, –10; ×2, +1, –10 . . . .

16. **(C)** The series is simply 9 10 11 12 13 . . . with the number 1 appearing between each step of the series.

17. **(A)** There are two alternating series. The first series starts with 48 and descends at the rate of –2. The alternating series starts with 10 and ascends at the rate of +7.

18. **(B)** The pattern is: repeat the number, +9, +9, repeat the number, +9, +9 . . . .

19. **(D)** The pattern is: –3, –6; –3, –6 . . . .

20. **(B)** The pattern is a 1 2 3 . . . with the numbers 7 8 intervening between members of the series.

21. **(A)** The series consists of repetitions of the sequence 1 2 2 1, or, if you see it otherwise, repetitions of 1 1; 2 2; 1 1; 2 2; 1 1 beginning in the middle of a repetition of 1's.

22. **(E)** The pattern is: +11, +12; +11, +12 . . . .

23. **(C)** The pattern is: +8, +2; +8, +2 . . . .

24. **(D)** The pattern is: ×2, ×2, repeat the number, ×2, ×2, repeat the number . . . .

Part D—Following Oral Instructions

Correctly Filled Answer Grid

1 Ⓐ Ⓑ Ⓒ Ⓓ Ⓔ	23 Ⓐ Ⓑ Ⓒ Ⓓ Ⓔ	45 ● Ⓑ Ⓒ Ⓓ Ⓔ	67 Ⓐ Ⓑ Ⓒ Ⓓ Ⓔ
2 Ⓐ Ⓑ Ⓒ Ⓓ Ⓔ	24 Ⓐ Ⓑ Ⓒ Ⓓ Ⓔ	46 Ⓐ Ⓑ Ⓒ Ⓓ Ⓔ	68 Ⓐ Ⓑ Ⓒ Ⓓ Ⓔ
3 Ⓐ Ⓑ Ⓒ ● Ⓔ	25 Ⓐ Ⓑ Ⓒ Ⓓ Ⓔ	47 Ⓐ Ⓑ Ⓒ Ⓓ Ⓔ	69 Ⓐ Ⓑ Ⓒ ● Ⓔ
4 Ⓐ Ⓑ Ⓒ Ⓓ ●	26 Ⓐ Ⓑ Ⓒ Ⓓ Ⓔ	48 Ⓐ Ⓑ Ⓒ Ⓓ Ⓔ	70 Ⓐ Ⓑ Ⓒ Ⓓ Ⓔ
5 Ⓐ Ⓑ Ⓒ Ⓓ Ⓔ	27 Ⓐ Ⓑ Ⓒ Ⓓ Ⓔ	49 Ⓐ Ⓑ Ⓒ Ⓓ Ⓔ	71 Ⓐ Ⓑ Ⓒ Ⓓ Ⓔ
6 Ⓐ Ⓑ Ⓒ Ⓓ Ⓔ	28 Ⓐ Ⓑ Ⓒ Ⓓ Ⓔ	50 Ⓐ Ⓑ Ⓒ Ⓓ Ⓔ	72 Ⓐ Ⓑ Ⓒ Ⓓ Ⓔ
7 Ⓐ Ⓑ Ⓒ Ⓓ Ⓔ	29 Ⓐ Ⓑ ● Ⓓ Ⓔ	51 Ⓐ Ⓑ Ⓒ Ⓓ ●	73 Ⓐ Ⓑ Ⓒ ● Ⓔ
8 Ⓐ Ⓑ Ⓒ Ⓓ ●	30 Ⓐ Ⓑ Ⓒ Ⓓ Ⓔ	52 ● Ⓑ Ⓒ Ⓓ Ⓔ	74 Ⓐ Ⓑ Ⓒ Ⓓ ●
9 Ⓐ Ⓑ Ⓒ Ⓓ ●	31 Ⓐ Ⓑ Ⓒ Ⓓ Ⓔ	53 Ⓐ Ⓑ Ⓒ Ⓓ Ⓔ	75 Ⓐ Ⓑ ● Ⓓ Ⓔ
10 ● Ⓑ Ⓒ Ⓓ Ⓔ	32 Ⓐ Ⓑ Ⓒ Ⓓ ●	54 Ⓐ Ⓑ Ⓒ Ⓓ Ⓔ	76 Ⓐ ● Ⓒ Ⓓ Ⓔ
11 Ⓐ Ⓑ Ⓒ Ⓓ Ⓔ	33 Ⓐ Ⓑ Ⓒ Ⓓ Ⓔ	55 Ⓐ Ⓑ Ⓒ Ⓓ Ⓔ	77 Ⓐ Ⓑ Ⓒ Ⓓ Ⓔ
12 Ⓐ Ⓑ Ⓒ Ⓓ ●	34 Ⓐ Ⓑ Ⓒ Ⓓ Ⓔ	56 Ⓐ ● Ⓒ Ⓓ Ⓔ	78 Ⓐ Ⓑ Ⓒ Ⓓ Ⓔ
13 Ⓐ Ⓑ Ⓒ ● Ⓔ	35 Ⓐ ● Ⓒ Ⓓ Ⓔ	57 Ⓐ Ⓑ ● Ⓓ Ⓔ	79 Ⓐ Ⓑ Ⓒ Ⓓ Ⓔ
14 Ⓐ Ⓑ Ⓒ Ⓓ Ⓔ	36 Ⓐ Ⓑ Ⓒ ● Ⓔ	58 Ⓐ Ⓑ Ⓒ Ⓓ Ⓔ	80 Ⓐ Ⓑ Ⓒ Ⓓ Ⓔ
15 Ⓐ ● Ⓒ Ⓓ Ⓔ	37 Ⓐ Ⓑ Ⓒ Ⓓ ●	59 Ⓐ Ⓑ Ⓒ Ⓓ Ⓔ	81 Ⓐ Ⓑ Ⓒ Ⓓ Ⓔ
16 Ⓐ Ⓑ Ⓒ Ⓓ Ⓔ	38 Ⓐ Ⓑ Ⓒ Ⓓ Ⓔ	60 Ⓐ Ⓑ Ⓒ Ⓓ Ⓔ	82 Ⓐ Ⓑ Ⓒ Ⓓ Ⓔ
17 Ⓐ Ⓑ Ⓒ Ⓓ Ⓔ	39 ● Ⓑ Ⓒ Ⓓ Ⓔ	61 Ⓐ Ⓑ Ⓒ Ⓓ Ⓔ	83 Ⓐ ● Ⓒ Ⓓ Ⓔ
18 Ⓐ Ⓑ Ⓒ Ⓓ Ⓔ	40 ● Ⓑ Ⓒ Ⓓ Ⓔ	62 Ⓐ Ⓑ Ⓒ ● Ⓔ	84 Ⓐ Ⓑ Ⓒ Ⓓ Ⓔ
19 Ⓐ Ⓑ Ⓒ Ⓓ Ⓔ	41 Ⓐ Ⓑ Ⓒ Ⓓ Ⓔ	63 Ⓐ Ⓑ Ⓒ Ⓓ Ⓔ	85 Ⓐ Ⓑ Ⓒ Ⓓ Ⓔ
20 Ⓐ Ⓑ ● Ⓓ Ⓔ	42 Ⓐ Ⓑ Ⓒ Ⓓ Ⓔ	64 Ⓐ Ⓑ Ⓒ Ⓓ Ⓔ	86 Ⓐ Ⓑ Ⓒ Ⓓ Ⓔ
21 Ⓐ Ⓑ Ⓒ Ⓓ Ⓔ	43 Ⓐ Ⓑ Ⓒ Ⓓ Ⓔ	65 Ⓐ Ⓑ Ⓒ Ⓓ Ⓔ	87 Ⓐ Ⓑ Ⓒ Ⓓ Ⓔ
22 ● Ⓑ Ⓒ Ⓓ Ⓔ	44 Ⓐ Ⓑ Ⓒ Ⓓ Ⓔ	66 ● Ⓑ Ⓒ Ⓓ Ⓔ	88 Ⓐ Ⓑ Ⓒ ● Ⓔ

Correctly Filled Worksheet

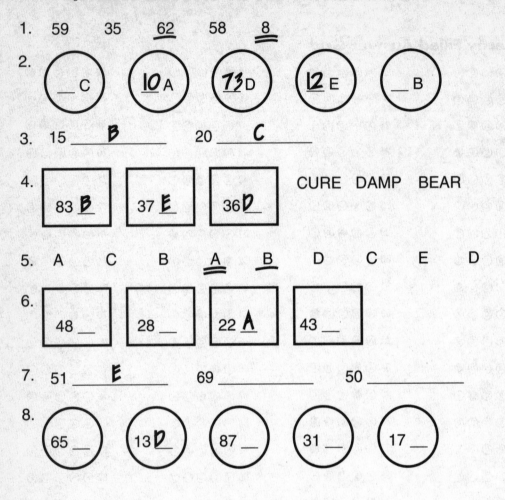

1. 59   35   <u>62</u>   58   <u>8</u>

2. (__C)   (10 A)   (73 D)   (12 E)   (__B)

3. 15 ____B____   20 ____C____

4. [83 B]   [37 E]   [36 D]   CURE DAMP BEAR

5. A   C   B   <u>A</u>   <u>B</u>   D   C   E   D

6. [48 __]   [28 __]   [22 A]   [43 __]

7. 51 ____E____   69 _____   50 _____

8. (65 __)   (13 D)   (87 __)   (31 __)   (17 __)

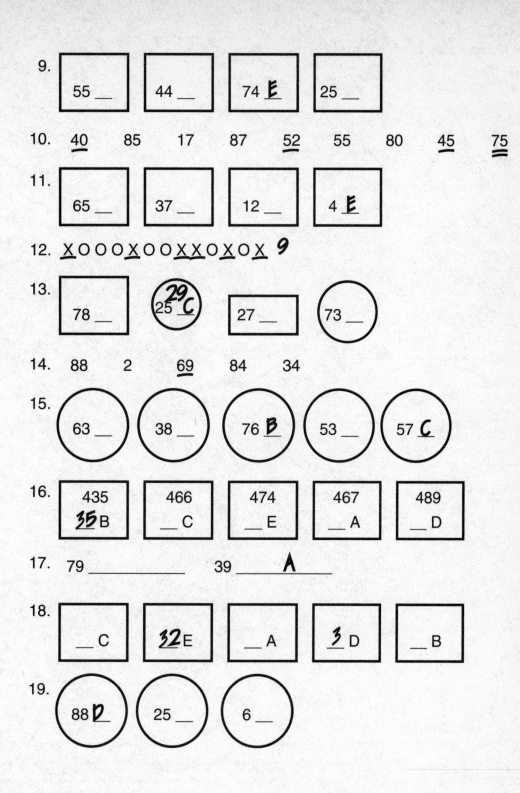

9.

| 55 __ | 44 __ | 74 _E_ | 25 __ |

10. <u>40</u> 85 17 87 <u>52</u> 55 80 <u>45</u> <u>75</u>

11.

| 65 __ | 37 __ | 12 __ | 4 _E_ |

12. <u>X</u> O O O <u>X</u> O O <u>X</u> <u>X</u> O <u>X</u> O <u>X</u> _9_

13.

| 78 __ | 25 _C_ _29_ | 27 __ | 73 __ |

14. 88 2 <u>69</u> 84 34

15.

| 63 __ | 38 __ | 76 _B_ | 53 __ | 57 _C_ |

16.

| 435 _35_ B | 466 __ C | 474 __ E | 467 __ A | 489 __ D |

17. 79 _____   39 _____ A _____

18.

| __ C | _32_ E | __ A | _3_ D | __ B |

19.

| 88 _D_ | 25 __ | 6 __ |

Fourth Model Exam
Answer Sheet

Part A—Address Checking

1. Ⓐ Ⓓ	20. Ⓐ Ⓓ	39. Ⓐ Ⓓ	58. Ⓐ Ⓓ	77. Ⓐ Ⓓ
2. Ⓐ Ⓓ	21. Ⓐ Ⓓ	40. Ⓐ Ⓓ	59. Ⓐ Ⓓ	78. Ⓐ Ⓓ
3. Ⓐ Ⓓ	22. Ⓐ Ⓓ	41. Ⓐ Ⓓ	60. Ⓐ Ⓓ	79. Ⓐ Ⓓ
4. Ⓐ Ⓓ	23. Ⓐ Ⓓ	42. Ⓐ Ⓓ	61. Ⓐ Ⓓ	80. Ⓐ Ⓓ
5. Ⓐ Ⓓ	24. Ⓐ Ⓓ	43. Ⓐ Ⓓ	62. Ⓐ Ⓓ	81. Ⓐ Ⓓ
6. Ⓐ Ⓓ	25. Ⓐ Ⓓ	44. Ⓐ Ⓓ	63. Ⓐ Ⓓ	82. Ⓐ Ⓓ
7. Ⓐ Ⓓ	26. Ⓐ Ⓓ	45. Ⓐ Ⓓ	64. Ⓐ Ⓓ	83. Ⓐ Ⓓ
8. Ⓐ Ⓓ	27. Ⓐ Ⓓ	46. Ⓐ Ⓓ	65. Ⓐ Ⓓ	84. Ⓐ Ⓓ
9. Ⓐ Ⓓ	28. Ⓐ Ⓓ	47. Ⓐ Ⓓ	66. Ⓐ Ⓓ	85. Ⓐ Ⓓ
10. Ⓐ Ⓓ	29. Ⓐ Ⓓ	48. Ⓐ Ⓓ	67. Ⓐ Ⓓ	86. Ⓐ Ⓓ
11. Ⓐ Ⓓ	30. Ⓐ Ⓓ	49. Ⓐ Ⓓ	68. Ⓐ Ⓓ	87. Ⓐ Ⓓ
12. Ⓐ Ⓓ	31. Ⓐ Ⓓ	50. Ⓐ Ⓓ	69. Ⓐ Ⓓ	88. Ⓐ Ⓓ
13. Ⓐ Ⓓ	32. Ⓐ Ⓓ	51. Ⓐ Ⓓ	70. Ⓐ Ⓓ	89. Ⓐ Ⓓ
14. Ⓐ Ⓓ	33. Ⓐ Ⓓ	52. Ⓐ Ⓓ	71. Ⓐ Ⓓ	90. Ⓐ Ⓓ
15. Ⓐ Ⓓ	34. Ⓐ Ⓓ	53. Ⓐ Ⓓ	72. Ⓐ Ⓓ	91. Ⓐ Ⓓ
16. Ⓐ Ⓓ	35. Ⓐ Ⓓ	54. Ⓐ Ⓓ	73. Ⓐ Ⓓ	92. Ⓐ Ⓓ
17. Ⓐ Ⓓ	36. Ⓐ Ⓓ	55. Ⓐ Ⓓ	74. Ⓐ Ⓓ	93. Ⓐ Ⓓ
18. Ⓐ Ⓓ	37. Ⓐ Ⓓ	56. Ⓐ Ⓓ	75. Ⓐ Ⓓ	94. Ⓐ Ⓓ
19. Ⓐ Ⓓ	38. Ⓐ Ⓓ	57. Ⓐ Ⓓ	76. Ⓐ Ⓓ	95. Ⓐ Ⓓ

Part B—Memory for Addresses

1 (A) (B) (C) (D) (E)
2 (A) (B) (C) (D) (E)
3 (A) (B) (C) (D) (E)
4 (A) (B) (C) (D) (E)
5 (A) (B) (C) (D) (E)
6 (A) (B) (C) (D) (E)
7 (A) (B) (C) (D) (E)
8 (A) (B) (C) (D) (E)
9 (A) (B) (C) (D) (E)
10 (A) (B) (C) (D) (E)
11 (A) (B) (C) (D) (E)
12 (A) (B) (C) (D) (E)
13 (A) (B) (C) (D) (E)
14 (A) (B) (C) (D) (E)
15 (A) (B) (C) (D) (E)
16 (A) (B) (C) (D) (E)
17 (A) (B) (C) (D) (E)
18 (A) (B) (C) (D) (E)
19 (A) (B) (C) (D) (E)
20 (A) (B) (C) (D) (E)
21 (A) (B) (C) (D) (E)
22 (A) (B) (C) (D) (E)

23 (A) (B) (C) (D) (E)
24 (A) (B) (C) (D) (E)
25 (A) (B) (C) (D) (E)
26 (A) (B) (C) (D) (E)
27 (A) (B) (C) (D) (E)
28 (A) (B) (C) (D) (E)
29 (A) (B) (C) (D) (E)
30 (A) (B) (C) (D) (E)
31 (A) (B) (C) (D) (E)
32 (A) (B) (C) (D) (E)
33 (A) (B) (C) (D) (E)
34 (A) (B) (C) (D) (E)
35 (A) (B) (C) (D) (E)
36 (A) (B) (C) (D) (E)
37 (A) (B) (C) (D) (E)
38 (A) (B) (C) (D) (E)
39 (A) (B) (C) (D) (E)
40 (A) (B) (C) (D) (E)
41 (A) (B) (C) (D) (E)
42 (A) (B) (C) (D) (E)
43 (A) (B) (C) (D) (E)
44 (A) (B) (C) (D) (E)

45 (A) (B) (C) (D) (E)
46 (A) (B) (C) (D) (E)
47 (A) (B) (C) (D) (E)
48 (A) (B) (C) (D) (E)
49 (A) (B) (C) (D) (E)
50 (A) (B) (C) (D) (E)
51 (A) (B) (C) (D) (E)
52 (A) (B) (C) (D) (E)
53 (A) (B) (C) (D) (E)
54 (A) (B) (C) (D) (E)
55 (A) (B) (C) (D) (E)
56 (A) (B) (C) (D) (E)
57 (A) (B) (C) (D) (E)
58 (A) (B) (C) (D) (E)
59 (A) (B) (C) (D) (E)
60 (A) (B) (C) (D) (E)
61 (A) (B) (C) (D) (E)
62 (A) (B) (C) (D) (E)
63 (A) (B) (C) (D) (E)
64 (A) (B) (C) (D) (E)
65 (A) (B) (C) (D) (E)
66 (A) (B) (C) (D) (E)

67 (A) (B) (C) (D) (E)
68 (A) (B) (C) (D) (E)
69 (A) (B) (C) (D) (E)
70 (A) (B) (C) (D) (E)
71 (A) (B) (C) (D) (E)
72 (A) (B) (C) (D) (E)
73 (A) (B) (C) (D) (E)
74 (A) (B) (C) (D) (E)
75 (A) (B) (C) (D) (E)
76 (A) (B) (C) (D) (E)
77 (A) (B) (C) (D) (E)
78 (A) (B) (C) (D) (E)
79 (A) (B) (C) (D) (E)
80 (A) (B) (C) (D) (E)
81 (A) (B) (C) (D) (E)
82 (A) (B) (C) (D) (E)
83 (A) (B) (C) (D) (E)
84 (A) (B) (C) (D) (E)
85 (A) (B) (C) (D) (E)
86 (A) (B) (C) (D) (E)
87 (A) (B) (C) (D) (E)
88 (A) (B) (C) (D) (E)

Part C—Number Series

1. (A) (B) (C) (D) (E)
2. (A) (B) (C) (D) (E)
3. (A) (B) (C) (D) (E)
4. (A) (B) (C) (D) (E)
5. (A) (B) (C) (D) (E)
6. (A) (B) (C) (D) (E)

7. (A) (B) (C) (D) (E)
8. (A) (B) (C) (D) (E)
9. (A) (B) (C) (D) (E)
10. (A) (B) (C) (D) (E)
11. (A) (B) (C) (D) (E)
12. (A) (B) (C) (D) (E)

13. (A) (B) (C) (D) (E)
14. (A) (B) (C) (D) (E)
15. (A) (B) (C) (D) (E)
16. (A) (B) (C) (D) (E)
17. (A) (B) (C) (D) (E)
18. (A) (B) (C) (D) (E)

19. (A) (B) (C) (D) (E)
20. (A) (B) (C) (D) (E)
21. (A) (B) (C) (D) (E)
22. (A) (B) (C) (D) (E)
23. (A) (B) (C) (D) (E)
24. (A) (B) (C) (D) (E)

Part D—Following Oral Instructions

TEAR HERE

1 Ⓐ Ⓑ Ⓒ Ⓓ Ⓔ
2 Ⓐ Ⓑ Ⓒ Ⓓ Ⓔ
3 Ⓐ Ⓑ Ⓒ Ⓓ Ⓔ
4 Ⓐ Ⓑ Ⓒ Ⓓ Ⓔ
5 Ⓐ Ⓑ Ⓒ Ⓓ Ⓔ
6 Ⓐ Ⓑ Ⓒ Ⓓ Ⓔ
7 Ⓐ Ⓑ Ⓒ Ⓓ Ⓔ
8 Ⓐ Ⓑ Ⓒ Ⓓ Ⓔ
9 Ⓐ Ⓑ Ⓒ Ⓓ Ⓔ
10 Ⓐ Ⓑ Ⓒ Ⓓ Ⓔ
11 Ⓐ Ⓑ Ⓒ Ⓓ Ⓔ
12 Ⓐ Ⓑ Ⓒ Ⓓ Ⓔ
13 Ⓐ Ⓑ Ⓒ Ⓓ Ⓔ
14 Ⓐ Ⓑ Ⓒ Ⓓ Ⓔ
15 Ⓐ Ⓑ Ⓒ Ⓓ Ⓔ
16 Ⓐ Ⓑ Ⓒ Ⓓ Ⓔ
17 Ⓐ Ⓑ Ⓒ Ⓓ Ⓔ
18 Ⓐ Ⓑ Ⓒ Ⓓ Ⓔ
19 Ⓐ Ⓑ Ⓒ Ⓓ Ⓔ
20 Ⓐ Ⓑ Ⓒ Ⓓ Ⓔ
21 Ⓐ Ⓑ Ⓒ Ⓓ Ⓔ
22 Ⓐ Ⓑ Ⓒ Ⓓ Ⓔ

23 Ⓐ Ⓑ Ⓒ Ⓓ Ⓔ
24 Ⓐ Ⓑ Ⓒ Ⓓ Ⓔ
25 Ⓐ Ⓑ Ⓒ Ⓓ Ⓔ
26 Ⓐ Ⓑ Ⓒ Ⓓ Ⓔ
27 Ⓐ Ⓑ Ⓒ Ⓓ Ⓔ
28 Ⓐ Ⓑ Ⓒ Ⓓ Ⓔ
29 Ⓐ Ⓑ Ⓒ Ⓓ Ⓔ
30 Ⓐ Ⓑ Ⓒ Ⓓ Ⓔ
31 Ⓐ Ⓑ Ⓒ Ⓓ Ⓔ
32 Ⓐ Ⓑ Ⓒ Ⓓ Ⓔ
33 Ⓐ Ⓑ Ⓒ Ⓓ Ⓔ
34 Ⓐ Ⓑ Ⓒ Ⓓ Ⓔ
35 Ⓐ Ⓑ Ⓒ Ⓓ Ⓔ
36 Ⓐ Ⓑ Ⓒ Ⓓ Ⓔ
37 Ⓐ Ⓑ Ⓒ Ⓓ Ⓔ
38 Ⓐ Ⓑ Ⓒ Ⓓ Ⓔ
39 Ⓐ Ⓑ Ⓒ Ⓓ Ⓔ
40 Ⓐ Ⓑ Ⓒ Ⓓ Ⓔ
41 Ⓐ Ⓑ Ⓒ Ⓓ Ⓔ
42 Ⓐ Ⓑ Ⓒ Ⓓ Ⓔ
43 Ⓐ Ⓑ Ⓒ Ⓓ Ⓔ
44 Ⓐ Ⓑ Ⓒ Ⓓ Ⓔ

45 Ⓐ Ⓑ Ⓒ Ⓓ Ⓔ
46 Ⓐ Ⓑ Ⓒ Ⓓ Ⓔ
47 Ⓐ Ⓑ Ⓒ Ⓓ Ⓔ
48 Ⓐ Ⓑ Ⓒ Ⓓ Ⓔ
49 Ⓐ Ⓑ Ⓒ Ⓓ Ⓔ
50 Ⓐ Ⓑ Ⓒ Ⓓ Ⓔ
51 Ⓐ Ⓑ Ⓒ Ⓓ Ⓔ
52 Ⓐ Ⓑ Ⓒ Ⓓ Ⓔ
53 Ⓐ Ⓑ Ⓒ Ⓓ Ⓔ
54 Ⓐ Ⓑ Ⓒ Ⓓ Ⓔ
55 Ⓐ Ⓑ Ⓒ Ⓓ Ⓔ
56 Ⓐ Ⓑ Ⓒ Ⓓ Ⓔ
57 Ⓐ Ⓑ Ⓒ Ⓓ Ⓔ
58 Ⓐ Ⓑ Ⓒ Ⓓ Ⓔ
59 Ⓐ Ⓑ Ⓒ Ⓓ Ⓔ
60 Ⓐ Ⓑ Ⓒ Ⓓ Ⓔ
61 Ⓐ Ⓑ Ⓒ Ⓓ Ⓔ
62 Ⓐ Ⓑ Ⓒ Ⓓ Ⓔ
63 Ⓐ Ⓑ Ⓒ Ⓓ Ⓔ
64 Ⓐ Ⓑ Ⓒ Ⓓ Ⓔ
65 Ⓐ Ⓑ Ⓒ Ⓓ Ⓔ
66 Ⓐ Ⓑ Ⓒ Ⓓ Ⓔ

67 Ⓐ Ⓑ Ⓒ Ⓓ Ⓔ
68 Ⓐ Ⓑ Ⓒ Ⓓ Ⓔ
69 Ⓐ Ⓑ Ⓒ Ⓓ Ⓔ
70 Ⓐ Ⓑ Ⓒ Ⓓ Ⓔ
71 Ⓐ Ⓑ Ⓒ Ⓓ Ⓔ
72 Ⓐ Ⓑ Ⓒ Ⓓ Ⓔ
73 Ⓐ Ⓑ Ⓒ Ⓓ Ⓔ
74 Ⓐ Ⓑ Ⓒ Ⓓ Ⓔ
75 Ⓐ Ⓑ Ⓒ Ⓓ Ⓔ
76 Ⓐ Ⓑ Ⓒ Ⓓ Ⓔ
77 Ⓐ Ⓑ Ⓒ Ⓓ Ⓔ
78 Ⓐ Ⓑ Ⓒ Ⓓ Ⓔ
79 Ⓐ Ⓑ Ⓒ Ⓓ Ⓔ
80 Ⓐ Ⓑ Ⓒ Ⓓ Ⓔ
81 Ⓐ Ⓑ Ⓒ Ⓓ Ⓔ
82 Ⓐ Ⓑ Ⓒ Ⓓ Ⓔ
83 Ⓐ Ⓑ Ⓒ Ⓓ Ⓔ
84 Ⓐ Ⓑ Ⓒ Ⓓ Ⓔ
85 Ⓐ Ⓑ Ⓒ Ⓓ Ⓔ
86 Ⓐ Ⓑ Ⓒ Ⓓ Ⓔ
87 Ⓐ Ⓑ Ⓒ Ⓓ Ⓔ
88 Ⓐ Ⓑ Ⓒ Ⓓ Ⓔ

Score Sheet

ADDRESS CHECKING: Your score on the Address Checking part is based upon the number of questions you answered correctly minus the number of questions you answered incorrectly. To determine your score, subtract the number of wrong answers from the number of correct answers.

Number Right	–	Number Wrong	=	Raw Score
_____	–	_____	=	_____

MEMORY FOR ADDRESSES: Your score on the Memory for Addresses part is based upon the number of questions you answered correctly minus one-fourth of the questions you answered incorrectly (number wrong divided by 4). Calculate this now:

Number Wrong ÷ 4 = _____ .

Number Right	–	Number Wrong	÷	4	=	Raw Score
_____	–	_____			=	_____

NUMBER SERIES: Your score on the Number Series part is based only on the number of questions you answered correctly. Wrong answers do not count against you.

Number Right	=	Raw Score
_____	=	_____

FOLLOWING ORAL INSTRUCTIONS: Your score on the Following Oral Instructions part is based only upon the number of questions you marked correctly on the answer sheet. The worksheet is not scored, and wrong answers on the answer sheet do not count against you.

Number Right	=	Raw Score
_____	=	_____

TOTAL SCORE: To find your total raw score, add together the raw scores for each section of the exam.

Address Checking Score   _____
\+
Memory for Addresses Score   _____
\+
Number Series Score   _____
\+
Following Oral Instructions Score   _____
=
     _____

Total Raw Score   _____

Self Evaluation Chart

Calculate your raw score for each test as shown above. Then check to see where your score falls on the scale from Poor to Excellent. Lightly shade in the boxes in which your scores fall.

Part	Excellent	Good	Average	Fair	Poor
Address Checking	80–95	65–79	50–64	35–49	1–34
Memory for Addresses	75–88	60–74	45–59	30–44	1–29
Number Series	21–24	18–20	14–17	11–13	1–10
Following Oral Instructions	27–31	23–26	19–22	14–18	1–13

Fourth Model Exam

Part A—Address Checking

Sample Questions

You will be allowed three minutes to read the directions and answer the five sample questions that follow. On the actual test, however, you will have only six minutes to answer 95 questions, so see how quickly you can compare addresses and still get the correct answer.

DIRECTIONS: Each question consists of two addresses. If the two addresses are alike in EVERY way, mark A on your answer sheet. If the two addresses are different in ANY way, mark D on your answer sheet.

1 ... Ft Collins CO 80523   Ft Collins CO 85023

2 ... 3626 Pennsylvania Ave NE   3626 Pennsylvania Ave NE

3 ... 2418 E 514th St   2418 E 515th St

4 ... 4437 Continental Tpke   4437 Continental Tpke

5 ... 682 Dunbarton Rd   682 Dunbarton Dr

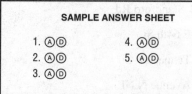

SAMPLE ANSWER SHEET

1. (A)(D)   4. (A)(D)
2. (A)(D)   5. (A)(D)
3. (A)(D)

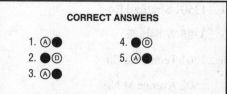

CORRECT ANSWERS

1. (A)●   4. ●(D)
2. ●(D)   5. (A)●
3. (A)●

191

Address Checking

Time: 6 Minutes. 95 Questions.

DIRECTIONS: For each question, compare the address in the left column with the address in the right column. If the two addresses are ALIKE IN EVERY WAY, blacken space A on your answer sheet. If the two addresses are DIFFERENT IN ANY WAY, blacken space D on your answer sheet. Correct answers for this test are on page 215.

1 ... 1897 Smicksburg Rd	1897 Smithsburg Rd
2 ... 3609 E Paseo Aldeano	3909 E Paseo Aldeano
3 ... 11787 Ornamental Ln	1787 Ornamental Ln
4 ... 1096 Camino Grande E	1096 Camino Grande E
5 ... 2544 E Radcliff Ave	2544 E Redcliff Ave
6 ... 5796 E Narragansett Dr	5796 E Narragasett Dr
7 ... 12475 Ebbtide Way W	12475 Ebbtide Way W
8 ... 14396 N Via Armando	14396 S Via Armando
9 ... 2155 S Del Giorgio Rd	2155 S Del Giorgio Rd
10 ... 16550 Bainbridge Cir	16505 Bainbridge Cir
11 ... 1826 Milneburg Rd	1826 Milneburg St
12 ... Eureka KS 67045	Eureka KY 67045
13 ... 4010 Glenaddie Ave	4010 Glenaddie Ave
14 ... 13501 Stratford Rd	13501 Standford Rd
15 ... 3296 W 64th St	3296 E 64th St
16 ... 2201 Tennessee Cir	2201 Tennessee Cir
17 ... 1502 Avenue M NE	1502 Avenue N NE
18 ... 1096 SE Longrone Dr	1096 SE Longrone Dr
19 ... 1267 Darthmouth Ct	1267 Darthmont Ct
20 ... 825 Ophanage Rd	825 Ophanage Rd
21 ... 1754 Golden Springs Rd	1754 Golden Springs Road
22 ... 1015 Tallwoods Ln	1015 Tallwoods Ln
23 ... 1097 Lambada Dr	1097 Lambadd Dr
24 ... Vredenburgh AL 36481	Verdenburgh AL 36481
25 ... 1800 Monticello Ave	1800 Monticello Ave
26 ... 1723 Yellowbird Ln	1723 Yellowbird Ct
27 ... 700 Valca Materials Rd	700 Valca Materials Rd
28 ... 1569 Ladywood Ln N	1569 Ladywood Ln W
29 ... 3256 Interurban Dr	3256 Interurban Dr

30 ... 1507 Haughton Cir	1507 Haughton Ct
31 ... 8971 Robertson Ave	8971 Robinson Ave
32 ... 3801 NE 49th Street	3801 NW 49th Street
33 ... 4102 Chalkville Rd	4102 Chalkview Rd
34 ... 1709 Ingersoll Cir	1709 Ingersoll Cir
35 ... 6800 N Nantucket Ln	6800 N Nantucket Ln
36 ... 12401 Tarrymore Dr	12401 Terrymore Dr
37 ... 1097 Huntsville Ave	1097 Huntsville Ave
38 ... 3566 Lornaridge Pl	3566 Lornaridge Pl
39 ... 2039 Klondike Ave SW	2039 Klondie Ave SW
40 ... 3267 Mayland Ln	3267 Maryland Ln
41 ... 12956 Strawberry Ln	12596 Strawberry Ln
42 ... De Armanville AL 36257	De Armanville AL 36257
43 ... 6015 Anniston Dr	6015 Anneston Dr
44 ... 1525 E 90th St	1525 E 90th St
45 ... 1299 Chappaque Rd	1266 Chappaque Rd
46 ... 2156 Juliette Dr	2156 Juliaetta Dr
47 ... 999 N Hollingsworth St	999 S Hollingsworth St
48 ... 16901 Odum Crest Ln	19601 Odum Crest Ln
49 ... 9787 Zellmark Dr	9787 Zealmark Dr
50 ... 11103 NE Feasell Ave	11103 NE Feasell Ave
51 ... 51121 N Mattison Rd	51121 S Mattison Rd
52 ... 8326 Blackjack Ln	8326 Blackjack Blvd
53 ... 18765 Lagarde Ave	18765 Lagrande Ave
54 ... 11297 Gallatin Ln	11297 Gallatin Ln
55 ... Wormleysburg PA 17043	Wormleysburg PA 17043
56 ... 22371 N Sprague Ave	22371 S Sprague Ave
57 ... 15014 Warrior River Rd	15014 Warrior River Rd
58 ... 45721 Hueytown Plaza	45721 Hueytowne Plaza
59 ... 8973 Tedescki Dr	8793 Tedescki Dr
60 ... 12995 Raimond Muscoda Pl	12995 Raimont Muscoda Pl
61 ... Phippsburg CO 80469	Phippsburg CA 80469
62 ... 52003 W 49th Ave	52003 W 46th Ave
63 ... 17201 Zenobia Cir	17210 Zenobia Cir

64	4800 Garrison Cir	4800 Garrison Dr
65	Los Angeles CA 90070	Los Angeles CA 90076
66	14798 W 62nd Ave	14198 W 62nd Ave
67	7191 E Eldridge Way	7191 E Eldridge Way
68	1279 S Quintard Dr	1279 S Guintard Dr
69	21899 Dellwood Ave	21899 Dillwood Ave
70	7191 Zenophone Cir	7191 Zenohone Cir
71	4301 Los Encinos Way	4301 Los Encinas Way
72	19700 Ostronic Dr NW	19700 Ostronic Dr NE
73	23291 Van Velsire Dr	23219 Van Velsire Dr
74	547 Paradise Valley Rd	547 Paradise Valley Ct
75	23167 Saltillo Ave	23167 Santillo Ave
76	43001 Mourning Dove Way	43001 Mourning Dove Way
77	21183 Declaration Ave	21183 Declaration Ave
78	10799 Via Sierra Ramal Ave	10799 Via Sierra Ramel Ave
79	16567 Hermosillia Ct	16597 Hermosillia Ct
80	Villamont VA 24178	Villamont VA 24178
81	18794 Villaboso Ave	18794 Villeboso Ave
82	24136 Ranthom Ave	24136 Ranthon Ave
83	13489 Golondrina Pl	13489 Golondrina St
84	6598 Adamsville Ave	6598 Adamsville Ave
85	12641 Indals Pl NE	12641 Indals Pl NW
86	19701 SE 2nd Avenue	19701 NE 2nd Avenue
87	22754 Cachalote Ln	22754 Cachalott Ln
88	12341 Kingfisher Rd	12341 Kingsfisher Rd
89	24168 Lorenzana Dr	24168 Lorenzano Dr
90	32480 Blackfriar Rd	32480 Blackfriar Rd
91	16355 Wheeler Dr	16355 Wheelen Dr
92	5100 Magna Carta Rd	5100 Magna Certa Rd
93	2341 N Federalist Pl	2341 N Federalist Pl
94	22200 Timpangos Rd	22200 Timpangos Rd
95	19704 Calderon Rd	19704 Calderon Rd

END OF ADDRESS CHECKING

Part B—Memory for Addresses

Sample Questions

The sample questions for this part are based upon the addresses in the five boxes below. Your task is to mark on your answer sheet the letter of the box in which each address belongs. You will have five minutes now to study the locations of the addresses. Then cover the boxes and try to mark the location of the sample questions. You may look back at the boxes if you cannot yet mark the address locations from memory.

The exam itself provides three practice sessions before the question set that really counts. Practice I and Practice III supply you with the boxes and permit you to refer to them if necessary. Practice II and the Memory for Addresses test itself do not permit you to look at the boxes. The test itself is based on memory.

A	B	C	D	E
8100–8399 Test	6800–6999 Test	7600–8099 Test	8400–8699 Test	7000–7599 Test
Pigeon	Vampire	Octopus	Ghost	Lever
7600–8099 City	7000–7599 City	8100–8399 City	6800–6999 City	8400–8699 City
Webb	Yak	Fleet	Hammer	Nougat
6800–6999 Mark	8400–8699 Mark	7000–7599 Mark	7600–8099 Mark	8100–8399 Mark

1. 7000–7599 Test
2. Octopus
3. Nougat
4. 8100–8399 Mark
5. 7000–7599 City
6. 8100–8399 City
7. Pigeon

8. 6800–6999 Mark
9. Vampire
10. Yak
11. 8400–8699 Test
12. 7600–8099 City
13. 7000–7599 Mark
14. Hammer

SAMPLE ANSWER SHEET

1. Ⓐ Ⓑ Ⓒ Ⓓ Ⓔ
2. Ⓐ Ⓑ Ⓒ Ⓓ Ⓔ
3. Ⓐ Ⓑ Ⓒ Ⓓ Ⓔ
4. Ⓐ Ⓑ Ⓒ Ⓓ Ⓔ
5. Ⓐ Ⓑ Ⓒ Ⓓ Ⓔ
6. Ⓐ Ⓑ Ⓒ Ⓓ Ⓔ
7. Ⓐ Ⓑ Ⓒ Ⓓ Ⓔ
8. Ⓐ Ⓑ Ⓒ Ⓓ Ⓔ
9. Ⓐ Ⓑ Ⓒ Ⓓ Ⓔ
10. Ⓐ Ⓑ Ⓒ Ⓓ Ⓔ
11. Ⓐ Ⓑ Ⓒ Ⓓ Ⓔ
12. Ⓐ Ⓑ Ⓒ Ⓓ Ⓔ
13. Ⓐ Ⓑ Ⓒ Ⓓ Ⓔ
14. Ⓐ Ⓑ Ⓒ Ⓓ Ⓔ

CORRECT ANSWERS

1. Ⓐ Ⓑ Ⓒ Ⓓ ●
2. Ⓐ Ⓑ ● Ⓓ Ⓔ
3. Ⓐ Ⓑ Ⓒ Ⓓ ●
4. Ⓐ Ⓑ Ⓒ Ⓓ ●
5. Ⓐ ● Ⓒ Ⓓ Ⓔ
6. Ⓐ Ⓑ ● Ⓓ Ⓔ
7. ● Ⓑ Ⓒ Ⓓ Ⓔ
8. ● Ⓑ Ⓒ Ⓓ Ⓔ
9. Ⓐ ● Ⓒ Ⓓ Ⓔ
10. Ⓐ ● Ⓒ Ⓓ Ⓔ
11. Ⓐ Ⓑ Ⓒ ● Ⓔ
12. ● Ⓑ Ⓒ Ⓓ Ⓔ
13. Ⓐ Ⓑ ● Ⓓ Ⓔ
14. Ⓐ Ⓑ Ⓒ ● Ⓔ

Practice for Memory for Addresses

DIRECTIONS: The five boxes below are labelled A, B, C, D, and E. In each box are three sets of number spans with names and two names that are not associated with numbers. In the next THREE MINUTES, you must try to memorize the box location of each name and number span. The position of a name or number span within its box is not important. You need only remember the letter of the box in which the item is to be found. You will use these names and numbers to answer three sets of practice questions that are NOT scored and one actual test that is scored. Correct answers are on pages 216 and 217.

A	B	C	D	E
8100–8399 Test	6800–6999 Test	7600–8099 Test	8400–8699 Test	7000–7599 Test
Pigeon	Vampire	Octopus	Ghost	Lever
7600–8099 City	7000–7599 City	8100–8399 City	6800–6999 City	8400–8699 City
Webb	Yak	Fleet	Hammer	Nougat
6800–6999 Mark	8400–8699 Mark	7000–7599 Mark	7600–8099 Mark	8100–8399 Mark

Practice I

DIRECTIONS: Use the next THREE MINUTES to mark on the Practice I answer sheet the letter of the box in which each item that follows is to be found. Try to mark each item without looking back at the boxes. If, however, you get stuck, you may refer to the boxes during this practice exercise. If you find that you must look at the boxes, try to memorize as you do so. This test is for practice only. It will not be scored.

1. 6800–6999 Test
2. 7000–7599 City
3. 8100–8399 Mark
4. Octopus
5. Webb
6. 7000–7599 Test
7. Nougat
8. 7600–8099 Mark
9. 7000–7599 City
10. Fleet
11. Hammer
12. 7000–7599 Mark
13. 7600–8099 City
14. 8400–8699 Test
15. 8400–8699 Mark
16. 7600–8099 City
17. Vampire
18. Lever
19. Ghost

20. 6800–6999 Mark
21. 8100–8399 City
22. 8400–8699 City
23. 8400–8699 Mark
24. Pigeon
25. Fleet
26. 8400–8699 Test
27. 7000–7599 Mark
28. 6800–6999 Test
29. 7600–8099 City
30. Yak
31. Nougat
32. 8100–8399 Test
33. 7000–7599 Test
34. Lever
35. 7000–7599 City
36. 7600–8099 Mark
37. Octopus
38. Webb

39. Hammer
40. 8100–8399 Mark
41. 7600–8099 Test
42. 6800–6999 City
43. 7600–8099 Test
44. Fleet
45. 6800–6999 Mark
46. 8100–8399 City
47. 8400–8699 City
48. 8400–8699 Mark
49. Yak
50. Vampire
51. 7000–7599 Test
52. 8100–8399 Mark
53. 8100–8399 Test
54. Ghost
55. Fleet
56. 6800–6999 Mark
57. 7000–7599 Mark

58. 7000–7599 City
59. Lever
60. Octopus
61. 7600–8099 Test
62. 8400–8699 Test
63. 7600–8099 City
64. Hammer
65. Pigeon
66. 7600–8099 Mark
67. 6800–6999 City
68. 6800–6999 Test

69. 8100–8399 City
70. Webb
71. Nougat
72. 7600–8099 Test
73. 8400–8699 City
74. 8400–8699 Mark
75. 8100–8399 Test
76. 7000–7599 City
77. 7000–7599 Mark
78. Hammer
79. Lever

80. Pigeon
81. 7600–8099 Test
82. 7000–7599 Test
83. 8100–8399 Mark
84. Vampire
85. Fleet
86. 7600–8099 City
87. 6800–6999 Mark
88. 8400–8699 City

Practice I Answer Sheet

1 Ⓐ Ⓑ Ⓒ Ⓓ Ⓔ
2 Ⓐ Ⓑ Ⓒ Ⓓ Ⓔ
3 Ⓐ Ⓑ Ⓒ Ⓓ Ⓔ
4 Ⓐ Ⓑ Ⓒ Ⓓ Ⓔ
5 Ⓐ Ⓑ Ⓒ Ⓓ Ⓔ
6 Ⓐ Ⓑ Ⓒ Ⓓ Ⓔ
7 Ⓐ Ⓑ Ⓒ Ⓓ Ⓔ
8 Ⓐ Ⓑ Ⓒ Ⓓ Ⓔ
9 Ⓐ Ⓑ Ⓒ Ⓓ Ⓔ
10 Ⓐ Ⓑ Ⓒ Ⓓ Ⓔ
11 Ⓐ Ⓑ Ⓒ Ⓓ Ⓔ
12 Ⓐ Ⓑ Ⓒ Ⓓ Ⓔ
13 Ⓐ Ⓑ Ⓒ Ⓓ Ⓔ
14 Ⓐ Ⓑ Ⓒ Ⓓ Ⓔ
15 Ⓐ Ⓑ Ⓒ Ⓓ Ⓔ
16 Ⓐ Ⓑ Ⓒ Ⓓ Ⓔ
17 Ⓐ Ⓑ Ⓒ Ⓓ Ⓔ
18 Ⓐ Ⓑ Ⓒ Ⓓ Ⓔ
19 Ⓐ Ⓑ Ⓒ Ⓓ Ⓔ
20 Ⓐ Ⓑ Ⓒ Ⓓ Ⓔ
21 Ⓐ Ⓑ Ⓒ Ⓓ Ⓔ
22 Ⓐ Ⓑ Ⓒ Ⓓ Ⓔ

23 Ⓐ Ⓑ Ⓒ Ⓓ Ⓔ
24 Ⓐ Ⓑ Ⓒ Ⓓ Ⓔ
25 Ⓐ Ⓑ Ⓒ Ⓓ Ⓔ
26 Ⓐ Ⓑ Ⓒ Ⓓ Ⓔ
27 Ⓐ Ⓑ Ⓒ Ⓓ Ⓔ
28 Ⓐ Ⓑ Ⓒ Ⓓ Ⓔ
29 Ⓐ Ⓑ Ⓒ Ⓓ Ⓔ
30 Ⓐ Ⓑ Ⓒ Ⓓ Ⓔ
31 Ⓐ Ⓑ Ⓒ Ⓓ Ⓔ
32 Ⓐ Ⓑ Ⓒ Ⓓ Ⓔ
33 Ⓐ Ⓑ Ⓒ Ⓓ Ⓔ
34 Ⓐ Ⓑ Ⓒ Ⓓ Ⓔ
35 Ⓐ Ⓑ Ⓒ Ⓓ Ⓔ
36 Ⓐ Ⓑ Ⓒ Ⓓ Ⓔ
37 Ⓐ Ⓑ Ⓒ Ⓓ Ⓔ
38 Ⓐ Ⓑ Ⓒ Ⓓ Ⓔ
39 Ⓐ Ⓑ Ⓒ Ⓓ Ⓔ
40 Ⓐ Ⓑ Ⓒ Ⓓ Ⓔ
41 Ⓐ Ⓑ Ⓒ Ⓓ Ⓔ
42 Ⓐ Ⓑ Ⓒ Ⓓ Ⓔ
43 Ⓐ Ⓑ Ⓒ Ⓓ Ⓔ
44 Ⓐ Ⓑ Ⓒ Ⓓ Ⓔ

45 Ⓐ Ⓑ Ⓒ Ⓓ Ⓔ
46 Ⓐ Ⓑ Ⓒ Ⓓ Ⓔ
47 Ⓐ Ⓑ Ⓒ Ⓓ Ⓔ
48 Ⓐ Ⓑ Ⓒ Ⓓ Ⓔ
49 Ⓐ Ⓑ Ⓒ Ⓓ Ⓔ
50 Ⓐ Ⓑ Ⓒ Ⓓ Ⓔ
51 Ⓐ Ⓑ Ⓒ Ⓓ Ⓔ
52 Ⓐ Ⓑ Ⓒ Ⓓ Ⓔ
53 Ⓐ Ⓑ Ⓒ Ⓓ Ⓔ
54 Ⓐ Ⓑ Ⓒ Ⓓ Ⓔ
55 Ⓐ Ⓑ Ⓒ Ⓓ Ⓔ
56 Ⓐ Ⓑ Ⓒ Ⓓ Ⓔ
57 Ⓐ Ⓑ Ⓒ Ⓓ Ⓔ
58 Ⓐ Ⓑ Ⓒ Ⓓ Ⓔ
59 Ⓐ Ⓑ Ⓒ Ⓓ Ⓔ
60 Ⓐ Ⓑ Ⓒ Ⓓ Ⓔ
61 Ⓐ Ⓑ Ⓒ Ⓓ Ⓔ
62 Ⓐ Ⓑ Ⓒ Ⓓ Ⓔ
63 Ⓐ Ⓑ Ⓒ Ⓓ Ⓔ
64 Ⓐ Ⓑ Ⓒ Ⓓ Ⓔ
65 Ⓐ Ⓑ Ⓒ Ⓓ Ⓔ
66 Ⓐ Ⓑ Ⓒ Ⓓ Ⓔ

67 Ⓐ Ⓑ Ⓒ Ⓓ Ⓔ
68 Ⓐ Ⓑ Ⓒ Ⓓ Ⓔ
69 Ⓐ Ⓑ Ⓒ Ⓓ Ⓔ
70 Ⓐ Ⓑ Ⓒ Ⓓ Ⓔ
71 Ⓐ Ⓑ Ⓒ Ⓓ Ⓔ
72 Ⓐ Ⓑ Ⓒ Ⓓ Ⓔ
73 Ⓐ Ⓑ Ⓒ Ⓓ Ⓔ
74 Ⓐ Ⓑ Ⓒ Ⓓ Ⓔ
75 Ⓐ Ⓑ Ⓒ Ⓓ Ⓔ
76 Ⓐ Ⓑ Ⓒ Ⓓ Ⓔ
77 Ⓐ Ⓑ Ⓒ Ⓓ Ⓔ
78 Ⓐ Ⓑ Ⓒ Ⓓ Ⓔ
79 Ⓐ Ⓑ Ⓒ Ⓓ Ⓔ
80 Ⓐ Ⓑ Ⓒ Ⓓ Ⓔ
81 Ⓐ Ⓑ Ⓒ Ⓓ Ⓔ
82 Ⓐ Ⓑ Ⓒ Ⓓ Ⓔ
83 Ⓐ Ⓑ Ⓒ Ⓓ Ⓔ
84 Ⓐ Ⓑ Ⓒ Ⓓ Ⓔ
85 Ⓐ Ⓑ Ⓒ Ⓓ Ⓔ
86 Ⓐ Ⓑ Ⓒ Ⓓ Ⓔ
87 Ⓐ Ⓑ Ⓒ Ⓓ Ⓔ
88 Ⓐ Ⓑ Ⓒ Ⓓ Ⓔ

Practice II

DIRECTIONS: The next 88 questions constitute another practice exercise. Mark your answers on the Practice II answer sheet. Again, the time limit is THREE MINUTES. This time, however, you must NOT look at the boxes while answering the questions. You must rely on your memory in marking the box location of each item. This practice test will not be scored.

1. 7000–7599 Mark
2. 6800–6999 City
3. 6800–6999 Test
4. Pigeon
5. Nougat
6. 8400–8699 Test
7. 7000–7599 City
8. 6800–6999 Mark
9. Hammer
10. Ghost
11. 7600–8099 City
12. 8100–8399 Mark
13. 7600–8099 Mark
14. 7600–8099 Test
15. Octopus
16. Webb
17. 8100–8399 City
18. 8400–8699 City
19. 6800–6999 Mark
20. Fleet
21. Lever
22. Yak
23. 8100–8399 Test
24. 7000–7599 Test
25. Vampire
26. Octopus
27. 6800–6999 Test
28. 6800–6999 City
29. 6800–6999 Mark
30. Lever

31. Nougat
32. 7000–7599 City
33. 8100–8399 Mark
34. 8100–8399 City
35. 8100–8399 Test
36. 8400–8699 Mark
37. Yak
38. Webb
39. 7600–8099 Test
40. 7000–7599 Mark
41. Fleet
42. 8400–8699 City
43. 7600–8099 City
44. 8400–8699 Test
45. Pigeon
46. Ghost
47. Hammer
48. 7600–8099 Mark
49. 7000–7599 Test
50. 8100–8399 Mark
51. 6800–6999 City
52. 7600–8099 Test
53. Lever
54. Hammer
55. 8100–8399 Test
56. 7000–7599 City
57. 7000–7599 Mark
58. Pigeon
59. Vampire
60. 8100–8399 City

61. 7600–8099 City
62. 7000–7599 Test
63. 6800–6999 Mark
64. Nougat
65. Yak
66. Webb
67. 8400–8699 Mark
68. 7600–8099 Mark
69. 8400–8699 City
70. 6800–6999 Test
71. Ghost
72. Octopus
73. Fleet
74. 8400–8699 Test
75. 7600–8099 Test
76. 6800–6999 Mark
77. 7600–8099 City
78. Nougat
79. Webb
80. 6800–6999 City
81. 6800–6999 Test
82. 7600–8099 Mark
83. Vampire
84. Octopus
85. 7000–7599 Test
86. 8100–8399 City
87. 6800–6999 Mark
88. 8100–8399 Test

Practice II Answer Sheet

1 Ⓐ Ⓑ Ⓒ Ⓓ Ⓔ	23 Ⓐ Ⓑ Ⓒ Ⓓ Ⓔ	45 Ⓐ Ⓑ Ⓒ Ⓓ Ⓔ	67 Ⓐ Ⓑ Ⓒ Ⓓ Ⓔ
2 Ⓐ Ⓑ Ⓒ Ⓓ Ⓔ	24 Ⓐ Ⓑ Ⓒ Ⓓ Ⓔ	46 Ⓐ Ⓑ Ⓒ Ⓓ Ⓔ	68 Ⓐ Ⓑ Ⓒ Ⓓ Ⓔ
3 Ⓐ Ⓑ Ⓒ Ⓓ Ⓔ	25 Ⓐ Ⓑ Ⓒ Ⓓ Ⓔ	47 Ⓐ Ⓑ Ⓒ Ⓓ Ⓔ	69 Ⓐ Ⓑ Ⓒ Ⓓ Ⓔ
4 Ⓐ Ⓑ Ⓒ Ⓓ Ⓔ	26 Ⓐ Ⓑ Ⓒ Ⓓ Ⓔ	48 Ⓐ Ⓑ Ⓒ Ⓓ Ⓔ	70 Ⓐ Ⓑ Ⓒ Ⓓ Ⓔ
5 Ⓐ Ⓑ Ⓒ Ⓓ Ⓔ	27 Ⓐ Ⓑ Ⓒ Ⓓ Ⓔ	49 Ⓐ Ⓑ Ⓒ Ⓓ Ⓔ	71 Ⓐ Ⓑ Ⓒ Ⓓ Ⓔ
6 Ⓐ Ⓑ Ⓒ Ⓓ Ⓔ	28 Ⓐ Ⓑ Ⓒ Ⓓ Ⓔ	50 Ⓐ Ⓑ Ⓒ Ⓓ Ⓔ	72 Ⓐ Ⓑ Ⓒ Ⓓ Ⓔ
7 Ⓐ Ⓑ Ⓒ Ⓓ Ⓔ	29 Ⓐ Ⓑ Ⓒ Ⓓ Ⓔ	51 Ⓐ Ⓑ Ⓒ Ⓓ Ⓔ	73 Ⓐ Ⓑ Ⓒ Ⓓ Ⓔ
8 Ⓐ Ⓑ Ⓒ Ⓓ Ⓔ	30 Ⓐ Ⓑ Ⓒ Ⓓ Ⓔ	52 Ⓐ Ⓑ Ⓒ Ⓓ Ⓔ	74 Ⓐ Ⓑ Ⓒ Ⓓ Ⓔ
9 Ⓐ Ⓑ Ⓒ Ⓓ Ⓔ	31 Ⓐ Ⓑ Ⓒ Ⓓ Ⓔ	53 Ⓐ Ⓑ Ⓒ Ⓓ Ⓔ	75 Ⓐ Ⓑ Ⓒ Ⓓ Ⓔ
10 Ⓐ Ⓑ Ⓒ Ⓓ Ⓔ	32 Ⓐ Ⓑ Ⓒ Ⓓ Ⓔ	54 Ⓐ Ⓑ Ⓒ Ⓓ Ⓔ	76 Ⓐ Ⓑ Ⓒ Ⓓ Ⓔ
11 Ⓐ Ⓑ Ⓒ Ⓓ Ⓔ	33 Ⓐ Ⓑ Ⓒ Ⓓ Ⓔ	55 Ⓐ Ⓑ Ⓒ Ⓓ Ⓔ	77 Ⓐ Ⓑ Ⓒ Ⓓ Ⓔ
12 Ⓐ Ⓑ Ⓒ Ⓓ Ⓔ	34 Ⓐ Ⓑ Ⓒ Ⓓ Ⓔ	56 Ⓐ Ⓑ Ⓒ Ⓓ Ⓔ	78 Ⓐ Ⓑ Ⓒ Ⓓ Ⓔ
13 Ⓐ Ⓑ Ⓒ Ⓓ Ⓔ	35 Ⓐ Ⓑ Ⓒ Ⓓ Ⓔ	57 Ⓐ Ⓑ Ⓒ Ⓓ Ⓔ	79 Ⓐ Ⓑ Ⓒ Ⓓ Ⓔ
14 Ⓐ Ⓑ Ⓒ Ⓓ Ⓔ	36 Ⓐ Ⓑ Ⓒ Ⓓ Ⓔ	58 Ⓐ Ⓑ Ⓒ Ⓓ Ⓔ	80 Ⓐ Ⓑ Ⓒ Ⓓ Ⓔ
15 Ⓐ Ⓑ Ⓒ Ⓓ Ⓔ	37 Ⓐ Ⓑ Ⓒ Ⓓ Ⓔ	59 Ⓐ Ⓑ Ⓒ Ⓓ Ⓔ	81 Ⓐ Ⓑ Ⓒ Ⓓ Ⓔ
16 Ⓐ Ⓑ Ⓒ Ⓓ Ⓔ	38 Ⓐ Ⓑ Ⓒ Ⓓ Ⓔ	60 Ⓐ Ⓑ Ⓒ Ⓓ Ⓔ	82 Ⓐ Ⓑ Ⓒ Ⓓ Ⓔ
17 Ⓐ Ⓑ Ⓒ Ⓓ Ⓔ	39 Ⓐ Ⓑ Ⓒ Ⓓ Ⓔ	61 Ⓐ Ⓑ Ⓒ Ⓓ Ⓔ	83 Ⓐ Ⓑ Ⓒ Ⓓ Ⓔ
18 Ⓐ Ⓑ Ⓒ Ⓓ Ⓔ	40 Ⓐ Ⓑ Ⓒ Ⓓ Ⓔ	62 Ⓐ Ⓑ Ⓒ Ⓓ Ⓔ	84 Ⓐ Ⓑ Ⓒ Ⓓ Ⓔ
19 Ⓐ Ⓑ Ⓒ Ⓓ Ⓔ	41 Ⓐ Ⓑ Ⓒ Ⓓ Ⓔ	63 Ⓐ Ⓑ Ⓒ Ⓓ Ⓔ	85 Ⓐ Ⓑ Ⓒ Ⓓ Ⓔ
20 Ⓐ Ⓑ Ⓒ Ⓓ Ⓔ	42 Ⓐ Ⓑ Ⓒ Ⓓ Ⓔ	64 Ⓐ Ⓑ Ⓒ Ⓓ Ⓔ	86 Ⓐ Ⓑ Ⓒ Ⓓ Ⓔ
21 Ⓐ Ⓑ Ⓒ Ⓓ Ⓔ	43 Ⓐ Ⓑ Ⓒ Ⓓ Ⓔ	65 Ⓐ Ⓑ Ⓒ Ⓓ Ⓔ	87 Ⓐ Ⓑ Ⓒ Ⓓ Ⓔ
22 Ⓐ Ⓑ Ⓒ Ⓓ Ⓔ	44 Ⓐ Ⓑ Ⓒ Ⓓ Ⓔ	66 Ⓐ Ⓑ Ⓒ Ⓓ Ⓔ	88 Ⓐ Ⓑ Ⓒ Ⓓ Ⓔ

Practice III

DIRECTIONS: The names and addresses are repeated for you in the boxes below. Each name and each number span is in the same box in which you found it in the original set. You will now be allowed FIVE MINUTES to study the locations again. Do your best to memorize the letter of the box in which each item is located. This is your last chance to see the boxes.

A	B	C	D	E
8100–8399 Test	6800–6999 Test	7600–8099 Test	8400–8699 Test	7000–7599 Test
Pigeon	Vampire	Octopus	Ghost	Lever
7600–8099 City	7000–7599 City	8100–8399 City	6800–6999 City	8400–8699 City
Webb	Yak	Fleet	Hammer	Nougat
6800–6999 Mark	8400–8699 Mark	7000–7599 Mark	7600–8099 Mark	8100–8399 Mark

DIRECTIONS: This is your last practice test. Mark the location of each of the 88 items on your answer sheet. You will have FIVE MINUTES to answer these questions. Do NOT look back at the boxes. This practice test will not be scored.

1. Fleet
2. Lever
3. 8400–8699 Test
4. 7000–7599 City
5. 6800–6999 Mark
6. Vampire
7. Pigeon
8. 8100–8399 Test
9. 8100–8399 Mark
10. 7000–7599 Test
11. 8100–8399 City
12. Octopus
13. Ghost
14. Yak
15. 6800–6999 City
16. 6800–6999 Test
17. 7600–8099 Mark
18. 7600–8099 City
19. Hammer
20. Nougat
21. 8400–8699 Mark

22. 8400–8699 City
23. 8400–8699 Test
24. 7000–7599 Mark
25. Octopus
26. Fleet
27. 8100–8399 City
28. 8100–8399 Test
29. 7000–7599 City
30. 7000–7599 Test
31. 8100–8399 Test
32. 7000–7599 City
33. 7000–7599 Mark
34. Nougat
35. Ghost
36. 6800–6999 City
37. 7000–7599 Test
38. 8100–8399 Mark
39. Pigeon
40. Webb
41. 7600–8099 City
42. 8100–8399 City

43. 8400–8699 Mark
44. Fleet
45. Vampire
46. 6800–6999 Test
47. 6800–6999 Mark
48. 7600–8099 Mark
49. Hammer
50. Yak
51. 8400–8699 City
52. 8400–8699 Test
53. 7600–8099 Test
54. Lever
55. Octopus
56. 7000–7599 Test
57. 7000–7599 Mark
58. 7000–7599 City
59. 8100–8399 Test
60. Vampire
61. 8100–8399 City
62. Hammer
63. 8100–8399 Mark

64. 7000–7599 Test
65. Ghost
66. Yak
67. 6800–6999 Mark
68. 7600–8099 City
69. Octopus
70. Fleet
71. 8400–8699 City
72. 7000-7599 Mark

73. 7600–8099 Test
74. 7600–8099 Mark
75. 6800–6999 City
76. 6800–6999 Test
77. Webb
78. Pigeon
79. Lever
80. 8400–8699 Test
81. 8400–8699 Mark

82. Nougat
83. 8400–8699 City
84. 7000–7599 City
85. 7000–7599 Test
86. Hammer
87. 6800–6999 Mark
88. Yak

Practice III Answer Sheet

1 Ⓐ Ⓑ Ⓒ Ⓓ Ⓔ
2 Ⓐ Ⓑ Ⓒ Ⓓ Ⓔ
3 Ⓐ Ⓑ Ⓒ Ⓓ Ⓔ
4 Ⓐ Ⓑ Ⓒ Ⓓ Ⓔ
5 Ⓐ Ⓑ Ⓒ Ⓓ Ⓔ
6 Ⓐ Ⓑ Ⓒ Ⓓ Ⓔ
7 Ⓐ Ⓑ Ⓒ Ⓓ Ⓔ
8 Ⓐ Ⓑ Ⓒ Ⓓ Ⓔ
9 Ⓐ Ⓑ Ⓒ Ⓓ Ⓔ
10 Ⓐ Ⓑ Ⓒ Ⓓ Ⓔ
11 Ⓐ Ⓑ Ⓒ Ⓓ Ⓔ
12 Ⓐ Ⓑ Ⓒ Ⓓ Ⓔ
13 Ⓐ Ⓑ Ⓒ Ⓓ Ⓔ
14 Ⓐ Ⓑ Ⓒ Ⓓ Ⓔ
15 Ⓐ Ⓑ Ⓒ Ⓓ Ⓔ
16 Ⓐ Ⓑ Ⓒ Ⓓ Ⓔ
17 Ⓐ Ⓑ Ⓒ Ⓓ Ⓔ
18 Ⓐ Ⓑ Ⓒ Ⓓ Ⓔ
19 Ⓐ Ⓑ Ⓒ Ⓓ Ⓔ
20 Ⓐ Ⓑ Ⓒ Ⓓ Ⓔ
21 Ⓐ Ⓑ Ⓒ Ⓓ Ⓔ
22 Ⓐ Ⓑ Ⓒ Ⓓ Ⓔ

23 Ⓐ Ⓑ Ⓒ Ⓓ Ⓔ
24 Ⓐ Ⓑ Ⓒ Ⓓ Ⓔ
25 Ⓐ Ⓑ Ⓒ Ⓓ Ⓔ
26 Ⓐ Ⓑ Ⓒ Ⓓ Ⓔ
27 Ⓐ Ⓑ Ⓒ Ⓓ Ⓔ
28 Ⓐ Ⓑ Ⓒ Ⓓ Ⓔ
29 Ⓐ Ⓑ Ⓒ Ⓓ Ⓔ
30 Ⓐ Ⓑ Ⓒ Ⓓ Ⓔ
31 Ⓐ Ⓑ Ⓒ Ⓓ Ⓔ
32 Ⓐ Ⓑ Ⓒ Ⓓ Ⓔ
33 Ⓐ Ⓑ Ⓒ Ⓓ Ⓔ
34 Ⓐ Ⓑ Ⓒ Ⓓ Ⓔ
35 Ⓐ Ⓑ Ⓒ Ⓓ Ⓔ
36 Ⓐ Ⓑ Ⓒ Ⓓ Ⓔ
37 Ⓐ Ⓑ Ⓒ Ⓓ Ⓔ
38 Ⓐ Ⓑ Ⓒ Ⓓ Ⓔ
39 Ⓐ Ⓑ Ⓒ Ⓓ Ⓔ
40 Ⓐ Ⓑ Ⓒ Ⓓ Ⓔ
41 Ⓐ Ⓑ Ⓒ Ⓓ Ⓔ
42 Ⓐ Ⓑ Ⓒ Ⓓ Ⓔ
43 Ⓐ Ⓑ Ⓒ Ⓓ Ⓔ
44 Ⓐ Ⓑ Ⓒ Ⓓ Ⓔ

45 Ⓐ Ⓑ Ⓒ Ⓓ Ⓔ
46 Ⓐ Ⓑ Ⓒ Ⓓ Ⓔ
47 Ⓐ Ⓑ Ⓒ Ⓓ Ⓔ
48 Ⓐ Ⓑ Ⓒ Ⓓ Ⓔ
49 Ⓐ Ⓑ Ⓒ Ⓓ Ⓔ
50 Ⓐ Ⓑ Ⓒ Ⓓ Ⓔ
51 Ⓐ Ⓑ Ⓒ Ⓓ Ⓔ
52 Ⓐ Ⓑ Ⓒ Ⓓ Ⓔ
53 Ⓐ Ⓑ Ⓒ Ⓓ Ⓔ
54 Ⓐ Ⓑ Ⓒ Ⓓ Ⓔ
55 Ⓐ Ⓑ Ⓒ Ⓓ Ⓔ
56 Ⓐ Ⓑ Ⓒ Ⓓ Ⓔ
57 Ⓐ Ⓑ Ⓒ Ⓓ Ⓔ
58 Ⓐ Ⓑ Ⓒ Ⓓ Ⓔ
59 Ⓐ Ⓑ Ⓒ Ⓓ Ⓔ
60 Ⓐ Ⓑ Ⓒ Ⓓ Ⓔ
61 Ⓐ Ⓑ Ⓒ Ⓓ Ⓔ
62 Ⓐ Ⓑ Ⓒ Ⓓ Ⓔ
63 Ⓐ Ⓑ Ⓒ Ⓓ Ⓔ
64 Ⓐ Ⓑ Ⓒ Ⓓ Ⓔ
65 Ⓐ Ⓑ Ⓒ Ⓓ Ⓔ
66 Ⓐ Ⓑ Ⓒ Ⓓ Ⓔ

67 Ⓐ Ⓑ Ⓒ Ⓓ Ⓔ
68 Ⓐ Ⓑ Ⓒ Ⓓ Ⓔ
69 Ⓐ Ⓑ Ⓒ Ⓓ Ⓔ
70 Ⓐ Ⓑ Ⓒ Ⓓ Ⓔ
71 Ⓐ Ⓑ Ⓒ Ⓓ Ⓔ
72 Ⓐ Ⓑ Ⓒ Ⓓ Ⓔ
73 Ⓐ Ⓑ Ⓒ Ⓓ Ⓔ
74 Ⓐ Ⓑ Ⓒ Ⓓ Ⓔ
75 Ⓐ Ⓑ Ⓒ Ⓓ Ⓔ
76 Ⓐ Ⓑ Ⓒ Ⓓ Ⓔ
77 Ⓐ Ⓑ Ⓒ Ⓓ Ⓔ
78 Ⓐ Ⓑ Ⓒ Ⓓ Ⓔ
79 Ⓐ Ⓑ Ⓒ Ⓓ Ⓔ
80 Ⓐ Ⓑ Ⓒ Ⓓ Ⓔ
81 Ⓐ Ⓑ Ⓒ Ⓓ Ⓔ
82 Ⓐ Ⓑ Ⓒ Ⓓ Ⓔ
83 Ⓐ Ⓑ Ⓒ Ⓓ Ⓔ
84 Ⓐ Ⓑ Ⓒ Ⓓ Ⓔ
85 Ⓐ Ⓑ Ⓒ Ⓓ Ⓔ
86 Ⓐ Ⓑ Ⓒ Ⓓ Ⓔ
87 Ⓐ Ⓑ Ⓒ Ⓓ Ⓔ
88 Ⓐ Ⓑ Ⓒ Ⓓ Ⓔ

Memory for Addresses

Time: 5 Minutes. 88 Questions.

DIRECTIONS: *Mark your answers on the answer sheet in the section headed "MEMORY FOR ADDRESSES." This test will be scored. You are NOT permitted to look at the boxes. Work from memory, as quickly and as accurately as you can. Correct answers are on page 217.*

1. 8400–8699 Test
2. 7000–7599 City
3. 8400–8699 Mark
4. Nougat
5. Pigeon
6. 6800–6999 Test
7. 8100–8399 Test
8. 8400–8699 City
9. 7000–7599 Mark
10. Ghost
11. Hammer
12. Vampire
13. 7600–8099 City
14. 7600–8099 Mark
15. 6800–6999 Mark
16. Octopus
17. Yak
18. 7600–8099 Test
19. 7000–7599 Test
20. 8400–8699 City
21. 8100–8399 Mark
22. Vampire
23. Lever
24. 7600–8099 Test
25. 7600–8099 City
26. 8100–8399 Mark
27. Webb
28. Ghost
29. 6800–6999 Mark
30. 7000–7599 Test

31. 8100–8399 City
32. 8400–8699 City
33. Pigeon
34. Yak
35. 7600–8099 Mark
36. 8400–8699 Mark
37. 8100–8399 Test
38. 6800–6999 City
39. Octopus
40. Hammer
41. Nougat
42. 7000–7599 City
43. 6800–6999 Test
44. 7600–8099 Mark
45. Nougat
46. 8400–8699 City
47. 6800–6999 Mark
48. 7600–8099 Test
49. 7000–7599 City
50. Ghost
51. Fleet
52. Yak
53. 7000–7599 Test
54. 8100–8399 City
55. 7600–8099 City
56. Pigeon
57. Octopus
58. 6800–6999 City
59. 8400–8699 Mark
60. 8100–8399 Mark

61. 8100–8399 Test
62. Webb
63. Hammer
64. 8400–8699 Test
65. 7000–7599 Mark
66. 8100–8399 City
67. Lever
68. Vampire
69. 8100–8399 Test
70. 8400–8699 City
71. 7000–7599 Test
72. 6800–6999 Mark
73. 8100–8399 City
74. 6800–6999 City
75. Yak
76. Nougat
77. Fleet
78. 6800–6999 Test
79. 7000–7599 Mark
80. 7000–7599 City
81. 8100–8399 Test
82. 8100–8399 Mark
83. Pigeon
84. Lever
85. Hammer
86. 8400–8699 Test
87. 8400–8699 Mark
88. 7600–8099 City

END OF MEMORY FOR ADDRESSES

Part C—Number Series

Sample Questions

The following sample questions show you the type of question that will be used in Part C. You will have three minutes to answer the sample questions and to study the explanations.

DIRECTIONS: Each number series question consists of a series of numbers that follows some definite order. The numbers progress from left to right according to some rule. One pair of numbers to the right of the series comprises the next two numbers in the series. Study each series to try to find a pattern to the series and to figure out the rule that governs the progression. Choose the answer pair that continues the series according to the pattern established and mark its letter on your answer sheet.

1. 75 75 72 72 69 69 66.......(A) 66 66   (B) 66 68   (C) 63 63   (D) 66 63   (E) 63 60

   The pattern established in this series is: repeat the number, –3; repeat the number, –3 . . . . To continue the series, repeat <u>66</u>, then subtract 3. The answer is (**D**).

2. 12 16 21 27 31 36 42.......(A) 48 56   (B) 44 48   (C) 48 52   (D) 46 52   (E) 46 51

   By marking the amount and direction of change from one number of the series to the next, you can see that the pattern is: +4, +5, +6; +4, +5, +6; +4, +5, +6. Continuing the series: 42 + 4 = 46 + 5 = 51. (**E**) is the correct answer.

3. 22 24 12 26 28 12 30.......(A) 12 32   (B) 32 34   (C) 32 12   (D) 12 12   (E) 32 36

   In this series the basic pattern is +2. The series may be read: 22 24 26 28 30 32. After each two numbers of the series we find the number <u>12</u>, which serves no function except for repetition. To continue the series, add 2 to <u>30</u> to get <u>32</u>. After <u>30</u> and <u>32</u>, you must put in the number <u>12</u>, so (**C**) is the correct answer.

4. 5 70 10 68 15 66 20.........(A) 25 64   (B) 64 25   (C) 24 63   (D) 25 30   (E) 64 62

   In this problem there are two distinct series alternating with one another. The first series is going up by a factor of +5. It reads: 10 15 20. The alternating series is going down by a factor of –2. It reads: 70 68 66. At the point where you must continue the series, the next number must be a member of the descending series, so it must be <u>64</u>. Following that number must come the next number of the ascending series, which is <u>25</u>. (**B**) is the answer.

5. 13 22 32 43 55 68 82.......(A) 97 113 (B) 100 115 (C) 96 110 (D) 95 105 (E) 99 112

   The numbers are large, but the progression is simple. If you mark the differences between numbers, you can readily recognize: +9, +10, +11, +12, +13, +14. Continuing the series: 82 + 15 = 97 + 16 = 113. (**A**) is the correct answer.

SAMPLE ANSWER SHEET	CORRECT ANSWERS
1. Ⓐ Ⓑ Ⓒ Ⓓ Ⓔ	1. Ⓐ Ⓑ Ⓒ ● Ⓔ
2. Ⓐ Ⓑ Ⓒ Ⓓ Ⓔ	2. Ⓐ Ⓑ Ⓒ Ⓓ ●
3. Ⓐ Ⓑ Ⓒ Ⓓ Ⓔ	3. Ⓐ Ⓑ ● Ⓓ Ⓔ
4. Ⓐ Ⓑ Ⓒ Ⓓ Ⓔ	4. Ⓐ ● Ⓒ Ⓓ Ⓔ
5. Ⓐ Ⓑ Ⓒ Ⓓ Ⓔ	5. ● Ⓑ Ⓒ Ⓓ Ⓔ

Number Series

Time: 20 Minutes. 24 Questions.

DIRECTIONS: Each number series question consists of a series of numbers that follows some definite order. The numbers progress from left to right according to some rule. One lettered pair of numbers comprises the next two numbers in the series. Study each series to try to find a pattern to the series and to figure the rule that governs the progression. Choose the answer pair that continues the series according to the pattern established and mark its letter on your answer sheet. Correct answers are on page 217.

1. 3 8 4 9 5 10 6 ....(A) 7 11   (B) 7 8   (C) 11 8 (D) 12 7 (E) 11 7

2. 18 14 19 17 20 20 21 ....(A) 22 24 (B) 14 19 (C) 24 21 (D) 21 23 (E) 23 22

3. 6 9 10 7 11 12 8 ....(A) 9 10   (B) 9 13 (C) 16 14 (D) 13 14 (E) 14 15

4. 7 5 3 9 7 5 11 ....(A) 13 12 (B) 7 5   (C) 9 7   (D) 13 7 (E) 9 9

5. 7 9 18 10 12 18 13 ....(A) 18 14 (B) 15 18 (C) 14 15 (D) 15 14 (E) 14 18

6. 2 6 4 8 6 10 8 ....(A) 12 10 (B) 6 10 (C) 10 12 (D) 12 16 (E) 6 4

7. 7 9 12 14 17 19 22 ....(A) 25 27 (B) 23 24 (C) 23 25 (D) 24 27 (E) 26 27

8. 3 23 5 25 7 27 9 ....(A) 10 11 (B) 27 29 (C) 29 11 (D) 11 28 (E) 28 10

9. 1 2 2 3 4 12 5 6 ....(A) 7 8   (B) 11 7 (C) 11 56 (D) 56 7 (E) 30 7

10. 1 2 3 6 4 5 6 6 7 ....(A) 6 5   (B) 8 9 (C) 6 8 (D) 7 6 (E) 8 6

11. 1 3 40 5 7 37 9 ....(A) 11 39 (B) 9 11 (C) 34 11 (D) 11 34 (E) 11 35

12. 25 27 29 31 33 35 37 ....(A) 39 41 (B) 38 39 (C) 37 39 (D) 37 38 (E) 39 40

13. 91 85 17 81 75 15 71 ....(A) 74 14 (B) 61 51 (C) 65 13 (D) 65 10 (E) 66 33

14. 41 37 46 42 51 47 56 ....(A) 51 70 (B) 52 61 (C) 49 60 (D) 60 43 (E) 55 65

15. 6 6 6 18 18 18 54 ....(A) 54 108 (B) 54 162 (C) 108 108 (D) 108 162 (E) 54 54

16. 13 23 14 22 15 21 16 ....(A) 17 20 (B) 20 17 (C) 17 18 (D) 20 19 (E) 16 20

17. 52 10 48 20 44 30 40 ....(A) 36 50 (B) 50 36 (C) 36 40 (D) 40 36 (E) 40 40

18. 94 84 75 67 60 54 49 ....(A) 45 42 (B) 49 45 (C) 44 40 (D) 46 42 (E) 45 40

19. 76 38 38 48 24 24 34 ....(A) 34 44 (B) 34 34 (C) 17 17 (D) 34 17 (E) 17 27

20. 83 38 84 48 85 58 86 ....(A) 86 68 (B) 87 78 (C) 59 95 (D) 68 88 (E) 68 87

21. 19 21 21 24 24 24 28 ....(A) 28 31 (B) 28 33 (C) 32 36 (D) 28 28 (E) 28 32

22. 52 45 38 32 26 21 16 ....(A) 16 12 (B) 12 8 (C) 11 6 (D) 11 7 (E) 12 9

23. 100 81 64 49 36 25 16 ....(A) 12 10 (B) 8 4 (C) 8 2 (D) 9 4 (E) 9 2

24. 4 40 44 5 50 55 6 ....(A) 60 66 (B) 6 60 (C) 6 66 (D) 7 70 (E) 70 77

END OF NUMBER SERIES

Part D—Following Oral Instructions

Directions and Sample Questions

LISTENING TO INSTRUCTIONS: When you are ready to try these sample questions, give the following instructions to a friend and have the friend read them aloud to you at the rate of 80 words per minute. Do not read them to yourself. Your friend will need a watch with a second hand. Listen carefully and do exactly what your friend tells you to do with the worksheet and answer sheet. Your friend will tell you some things to do with each item on the worksheet. After each set of instructions, your friend will give you time to mark your answer by darkening a circle on the sample answer sheet. Since B and D sound very much alike, your friend will say "B as in baker" when he or she means B and "D as in dog" when he or she means D.

Before proceeding further, tear out the worksheet on page 207. Then hand this book to your friend.

TO THE PERSON WHO IS TO READ THE INSTRUCTIONS: The instructions are to be read at the rate of 80 words per minute. Do not read aloud the material that is in parentheses. Do not repeat any instructions.

Read Aloud to the Candidate

Look at line 1 on your worksheet. (Pause slightly.) Draw a line under the third letter in the line. (Pause 2 seconds.) Now, on your answer sheet, find the number that is 2 less than 17 and darken the space for the letter which you drew a line under. (Pause 10 seconds.)

Look at line 2 on your worksheet. (Pause slightly.) Locate the smallest number and draw a circle around it. (Pause 5 seconds.) Now, on your answer sheet, darken the space next to letter C for the number you have circled. (Pause 5 seconds.)

Look at line 3 on your worksheet. (Pause slightly.) There are 5 boxes. Each box has a number. In each box containing a number that can be found on a foot-long ruler, write the letter E. (Pause 10 seconds.) Now, on your answer sheet, darken the space for the number-letter combination that is in each box you wrote in. (Pause 10 seconds.)

Look at line 4 on your worksheet. (Pause slightly.) If in a week Wednesday comes before Thursday, write D as in dog in the box with the largest number. (Pause 5 seconds.) If it does not, write E in the box of the second-to-largest number. (Pause 5 seconds.) Now, on your answer sheet, darken the space for the number-letter combination that is in the box you just wrote in. (Pause 5 seconds.)

Sample Worksheet

DIRECTIONS: *Listening carefully to each set of instructions, mark each item on this worksheet as directed. Then complete each question by marking the sample answer sheet below as directed. For each answer you will darken the answer for a number-letter combination. Should you fall behind and miss an instruction, don't become excited. Let that one go and listen for the next one. If, when you start to darken a space for a number, you find that you have already darkened another space for that number, either erase the first mark and darken the space for the new combination or let the first mark stay and do not darken a space for the new combination. Write with a pencil that has a clean eraser. When you finish, you should have no more than one space darkened for each number.*

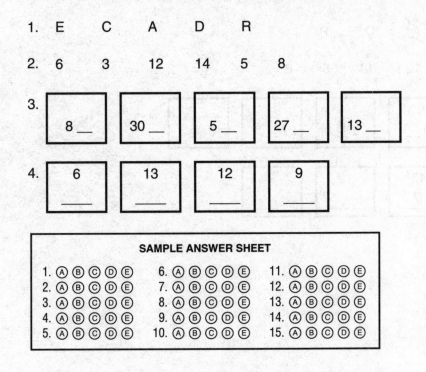

1. E   C   A   D   R

2. 6   3   12   14   5   8

3. | 8 __ | 30 __ | 5 __ | 27 __ | 13 __ |

4. | 6 ___ | 13 ___ | 12 ___ | 9 ___ |

SAMPLE ANSWER SHEET

1. Ⓐ Ⓑ Ⓒ Ⓓ Ⓔ   6. Ⓐ Ⓑ Ⓒ Ⓓ Ⓔ   11. Ⓐ Ⓑ Ⓒ Ⓓ Ⓔ
2. Ⓐ Ⓑ Ⓒ Ⓓ Ⓔ   7. Ⓐ Ⓑ Ⓒ Ⓓ Ⓔ   12. Ⓐ Ⓑ Ⓒ Ⓓ Ⓔ
3. Ⓐ Ⓑ Ⓒ Ⓓ Ⓔ   8. Ⓐ Ⓑ Ⓒ Ⓓ Ⓔ   13. Ⓐ Ⓑ Ⓒ Ⓓ Ⓔ
4. Ⓐ Ⓑ Ⓒ Ⓓ Ⓔ   9. Ⓐ Ⓑ Ⓒ Ⓓ Ⓔ   14. Ⓐ Ⓑ Ⓒ Ⓓ Ⓔ
5. Ⓐ Ⓑ Ⓒ Ⓓ Ⓔ   10. Ⓐ Ⓑ Ⓒ Ⓓ Ⓔ   15. Ⓐ Ⓑ Ⓒ Ⓓ Ⓔ

TEAR HERE

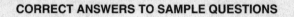

CORRECT ANSWERS TO SAMPLE QUESTIONS		
1. Ⓐ Ⓑ Ⓒ Ⓓ Ⓔ	6. Ⓐ Ⓑ Ⓒ Ⓓ Ⓔ	11. Ⓐ Ⓑ Ⓒ Ⓓ Ⓔ
2. Ⓐ Ⓑ Ⓒ Ⓓ Ⓔ	7. Ⓐ Ⓑ Ⓒ Ⓓ Ⓔ	12. Ⓐ Ⓑ Ⓒ Ⓓ Ⓔ
3. Ⓐ Ⓑ ● Ⓓ Ⓔ	8. Ⓐ Ⓑ Ⓒ Ⓓ ●	13. Ⓐ Ⓑ Ⓒ ● Ⓔ
4. Ⓐ Ⓑ Ⓒ Ⓓ Ⓔ	9. Ⓐ Ⓑ Ⓒ Ⓓ Ⓔ	14. Ⓐ Ⓑ Ⓒ Ⓓ Ⓔ
5. Ⓐ Ⓑ Ⓒ Ⓓ ●	10. Ⓐ Ⓑ Ⓒ Ⓓ Ⓔ	15. ● Ⓑ Ⓒ Ⓓ Ⓔ

Correctly Filled Worksheet

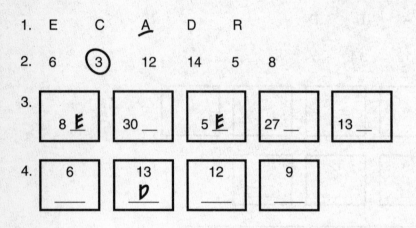

1. E   C   A̲   D   R

2. 6   ③   12   14   5   8

3. | 8 E̲ | 30 __ | 5 E̲ | 27 __ | 13 __ |

4. | 6 __ | 13 D̲ | 12 | 9 __ |

Following Oral Instructions

Time: 25 Minutes.

Listening to Instructions

DIRECTIONS: When you are ready to try this test of the Model Exam, give the following instructions to a friend and have the friend read them aloud to you at the rate of 80 words per minute. Do NOT read them to yourself. Your friend will need a watch with a second hand. Listen carefully and do exactly what your friend tells you to do with the worksheet and with the answer sheet. Your friend will tell you some things to do with each item on the worksheet. After each set of instructions, your friend will give you time to mark your answer by darkening a circle on the answer sheet. Since B and D sound very much alike, your friend will say "B as in baker" when he or she means B and "D as in dog" when he or she means D.

> **Before proceeding further, tear out the worksheet on page 213 of this test. Then hand this book to your friend.**

TO THE PERSON WHO IS TO READ THE INSTRUCTIONS: The instructions are to be read at the rate of 80 words per minute. Do not read aloud the material that is in parentheses. Once you have begun the test itself, do not repeat any instructions. The next three paragraphs consist of approximately 120 words. Read these three paragraphs aloud to the candidate in about one and one-half minutes. You may reread these paragraphs as often as necessary to establish an 80-words-per-minute reading speed.

Read Aloud to the Candidate

On the job you will have to listen to directions and then do what you have been told to do. In this test, I will read instructions to you. Try to understand them as I read them; I cannot repeat them. Once we begin, you may not ask any questions until the end of the test.

On the job you won't have to deal with pictures, numbers, and letters like those in the test, but you will have to listen to instructions and follow them. We are using this test to see how well you can follow instructions.

You are to mark your test booklet according to the instructions that I'll read to you. After each set of instructions, I'll give you time to record your answers on the separate answer sheet.

The actual test begins now.

Look at line 1 on your worksheet. (Pause slightly.) Underline the fifth number on line 1. (Pause 2 seconds.) Now, on your answer sheet, find the number you have underlined and mark D as in dog. (Pause 5 seconds.)

Now look at line 2 on your worksheet. (Pause slightly.) In each box that contains a vowel, write that vowel next to the number in the box. (Pause 5 seconds.) Now, on your answer sheet, blacken the spaces for the number-letter combinations in the box or boxes in which you just wrote. (Pause 10 seconds.)

Look at line 3 on your worksheet. (Pause slightly.) Find the smallest number on line 3 and multiply it by 2. Write the number at the end of line 3. (Pause 5 seconds.) Now, on your answer sheet, darken space C for that number. (Pause 5 seconds.)

Look at line 3 again. (Pause slightly.) Divide the third number by 10 and write that number at the end of the line. (Pause 2 seconds.) Now, on your answer sheet, darken space A for the number you just wrote. (Pause 5 seconds.)

Now look at line 4 on your worksheet. (Pause slightly.) Mail for Detroit and Hartford is to be put in box 3. (Pause slightly.) Mail for Cleveland and St. Louis is to be put in box 26. (Pause slightly.) Write C in the box in which you put mail for St. Louis. (Pause 2 seconds.) Now, on your answer sheet, darken the space for the number-letter combination that is in the box you just wrote in. (Pause 5 seconds.)

Look at line 5 on your worksheet. (Pause slightly.) Write B as in baker on the line next to the highest number. (Pause 2 seconds.) Now, on your answer sheet, blacken the space for the number-letter combination in the circle in which you just wrote. (Pause 5 seconds.)

Look at line 5 again. (Pause slightly.) Write the letter C on the line next to the lowest number. (Pause 2 seconds.) Now, on your answer sheet, blacken the space for the number-letter combination in the circle in which you just wrote. (Pause 5 seconds.)

Look at the boxes and words on line 6 of your worksheet. (Pause 2 seconds.) In Box 1, write the first letter of the third word. (Pause 5 seconds.) In Box 2, write the last letter of the first word. (Pause 5 seconds.) In Box 3, write the last letter of the second word. (Pause 5 seconds.) Now, on your answer sheet, blacken spaces for the number-letter combinations in all three boxes. (Pause 15 seconds.)

Look at line 7 on your worksheet. (Pause slightly.) Write the number 33 next to the letter in the mid-size circle. (Pause 2 seconds.) Now, on your answer sheet, darken the space for the number-letter combination in the circle in which you just wrote. (Pause 5 seconds.)

Look at line 8 on your worksheet. (Pause slightly.) If July comes before June, write D as in dog on the line after the second number; if not, write A on the line after the first number. (Pause 10 seconds.) Now, on your answer sheet, darken the space for the number-letter combination you just wrote. (Pause 5 seconds.)

Look at line 9 on your worksheet. (Pause slightly.) The number on each sack represents the number of pieces of mail in that sack. Next to the letter, write the last two figures of the sack containing the most pieces of mail. (Pause 2 seconds.) On your answer sheet, darken the space for the number-letter combination in the sack you just wrote in. (Pause 5 seconds.)

Look at line 9 again. (Pause slightly.) Now, write next to the letter the first two figures in the sack containing the fewest pieces of mail. (Pause 2 seconds.) On your answer sheet, darken the space for the number-letter combination in the sack you just wrote in. (Pause 5 seconds.)

Look at line 10 on your worksheet. (Pause slightly.) Answer this question: What is the sum of 8 plus 13? (Pause 2 seconds.) If the answer is 25, write 25 in the second box; if not, write the correct answer in the fourth box. (Pause 2 seconds.) Now, on your answer sheet, blacken the number-letter combination in the box you just wrote in. (Pause 5 seconds.)

Look at line 10 again. (Pause slightly.) In the fifth box, write the number of ounces in a pound. (Pause 2 seconds.) Now, on your answer sheet, blacken the number-letter combination in the box you just wrote in. (Pause 5 seconds.)

Look at line 11 on your worksheet. (Pause slightly.) If the number in the circle is greater than the number in the star, write B as in baker in the triangle; if not, write E in the box. (Pause 5 seconds.) Now, on your answer sheet, darken the number-letter combination in the figure you just wrote in. (Pause 5 seconds.)

Look at line 12 on your worksheet. (Pause slightly.) Draw one line under each P in line 12. (Pause 5 seconds.) Draw two lines under each Q in line 12. (Pause 5 seconds.) Count the number of P's and the number of Q's. (Pause 5 seconds.) If there are more P's than Q's, blacken 71A on your answer sheet; if there are not more P's than Q's, blacken 71C on your answer sheet. (Pause 5 seconds.)

Look at line 13 on your worksheet. (Pause slightly.) Circle each odd number that falls between 65 and 85. (Pause 10 seconds.) Now, on your answer sheet, darken space D as in dog for each number that you circled. (Pause 10 seconds.)

Look at line 13 again. (Pause slightly.) Find the number that is divisible by 6 and underline it. (Pause 2 seconds.) Now, on your answer sheet, darken space A for that number. (Pause 5 seconds.)

Look at line 14 on your worksheet. (Pause slightly.) Each circled time represents a pickup time from a street letter box. Find the pickup time which is farthest from noon and write the last two figures of that time on the line in the circle. (Pause 2 seconds.) Now, on your answer sheet, darken the number-letter combination that is in the circle you just wrote in. (Pause 5 seconds.)

Look at line 14 again. (Pause slightly.) Find the pickup time that is closest to noon and write the last two figures of that time on the line in the circle. (Pause 2 seconds.) Now, on your answer sheet, darken the number-letter combination that is in the circle you just wrote in. (Pause 5 seconds.)

Look at line 15 on your worksheet. (Pause slightly.) Write the highest number in the small box. (Pause 2 seconds.) Write the lowest number in the large box. (Pause 2 seconds.) Now, on your answer sheet, darken the number-letter combinations in the boxes you just wrote in. (Pause 10 seconds.)

Look at line 16 on your worksheet. (Pause slightly.) If, in the alphabet, the fourth letter on line 16 comes before the first letter on line 16, draw a line under the fourth letter (pause 2 seconds); if not, draw a line under the first letter on line 16. (Pause 2 seconds.) Now, on your answer sheet, find number 39 and blacken the space for the letter you underlined. (Pause 5 seconds.)

Look at line 17 on your worksheet. (Pause slightly.) Find the number that does not belong on line 17 and circle that number. (Pause 2 seconds.) Now, on your answer sheet, darken D as in dog for the number you just circled. (Pause 5 seconds.)

Look at line 17 again. (Pause slightly.) Find the number that answers this question: 60 minus 20 equals . . . and draw two lines under that number. (Pause 2 seconds.) Now, on your answer sheet, darken space C for the number under which you just drew two lines. (Pause 5 seconds.)

Look at line 18 on your worksheet. (Pause slightly.) If 3 is less than 7 and 4 is more than 6, write the number 12 in the first box (pause 5 seconds); if not, write the number 48 in the third box. (Pause 5 seconds.) Now, on your answer sheet, darken the space for the number-letter combination in the box you just wrote in. (Pause 5 seconds.)

Look at line 19 on your worksheet. (Pause slightly.) Draw a circle around the number that represents the product of 5 × 6. (Pause 5 seconds.) Now, on your answer sheet, find the number that you just circled and darken space A for that number. (Pause 5 seconds.)

Correct Answers for Fourth Model Exam

Part A—Address Checking

1. D	13. A	25. A	37. A	49. D	61. D	73. D	85. D
2. D	14. D	26. D	38. A	50. A	62. D	74. D	86. D
3. D	15. D	27. A	39. D	51. D	63. D	75. D	87. D
4. A	16. A	28. D	40. A	52. D	64. D	76. A	88. D
5. D	17. D	29. A	41. D	53. D	65. D	77. A	89. D
6. D	18. A	30. D	42. A	54. A	66. D	78. D	90. A
7. A	19. D	31. D	43. D	55. A	67. A	79. D	91. D
8. D	20. A	32. D	44. A	56. D	68. D	80. A	92. D
9. A	21. D	33. D	45. D	57. A	69. D	81. D	93. A
10. D	22. A	34. A	46. D	58. D	70. D	82. D	94. A
11. D	23. D	35. A	47. D	59. D	71. D	83. D	95. A
12. D	24. D	36. D	48. D	60. D	72. D	84. A	

Analyzing Your Errors

Type of Error	Tally	Total Number
Number of addresses that were alike and you incorrectly marked "different"		
Number of addresses that were different and you incorrectly marked "alike"		
Number of addresses in which you missed a difference in NUMBERS		
Number of addresses in which you missed a difference in ABBREVIATIONS		
Number of addresses in which you missed a difference in NAMES		

Part B—Memory for Addresses

Practice I

1. B	12. C	23. B	34. E	45. A	56. A	67. D	78. D
2. B	13. A	24. A	35. B	46. C	57. C	68. B	79. E
3. E	14. D	25. C	36. D	47. E	58. B	69. C	80. A
4. C	15. B	26. D	37. C	48. B	59. E	70. A	81. C
5. A	16. A	27. C	38. A	49. B	60. C	71. E	82. E
6. E	17. B	28. B	39. D	50. B	61. C	72. C	83. E
7. E	18. E	29. A	40. E	51. E	62. D	73. E	84. B
8. D	19. D	30. B	41. C	52. E	63. A	74. B	85. C
9. B	20. A	31. E	42. D	53. A	64. D	75. A	86. A
10. C	21. C	32. A	43. C	54. D	65. A	76. B	87. A
11. D	22. E	33. E	44. C	55. C	66. D	77. C	88. E

Practice II

1. C	12. E	23. A	34. C	45. A	56. B	67. B	78. E
2. D	13. D	24. E	35. A	46. D	57. C	68. D	79. A
3. B	14. C	25. B	36. B	47. D	58. A	69. E	80. D
4. A	15. C	26. C	37. B	48. D	59. B	70. B	81. B
5. E	16. A	27. B	38. A	49. E	60. C	71. D	82. D
6. D	17. C	28. D	39. C	50. E	61. A	72. C	83. B
7. B	18. E	29. A	40. C	51. D	62. E	73. C	84. C
8. A	19. A	30. E	41. C	52. C	63. A	74. D	85. E
9. D	20. C	31. E	42. E	53. E	64. E	75. C	86. C
10. D	21. E	32. B	43. A	54. D	65. B	76. A	87. A
11. A	22. B	33. E	44. D	55. A	66. A	77. A	88. A

Practice III

1. C	12. C	23. D	34. E	45. B	56. E	67. A	78. A
2. E	13. D	24. C	35. D	46. B	57. C	68. A	79. E
3. D	14. B	25. C	36. D	47. A	58. B	69. C	80. D
4. B	15. D	26. C	37. E	48. D	59. A	70. C	81. B
5. A	16. B	27. C	38. E	49. D	60. B	71. E	82. E
6. B	17. D	28. A	39. A	50. B	61. C	72. C	83. E
7. A	18. A	29. B	40. A	51. E	62. D	73. C	84. B
8. A	19. D	30. E	41. A	52. D	63. E	74. D	85. E
9. E	20. E	31. A	42. C	53. C	64. E	75. D	86. D
10. E	21. B	32. B	43. B	54. E	65. D	76. B	87. A
11. C	22. E	33. C	44. C	55. C	66. B	77. A	88. B

Memory for Addresses

1. D	12. B	23. E	34. B	45. E	56. A	67. E	78. B
2. B	13. A	24. C	35. D	46. E	57. C	68. B	79. C
3. B	14. D	25. A	36. B	47. A	58. D	69. A	80. B
4. E	15. A	26. E	37. A	48. C	59. B	70. E	81. A
5. A	16. C	27. A	38. D	49. B	60. E	71. E	82. E
6. B	17. B	28. D	39. C	50. D	61. A	72. A	83. A
7. A	18. C	29. A	40. D	51. C	62. A	73. C	84. E
8. E	19. E	30. E	41. E	52. B	63. D	74. D	85. D
9. C	20. E	31. C	42. B	53. E	64. D	75. B	86. D
10. D	21. E	32. E	43. B	54. C	65. C	76. E	87. B
11. D	22. B	33. A	44. D	55. A	66. C	77. C	88. A

Part C—Number Series

1. E	4. C	7. D	10. B	13. C	16. B	19. C	22. B
2. E	5. B	8. C	11. D	14. B	17. D	20. E	23. D
3. D	6. A	9. E	12. A	15. E	18. A	21. D	24. A

Explanations

1. **(E)** There are two alternating series, each ascending by +1. One series begins with <u>3</u>, the other with <u>8</u>.

2. **(E)** The two alternating series progress at different rates. The first, beginning with <u>18</u>, moves up one number at a time. The alternating series, beginning with <u>14</u>, increases by +3.

3. **(D)** There are two alternating series, but this time two numbers of one series interpose between steps of the other series. Thus, one series reads 6 7 8 while the other reads 9 10 11 12 13 14.

4. **(C)** Here we have a series of mini-series. The pattern in each mini-series is –2, –2. Then the pattern repeats with the first number of the next mini-series two numbers higher than the first number of the preceding mini-series.

5. **(B)** The series really is +2, +1, with the number <u>18</u> appearing between the two numbers at the +1 phase.

6. **(A)** Two series alternate, both ascending by +2.

7. **(D)** Here the progression is +2, +3; +2, +3; and so on.

8. **(C)** Both alternating series move up by +2.

9. **(E)** The series is essentially 1 2 3 4 5 6 7, but after each two numbers in the series we find the product of the multiplication of those two numbers: $1 \times 2 = 2$; $3 \times 4 = 12$; $5 \times 6 = 30$; 7 . . . .

10. **(B)** The series is simply 1 2 3 4 5 6 7 8 9. After each three numbers of the series, we find the number <u>6</u>.

11. **(D)** There are two series. The ascending series increases by +2. The descending series intervenes after every two members of the ascending series. The descending series moves in steps of –3.

12. **(A)** Weren't you ready for an easy one? There is no catch. The series moves by +2.

13. **(C)** You may feel the rhythm of this series and spot the pattern without playing around with the numbers. If you cannot solve the problem by inspection, then you might see three parallel series. The first series descends by –10 (91 81 71); the second series, also descends by minus 10 (85 75 65); the third series descends by –2 (17 15 13). Or, you might see a series of mini-series. Each mini-series begins with a number 10 lower than the first number of the previous mini-series. Within each mini-series the pattern is –6, ÷5.

14. **(B)** The pattern is –4, +9; –4, +9 . . . Or, there are two alternating series. The first series ascends at the rate of +5; the alternating series also ascends at the rate of +5.

15. **(E)** Each number appears three times, then is multiplied by 3.

16. **(B)** There are two alternating series. One starts at <u>13</u> and moves up by +1, and the other starts at <u>23</u> and moves down by –1.

17. **(D)** There are two alternating series. The first series begins with <u>52</u> and descends at the rate of –4. The alternating series begins with <u>10</u> and ascends at the rate of +10.

18. **(A)** The pattern is: –10, –9, –8, –7, –6, –5, –4, –3.

19. **(C)** The pattern is: ÷2, repeat the number, +10; ÷2, repeat the number, +10; ÷2, repeat the number, +10.

20. **(E)** You see a simple series, 83 84 85 86 . . . . After each number in this series you see its mirror image, that is, the mirror image of 83 is 38; the mirror image of 84 is 48 and so forth. Or you might see a series that increases by +1 alternating with a series that increases by +10.

21. **(D)** The pattern is: +2, repeat the number 2 times; +3, repeat the number 3 times; +4, repeat the number 4 times.

22. **(B)** The pattern is –7, –7, –6, –6, –5, –5, –4, –4.

23. **(D)** The series consists of the squares of the whole numbers in descending order.

24. **(A)** You can probably get this one by inspection. If not, notice the series of mini-series. In each mini-series the pattern is 10 times the first number, 11 times the first number.

Part D—Following Oral Instructions

Correctly Filled Answer Grid

1 ⒶⒷⒸⒹⒺ	23 ⒶⒷⒸⒹⒺ	45 ⒶⒷⒸ●Ⓔ	67 ⒶⒷⒸⒹⒺ
2 ⒶⒷⒸⒹⒺ	24 ⒶⒷⒸⒹⒺ	46 ⒶⒷⒸⒹⒺ	68 ⒶⒷⒸⒹⒺ
3 ●ⒷⒸⒹⒺ	25 ⒶⒷⒸⒹⒺ	47 ⒶⒷⒸⒹⒺ	69 ⒶⒷ●ⒹⒺ
4 ⒶⒷⒸⒹ●	26 ⒶⒷ●ⒹⒺ	48 ⒶⒷⒸⒹ●	70 ⒶⒷⒸⒹⒺ
5 ⒶⒷⒸⒹⒺ	27 ⒶⒷⒸⒹⒺ	49 ⒶⒷⒸⒹⒺ	71 ⒶⒷ●ⒹⒺ
6 ⒶⒷⒸⒹⒺ	28 ⒶⒷⒸⒹⒺ	50 ⒶⒷⒸⒹⒺ	72 ⒶⒷⒸⒹⒺ
7 ●ⒷⒸⒹⒺ	29 ⒶⒷⒸⒹⒺ	51 ⒶⒷⒸⒹⒺ	73 ⒶⒷⒸⒹⒺ
8 Ⓐ Ⓑ ● Ⓓ Ⓔ	30 ●ⒷⒸⒹⒺ	52 ⒶⒷⒸⒹⒺ	74 ⒶⒷⒸⒹⒺ
9 ⒶⒷⒸⒹ●	31 ⒶⒷⒸⒹⒺ	53 ⒶⒷⒸⒹ●	75 ⒶⒷⒸ●Ⓔ
10 ⒶⒷⒸⒹⒺ	32 ⒶⒷⒸⒹⒺ	54 ⒶⒷⒸⒹⒺ	76 Ⓐ●ⒸⒹⒺ
11 ⒶⒷⒸⒹⒺ	33 ●ⒷⒸⒹⒺ	55 ⒶⒷⒸⒹⒺ	77 ⒶⒷⒸⒹⒺ
12 Ⓐ●ⒸⒹⒺ	34 ⒶⒷⒸⒹⒺ	56 ⒶⒷⒸ●Ⓔ	78 ⒶⒷⒸⒹⒺ
13 ⒶⒷⒸⒹⒺ	35 ⒶⒷⒸⒹⒺ	57 ⒶⒷⒸ●Ⓔ	79 ⒶⒷⒸⒹⒺ
14 ⒶⒷⒸⒹⒺ	36 Ⓐ●ⒸⒹⒺ	58 ⒶⒷⒸⒹⒺ	80 ⒶⒷⒸⒹⒺ
15 ⒶⒷⒸⒹⒺ	37 ⒶⒷⒸⒹⒺ	59 ⒶⒷⒸⒹⒺ	81 ⒶⒷⒸⒹⒺ
16 ⒶⒷⒸⒹ●	38 ⒶⒷⒸⒹⒺ	60 ⒶⒷⒸⒹⒺ	82 ●ⒷⒸⒹⒺ
17 ⒶⒷⒸⒹⒺ	39 Ⓐ●ⒸⒹⒺ	61 ⒶⒷⒸⒹⒺ	83 ⒶⒷⒸ●Ⓔ
18 Ⓐ Ⓑ ● Ⓓ Ⓔ	40 ⒶⒷ●ⒹⒺ	62 ⒶⒷⒸⒹⒺ	84 ⒶⒷⒸⒹⒺ
19 ⒶⒷⒸⒹⒺ	41 ⒶⒷⒸⒹⒺ	63 ⒶⒷ●ⒹⒺ	85 ⒶⒷⒸⒹⒺ
20 ⒶⒷⒸⒹⒺ	42 ●ⒷⒸⒹⒺ	64 ⒶⒷⒸⒹⒺ	86 ⒶⒷⒸⒹⒺ
21 Ⓐ●ⒸⒹⒺ	43 ⒶⒷⒸⒹⒺ	65 ⒶⒷⒸⒹⒺ	87 ⒶⒷⒸⒹ●
22 Ⓐ●ⒸⒹⒺ	44 ⒶⒷⒸⒹⒺ	66 ●ⒷⒸⒹⒺ	88 ⒶⒷⒸⒹⒺ

Correctly Filled Worksheet

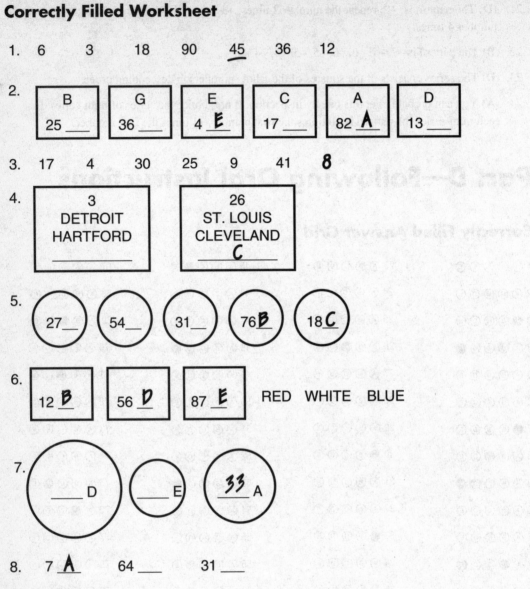

1. 6   3   18   90   <u>45</u>   36   12

2.
B	G	E	C	A	D
25 ___	36 ___	4 **E**	17 ___	82 **A**	13 ___

3. 17   4   30   25   9   41   **8**

4.
3 DETROIT HARTFORD ___	26 ST. LOUIS CLEVELAND **C**

5. 27___   54___   31___   76**B**   18**C**

6. 12 **B**   56 **D**   87 **E**   RED   WHITE   BLUE

7. ___D   ___E   **33** A

8. 7 **A**   64 ___   31 ___

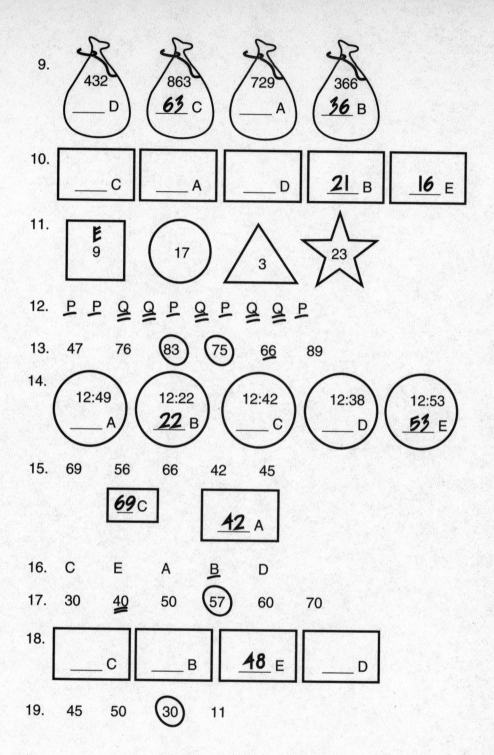

9. 432 ____ D   863 *63* C   729 ____ A   366 *36* B

10. ____ C   ____ A   ____ D   *21* B   *16* E

11. *E* 9   17   3   23

12. P P Q Q P Q P Q Q P

13. 47   76   83   75   66   89

14. 12:49 ____ A   12:22 *22* B   12:42 ____ C   12:38 ____ D   12:53 *53* E

15. 69   56   66   42   45
    69 C   *42* A

16. C   E   A   B   D

17. 30   40   50   57   60   70

18. ____ C   ____ B   *48* E   ____ D

19. 45   50   30   11

Fifth Model Exam
Answer Sheet

Part A—Address Checking

1. Ⓐ Ⓓ	20. Ⓐ Ⓓ	39. Ⓐ Ⓓ	58. Ⓐ Ⓓ	77. Ⓐ Ⓓ
2. Ⓐ Ⓓ	21. Ⓐ Ⓓ	40. Ⓐ Ⓓ	59. Ⓐ Ⓓ	78. Ⓐ Ⓓ
3. Ⓐ Ⓓ	22. Ⓐ Ⓓ	41. Ⓐ Ⓓ	60. Ⓐ Ⓓ	79. Ⓐ Ⓓ
4. Ⓐ Ⓓ	23. Ⓐ Ⓓ	42. Ⓐ Ⓓ	61. Ⓐ Ⓓ	80. Ⓐ Ⓓ
5. Ⓐ Ⓓ	24. Ⓐ Ⓓ	43. Ⓐ Ⓓ	62. Ⓐ Ⓓ	81. Ⓐ Ⓓ
6. Ⓐ Ⓓ	25. Ⓐ Ⓓ	44. Ⓐ Ⓓ	63. Ⓐ Ⓓ	82. Ⓐ Ⓓ
7. Ⓐ Ⓓ	26. Ⓐ Ⓓ	45. Ⓐ Ⓓ	64. Ⓐ Ⓓ	83. Ⓐ Ⓓ
8. Ⓐ Ⓓ	27. Ⓐ Ⓓ	46. Ⓐ Ⓓ	65. Ⓐ Ⓓ	84. Ⓐ Ⓓ
9. Ⓐ Ⓓ	28. Ⓐ Ⓓ	47. Ⓐ Ⓓ	66. Ⓐ Ⓓ	85. Ⓐ Ⓓ
10. Ⓐ Ⓓ	29. Ⓐ Ⓓ	48. Ⓐ Ⓓ	67. Ⓐ Ⓓ	86. Ⓐ Ⓓ
11. Ⓐ Ⓓ	30. Ⓐ Ⓓ	49. Ⓐ Ⓓ	68. Ⓐ Ⓓ	87. Ⓐ Ⓓ
12. Ⓐ Ⓓ	31. Ⓐ Ⓓ	50. Ⓐ Ⓓ	69. Ⓐ Ⓓ	88. Ⓐ Ⓓ
13. Ⓐ Ⓓ	32. Ⓐ Ⓓ	51. Ⓐ Ⓓ	70. Ⓐ Ⓓ	89. Ⓐ Ⓓ
14. Ⓐ Ⓓ	33. Ⓐ Ⓓ	52. Ⓐ Ⓓ	71. Ⓐ Ⓓ	90. Ⓐ Ⓓ
15. Ⓐ Ⓓ	34. Ⓐ Ⓓ	53. Ⓐ Ⓓ	72. Ⓐ Ⓓ	91. Ⓐ Ⓓ
16. Ⓐ Ⓓ	35. Ⓐ Ⓓ	54. Ⓐ Ⓓ	73. Ⓐ Ⓓ	92. Ⓐ Ⓓ
17. Ⓐ Ⓓ	36. Ⓐ Ⓓ	55. Ⓐ Ⓓ	74. Ⓐ Ⓓ	93. Ⓐ Ⓓ
18. Ⓐ Ⓓ	37. Ⓐ Ⓓ	56. Ⓐ Ⓓ	75. Ⓐ Ⓓ	94. Ⓐ Ⓓ
19. Ⓐ Ⓓ	38. Ⓐ Ⓓ	57. Ⓐ Ⓓ	76. Ⓐ Ⓓ	95. Ⓐ Ⓓ

Part B—Memory for Addresses

1 Ⓐ Ⓑ Ⓒ Ⓓ Ⓔ   23 Ⓐ Ⓑ Ⓒ Ⓓ Ⓔ   45 Ⓐ Ⓑ Ⓒ Ⓓ Ⓔ   67 Ⓐ Ⓑ Ⓒ Ⓓ Ⓔ
2 Ⓐ Ⓑ Ⓒ Ⓓ Ⓔ   24 Ⓐ Ⓑ Ⓒ Ⓓ Ⓔ   46 Ⓐ Ⓑ Ⓒ Ⓓ Ⓔ   68 Ⓐ Ⓑ Ⓒ Ⓓ Ⓔ
3 Ⓐ Ⓑ Ⓒ Ⓓ Ⓔ   25 Ⓐ Ⓑ Ⓒ Ⓓ Ⓔ   47 Ⓐ Ⓑ Ⓒ Ⓓ Ⓔ   69 Ⓐ Ⓑ Ⓒ Ⓓ Ⓔ
4 Ⓐ Ⓑ Ⓒ Ⓓ Ⓔ   26 Ⓐ Ⓑ Ⓒ Ⓓ Ⓔ   48 Ⓐ Ⓑ Ⓒ Ⓓ Ⓔ   70 Ⓐ Ⓑ Ⓒ Ⓓ Ⓔ
5 Ⓐ Ⓑ Ⓒ Ⓓ Ⓔ   27 Ⓐ Ⓑ Ⓒ Ⓓ Ⓔ   49 Ⓐ Ⓑ Ⓒ Ⓓ Ⓔ   71 Ⓐ Ⓑ Ⓒ Ⓓ Ⓔ
6 Ⓐ Ⓑ Ⓒ Ⓓ Ⓔ   28 Ⓐ Ⓑ Ⓒ Ⓓ Ⓔ   50 Ⓐ Ⓑ Ⓒ Ⓓ Ⓔ   72 Ⓐ Ⓑ Ⓒ Ⓓ Ⓔ
7 Ⓐ Ⓑ Ⓒ Ⓓ Ⓔ   29 Ⓐ Ⓑ Ⓒ Ⓓ Ⓔ   51 Ⓐ Ⓑ Ⓒ Ⓓ Ⓔ   73 Ⓐ Ⓑ Ⓒ Ⓓ Ⓔ
8 Ⓐ Ⓑ Ⓒ Ⓓ Ⓔ   30 Ⓐ Ⓑ Ⓒ Ⓓ Ⓔ   52 Ⓐ Ⓑ Ⓒ Ⓓ Ⓔ   74 Ⓐ Ⓑ Ⓒ Ⓓ Ⓔ
9 Ⓐ Ⓑ Ⓒ Ⓓ Ⓔ   31 Ⓐ Ⓑ Ⓒ Ⓓ Ⓔ   53 Ⓐ Ⓑ Ⓒ Ⓓ Ⓔ   75 Ⓐ Ⓑ Ⓒ Ⓓ Ⓔ
10 Ⓐ Ⓑ Ⓒ Ⓓ Ⓔ   32 Ⓐ Ⓑ Ⓒ Ⓓ Ⓔ   54 Ⓐ Ⓑ Ⓒ Ⓓ Ⓔ   76 Ⓐ Ⓑ Ⓒ Ⓓ Ⓔ
11 Ⓐ Ⓑ Ⓒ Ⓓ Ⓔ   33 Ⓐ Ⓑ Ⓒ Ⓓ Ⓔ   55 Ⓐ Ⓑ Ⓒ Ⓓ Ⓔ   77 Ⓐ Ⓑ Ⓒ Ⓓ Ⓔ
12 Ⓐ Ⓑ Ⓒ Ⓓ Ⓔ   34 Ⓐ Ⓑ Ⓒ Ⓓ Ⓔ   56 Ⓐ Ⓑ Ⓒ Ⓓ Ⓔ   78 Ⓐ Ⓑ Ⓒ Ⓓ Ⓔ
13 Ⓐ Ⓑ Ⓒ Ⓓ Ⓔ   35 Ⓐ Ⓑ Ⓒ Ⓓ Ⓔ   57 Ⓐ Ⓑ Ⓒ Ⓓ Ⓔ   79 Ⓐ Ⓑ Ⓒ Ⓓ Ⓔ
14 Ⓐ Ⓑ Ⓒ Ⓓ Ⓔ   36 Ⓐ Ⓑ Ⓒ Ⓓ Ⓔ   58 Ⓐ Ⓑ Ⓒ Ⓓ Ⓔ   80 Ⓐ Ⓑ Ⓒ Ⓓ Ⓔ
15 Ⓐ Ⓑ Ⓒ Ⓓ Ⓔ   37 Ⓐ Ⓑ Ⓒ Ⓓ Ⓔ   59 Ⓐ Ⓑ Ⓒ Ⓓ Ⓔ   81 Ⓐ Ⓑ Ⓒ Ⓓ Ⓔ
16 Ⓐ Ⓑ Ⓒ Ⓓ Ⓔ   38 Ⓐ Ⓑ Ⓒ Ⓓ Ⓔ   60 Ⓐ Ⓑ Ⓒ Ⓓ Ⓔ   82 Ⓐ Ⓑ Ⓒ Ⓓ Ⓔ
17 Ⓐ Ⓑ Ⓒ Ⓓ Ⓔ   39 Ⓐ Ⓑ Ⓒ Ⓓ Ⓔ   61 Ⓐ Ⓑ Ⓒ Ⓓ Ⓔ   83 Ⓐ Ⓑ Ⓒ Ⓓ Ⓔ
18 Ⓐ Ⓑ Ⓒ Ⓓ Ⓔ   40 Ⓐ Ⓑ Ⓒ Ⓓ Ⓔ   62 Ⓐ Ⓑ Ⓒ Ⓓ Ⓔ   84 Ⓐ Ⓑ Ⓒ Ⓓ Ⓔ
19 Ⓐ Ⓑ Ⓒ Ⓓ Ⓔ   41 Ⓐ Ⓑ Ⓒ Ⓓ Ⓔ   63 Ⓐ Ⓑ Ⓒ Ⓓ Ⓔ   85 Ⓐ Ⓑ Ⓒ Ⓓ Ⓔ
20 Ⓐ Ⓑ Ⓒ Ⓓ Ⓔ   42 Ⓐ Ⓑ Ⓒ Ⓓ Ⓔ   64 Ⓐ Ⓑ Ⓒ Ⓓ Ⓔ   86 Ⓐ Ⓑ Ⓒ Ⓓ Ⓔ
21 Ⓐ Ⓑ Ⓒ Ⓓ Ⓔ   43 Ⓐ Ⓑ Ⓒ Ⓓ Ⓔ   65 Ⓐ Ⓑ Ⓒ Ⓓ Ⓔ   87 Ⓐ Ⓑ Ⓒ Ⓓ Ⓔ
22 Ⓐ Ⓑ Ⓒ Ⓓ Ⓔ   44 Ⓐ Ⓑ Ⓒ Ⓓ Ⓔ   66 Ⓐ Ⓑ Ⓒ Ⓓ Ⓔ   88 Ⓐ Ⓑ Ⓒ Ⓓ Ⓔ

Part C—Number Series

1. Ⓐ Ⓑ Ⓒ Ⓓ Ⓔ   7. Ⓐ Ⓑ Ⓒ Ⓓ Ⓔ   13. Ⓐ Ⓑ Ⓒ Ⓓ Ⓔ   19. Ⓐ Ⓑ Ⓒ Ⓓ Ⓔ
2. Ⓐ Ⓑ Ⓒ Ⓓ Ⓔ   8. Ⓐ Ⓑ Ⓒ Ⓓ Ⓔ   14. Ⓐ Ⓑ Ⓒ Ⓓ Ⓔ   20. Ⓐ Ⓑ Ⓒ Ⓓ Ⓔ
3. Ⓐ Ⓑ Ⓒ Ⓓ Ⓔ   9. Ⓐ Ⓑ Ⓒ Ⓓ Ⓔ   15. Ⓐ Ⓑ Ⓒ Ⓓ Ⓔ   21. Ⓐ Ⓑ Ⓒ Ⓓ Ⓔ
4. Ⓐ Ⓑ Ⓒ Ⓓ Ⓔ   10. Ⓐ Ⓑ Ⓒ Ⓓ Ⓔ   16. Ⓐ Ⓑ Ⓒ Ⓓ Ⓔ   22. Ⓐ Ⓑ Ⓒ Ⓓ Ⓔ
5. Ⓐ Ⓑ Ⓒ Ⓓ Ⓔ   11. Ⓐ Ⓑ Ⓒ Ⓓ Ⓔ   17. Ⓐ Ⓑ Ⓒ Ⓓ Ⓔ   23. Ⓐ Ⓑ Ⓒ Ⓓ Ⓔ
6. Ⓐ Ⓑ Ⓒ Ⓓ Ⓔ   12. Ⓐ Ⓑ Ⓒ Ⓓ Ⓔ   18. Ⓐ Ⓑ Ⓒ Ⓓ Ⓔ   24. Ⓐ Ⓑ Ⓒ Ⓓ Ⓔ

Part D—Following Oral Instructions

1 Ⓐ Ⓑ Ⓒ Ⓓ Ⓔ   23 Ⓐ Ⓑ Ⓒ Ⓓ Ⓔ   45 Ⓐ Ⓑ Ⓒ Ⓓ Ⓔ   67 Ⓐ Ⓑ Ⓒ Ⓓ Ⓔ

2 Ⓐ Ⓑ Ⓒ Ⓓ Ⓔ   24 Ⓐ Ⓑ Ⓒ Ⓓ Ⓔ   46 Ⓐ Ⓑ Ⓒ Ⓓ Ⓔ   68 Ⓐ Ⓑ Ⓒ Ⓓ Ⓔ

3 Ⓐ Ⓑ Ⓒ Ⓓ Ⓔ   25 Ⓐ Ⓑ Ⓒ Ⓓ Ⓔ   47 Ⓐ Ⓑ Ⓒ Ⓓ Ⓔ   69 Ⓐ Ⓑ Ⓒ Ⓓ Ⓔ

4 Ⓐ Ⓑ Ⓒ Ⓓ Ⓔ   26 Ⓐ Ⓑ Ⓒ Ⓓ Ⓔ   48 Ⓐ Ⓑ Ⓒ Ⓓ Ⓔ   70 Ⓐ Ⓑ Ⓒ Ⓓ Ⓔ

5 Ⓐ Ⓑ Ⓒ Ⓓ Ⓔ   27 Ⓐ Ⓑ Ⓒ Ⓓ Ⓔ   49 Ⓐ Ⓑ Ⓒ Ⓓ Ⓔ   71 Ⓐ Ⓑ Ⓒ Ⓓ Ⓔ

6 Ⓐ Ⓑ Ⓒ Ⓓ Ⓔ   28 Ⓐ Ⓑ Ⓒ Ⓓ Ⓔ   50 Ⓐ Ⓑ Ⓒ Ⓓ Ⓔ   72 Ⓐ Ⓑ Ⓒ Ⓓ Ⓔ

7 Ⓐ Ⓑ Ⓒ Ⓓ Ⓔ   29 Ⓐ Ⓑ Ⓒ Ⓓ Ⓔ   51 Ⓐ Ⓑ Ⓒ Ⓓ Ⓔ   73 Ⓐ Ⓑ Ⓒ Ⓓ Ⓔ

8 Ⓐ Ⓑ Ⓒ Ⓓ Ⓔ   30 Ⓐ Ⓑ Ⓒ Ⓓ Ⓔ   52 Ⓐ Ⓑ Ⓒ Ⓓ Ⓔ   74 Ⓐ Ⓑ Ⓒ Ⓓ Ⓔ

9 Ⓐ Ⓑ Ⓒ Ⓓ Ⓔ   31 Ⓐ Ⓑ Ⓒ Ⓓ Ⓔ   53 Ⓐ Ⓑ Ⓒ Ⓓ Ⓔ   75 Ⓐ Ⓑ Ⓒ Ⓓ Ⓔ

10 Ⓐ Ⓑ Ⓒ Ⓓ Ⓔ   32 Ⓐ Ⓑ Ⓒ Ⓓ Ⓔ   54 Ⓐ Ⓑ Ⓒ Ⓓ Ⓔ   76 Ⓐ Ⓑ Ⓒ Ⓓ Ⓔ

11 Ⓐ Ⓑ Ⓒ Ⓓ Ⓔ   33 Ⓐ Ⓑ Ⓒ Ⓓ Ⓔ   55 Ⓐ Ⓑ Ⓒ Ⓓ Ⓔ   77 Ⓐ Ⓑ Ⓒ Ⓓ Ⓔ

12 Ⓐ Ⓑ Ⓒ Ⓓ Ⓔ   34 Ⓐ Ⓑ Ⓒ Ⓓ Ⓔ   56 Ⓐ Ⓑ Ⓒ Ⓓ Ⓔ   78 Ⓐ Ⓑ Ⓒ Ⓓ Ⓔ

13 Ⓐ Ⓑ Ⓒ Ⓓ Ⓔ   35 Ⓐ Ⓑ Ⓒ Ⓓ Ⓔ   57 Ⓐ Ⓑ Ⓒ Ⓓ Ⓔ   79 Ⓐ Ⓑ Ⓒ Ⓓ Ⓔ

14 Ⓐ Ⓑ Ⓒ Ⓓ Ⓔ   36 Ⓐ Ⓑ Ⓒ Ⓓ Ⓔ   58 Ⓐ Ⓑ Ⓒ Ⓓ Ⓔ   80 Ⓐ Ⓑ Ⓒ Ⓓ Ⓔ

15 Ⓐ Ⓑ Ⓒ Ⓓ Ⓔ   37 Ⓐ Ⓑ Ⓒ Ⓓ Ⓔ   59 Ⓐ Ⓑ Ⓒ Ⓓ Ⓔ   81 Ⓐ Ⓑ Ⓒ Ⓓ Ⓔ

16 Ⓐ Ⓑ Ⓒ Ⓓ Ⓔ   38 Ⓐ Ⓑ Ⓒ Ⓓ Ⓔ   60 Ⓐ Ⓑ Ⓒ Ⓓ Ⓔ   82 Ⓐ Ⓑ Ⓒ Ⓓ Ⓔ

17 Ⓐ Ⓑ Ⓒ Ⓓ Ⓔ   39 Ⓐ Ⓑ Ⓒ Ⓓ Ⓔ   61 Ⓐ Ⓑ Ⓒ Ⓓ Ⓔ   83 Ⓐ Ⓑ Ⓒ Ⓓ Ⓔ

18 Ⓐ Ⓑ Ⓒ Ⓓ Ⓔ   40 Ⓐ Ⓑ Ⓒ Ⓓ Ⓔ   62 Ⓐ Ⓑ Ⓒ Ⓓ Ⓔ   84 Ⓐ Ⓑ Ⓒ Ⓓ Ⓔ

19 Ⓐ Ⓑ Ⓒ Ⓓ Ⓔ   41 Ⓐ Ⓑ Ⓒ Ⓓ Ⓔ   63 Ⓐ Ⓑ Ⓒ Ⓓ Ⓔ   85 Ⓐ Ⓑ Ⓒ Ⓓ Ⓔ

20 Ⓐ Ⓑ Ⓒ Ⓓ Ⓔ   42 Ⓐ Ⓑ Ⓒ Ⓓ Ⓔ   64 Ⓐ Ⓑ Ⓒ Ⓓ Ⓔ   86 Ⓐ Ⓑ Ⓒ Ⓓ Ⓔ

21 Ⓐ Ⓑ Ⓒ Ⓓ Ⓔ   43 Ⓐ Ⓑ Ⓒ Ⓓ Ⓔ   65 Ⓐ Ⓑ Ⓒ Ⓓ Ⓔ   87 Ⓐ Ⓑ Ⓒ Ⓓ Ⓔ

22 Ⓐ Ⓑ Ⓒ Ⓓ Ⓔ   44 Ⓐ Ⓑ Ⓒ Ⓓ Ⓔ   66 Ⓐ Ⓑ Ⓒ Ⓓ Ⓔ   88 Ⓐ Ⓑ Ⓒ Ⓓ Ⓔ

TEAR HERE

SCORE SHEET

ADDRESS CHECKING: Your score on the Address Checking part is based upon the number of questions you answered correctly minus the number of questions you answered incorrectly. To determine your score, subtract the number of wrong answers from the number of correct answers.

Number Right   –   Number Wrong   =   Raw Score

_____ – _____ = _____

MEMORY FOR ADDRESSES: Your score on the Memory for Addresses part is based upon the number of questions you answered correctly minus one-fourth of the questions you answered incorrectly (number wrong divided by 4). Calculate this now:

Number Wrong ÷ 4 =   .

Number Right   –   Number Wrong ÷ 4   =   Raw Score

_____ – _____ = _____

NUMBER SERIES: Your score on the Number Series part is based only on the number of questions you answered correctly. Wrong answers do not count against you.

Number Right   =   Raw Score

_____ = _____

FOLLOWING ORAL INSTRUCTIONS: Your score on the Following Oral Instructions part is based only upon the number of questions you marked correctly on the answer sheet. The worksheet is not scored, and wrong answers on the answer sheet do not count against you.

Number Right   =   Raw Score

_____ = _____

TOTAL SCORE: To find your total raw score, add together the raw scores for each section of the exam.

Address Checking Score   _____

+

Memory for Addresses Score   _____

+

Number Series Score   _____

+

Following Oral Instructions Score   _____

=   _____

Total Raw Score   _____

Self Evaluation Chart

Calculate your raw score for each test as shown above. Then check to see where your score falls on the scale from Poor to Excellent. Lightly shade in the boxes in which your scores fall.

Part	Excellent	Good	Average	Fair	Poor
Address Checking	80–95	65–79	50–64	35–49	1–34
Memory for Addresses	75–88	60–74	45–59	30–44	1–29
Number Series	21–24	18–20	14–17	11–13	1–10
Following Oral Instructions	27–31	23–26	19–22	14–18	1–13

Fifth Model Exam

Part A—Address Checking

Sample Questions

You will be allowed three minutes to read the directions and answer the five sample questions that follow. On the actual test, however, you will have only six minutes to answer 95 questions, so see how quickly you can compare addresses and still get the correct answer.

DIRECTIONS: Each question consists of two addresses. If the two addresses are alike in EVERY *way, mark A on your answer sheet. If the two addresses are* different in ANY *way, mark D on your answer sheet.*

1 ...3969 Ardsley Rd	3696 Ardsley Rd
2 ...Bryn Mawr PA 19010	Bryn Mawr PA 19010
3 ...1684 Beechwood Rd	1684 Beachwood Rd
4 ...1885 Black Birch La	1885 Black Birch La
5 ...Indianapolis IN 46208	Indianapollis IN 46208

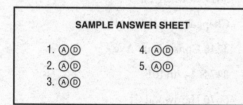

SAMPLE ANSWER SHEET

1. Ⓐ Ⓓ   4. Ⓐ Ⓓ
2. Ⓐ Ⓓ   5. Ⓐ Ⓓ
3. Ⓐ Ⓓ

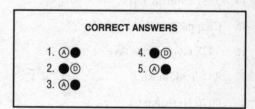

CORRECT ANSWERS

1. Ⓐ ●   4. ● Ⓓ
2. ● Ⓓ   5. Ⓐ ●
3. Ⓐ ●

Address Checking

Time: 6 Minutes. 95 Questions.

DIRECTIONS: For each question compare the address in the left column with the address in the right column. If the addresses are ALIKE IN EVERY WAY, blacken space A on your answer sheet. If the two addresses are DIFFERENT IN ANY WAY, blacken space D on your answer sheet. Correct answers for this test are on page 251.

1	4623 Grand Concourse	4623 Grand Concourse
2	6179 Ridgecroft Rd	6719 Ridgecroft Rd
3	5291 Hanover Cir	5291 Hangover Cir
4	2333 Palmer Ave	233 Palmer Ave
5	1859 SE 148th St	1859 SE 148th St
6	Dowagiac MI 49047	Dowagiac MI 49047
7	4147 Wykagyl Terr	4147 Wykagyl Terr
8	1504 N 10th Ave	1504 N 10th St
9	2967 Montross Ave	2967 Montrose Ave
10	Chicago IL 60601	Chicago IL 60601
11	2073 Defoe Ct	2073 Defoe Ct
12	2433 Westchester Plz	2343 Westchester Plz
13	6094 Carpenter Ave	6094 Charpenter Ave
14	5677 Bolman Twrs	5677 Bolman Twrs
15	Chappaqua NY 10514	Chappaqua NY 10541
16	3428 Constantine Ave	3248 Constantine Ave
17	847 S 147th Rd	847 S 147th Rd
18	6676 Harwood Ct	6676 Hardwood Ct
19	3486 Mosholu Pky	3486 Mosholu Pkwy
20	Mindenmines MO 64769	Mindenmines MO 64679
21	816 Oscawana Lake Rd	816 Ocsawana Lake Rd
22	9159 Battle Hill Rd	9195 Battle Hill Rd
23	7558 Winston Ln	7558 Winston Ln
24	3856 W 385th St	3856 W 386th St
25	3679 W Alpine Pl	3679 W Alpine Pl
26	Hartford CT 06115	Hartford CN 06115
27	6103 Locust Hill Wy	6013 Locust Hill Wy
28	4941 Annrock Dr	4941 Annrock Dr
29	2018 N St Andrews Pl	2018 N St Andrews Pl

30 ... 8111 Drewville Rd	8111 Drewsville Rd
31 ... 463 Peaceable Hill Rd	463 Peaceable Hill Rd
32 ... Biloxi MS 39532	Biloxi MS 39532
33 ... 3743 Point Dr S	3734 Point Dr S
34 ... 5665 Barnington Rd	5665 Barnington Rd
35 ... 2246 E Sheldrake Ave	2246 W Sheldrake Ave
36 ... 1443 Bloomingdale Rd	1443 Bloomingdales Rd
37 ... 2064 Chalford Ln	2064 Chalford Ln
38 ... McMinnville OR 97128	McMinville OR 97128
39 ... 6160 Shadybrook Ln	6160 Shadybrook Ln
40 ... 2947 E Lake Blvd	2947 E Lake Blvd
41 ... 3907 Evergreen Row	3907 Evergreen Row
42 ... 2192 SE Hotel Dr	2192 SE Hotel Dr
43 ... 8844 Fremont St	8844 Fremont Rd
44 ... 8487 Wolfshead Rd	8487 Wolfshead Rd
45 ... Anamosa IA 52205	Anamoosa IA 52205
46 ... 4055 Katonah Ave	4055 Katonah Ave
47 ... 1977 Buckingham Apts	1979 Buckingham Apts
48 ... 983 W 139th Way	983 W 139th Wy
49 ... 7822 Bayliss Ln	7822 Bayliss Ln
50 ... 8937 Banksville Rd	8937 Banksville Rd
51 ... 4759 Strathmore Rd	4579 Strathmore Rd
52 ... 2221 E Main St	221 E Main St
53 ... South Orange NJ 07079	South Orange NJ 07079
54 ... 4586 Sylvia Wy	4586 Sylvan Wy
55 ... 6335 Soundview Ave	6335 SoundView Ave
56 ... 3743 Popham Rd	3743 Poppam Rd
57 ... 2845 Brookfield Dr	2485 Brookfield Dr
58 ... 3845 Fort Slocum Rd	3845 Fort Slocum St
59 ... 9268 Jochum Ave	9268 Jochum Ave
60 ... Bloomington MN 55437	Bloomington MN 54537
61 ... 6903 S 184th St	6903 S 184th St
62 ... 7486 Rossmor Rd	7486 Rosemor Rd
63 ... 4176 Whitlockville Rd	4176 Whitlockville Wy

64 ... 4286 Megquire Ln	4286 Megquire Ln
65 ... 6270 Tamarock Rd	6270 Tammarock Rd
66 ... 3630 Bulkley Mnr	3630 Bulkley Mnr
67 ... 7158 Scarswold Apts	7185 Scarswold Apts
68 ... Brooklyn NY 11218	Brooklyn NY 11128
69 ... 9598 Prince Edward Rd	9598 Prince Edward Rd
70 ... 8439 S 145th St	8439 S 154th St
71 ... 9795 Shady Glen Ct	9795 Shady Grove Ct
72 ... 7614 Ganung St	7614 Ganung St
73 ... Teaneck NJ 07666	Teaneck NH 07666
74 ... 6359 Dempster Rd	6359 Dumpster Rd
75 ... 1065 Colchester Hl	1065 Colchester Hl
76 ... 5381 Phillipse Pl	5381 Philipse Pl
77 ... 6484 Rochester Terr	6484 Rochester Terr
78 ... 2956 Quinin St	2956 Quinin St
79 ... Tarzana CA 91356	Tarzana CA 91536
80 ... 7558 Winston Ln	7558 Whinston Ln
81 ... 1862 W 293rd St	1862 W 393rd St
82 ... 8534 S Huntington Ave	8534 N Huntington Ave
83 ... 9070 Wild Oaks Vlg	9070 Wild Oakes Vlg
84 ... 4860 Smadbeck Ave	4680 Smadbeck Ave
85 ... 8596 E Commonwealth Ave	8596 E Commonwealth Ave
86 ... Ridgefield NJ 07657	Ridgefield NJ 07657
87 ... 1478 Charter Cir	1478 W Charter Cir
88 ... 3963 Priscilla Ave	3963 Pricsilla Ave
89 ... 4897 Winding Ln	4897 Winding Ln
90 ... 847 Windmill Terr	847 Windmill Terr
91 ... 1662 Wixon St W	1662 Wixon St W
92 ... West Hartford CT 06107	West Hartford CT 06107
93 ... 6494 Rochelle Terr	9464 Rochelle Terr
94 ... 4228 Pocantico Rd	4228 Pocantico Rd
95 ... 1783 S 486th Ave	1783 S 486th Ave

END OF ADDRESS CHECKING

Part B—Memory for Addresses

Sample Questions

The sample questions for this part are based upon the addresses in the five boxes below. Your task is to mark on your answer sheet the letter of the box in which each address belongs. You will have five minutes now to study the locations of the addresses. Then cover the boxes and try to mark the location of the sample questions. You may look back at the boxes if you cannot yet mark the address locations from memory.

The exam itself provides three practice sessions before the question set that really counts. Practice I and Practice III supply you with the boxes and permit you to refer to them if necessary. Practice II and the Memory for Addresses test itself do not permit you to look at the boxes. The test itself is based on memory.

A	B	C	D	E
2600–3899 Hart	1400–2099 Hart	3900–4199 Hart	4200–5399 Hart	2100–2599 Hart
Linda	Ashley	Farmer	Monroe	Nolan
4200–5399 Dorp	3900–4199 Dorp	2600–3899 Dorp	2100–2599 Dorp	1400–2099 Dorp
Croft	Walton	Brendan	Orton	Gould
2100–2599 Noon	2600–3899 Noon	1400–2099 Noon	3900–4199 Noon	4200–5399 Noon

1. 3900–4199 Noon

2. 4200–5399 Dorp

3. Nolan

4. Farmer

5. 1400–2099 Hart

6. 2100–2599 Hart

7. 1400–2099 Noon

8. Monroe

9. Ashley

10. 2100–2599 Dorp

11. 2600–3899 Hart

12. 2100–2599 Noon

13. Orton

14. 2600–3899 Dorp

SAMPLE ANSWER SHEET		CORRECT ANSWERS	
1. Ⓐ Ⓑ Ⓒ Ⓓ Ⓔ	8. Ⓐ Ⓑ Ⓒ Ⓓ Ⓔ	1. Ⓐ Ⓑ Ⓒ ● Ⓔ	8. Ⓐ Ⓑ Ⓒ ● Ⓔ
2. Ⓐ Ⓑ Ⓒ Ⓓ Ⓔ	9. Ⓐ Ⓑ Ⓒ Ⓓ Ⓔ	2. ● Ⓑ Ⓒ Ⓓ Ⓔ	9. Ⓐ ● Ⓒ Ⓓ Ⓔ
3. Ⓐ Ⓑ Ⓒ Ⓓ Ⓔ	10. Ⓐ Ⓑ Ⓒ Ⓓ Ⓔ	3. Ⓐ Ⓑ Ⓒ Ⓓ ●	10. Ⓐ Ⓑ Ⓒ ● Ⓔ
4. Ⓐ Ⓑ Ⓒ Ⓓ Ⓔ	11. Ⓐ Ⓑ Ⓒ Ⓓ Ⓔ	4. Ⓐ Ⓑ ● Ⓓ Ⓔ	11. ● Ⓑ Ⓒ Ⓓ Ⓔ
5. Ⓐ Ⓑ Ⓒ Ⓓ Ⓔ	12. Ⓐ Ⓑ Ⓒ Ⓓ Ⓔ	5. Ⓐ ● Ⓒ Ⓓ Ⓔ	12. ● Ⓑ Ⓒ Ⓓ Ⓔ
6. Ⓐ Ⓑ Ⓒ Ⓓ Ⓔ	13. Ⓐ Ⓑ Ⓒ Ⓓ Ⓔ	6. Ⓐ Ⓑ Ⓒ Ⓓ ●	13. Ⓐ Ⓑ Ⓒ ● Ⓔ
7. Ⓐ Ⓑ Ⓒ Ⓓ Ⓔ	14. Ⓐ Ⓑ Ⓒ Ⓓ Ⓔ	7. Ⓐ Ⓑ ● Ⓓ Ⓔ	14. Ⓐ Ⓑ ● Ⓓ Ⓔ

Practice for Memory for Addresses

DIRECTIONS: *The five boxes below are labelled A, B, C, D, and E. In each box are three sets of number spans with names and two names that are not associated with numbers. In the next THREE MINUTES, you must try to memorize the box location of each name and number span. The position of a name or number span within its box is not important. You need only remember the letter of the box in which the item is to be found. You will use these names and numbers to answer three sets of practice questions that are NOT scored and one actual test that is scored. Correct answers are on pages 252 and 253.*

A	B	C	D	E
2600–3899 Hart	1400–2099 Hart	3900–4199 Hart	4200–5399 Hart	2100–2599 Hart
Linda	Ashley	Farmer	Monroe	Nolan
4200–5399 Dorp	3900–4199 Dorp	2600–3899 Dorp	2100–2599 Dorp	1400–2099 Dorp
Croft	Walton	Brendan	Orton	Gould
2100–2599 Noon	2600–3899 Noon	1400–2099 Noon	3900–4199 Noon	4200–5399 Noon

Practice I

DIRECTIONS: *Use the next THREE MINUTES to mark on the Practice I answer sheet the letter of the box in which each item that follows is to be found. Try to mark each item without looking back at the boxes. If, however, you get stuck, you may refer to the boxes during this practice exercise. If you find that you must look at the boxes, try to memorize as you do so. This test is for practice only. It will not be scored.*

1. 4200–5399 Dorp
2. 3900–4199 Hart
3. 4200–5399 Noon
4. Walton
5. Monroe
6. 2100–2599 Noon
7. 1400–2199 Hart
8. Gould
9. 1400–2099 Dorp
10. 2100–2599 Dorp
11. 1400–2099 Noon
12. Linda
13. Croft
14. Brendan
15. 3900–4199 Dorp
16. 2600–3899 Noon
17. 2100–2599 Hart
18. 2600–3899 Hart
19. 1400–2099 Dorp

20. Farmer
21. Ashley
22. 3900–4199 Noon
23. 2100–2599 Dorp
24. 2100–2599 Noon
25. Nolan
26. Croft
27. 4200–5399 Dorp
28. 1400–2099 Noon
29. 4200–5399 Hart
30. Monroe
31. Gould
32. 1400–2099 Hart
33. 2600–3899 Dorp
34. 2600–3899 Noon
35. Linda
36. Walton
37. Orton
38. 3900–4199 Dorp

39. 4200–5399 Noon
40. 3900–4199 Hart
41. Brendan
42. 1400–2099 Dorp
43. 2600–3899 Noon
44. Ashley
45. 4200–5399 Hart
46. 2600–3899 Hart
47. 3900–4199 Dorp
48. Orton
49. Monroe
50. 3900–4199 Noon
51. 2100–2599 Hart
52. 4200–5399 Noon
53. 2100–2599 Noon
54. Walton
55. Farmer
56. 2600–3899 Dorp
57. 3900–4199 Hart

58. 2100–2599 Dorp

59. Gould

60. Brendan

61. 1400–2099 Hart

62. 2600–3899 Noon

63. Ashley

64. 1400–2099 Dorp

65. 4200–5399 Dorp

66. 4200–5399 Hart

67. Linda

68. Croft

69. Nolan

70. 1400–2099 Noon

71. 3900–4199 Hart

72. 2100–2599 Dorp

73. 2600–3899 Noon

74. Walton

75. 2600–3899 Dorp

76. 2600–3899 Hart

77. 4200–5399 Noon

78. Monroe

79. Ashley

80. 2100–2599 Noon

81. 2100–2599 Hart

82. 3900–4199 Hart

83. Brendan

84. Nolan

85. Croft

86. 3900–4199 Dorp

87. 2100–2599 Dorp

88. 1400–2099 Noon

Practice I Answer Sheet

1 Ⓐ Ⓑ Ⓒ Ⓓ Ⓔ   23 Ⓐ Ⓑ Ⓒ Ⓓ Ⓔ   45 Ⓐ Ⓑ Ⓒ Ⓓ Ⓔ   67 Ⓐ Ⓑ Ⓒ Ⓓ Ⓔ

2 Ⓐ Ⓑ Ⓒ Ⓓ Ⓔ   24 Ⓐ Ⓑ Ⓒ Ⓓ Ⓔ   46 Ⓐ Ⓑ Ⓒ Ⓓ Ⓔ   68 Ⓐ Ⓑ Ⓒ Ⓓ Ⓔ

3 Ⓐ Ⓑ Ⓒ Ⓓ Ⓔ   25 Ⓐ Ⓑ Ⓒ Ⓓ Ⓔ   47 Ⓐ Ⓑ Ⓒ Ⓓ Ⓔ   69 Ⓐ Ⓑ Ⓒ Ⓓ Ⓔ

4 Ⓐ Ⓑ Ⓒ Ⓓ Ⓔ   26 Ⓐ Ⓑ Ⓒ Ⓓ Ⓔ   48 Ⓐ Ⓑ Ⓒ Ⓓ Ⓔ   70 Ⓐ Ⓑ Ⓒ Ⓓ Ⓔ

5 Ⓐ Ⓑ Ⓒ Ⓓ Ⓔ   27 Ⓐ Ⓑ Ⓒ Ⓓ Ⓔ   49 Ⓐ Ⓑ Ⓒ Ⓓ Ⓔ   71 Ⓐ Ⓑ Ⓒ Ⓓ Ⓔ

6 Ⓐ Ⓑ Ⓒ Ⓓ Ⓔ   28 Ⓐ Ⓑ Ⓒ Ⓓ Ⓔ   50 Ⓐ Ⓑ Ⓒ Ⓓ Ⓔ   72 Ⓐ Ⓑ Ⓒ Ⓓ Ⓔ

7 Ⓐ Ⓑ Ⓒ Ⓓ Ⓔ   29 Ⓐ Ⓑ Ⓒ Ⓓ Ⓔ   51 Ⓐ Ⓑ Ⓒ Ⓓ Ⓔ   73 Ⓐ Ⓑ Ⓒ Ⓓ Ⓔ

8 Ⓐ Ⓑ Ⓒ Ⓓ Ⓔ   30 Ⓐ Ⓑ Ⓒ Ⓓ Ⓔ   52 Ⓐ Ⓑ Ⓒ Ⓓ Ⓔ   74 Ⓐ Ⓑ Ⓒ Ⓓ Ⓔ

9 Ⓐ Ⓑ Ⓒ Ⓓ Ⓔ   31 Ⓐ Ⓑ Ⓒ Ⓓ Ⓔ   53 Ⓐ Ⓑ Ⓒ Ⓓ Ⓔ   75 Ⓐ Ⓑ Ⓒ Ⓓ Ⓔ

10 Ⓐ Ⓑ Ⓒ Ⓓ Ⓔ   32 Ⓐ Ⓑ Ⓒ Ⓓ Ⓔ   54 Ⓐ Ⓑ Ⓒ Ⓓ Ⓔ   76 Ⓐ Ⓑ Ⓒ Ⓓ Ⓔ

11 Ⓐ Ⓑ Ⓒ Ⓓ Ⓔ   33 Ⓐ Ⓑ Ⓒ Ⓓ Ⓔ   55 Ⓐ Ⓑ Ⓒ Ⓓ Ⓔ   77 Ⓐ Ⓑ Ⓒ Ⓓ Ⓔ

12 Ⓐ Ⓑ Ⓒ Ⓓ Ⓔ   34 Ⓐ Ⓑ Ⓒ Ⓓ Ⓔ   56 Ⓐ Ⓑ Ⓒ Ⓓ Ⓔ   78 Ⓐ Ⓑ Ⓒ Ⓓ Ⓔ

13 Ⓐ Ⓑ Ⓒ Ⓓ Ⓔ   35 Ⓐ Ⓑ Ⓒ Ⓓ Ⓔ   57 Ⓐ Ⓑ Ⓒ Ⓓ Ⓔ   79 Ⓐ Ⓑ Ⓒ Ⓓ Ⓔ

14 Ⓐ Ⓑ Ⓒ Ⓓ Ⓔ   36 Ⓐ Ⓑ Ⓒ Ⓓ Ⓔ   58 Ⓐ Ⓑ Ⓒ Ⓓ Ⓔ   80 Ⓐ Ⓑ Ⓒ Ⓓ Ⓔ

15 Ⓐ Ⓑ Ⓒ Ⓓ Ⓔ   37 Ⓐ Ⓑ Ⓒ Ⓓ Ⓔ   59 Ⓐ Ⓑ Ⓒ Ⓓ Ⓔ   81 Ⓐ Ⓑ Ⓒ Ⓓ Ⓔ

16 Ⓐ Ⓑ Ⓒ Ⓓ Ⓔ   38 Ⓐ Ⓑ Ⓒ Ⓓ Ⓔ   60 Ⓐ Ⓑ Ⓒ Ⓓ Ⓔ   82 Ⓐ Ⓑ Ⓒ Ⓓ Ⓔ

17 Ⓐ Ⓑ Ⓒ Ⓓ Ⓔ   39 Ⓐ Ⓑ Ⓒ Ⓓ Ⓔ   61 Ⓐ Ⓑ Ⓒ Ⓓ Ⓔ   83 Ⓐ Ⓑ Ⓒ Ⓓ Ⓔ

18 Ⓐ Ⓑ Ⓒ Ⓓ Ⓔ   40 Ⓐ Ⓑ Ⓒ Ⓓ Ⓔ   62 Ⓐ Ⓑ Ⓒ Ⓓ Ⓔ   84 Ⓐ Ⓑ Ⓒ Ⓓ Ⓔ

19 Ⓐ Ⓑ Ⓒ Ⓓ Ⓔ   41 Ⓐ Ⓑ Ⓒ Ⓓ Ⓔ   63 Ⓐ Ⓑ Ⓒ Ⓓ Ⓔ   85 Ⓐ Ⓑ Ⓒ Ⓓ Ⓔ

20 Ⓐ Ⓑ Ⓒ Ⓓ Ⓔ   42 Ⓐ Ⓑ Ⓒ Ⓓ Ⓔ   64 Ⓐ Ⓑ Ⓒ Ⓓ Ⓔ   86 Ⓐ Ⓑ Ⓒ Ⓓ Ⓔ

21 Ⓐ Ⓑ Ⓒ Ⓓ Ⓔ   43 Ⓐ Ⓑ Ⓒ Ⓓ Ⓔ   65 Ⓐ Ⓑ Ⓒ Ⓓ Ⓔ   87 Ⓐ Ⓑ Ⓒ Ⓓ Ⓔ

22 Ⓐ Ⓑ Ⓒ Ⓓ Ⓔ   44 Ⓐ Ⓑ Ⓒ Ⓓ Ⓔ   66 Ⓐ Ⓑ Ⓒ Ⓓ Ⓔ   88 Ⓐ Ⓑ Ⓒ Ⓓ Ⓔ

Practice II

DIRECTIONS: This is another practice test. Again, the time limit is THREE MINUTES. This time you must NOT look back at the boxes while answering the questions. This practice test will NOT be scored.

1. 3900–4199 Hart
2. 3900–4199 Dorp
3. 2100–2599 Noon
4. Nolan
5. Orton
6. 4200–5399 Noon
7. 4200–5399 Hart
8. 1400–2099 Noon
9. Croft
10. Ashley
11. 2600–3899 Hart
12. 4200–5399 Dorp
13. 1400–2099 Dorp
14. 1400–2099 Hart
15. Farmer
16. Brendan
17. 2600–3899 Dorp
18. 2100–2599 Dorp
19. 2100–2599 Hart
20. Monroe
21. 4200–5399 Hart
22. Linda
23. 2600–3899 Noon
24. 3900–4199 Noon
25. Walton
26. Monroe
27. Ashley
28. 1400–2099 Dorp
29. 3900–4199 Hart
30. 2100–2599 Noon

31. Brendan
32. Linda
33. 2600–3899 Hart
34. 3900–4199 Dorp
35. 1400–2099 Noon
36. Nolan
37. Farmer
38. 4200–5399 Noon
39. 2100–2599 Dorp
40. 1400–2099 Hart
41. Croft
42. Walton
43. 2100–2599 Hart
44. 2600–3899 Noon
45. 2600–3899 Dorp
46. Gould
47. Orton
48. 3900–4199 Noon
49. 4200–5399 Dorp
50. 4200–5399 Hart
51. 2600–3899 Dorp
52. Linda
53. 2100–2599 Noon
54. Ashley
55. Gould
56. 4200–5399 Noon
57. 3900–4199 Noon
58. 3900–4199 Dorp
59. Nolan
60. Croft

61. 2600–3899 Hart
62. 2100–2599 Dorp
63. 3900–4199 Hart
64. Farmer
65. Orton
66. 4200–5399 Dorp
67. 1400–2099 Dorp
68. 1400–2099 Hart
69. Brendan
70. Linda
71. 1400–2099 Noon
72. 2600–3899 Noon
73. 4200–5399 Hart
74. Walton
75. Monroe
76. 3900–4199 Dorp
77. 2100–2599 Hart
78. 2100–2599 Noon
79. Ashley
80. Gould
81. Orton
82. 2600–3899 Noon
83. 1400–2099 Hart
84. 2600–3899 Dorp
85. 3900–4199 Noon
86. 2600–3899 Hart
87. Brendan
88. Croft

Practice II Answer Sheet

1 Ⓐ Ⓑ Ⓒ Ⓓ Ⓔ   23 Ⓐ Ⓑ Ⓒ Ⓓ Ⓔ   45 Ⓐ Ⓑ Ⓒ Ⓓ Ⓔ   67 Ⓐ Ⓑ Ⓒ Ⓓ Ⓔ

2 Ⓐ Ⓑ Ⓒ Ⓓ Ⓔ   24 Ⓐ Ⓑ Ⓒ Ⓓ Ⓔ   46 Ⓐ Ⓑ Ⓒ Ⓓ Ⓔ   68 Ⓐ Ⓑ Ⓒ Ⓓ Ⓔ

3 Ⓐ Ⓑ Ⓒ Ⓓ Ⓔ   25 Ⓐ Ⓑ Ⓒ Ⓓ Ⓔ   47 Ⓐ Ⓑ Ⓒ Ⓓ Ⓔ   69 Ⓐ Ⓑ Ⓒ Ⓓ Ⓔ

4 Ⓐ Ⓑ Ⓒ Ⓓ Ⓔ   26 Ⓐ Ⓑ Ⓒ Ⓓ Ⓔ   48 Ⓐ Ⓑ Ⓒ Ⓓ Ⓔ   70 Ⓐ Ⓑ Ⓒ Ⓓ Ⓔ

5 Ⓐ Ⓑ Ⓒ Ⓓ Ⓔ   27 Ⓐ Ⓑ Ⓒ Ⓓ Ⓔ   49 Ⓐ Ⓑ Ⓒ Ⓓ Ⓔ   71 Ⓐ Ⓑ Ⓒ Ⓓ Ⓔ

6 Ⓐ Ⓑ Ⓒ Ⓓ Ⓔ   28 Ⓐ Ⓑ Ⓒ Ⓓ Ⓔ   50 Ⓐ Ⓑ Ⓒ Ⓓ Ⓔ   72 Ⓐ Ⓑ Ⓒ Ⓓ Ⓔ

7 Ⓐ Ⓑ Ⓒ Ⓓ Ⓔ   29 Ⓐ Ⓑ Ⓒ Ⓓ Ⓔ   51 Ⓐ Ⓑ Ⓒ Ⓓ Ⓔ   73 Ⓐ Ⓑ Ⓒ Ⓓ Ⓔ

8 Ⓐ Ⓑ Ⓒ Ⓓ Ⓔ   30 Ⓐ Ⓑ Ⓒ Ⓓ Ⓔ   52 Ⓐ Ⓑ Ⓒ Ⓓ Ⓔ   74 Ⓐ Ⓑ Ⓒ Ⓓ Ⓔ

9 Ⓐ Ⓑ Ⓒ Ⓓ Ⓔ   31 Ⓐ Ⓑ Ⓒ Ⓓ Ⓔ   53 Ⓐ Ⓑ Ⓒ Ⓓ Ⓔ   75 Ⓐ Ⓑ Ⓒ Ⓓ Ⓔ

10 Ⓐ Ⓑ Ⓒ Ⓓ Ⓔ   32 Ⓐ Ⓑ Ⓒ Ⓓ Ⓔ   54 Ⓐ Ⓑ Ⓒ Ⓓ Ⓔ   76 Ⓐ Ⓑ Ⓒ Ⓓ Ⓔ

11 Ⓐ Ⓑ Ⓒ Ⓓ Ⓔ   33 Ⓐ Ⓑ Ⓒ Ⓓ Ⓔ   55 Ⓐ Ⓑ Ⓒ Ⓓ Ⓔ   77 Ⓐ Ⓑ Ⓒ Ⓓ Ⓔ

12 Ⓐ Ⓑ Ⓒ Ⓓ Ⓔ   34 Ⓐ Ⓑ Ⓒ Ⓓ Ⓔ   56 Ⓐ Ⓑ Ⓒ Ⓓ Ⓔ   78 Ⓐ Ⓑ Ⓒ Ⓓ Ⓔ

13 Ⓐ Ⓑ Ⓒ Ⓓ Ⓔ   35 Ⓐ Ⓑ Ⓒ Ⓓ Ⓔ   57 Ⓐ Ⓑ Ⓒ Ⓓ Ⓔ   79 Ⓐ Ⓑ Ⓒ Ⓓ Ⓔ

14 Ⓐ Ⓑ Ⓒ Ⓓ Ⓔ   36 Ⓐ Ⓑ Ⓒ Ⓓ Ⓔ   58 Ⓐ Ⓑ Ⓒ Ⓓ Ⓔ   80 Ⓐ Ⓑ Ⓒ Ⓓ Ⓔ

15 Ⓐ Ⓑ Ⓒ Ⓓ Ⓔ   37 Ⓐ Ⓑ Ⓒ Ⓓ Ⓔ   59 Ⓐ Ⓑ Ⓒ Ⓓ Ⓔ   81 Ⓐ Ⓑ Ⓒ Ⓓ Ⓔ

16 Ⓐ Ⓑ Ⓒ Ⓓ Ⓔ   38 Ⓐ Ⓑ Ⓒ Ⓓ Ⓔ   60 Ⓐ Ⓑ Ⓒ Ⓓ Ⓔ   82 Ⓐ Ⓑ Ⓒ Ⓓ Ⓔ

17 Ⓐ Ⓑ Ⓒ Ⓓ Ⓔ   39 Ⓐ Ⓑ Ⓒ Ⓓ Ⓔ   61 Ⓐ Ⓑ Ⓒ Ⓓ Ⓔ   83 Ⓐ Ⓑ Ⓒ Ⓓ Ⓔ

18 Ⓐ Ⓑ Ⓒ Ⓓ Ⓔ   40 Ⓐ Ⓑ Ⓒ Ⓓ Ⓔ   62 Ⓐ Ⓑ Ⓒ Ⓓ Ⓔ   84 Ⓐ Ⓑ Ⓒ Ⓓ Ⓔ

19 Ⓐ Ⓑ Ⓒ Ⓓ Ⓔ   41 Ⓐ Ⓑ Ⓒ Ⓓ Ⓔ   63 Ⓐ Ⓑ Ⓒ Ⓓ Ⓔ   85 Ⓐ Ⓑ Ⓒ Ⓓ Ⓔ

20 Ⓐ Ⓑ Ⓒ Ⓓ Ⓔ   42 Ⓐ Ⓑ Ⓒ Ⓓ Ⓔ   64 Ⓐ Ⓑ Ⓒ Ⓓ Ⓔ   86 Ⓐ Ⓑ Ⓒ Ⓓ Ⓔ

21 Ⓐ Ⓑ Ⓒ Ⓓ Ⓔ   43 Ⓐ Ⓑ Ⓒ Ⓓ Ⓔ   65 Ⓐ Ⓑ Ⓒ Ⓓ Ⓔ   87 Ⓐ Ⓑ Ⓒ Ⓓ Ⓔ

22 Ⓐ Ⓑ Ⓒ Ⓓ Ⓔ   44 Ⓐ Ⓑ Ⓒ Ⓓ Ⓔ   66 Ⓐ Ⓑ Ⓒ Ⓓ Ⓔ   88 Ⓐ Ⓑ Ⓒ Ⓓ Ⓔ

Practice III

DIRECTIONS: *The names and addresses are repeated for you in the boxes below. Each name and each number span is in the same box in which you found it in the original set. You will now be allowed FIVE MINUTES to study the locations again. Do your best to memorize the letter of the box in which each item is located. This is your last chance to see the boxes.*

A	B	C	D	E
2600–3899 Hart Linda 4200–5399 Dorp Croft 2100–2599 Noon	1400–2099 Hart Ashley 3900–4199 Dorp Walton 2600–3899 Noon	3900–4199 Hart Farmer 2600–3899 Dorp Brendan 1400–2099 Noon	4200–5399 Hart Monroe 2100–2599 Dorp Orton 3900–4199 Noon	2100–2599 Hart Nolan 1400–2099 Dorp Gould 4200–5399 Noon

DIRECTIONS: *This is your last practice test. Mark the location of each of the 88 items on the Practice III answer sheet. You will have FIVE MINUTES to answer these questions. Do NOT look back at the boxes. This practice test will not be scored.*

1. 2600–3899 Hart
2. 2600–3899 Dorp
3. 2600–3899 Noon
4. Walton
5. Nolan
6. 4200–5399 Noon
7. 2100–2599 Dorp
8. 1400–2099 Noon
9. Gould
10. Monroe
11. 3900–4199 Hart
12. 2100–2599 Hart
13. 3900–4199 Dorp
14. Brendan
15. Ashley
16. 1400–2099 Hart
17. 1400–2099 Dorp
18. 4200–5399 Dorp
19. Farmer
20. Monroe
21. Linda
22. 2100–2599 Noon

23. 3900–4199 Hart
24. 4200–5399 Hart
25. Croft
26. Ashley
27. 3900–4199 Dorp
28. 2600–3899 Noon
29. 2600–3899 Hart
30. Nolan
31. 2100–2599 Dorp
32. 4200–5399 Hart
33. 2600–3899 Noon
34. Monroe
35. Farmer
36. 3900–4199 Noon
37. 3900–4199 Dorp
38. 2600–3899 Hart
39. Nolan
40. Walton
41. 4200–5399 Dorp
42. 4200–5399 Noon
43. 1400–2099 Hart
44. Linda

45. Gould
46. 2100–2599 Hart
47. 3900–4199 Hart
48. 2600–3899 Dorp
49. Ashley
50. Croft
51. 1400–2099 Dorp
52. 1400–2099 Noon
53. 2100–2599 Noon
54. Orton
55. Brendan
56. 2600–3899 Hart
57. 3900–4199 Dorp
58. 4200–5399 Noon
59. 3900–4199 Hart
60. 1400–2099 Noon
61. Ashley
62. Brendan
63. Monroe
64. 1400–2099 Hart
65. 3900–4199 Noon
66. 4200–5399 Hart

67. 3900–4199 Dorp   75. Gould   83. Croft

68. Nolan   76. Linda   84. Orton

69. Walton   77. Farmer   85. 2100–2599 Noon

70. 4200–5399 Dorp   78. 2600–3899 Hart 86. 3900–4199 Hart

71. 1400–2099 Dorp   79. 2600–3899 Noon 87. 1400–2099 Dorp

72. 1400–2099 Noon   80. 4200–5399 Noon 88. 4200–5399 Noon

73. 3900–4199 Hart   81. 2600–3899 Dorp

74. 2100–2599 Hart   82. 2100–2599 Dorp

Practice III Answer Sheet

1 Ⓐ Ⓑ Ⓒ Ⓓ Ⓔ	23 Ⓐ Ⓑ Ⓒ Ⓓ Ⓔ	45 Ⓐ Ⓑ Ⓒ Ⓓ Ⓔ	67 Ⓐ Ⓑ Ⓒ Ⓓ Ⓔ
2 Ⓐ Ⓑ Ⓒ Ⓓ Ⓔ	24 Ⓐ Ⓑ Ⓒ Ⓓ Ⓔ	46 Ⓐ Ⓑ Ⓒ Ⓓ Ⓔ	68 Ⓐ Ⓑ Ⓒ Ⓓ Ⓔ
3 Ⓐ Ⓑ Ⓒ Ⓓ Ⓔ	25 Ⓐ Ⓑ Ⓒ Ⓓ Ⓔ	47 Ⓐ Ⓑ Ⓒ Ⓓ Ⓔ	69 Ⓐ Ⓑ Ⓒ Ⓓ Ⓔ
4 Ⓐ Ⓑ Ⓒ Ⓓ Ⓔ	26 Ⓐ Ⓑ Ⓒ Ⓓ Ⓔ	48 Ⓐ Ⓑ Ⓒ Ⓓ Ⓔ	70 Ⓐ Ⓑ Ⓒ Ⓓ Ⓔ
5 Ⓐ Ⓑ Ⓒ Ⓓ Ⓔ	27 Ⓐ Ⓑ Ⓒ Ⓓ Ⓔ	49 Ⓐ Ⓑ Ⓒ Ⓓ Ⓔ	71 Ⓐ Ⓑ Ⓒ Ⓓ Ⓔ
6 Ⓐ Ⓑ Ⓒ Ⓓ Ⓔ	28 Ⓐ Ⓑ Ⓒ Ⓓ Ⓔ	50 Ⓐ Ⓑ Ⓒ Ⓓ Ⓔ	72 Ⓐ Ⓑ Ⓒ Ⓓ Ⓔ
7 Ⓐ Ⓑ Ⓒ Ⓓ Ⓔ	29 Ⓐ Ⓑ Ⓒ Ⓓ Ⓔ	51 Ⓐ Ⓑ Ⓒ Ⓓ Ⓔ	73 Ⓐ Ⓑ Ⓒ Ⓓ Ⓔ
8 Ⓐ Ⓑ Ⓒ Ⓓ Ⓔ	30 Ⓐ Ⓑ Ⓒ Ⓓ Ⓔ	52 Ⓐ Ⓑ Ⓒ Ⓓ Ⓔ	74 Ⓐ Ⓑ Ⓒ Ⓓ Ⓔ
9 Ⓐ Ⓑ Ⓒ Ⓓ Ⓔ	31 Ⓐ Ⓑ Ⓒ Ⓓ Ⓔ	53 Ⓐ Ⓑ Ⓒ Ⓓ Ⓔ	75 Ⓐ Ⓑ Ⓒ Ⓓ Ⓔ
10 Ⓐ Ⓑ Ⓒ Ⓓ Ⓔ	32 Ⓐ Ⓑ Ⓒ Ⓓ Ⓔ	54 Ⓐ Ⓑ Ⓒ Ⓓ Ⓔ	76 Ⓐ Ⓑ Ⓒ Ⓓ Ⓔ
11 Ⓐ Ⓑ Ⓒ Ⓓ Ⓔ	33 Ⓐ Ⓑ Ⓒ Ⓓ Ⓔ	55 Ⓐ Ⓑ Ⓒ Ⓓ Ⓔ	77 Ⓐ Ⓑ Ⓒ Ⓓ Ⓔ
12 Ⓐ Ⓑ Ⓒ Ⓓ Ⓔ	34 Ⓐ Ⓑ Ⓒ Ⓓ Ⓔ	56 Ⓐ Ⓑ Ⓒ Ⓓ Ⓔ	78 Ⓐ Ⓑ Ⓒ Ⓓ Ⓔ
13 Ⓐ Ⓑ Ⓒ Ⓓ Ⓔ	35 Ⓐ Ⓑ Ⓒ Ⓓ Ⓔ	57 Ⓐ Ⓑ Ⓒ Ⓓ Ⓔ	79 Ⓐ Ⓑ Ⓒ Ⓓ Ⓔ
14 Ⓐ Ⓑ Ⓒ Ⓓ Ⓔ	36 Ⓐ Ⓑ Ⓒ Ⓓ Ⓔ	58 Ⓐ Ⓑ Ⓒ Ⓓ Ⓔ	80 Ⓐ Ⓑ Ⓒ Ⓓ Ⓔ
15 Ⓐ Ⓑ Ⓒ Ⓓ Ⓔ	37 Ⓐ Ⓑ Ⓒ Ⓓ Ⓔ	59 Ⓐ Ⓑ Ⓒ Ⓓ Ⓔ	81 Ⓐ Ⓑ Ⓒ Ⓓ Ⓔ
16 Ⓐ Ⓑ Ⓒ Ⓓ Ⓔ	38 Ⓐ Ⓑ Ⓒ Ⓓ Ⓔ	60 Ⓐ Ⓑ Ⓒ Ⓓ Ⓔ	82 Ⓐ Ⓑ Ⓒ Ⓓ Ⓔ
17 Ⓐ Ⓑ Ⓒ Ⓓ Ⓔ	39 Ⓐ Ⓑ Ⓒ Ⓓ Ⓔ	61 Ⓐ Ⓑ Ⓒ Ⓓ Ⓔ	83 Ⓐ Ⓑ Ⓒ Ⓓ Ⓔ
18 Ⓐ Ⓑ Ⓒ Ⓓ Ⓔ	40 Ⓐ Ⓑ Ⓒ Ⓓ Ⓔ	62 Ⓐ Ⓑ Ⓒ Ⓓ Ⓔ	84 Ⓐ Ⓑ Ⓒ Ⓓ Ⓔ
19 Ⓐ Ⓑ Ⓒ Ⓓ Ⓔ	41 Ⓐ Ⓑ Ⓒ Ⓓ Ⓔ	63 Ⓐ Ⓑ Ⓒ Ⓓ Ⓔ	85 Ⓐ Ⓑ Ⓒ Ⓓ Ⓔ
20 Ⓐ Ⓑ Ⓒ Ⓓ Ⓔ	42 Ⓐ Ⓑ Ⓒ Ⓓ Ⓔ	64 Ⓐ Ⓑ Ⓒ Ⓓ Ⓔ	86 Ⓐ Ⓑ Ⓒ Ⓓ Ⓔ
21 Ⓐ Ⓑ Ⓒ Ⓓ Ⓔ	43 Ⓐ Ⓑ Ⓒ Ⓓ Ⓔ	65 Ⓐ Ⓑ Ⓒ Ⓓ Ⓔ	87 Ⓐ Ⓑ Ⓒ Ⓓ Ⓔ
22 Ⓐ Ⓑ Ⓒ Ⓓ Ⓔ	44 Ⓐ Ⓑ Ⓒ Ⓓ Ⓔ	66 Ⓐ Ⓑ Ⓒ Ⓓ Ⓔ	88 Ⓐ Ⓑ Ⓒ Ⓓ Ⓔ

Memory for Addresses

Time: 5 Minutes. 88 Questions.

DIRECTIONS: Mark your answers on the answer sheet in the section headed "MEMORY FOR ADDRESSES." This test will be scored. You are NOT permitted to look at the boxes. Work from memory, as quickly and as accurately as you can. Correct answers are on page 253.

1. Monroe
2. Walton
3. 2600–3899 Dorp
4. 2100–2599 Noon
5. 2100–2599 Hart
6. Linda
7. Gould
8. 4200–5399 Noon
9. 1400–2099 Dorp
10. 2600–3899 Hart
11. Ashley
12. Orton
13. 3900–4199 Hart
14. 1400–2099 Noon
15. 4200–5399 Dorp
16. 4200–5399 Hart
17. 2600–3899 Noon
18. 2100–2599 Dorp
19. Croft
20. Brendan
21. Nolan
22. Farmer
23. 3900–4199 Dorp
24. 3900–4199 Noon
25. 1400–3899 Hart
26. Linda
27. 2100–2599 Hart
28. 3900–4199 Hart
29. Monroe
30. 2600–3899 Dorp

31. 1400–3899 Noon
32. Brendan
33. Ashley
34. 2600–3899 Hart
35. 2100–2599 Noon
36. 1400–2099 Dorp
37. 2100–2599 Dorp
38. 4200–5399 Noon
39. Orton
40. Croft
41. 4200–5399 Hart
42. 2600–3899 Noon
43. 4200–5399 Dorp
44. Gould
45. 3900–4199 Noon
46. 2600–3899 Dorp
47. 1400–2099 Hart
48. Linda
49. Gould
50. 2100–2599 Hart
51. 2100–2599 Dorp
52. 3900–4199 Dorp
53. 2100–2599 Noon
54. Brendan
55. Farmer
56. 2600–3899 Hart
57. 4200–5399 Noon
58. 1400–2099 Dorp
59. Nolan
60. Croft

61. 4200–5399 Dorp
62. 1400–2099 Noon
63. 2600–3899 Noon
64. Monroe
65. Ashley
66. 3900–4199 Hart
67. 4200–5399 Hart
68. Orton
69. Walton
70. 2100–2599 Hart
71. 4200–5399 Dorp
72. 3900–4199 Noon
73. 2100–2599 Noon
74. 2600–3899 Dorp
75. 3900–4199 Hart
76. Croft
77. Farmer
78. 2100–2599 Hart
79. 4200–5399 Noon
80. 4200–5399 Dorp
81. Brendan
82. Monroe
83. 1400–2099 Noon
84. 3900–4199 Dorp
85. 4200–5399 Hart
86. Linda
87. Ashley
88. 1400–2099 Dorp

END OF MEMORY FOR ADDRESSES

Part C—Number Series

Sample Questions

The following sample questions show you the type of question that will be used in Part C. You will have three minutes to answer the sample questions and to study the explanations.

DIRECTIONS: Each number series question consists of a series of numbers that follows some definite order. The numbers progress from left to right according to some rule. One pair of numbers to the right of the series comprises the next two numbers in the series. Study each series to try to find a pattern to the series and to figure out the rule that governs the progression. Choose the answer pair that continues the series according to the pattern established and mark its letter on your answer sheet.

1. 23 23 25 23 28 23 32 .... (A) 32 37 (B) 23 27 (C) 32 23 (D) 37 23 (E) 23 36

   The pattern of this series is +2, +3, +4, +5 with the number 23 intervening after each number in the main series. Do not be confused by what appears to be an initial repetition of the number 23. It is coincidental that the series happens to begin with the same number that then intervenes during the series. The answer is (**B**): intervening 23, then 32 + 5 = 37.

2. 40 35 31 30 25 21 20 15 .... (A) 10 6 (B) 14 9 (C) 14 10 (D) 11 7 (E) 11 10

   The pattern is: −5, −4, −1; −5, −4, −1; −5, −4, −1. The answer is (**E**) because 15−4 = 11 − 1 = 10.

3. 98 24 92 28 86 32 80 .... (A) 74 36 (B) 26 84 (C) 38 84 (D) 36 75 (E) 36 74

   There are two separate and distinct alternating series within this series. The first series progresses at the rate of −6: 98 92 86 80 74. The alternating series progresses at the rate of +4: 24 28 32 36. The correct answer is (**E**).

4. 17 17 28 28 40 40 53 .... (A) 53 66 (B) 53 53 (C) 66 66 (D) 53 67 (E) 67 67

   The pattern being established is: repeat the number, +11, repeat the number, +12, repeat the number, +13, repeat the number, +14. The answer is (**D**): repeat the 53, then 53 + 14 = 67.

5. 19 15 10 19 15 10 19 .... (A) 15 10 (B) 10 15 (C) 19 15 (D) 19 10 (E) 15 19

   The sequence 19 15 10 repeats itself over and over again. The answer is (**A**).

<table>
<tr><td>

SAMPLE ANSWER SHEET

1. (A) (B) (C) (D) (E)
2. (A) (B) (C) (D) (E)
3. (A) (B) (C) (D) (E)
4. (A) (B) (C) (D) (E)
5. (A) (B) (C) (D) (E)

</td><td>

CORRECT ANSWERS

1. (A) ● (C) (D) (E)
2. (A) (B) (C) (D) ●
3. (A) (B) (C) (D) ●
4. (A) (B) (C) ● (E)
5. ● (B) (C) (D) (E)

</td></tr>
</table>

Number Series

Time: 20 Minutes. 24 Questions.

DIRECTIONS: Each number series question consists of a series of numbers that follows some definite order. The numbers progress from left to right according to some rule. One lettered pair of numbers to the right of the series comprises the next two numbers in the series. Study each series to try to find a pattern to the series and to figure out the rule that governs the progression. Choose the answer pair that continues the series according to the pattern established and mark its letter on your answer sheet. Correct answers are on page 253.

1. 19 18 12 17 16 13 15 ...(A) 16 12   (B) 14 14   (C) 12 14   (D) 14 12   (E) 12 16

2. 7 15 12 8 16 13 9 ....(A) 17 14   (B) 17 10   (C) 14 10   (D) 14 17   (E) 10 14

3. 18 15 6 16 14 6 14 ....(A) 12 6   (B) 14 13   (C) 6 12   (D) 13 12   (E) 33 6

4. 6 6 5 8 8 7 10 10 ....(A) 8 12   (B) 9 12   (C) 22 12   (D) 12 9   (E) 9 9

5. 17 20 23 26 29 32 35 ...(A) 37 40   (B) 41 44   (C) 38 41   (D) 38 42   (E) 36 39

6. 15 5 7 16 9 11 17 ....(A) 18 13   (B) 15 17   (C) 12 19   (D) 13 15   (E) 12 13

7. 19 17 16 16 13 15 10 ...(A) 14 7   (B) 12 9   (C) 14 9   (D) 7 12   (E) 10 14

8. 11 1 16 10 6 21 9 ....(A) 12 26   (B) 26 8   (C) 11 26   (D) 11 8   (E) 8 11

9. 15 22 19 26 23 30 27 ...(A) 28 34   (B) 27 35   (C) 31 34   (D) 29 33   (E) 34 31

10. 99 9 88 8 77 7 66 ....(A) 55 5   (B) 6 55   (C) 66 5   (D) 55 6   (E) 55 44

11. 25 29 29 33 37 37 41 ...(A) 41 41   (B) 41 45   (C) 45 49   (D) 45 45   (E) 49 49

12. 81 71 61 52 43 35 27 ....(A) 27 20   (B) 21 14   (C) 20 14   (D) 21 15   (E) 20 13

13. 12 14 16 48 50 52 156 ....(A) 468 470   (B) 158 316   (C) 158 474   (D) 158 160   (E) 158 158

14. 47 42 38 35 30 26 23 ...(A) 18 14   (B) 21 19   (C) 23 18   (D) 19 14   (E) 19 13

15. 84 84 91 91 97 97 102 ....(A) 102 102   (B) 102 104   (C) 104 106   (D) 106 106   (E) 102 106

16. 66 13 62 21 58 29 54 ..(A) 50 48   (B) 62 66   (C) 34 42   (D) 37 50   (E) 58 21

17. 14 12 10 10 20 18 16 16 ....(A) 32 32   (B) 32 30   (C) 30 28   (D) 16 32   (E) 16 14

18. 25 30 35 30 25 30 35 ...(A) 30 40   (B) 25 30   (C) 25 20   (D) 35 30   (E) 30 25

19. 19 19 19 57 57 57 171 ..(A) 171 513   (B) 513 513   (C) 171 171   (D) 171 57   (E) 57 18

20. 75 69 63 57 51 45 39 ...(A) 36 33   (B) 39 36   (C) 39 33   (D) 33 27   (E) 33 33

21. 6 15 23 30 36 41 45 ....(A) 48 50   (B) 49 53   (C) 45 41   (D) 46 47   (E) 47 49

22. 12 58 25 51 38 44 51 ...(A) 64 37   (B) 37 64   (C) 51 51   (D) 51 64   (E) 51 37

23. 1 2 4 8 16 32 64 ....(A) 64 32   (B) 64 64   (C) 64 128   (D) 128 256   (E) 128 128

24. 5 86 7 81 10 77 14 ....(A) 16 80   (B) 70 25   (C) 79 13   (D) 19 74   (E) 74 19

END OF NUMBER SERIES

Part D—Following Oral Instructions

Directions and Sample Questions

LISTENING TO INSTRUCTIONS: When you are ready to try these sample questions, give the following instructions to a friend and have the friend read them aloud to you at the rate of 80 words per minute. Do not read them to yourself. Your friend will need a watch with a second hand. Listen carefully and do exactly what your friend tells you to do with the worksheet and answer sheet. Your friend will tell you some things to do with each item on the worksheet. After each set of instructions, your friend will give you time to mark your answer by darkening a circle on the sample answer sheet. Since B and D sound very much alike, your friend will say "B as in baker" when he or she means B and "D as in dog" when he or she means D.

Before proceeding further, tear out the worksheet on page 243. Then hand this book to your friend.

TO THE PERSON WHO IS TO READ THE INSTRUCTIONS: The instructions are to be read at the rate of 80 words per minute. Do not read aloud the material that is in parentheses. Do not repeat any instructions.

Read Aloud to the Candidate

Look at line 1 on the worksheet. (Pause slightly.) Draw a line under the second number in the line. (Pause 2 seconds.) Now, on your answer sheet, find the number under which you just drew the line and darken space B as in baker for that number. (Pause 5 seconds.)

Look at the letters in line 2 on the worksheet. (Pause slightly.) Draw a line under the second letter in the line. Now, on your answer sheet, find number 6 (pause 2 seconds) and darken the space for the letter under which you drew a line. (Pause 5 seconds.)

Look at the letters in line 2 again. (Pause slightly.) Now draw two lines under the first letter in the line. (Pause 2 seconds.) Now, on your answer sheet, find number 12 (pause 2 seconds) and darken the space for the letter under which you drew two lines. (Pause 5 seconds.)

Look at line 3. (Pause slightly.) Draw a circle around the number that is the smallest in the line. (Pause 2 seconds.) Now, on your answer sheet, find the number you just drew a circle around and darken the space A for that number. (Pause 5 seconds.)

Now look at line 4 on your worksheet. There are 3 boxes with words and letters in them. (Pause slightly.) Each box represents a station in a large city. Station A delivers mail in the Regent Street area, Station B delivers mail in Broadway Plaza, and Station C delivers mail in Sunset Park. Ms. Kelly lives in Sunset Park. Write the number 2 on the line inside the box that represents the station that delivers Ms. Kelly's mail. (Pause 2 seconds.) Now, on your answer sheet, find the number 2 and darken the space for the letter that is in the box you just wrote in. (Pause 5 seconds.)

Sample Worksheet

DIRECTIONS: Listening carefully to each set of instructions, mark each item on this worksheet as directed. Then complete each question by marking the sample answer sheet below as directed. For each answer you will darken the answer for a number-letter combination. Should you fall behind and miss an instruction, don't become excited. Let that one go and listen for the next one. If, when you start to darken a space for a number, you find that you have already darkened another space for that number, either erase the first mark and darken the space for the new combination or let the first mark stay and do not darken a space for the new combination. Write with a pencil that has a clean eraser. When you finish, you should have no more than one space darkened for each number.

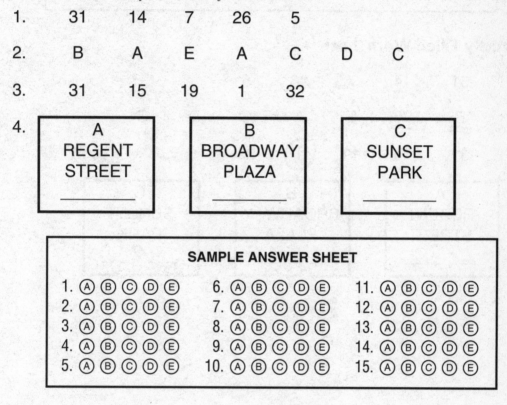

1.   31   14   7   26   5

2.   B   A   E   A   C   D   C

3.   31   15   19   1   32

4.

A REGENT STREET	B BROADWAY PLAZA	C SUNSET PARK
_____	_____	_____

SAMPLE ANSWER SHEET

1. Ⓐ Ⓑ Ⓒ Ⓓ Ⓔ   6. Ⓐ Ⓑ Ⓒ Ⓓ Ⓔ   11. Ⓐ Ⓑ Ⓒ Ⓓ Ⓔ
2. Ⓐ Ⓑ Ⓒ Ⓓ Ⓔ   7. Ⓐ Ⓑ Ⓒ Ⓓ Ⓔ   12. Ⓐ Ⓑ Ⓒ Ⓓ Ⓔ
3. Ⓐ Ⓑ Ⓒ Ⓓ Ⓔ   8. Ⓐ Ⓑ Ⓒ Ⓓ Ⓔ   13. Ⓐ Ⓑ Ⓒ Ⓓ Ⓔ
4. Ⓐ Ⓑ Ⓒ Ⓓ Ⓔ   9. Ⓐ Ⓑ Ⓒ Ⓓ Ⓔ   14. Ⓐ Ⓑ Ⓒ Ⓓ Ⓔ
5. Ⓐ Ⓑ Ⓒ Ⓓ Ⓔ   10. Ⓐ Ⓑ Ⓒ Ⓓ Ⓔ   15. Ⓐ Ⓑ Ⓒ Ⓓ Ⓔ

CORRECT ANSWERS TO SAMPLE QUESTIONS

1. ● Ⓑ Ⓒ Ⓓ Ⓔ   6. ● Ⓑ Ⓒ Ⓓ Ⓔ   11. Ⓐ Ⓑ Ⓒ Ⓓ Ⓔ
2. Ⓐ Ⓑ ● Ⓓ Ⓔ   7. Ⓐ Ⓑ Ⓒ Ⓓ Ⓔ   12. Ⓐ ● Ⓒ Ⓓ Ⓔ
3. Ⓐ Ⓑ Ⓒ Ⓓ Ⓔ   8. Ⓐ Ⓑ Ⓒ Ⓓ Ⓔ   13. Ⓐ Ⓑ Ⓒ Ⓓ Ⓔ
4. Ⓐ Ⓑ Ⓒ Ⓓ Ⓔ   9. Ⓐ Ⓑ Ⓒ Ⓓ Ⓔ   14. Ⓐ ● Ⓒ Ⓓ Ⓔ
5. Ⓐ Ⓑ Ⓒ Ⓓ Ⓔ   10. Ⓐ Ⓑ Ⓒ Ⓓ Ⓔ   15. Ⓐ Ⓑ Ⓒ Ⓓ Ⓔ

Correctly Filled Worksheet

1.   31   <u>14</u>   7   26   5

2.   <u>B̲</u>   <u>A</u>   E   A   C   D   C

3.   31   15   19   ①   32

4.
| A REGENT STREET | B BROADWAY PLAZA | C SUNSET PARK **2** |

Following Oral Instructions

Time: 25 Minutes.

Listening to Instructions

DIRECTIONS: When you are ready to try this test of the Model Exam, give the following instructions to a friend and have the friend read them aloud to you at the rate of 80 words per minute. Do NOT read them to yourself. Your friend will need a watch with a second hand. Listen carefully and do exactly what your friend tells you to do with the worksheet and with the answer sheet. Your friend will tell you some things to do with each item on the worksheet. After each set of instructions, your friend will give you time to mark your answer by darkening a circle on the answer sheet. Since B and D sound very much alike, your friend will say "B as in baker" when he or she means B and "D as in dog" when he or she means D.

Before proceeding further, tear out the worksheet on page 249 of this test. Then hand this book to your friend.

TO THE PERSON WHO IS TO READ THE INSTRUCTIONS: The instructions are to be read at the rate of 80 words per minute. Do not read aloud the material that is in parentheses. Once you have begun the test itself, do not repeat any instructions. The next three paragraphs consist of approximately 120 words. Read these three paragraphs aloud to the candidate in about one and one-half minutes. You may reread these paragraphs as often as necessary to establish an 80-words-per-minute reading speed.

Read Aloud to the Candidate

On the job you will have to listen to directions and then do what you have been told to do. In this test, I will read instructions to you. Try to understand them as I read them; I cannot repeat them. Once we begin, you may not ask any questions until the end of the test.

On the job you won't have to deal with pictures, numbers, and letters like those in the test, but you will have to listen to instructions and follow them. We are using this test to see how well you can follow instructions.

You are to mark your test booklet according to the instructions that I'll read to you. After each set of instructions, I'll give you time to record your answers on the separate answer sheet.

The actual test begins now.

Look at line 1 on your worksheet. (Pause slightly.) Draw a line under the fourth letter in the line. (Pause 2 seconds.) Now, on your answer sheet, find number 21 and darken the space for the letter under which you drew a line. (Pause 5 seconds.)

Now look at line 2 on your worksheet. (Pause slightly.) Draw a line under each star on line 2. (Pause 5 seconds.) Count the number of lines you have drawn and write that number at the end of line 2. (Pause 5 seconds.) Now, on your answer sheet, find that number and darken space A. (Pause 5 seconds.)

Look at line 3 on your worksheet. (Pause slightly.) Find the largest circle and write the letter D as in dog on the line in the circle. (Pause 2 seconds.) Now, on your answer sheet, find the number that is in the circle and darken the number-letter combination that is in that circle. (Pause 5 seconds.)

Look at line 3 again. (Pause slightly.) Find the largest square. (Pause 2 seconds.) Draw a line through the number in the square, subtract 4 from that number, and write your answer on the line beside the number. (Pause 5 seconds.) Now, on your answer sheet, darken space E for the number that you wrote in the box. (Pause 5 seconds.)

Look at line 4 on your worksheet. (Pause slightly.) Draw two lines under the fifth number on line 4. (Pause 2 seconds.) If the number under which you drew two lines is an even number, darken space B as in baker for that number on your answer sheet. If the number under which you drew two lines is an odd number, darken space A. (Pause 10 seconds.)

Look at line 4 again. (Pause slightly.) Circle the middle number in the line. (Pause 2 seconds.) Now, on your answer sheet, darken space B as in baker for the number you circled. (Pause 5 seconds.)

Look at line 5 on your worksheet. (Pause slightly.)There are five mail sacks on the line with a time printed on each mail sack. The train carrying the mail leaves the station promptly at 4:00 P.M., so mail must be on the platform before that time. Find the mail sack with the latest possible time for arrival at the station, and write the last two digits of the time on the line in the mail sack. (Pause 5 seconds.) Now, on your answer sheet, find the number you wrote and darken the space for the number-letter combination in the mail sack. (Pause 5 seconds.)

Look at line 6 on your worksheet. (Pause slightly.) If the number 35 is divisible by 2, write the letter C in the third box. If not, write the letter D as in dog in the fifth box. (Pause 5 seconds.) Now, on your answer sheet, darken the space for the number-letter combination in the box. (Pause 5 seconds.)

Look at line 6 again. (Pause slightly.) Find the box with the highest number and write the letter A on the line in that box. (Pause 2 seconds.) Now, on your answer sheet, darken the space for the number-letter combination in that box. (Pause 5 seconds.)

Look at line 7 on your worksheet. (Pause slightly.) Count up the number of even numbers on line 7 and write that number at the end of the line. (Pause 5 seconds.) If the number you wrote is greater than 3, circle the fourth number on the line. If the number you wrote is less than 3, circle the fifth number on line 7. (Pause 5 seconds.) Now, on your answer sheet, darken space B as in baker for the number that you circled. (Pause 5 seconds.)

Look at line 8 on your worksheet. (Pause slightly.) There are three words and three boxes with numbers on the line. Write the second letter of the third word in the first box. (Pause 5 seconds.) Write the first letter of the second word in the third box. (Pause 5 seconds.) Now, on your answer sheet, darken the spaces for the number-letter combinations in both boxes. (Pause 10 seconds.)

Look at line 8 again. (Pause slightly.) Find the letter of the alphabet that appears more than two times in the three words and circle that letter in each word. (Pause 2 seconds.) Now, on your answer sheet, darken that letter for space 13. (Pause 5 seconds.)

Look at line 9 on your worksheet. (Pause slightly.) If Monday comes before Wednesday and if 11 is greater than 7, write the letter B as in baker in the second triangle. Otherwise, write the letter D as in dog in the square. (Pause 10 seconds.) Now, on your answer sheet, darken the space for the number-letter combination you just wrote. (Pause 5 seconds.)

Look at line 9 again. (Pause slightly.) Write the letter C in the figure with the most sides. (Pause 2 seconds.) Now add the number 10 to the number in the figure in which you just wrote the letter C and darken the space for that number-letter combination on your answer sheet. (Pause 10 seconds.)

Look at line 10 on your worksheet. (Pause slightly.) Draw one line under the third even number on line 10. (Pause 2 seconds.) Now, on your answer sheet, darken space D as in dog for the number under which you just drew one line. (Pause 5 seconds.)

Look at line 10 again. (Pause slightly.) Draw two lines under the first number in the line. (Pause 2 seconds.) Multiply that number by 5 and write the number at the end of line 10. (Pause 2 seconds.) Now, on your answer sheet, darken space A for the number you wrote at the end of the line. (Pause 5 seconds.)

Look at line 11 on your worksheet. (Pause slightly.) If the number in the smallest box is smaller than the number in the first box, write the letter C in the smallest box. If not, write the letter E in the largest box. (Pause 5 seconds.) Now, on your answer sheet, darken the space for the number-letter combination in the box you just wrote in. (Pause 5 seconds.)

Look at line 12 on your worksheet. (Pause slightly.) Write the number of days in the month of February in a year that is not a leap year next to the fourth letter on line 12. (Pause 2 seconds.) Now, on your answer sheet, darken the space for that number-letter combination. (Pause 5 seconds.)

Look at line 13 on your worksheet. (Pause slightly.) In the fourth box write the answer to this question: Which of the following is the largest number: 72, 12, 85, 51, or 67? (Pause 2 seconds.) Now, on your answer sheet, darken the space for the number-letter combination in the box you just wrote in. (Pause 5 seconds.)

Look at line 13 again. (Pause slightly.) If the number of minutes in an hour is equal to the number of seconds in a minute, write the number 24 in the middle box. If not, write the number 60 in the first box. (Pause 5 seconds.) Now, on your answer sheet, darken the space for the number-letter combination in the box you just wrote in. (Pause 5 seconds.)

Look at line 14 on your worksheet. (Pause slightly.) Mail for individual carrier routes is sorted into individual boxes as indicated by the names in the boxes. The numbers on the boxes are the numbers of the carrier routes. Write the letter E in the box for the carrier route to which mail for Dempsey is assigned. (Pause 2 seconds.) Now, on your answer sheet, darken the space for the number-letter combination in the box you just wrote in. (Pause 5 seconds.)

Look at line 15 on your worksheet. (Pause slightly.) Count the number of diamonds that are partially shaded, multiply that number by 4, and write the new number in the first unshaded diamond. (Pause 2 seconds.) Now, on your answer sheet, darken space B as in baker for the number you wrote in the first unshaded diamond. (Pause 5 seconds.)

Look at line 15 again. (Pause slightly.) If there are more diamonds fully shaded than fully unshaded, write the number 79 in the first diamond. If not, write the number 10 in the last diamond. Now, on your answer sheet, darken space D as in dog for the number you just wrote. (Pause 5 seconds.)

Look at line 16 on your worksheet. (Pause slightly.) Draw a line under every number that is 55 or greater but less than 75. (Pause 5 seconds.) Now, on your answer sheet, darken the letter C for every number under which you drew a line. (Pause 10 seconds.)

Look at line 17 on your worksheet. (Pause slightly.) Write the letter A in the middle square in the bottom row of mailboxes. (Pause 2 seconds.) Now, on your answer sheet, darken the space for the number-letter combination in the mailbox you just wrote in. (Pause 5 seconds.)

Look at line 17 again. (Pause slightly.) If the sum of 5 plus 3 is 8 and the sum of 7 plus 2 is 9, write B as in baker in the upper right hand mailbox. Otherwise, write C in the lower right hand mailbox. (Pause 5 seconds.) Now, on your answer sheet, darken the space for the number-letter combination in the mailbox you just wrote in. (Pause 5 seconds.)

Look at line 18 on your worksheet. (Pause slightly.) Find the figure with the greatest number of corners. Add 70 to the number of corners and write the sum on the line in the figure. (Pause 5 seconds.) Now, on your answer sheet, darken the space for the number-letter combination in the figure in which you just wrote. (Pause 5 seconds.)

Look at line 18 again. (Pause slightly.) If the second figure is larger than the first figure, write the number 40 on the line in the second figure. (Pause 2 seconds.) Otherwise, write the number 40 on the line in the fifth figure. (Pause 2 seconds.) Now, on your answer sheet, darken the space for the number-letter combination in the figure you just wrote in. (Pause 5 seconds.)

Look at line 19 on your worksheet. (Pause slightly.) Draw a circle around each number on line 19 that is a multiple of 10. (Pause 5 seconds.) Now, on your answer sheet, darken the letter E for each number around which you drew a circle. (Pause 10 seconds.)

Following Oral Instructions

Worksheet

DIRECTIONS: Listening carefully to each set of instructions, mark each item on this worksheet as directed. Then complete each question by marking the answer sheet as directed. For each answer you will darken the answer for a number-letter combination. Should you fall behind and miss an instruction, don't become excited. Let that one go and listen for the next one. If, when you start to darken a space for a number, you find that you have already darkened another space for that number, either erase the first mark and darken the space for the new combination or let the first mark stay and do not darken a space for the new combination. Write with a pencil that has a clean eraser. When you finish, you should have no more than one space darkened for each number. Correct answers are on page 256.

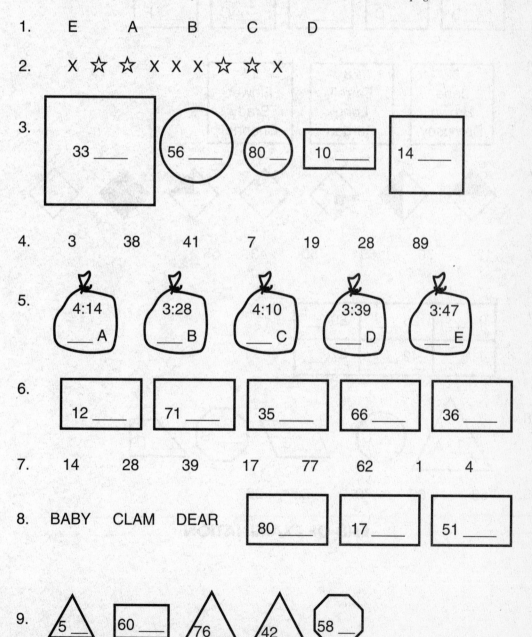

1. E   A   B   C   D

2. X ☆ ☆ X X X ☆ ☆ X

3. 33 ____   56 ____   80 __   10 ____   14 ____

4. 3   38   41   7   19   28   89

5. 4:14 __ A   3:28 __ B   4:10 __ C   3:39 __ D   3:47 __ E

6. 12 ____   71 ____   35 ____   66 ____   36 ____

7. 14   28   39   17   77   62   1   4

8. BABY   CLAM   DEAR   80 ____   17 ____   51 ____

9. 5 __   60 __   76 __   42 __   58 __

TEAR HERE

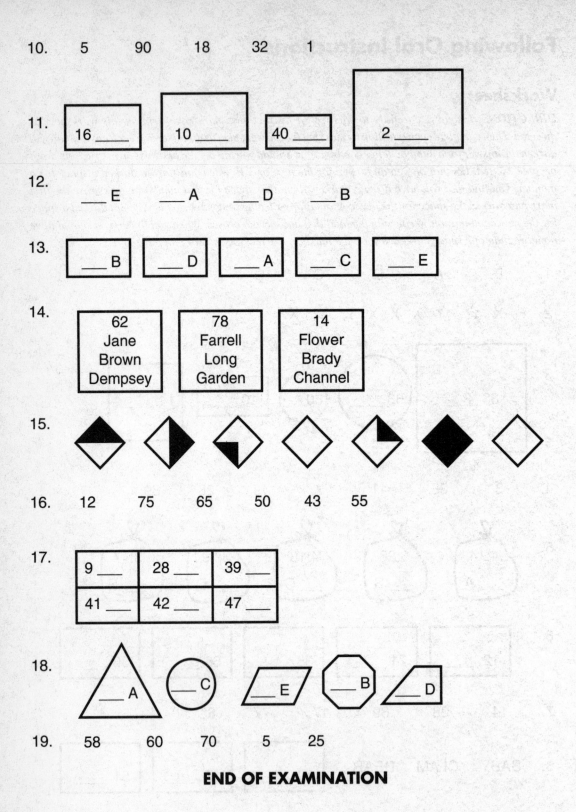

10.   5   90   18   32   1

11.   16 ____   10 ____   40 ____   2 ____

12.   ___ E   ___ A   ___ D   ___ B

13.   ___ B   ___ D   ___ A   ___ C   ___ E

14.
62 Jane Brown Dempsey	78 Farrell Long Garden	14 Flower Brady Channel

15.

16.   12   75   65   50   43   55

17.
9 ___	28 ___	39 ___
41 ___	42 ___	47 ___

18.   ___ A   ___ C   ___ E   ___ B   ___ D

19.   58   60   70   5   25

END OF EXAMINATION

Correct Answers for Fifth Model Exam

Part A—Address Checking

1. A	13. D	25. A	37. A	49. A	61. A	73. D	85. A
2. D	14. A	26. D	38. D	50. A	62. D	74. D	86. A
3. D	15. D	27. D	39. A	51. D	63. D	75. A	87. D
4. D	16. D	28. A	40. A	52. D	64. A	76. D	88. D
5. A	17. A	29. A	41. A	53. A	65. D	77. A	89. A
6. A	18. D	30. D	42. A	54. D	66. A	78. A	90. A
7. A	19. D	31. A	43. D	55. D	67. D	79. D	91. A
8. D	20. D	32. A	44. A	56. D	68. D	80. D	92. A
9. D	21. D	33. D	45. D	57. D	69. A	81. D	93. D
10. A	22. D	34. A	46. A	58. D	70. D	82. A	94. A
11. A	23. A	35. D	47. D	59. A	71. D	83. D	95. A
12. D	24. D	36. D	48. D	60. D	72. A	84. D	

Analyzing Your Errors

Type of Error	Tally	Total Number
Number of addresses that were alike and you incorrectly marked "different"		
Number of addresses that were different and you incorrectly marked "alike"		
Number of addresses in which you missed a difference in NUMBERS		
Number of addresses in which you missed a difference in ABBREVIATIONS		
Number of addresses in which you missed a difference in NAMES		

Part B—Memory for Addresses

Practice I

1. A	12. A	23. D	34. B	45. D	56. C	67. A	78. D
2. C	13. A	24. A	35. A	46. A	57. C	68. A	79. B
3. E	14. C	25. E	36. B	47. B	58. D	69. E	80. A
4. B	15. B	26. A	37. D	48. D	59. E	70. C	81. E
5. D	16. B	27. A	38. B	49. D	60. C	71. C	82. C
6. A	17. E	28. C	39. E	50. D	61. B	72. D	83. C
7. B	18. A	29. D	40. C	51. E	62. B	73. B	84. E
8. E	19. E	30. D	41. C	52. E	63. B	74. B	85. A
9. E	20. C	31. E	42. E	53. A	64. E	75. C	86. B
10. D	21. B	32. B	43. B	54. B	65. A	76. A	87. D
11. C	22. D	33. C	44. B	55. C	66. D	77. E	88. C

Practice II

1. C	12. A	23. B	34. B	45. C	56. E	67. E	78. A
2. B	13. E	24. D	35. C	46. E	57. D	68. B	79. B
3. A	14. B	25. B	36. E	47. D	58. B	69. C	80. E
4. E	15. C	26. D	37. C	48. D	59. E	70. A	81. D
5. D	16. C	27. B	38. E	49. A	60. A	71. C	82. B
6. E	17. C	28. E	39. D	50. D	61. A	72. B	83. B
7. D	18. D	29. C	40. B	51. C	62. D	73. D	84. C
8. C	19. E	30. A	41. A	52. A	63. C	74. B	85. D
9. A	20. D	31. C	42. B	53. A	64. C	75. D	86. A
10. B	21. D	32. A	43. E	54. B	65. D	76. B	87. C
11. A	22. A	33. A	44. B	55. E	66. A	77. E	88. A

Practice III

1. A	12. E	23. C	34. D	45. E	56. A	67. B	78. A
2. C	13. B	24. D	35. C	46. E	57. B	68. E	79. B
3. B	14. C	25. A	36. D	47. C	58. E	69. B	80. E
4. B	15. B	26. B	37. B	48. C	59. C	70. A	81. C
5. E	16. B	27. B	38. A	49. B	60. C	71. E	82. D
6. E	17. E	28. B	39. E	50. A	61. B	72. C	83. A
7. D	18. A	29. A	40. B	51. E	62. C	73. C	84. D
8. C	19. C	30. E	41. A	52. C	63. D	74. E	85. A
9. E	20. D	31. D	42. E	53. A	64. B	75. E	86. C
10. D	21. A	32. D	43. B	54. D	65. D	76. A	87. E
11. C	22. A	33. B	44. A	55. C	66. D	77. C	88. E

Memory for Addresses

1. D	12. D	23. B	34. A	45. D	56. A	67. D	78. E
2. B	13. C	24. D	35. A	46. C	57. E	68. D	79. E
3. C	14. C	25. B	36. E	47. B	58. E	69. B	80. A
4. A	15. A	26. A	37. D	48. A	59. E	70. E	81. C
5. E	16. D	27. E	38. E	49. E	60. A	71. A	82. D
6. A	17. B	28. C	39. D	50. E	61. A	72. D	83. C
7. E	18. D	29. D	40. A	51. D	62. C	73. A	84. B
8. E	19. A	30. C	41. D	52. B	63. B	74. C	85. D
9. E	20. C	31. C	42. B	53. A	64. D	75. C	86. A
10. A	21. E	32. D	43. A	54. C	65. B	76. A	87. B
11. B	22. C	33. B	44. E	55. C	66. C	77. C	88. E

Part C—Number Series

1. B	4. B	7. A	10. B	13. D	16. D	19. C	22. B
2. A	5. C	8. C	11. D	14. A	17. B	20. D	23. D
3. E	6. D	9. E	12. E	15. E	18. E	21. A	24. E

Explanations

1. **(B)** There are two series. The first series descends one number at a time, beginning with 19. The second series enters between each two numbers of the first series. The second series increases by +1. Thus, the series are: 19 18 17 16 15 14 and 12 13 14.

2. **(A)** The repeating pattern is +8, –3, –5.

3. **(E)** This is a difficult problem. The first series begins with 18 and decreases by –2: 18 16 14 . . . . The second series begins with 15 and descends by –1: 15 14 13 . . . . The number 6 separates each pair of descending numbers.

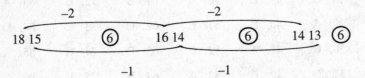

4. **(B)** The even numbers repeat themselves as they increase; the odd numbers simply increase by +2, alternating with the evens.

5. **(C)** Just add three to each number to get the next number.

6. **(D)** One series increases by +1: 15 16 17 18. The other series, which intervenes with two numbers to the first series' one, increases by +2: 5 7 9 11 13.

7. **(A)** The rule for the first series is –3. The rule for the alternating series is –1.

8. **(C)** There are two series here. The first reads 11 10 9. The second series starts at 1 and follows the rule +15, –10, +15, –10. The second series takes two steps to the first series' one. The solution to this problem is best seen by diagramming.

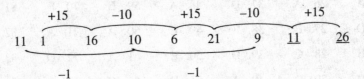

9. **(E)** The pattern is: +7, –3; +7, –3; . . . . Or, you might see alternating series, both increasing by +4.

10. **(B)** You might see two series. One series decreases at the rate of –11; the other decreases at the rate of –1. Or, you might see a series of the multiples of 11 each divided by 11.

11. **(D)** The pattern is +4, repeat the number, +4; +4, repeat the number, +4; +4, repeat the number, +4 . . . .

12. **(E)** The pattern is: –10, –10, –9, –9, –8, –8, –7, –7, –6 . . . .

13. **(D)** The pattern is: +2, +2, ×3; +2, +2, ×3 . . . .

14. **(A)** The pattern is: –5, –4, –3; –5, –4, –3; –5 . . . .

15. **(E)** The pattern is: repeat the number, +7, repeat the number, +6, repeat the number, +5, repeat the number, +4 . . . .

16. **(D)** There are two alternating series. The first series descends at the rate of –4. The alternating series ascends at the rate of +8.

17. **(B)** The pattern is: –2, –2, repeat the number, ×2; –2, –2, repeat the number, ×2; –2 . . . .

18. **(E)** The pattern is: +5, +5, –5, –5; +5, +5, –5, –5; +5 . . . . Or you might see the repeat of the four numbers 25, 30, 35, 30.

19. **(C)** The pattern is: repeat the number three times, ×3; repeat the number three times, ×3; repeat the number three times, ×3.

20. **(D)** The pattern is simply: –6, –6, –6 . . . .

21. **(A)** The pattern is: +9, +8, +7, +6, +5, +4, +3, +2, +1.

22. **(B)** There are two alternating series. The first series increases at the rate of +13. The alternating series decreases at the rate of –7.

23. **(D)** The pattern is: ×2, ×2, ×2 . . . .

24. **(E)** There are two alternating series. The pattern of the first series is: +2, +3, +4, +5. The pattern of the alternating series is: –5, –4, –3, –2.

Part D—Following Oral Instructions

Correctly Filled Answer Grid

1 Ⓐ Ⓑ Ⓒ Ⓓ Ⓔ	23 Ⓐ Ⓑ Ⓒ Ⓓ Ⓔ	45 Ⓐ Ⓑ Ⓒ Ⓓ Ⓔ	67 Ⓐ Ⓑ Ⓒ Ⓓ Ⓔ
2 Ⓐ Ⓑ Ⓒ Ⓓ ●	24 ● Ⓑ Ⓒ Ⓓ Ⓔ	46 Ⓐ Ⓑ Ⓒ Ⓓ Ⓔ	68 Ⓐ Ⓑ ● Ⓓ Ⓔ
3 Ⓐ Ⓑ Ⓒ Ⓓ Ⓔ	25 ● Ⓑ Ⓒ Ⓓ Ⓔ	47 Ⓐ Ⓑ Ⓒ Ⓓ ●	69 Ⓐ Ⓑ Ⓒ Ⓓ Ⓔ
4 ● Ⓑ Ⓒ Ⓓ Ⓔ	26 Ⓐ Ⓑ Ⓒ Ⓓ Ⓔ	48 Ⓐ Ⓑ Ⓒ Ⓓ Ⓔ	70 Ⓐ Ⓑ Ⓒ Ⓓ ●
5 Ⓐ Ⓑ Ⓒ Ⓓ Ⓔ	27 Ⓐ Ⓑ Ⓒ Ⓓ Ⓔ	49 Ⓐ Ⓑ Ⓒ Ⓓ Ⓔ	71 ● Ⓑ Ⓒ Ⓓ Ⓔ
6 Ⓐ Ⓑ Ⓒ Ⓓ Ⓔ	28 Ⓐ ● Ⓒ Ⓓ Ⓔ	50 Ⓐ Ⓑ Ⓒ Ⓓ Ⓔ	72 Ⓐ Ⓑ Ⓒ Ⓓ Ⓔ
7 Ⓐ ● Ⓒ Ⓓ Ⓔ	29 Ⓐ Ⓑ Ⓒ Ⓓ ●	51 Ⓐ Ⓑ ● Ⓓ Ⓔ	73 Ⓐ Ⓑ Ⓒ Ⓓ Ⓔ
8 Ⓐ Ⓑ Ⓒ Ⓓ Ⓔ	30 Ⓐ Ⓑ Ⓒ Ⓓ Ⓔ	52 Ⓐ Ⓑ Ⓒ Ⓓ Ⓔ	74 Ⓐ Ⓑ Ⓒ Ⓓ Ⓔ
9 Ⓐ Ⓑ Ⓒ Ⓓ Ⓔ	31 Ⓐ Ⓑ Ⓒ Ⓓ Ⓔ	53 Ⓐ Ⓑ Ⓒ Ⓓ Ⓔ	75 Ⓐ Ⓑ Ⓒ Ⓓ Ⓔ
10 Ⓐ Ⓑ Ⓒ ● Ⓔ	32 Ⓐ Ⓑ Ⓒ ● Ⓔ	54 Ⓐ Ⓑ Ⓒ Ⓓ Ⓔ	76 Ⓐ ● Ⓒ Ⓓ Ⓔ
11 Ⓐ Ⓑ Ⓒ Ⓓ Ⓔ	33 Ⓐ Ⓑ Ⓒ Ⓓ Ⓔ	55 Ⓐ Ⓑ ● Ⓓ Ⓔ	77 Ⓐ Ⓑ Ⓒ Ⓓ Ⓔ
12 Ⓐ Ⓑ Ⓒ Ⓓ Ⓔ	34 Ⓐ Ⓑ Ⓒ Ⓓ Ⓔ	56 Ⓐ Ⓑ Ⓒ ● Ⓔ	78 Ⓐ ● Ⓒ Ⓓ Ⓔ
13 ● Ⓑ Ⓒ Ⓓ Ⓔ	35 Ⓐ Ⓑ Ⓒ Ⓓ Ⓔ	57 Ⓐ Ⓑ Ⓒ Ⓓ Ⓔ	79 Ⓐ Ⓑ Ⓒ Ⓓ Ⓔ
14 Ⓐ Ⓑ Ⓒ Ⓓ Ⓔ	36 Ⓐ Ⓑ Ⓒ ● Ⓔ	58 Ⓐ Ⓑ Ⓒ Ⓓ Ⓔ	80 Ⓐ Ⓑ Ⓒ Ⓓ ●
15 Ⓐ Ⓑ Ⓒ Ⓓ Ⓔ	37 Ⓐ Ⓑ Ⓒ Ⓓ Ⓔ	59 Ⓐ Ⓑ Ⓒ Ⓓ Ⓔ	81 Ⓐ Ⓑ Ⓒ Ⓓ Ⓔ
16 Ⓐ ● Ⓒ Ⓓ Ⓔ	38 Ⓐ Ⓑ Ⓒ Ⓓ Ⓔ	60 Ⓐ Ⓑ Ⓒ Ⓓ ●	82 Ⓐ Ⓑ Ⓒ Ⓓ Ⓔ
17 Ⓐ ● Ⓒ Ⓓ Ⓔ	39 Ⓐ ● Ⓒ Ⓓ Ⓔ	61 Ⓐ Ⓑ Ⓒ Ⓓ Ⓔ	83 Ⓐ Ⓑ Ⓒ Ⓓ Ⓔ
18 Ⓐ Ⓑ Ⓒ Ⓓ Ⓔ	40 Ⓐ Ⓑ Ⓒ ● Ⓔ	62 Ⓐ Ⓑ Ⓒ Ⓓ ●	84 Ⓐ Ⓑ Ⓒ Ⓓ Ⓔ
19 ● Ⓑ Ⓒ Ⓓ Ⓔ	41 Ⓐ Ⓑ Ⓒ Ⓓ Ⓔ	63 Ⓐ Ⓑ Ⓒ Ⓓ Ⓔ	85 Ⓐ Ⓑ ● Ⓓ Ⓔ
20 Ⓐ Ⓑ Ⓒ Ⓓ Ⓔ	42 ● Ⓑ Ⓒ Ⓓ Ⓔ	64 Ⓐ Ⓑ Ⓒ Ⓓ Ⓔ	86 Ⓐ Ⓑ Ⓒ Ⓓ Ⓔ
21 Ⓐ Ⓑ ● Ⓓ Ⓔ	43 Ⓐ Ⓑ Ⓒ Ⓓ Ⓔ	65 Ⓐ Ⓑ ● Ⓓ Ⓔ	87 Ⓐ Ⓑ Ⓒ Ⓓ Ⓔ
22 Ⓐ Ⓑ Ⓒ Ⓓ Ⓔ	44 Ⓐ Ⓑ Ⓒ Ⓓ Ⓔ	66 Ⓐ Ⓑ Ⓒ Ⓓ Ⓔ	88 Ⓐ Ⓑ Ⓒ Ⓓ Ⓔ

Correctly Filled Worksheet

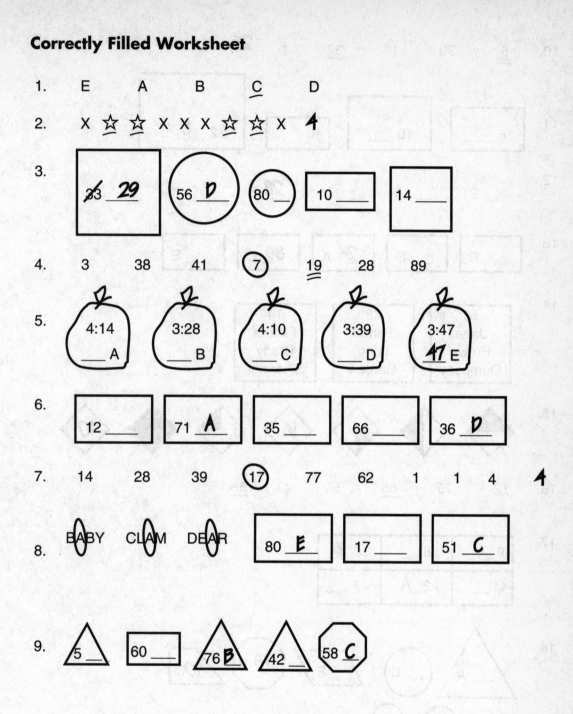

1.   E   A   B   <u>C</u>   D

2.   X   ☆   ☆   X   X   ☆   ☆   X   **4**

3.   33 29 | 56 D | 80 ___ | 10 ___ | 14 ___

4.   3   38   41   ⑦   19   28   89

5.   4:14 ___ A | 3:28 ___ B | 4:10 ___ C | 3:39 ___ D | 3:47 41 E

6.   12 ___ | 71 **A** | 35 ___ | 66 ___ | 36 **D**

7.   14   28   39   ⑰   77   62   1   1   4   **4**

8.   BABY   CLAM   DEAR | 80 **E** | 17 ___ | 51 **C**

9.   5 ___ | 60 ___ | 76 **B** | 42 ___ | 58 **C**

10. <u>5</u>   90   18   <u>32</u>   1   *25*

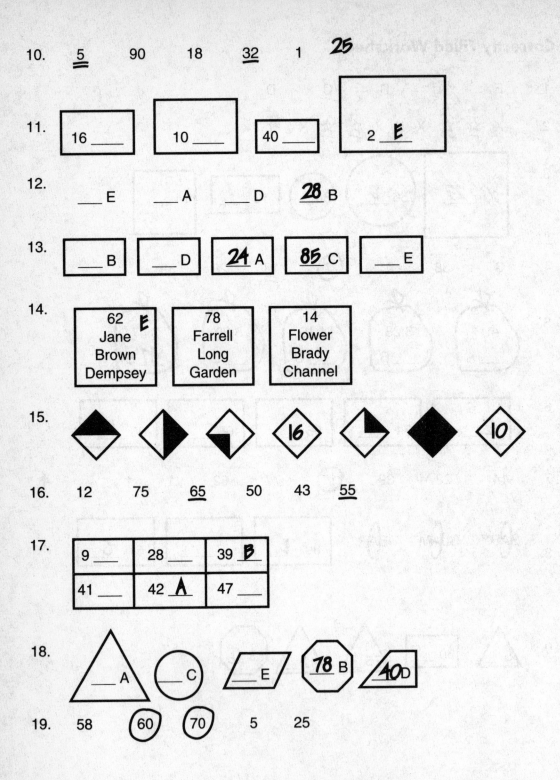

11. [16 ____]   [10 ____]   [40 ____]   [2 __*E*]

12. ___E   ___A   ___D   *28* B

13. [___B]   [___D]   [*24* A]   [*85* C]   [___E]

14. | 62 *E*
Jane
Brown
Dempsey | 78
Farrell
Long
Garden | 14
Flower
Brady
Channel |

15.

16. 12   75   <u>65</u>   50   43   <u>55</u>

17. | 9 ___ | 28 ___ | 39 *B* |
     | 41 ___ | 42 *A* | 47 ___ |

18. ___A   ___C   ___E   *78* B   *40* D

19. 58   60   70   5   25

Final Model Exam
Answer Sheet

Part A—Address Checking

1. Ⓐ Ⓓ	20. Ⓐ Ⓓ	39. Ⓐ Ⓓ	58. Ⓐ Ⓓ	77. Ⓐ Ⓓ
2. Ⓐ Ⓓ	21. Ⓐ Ⓓ	40. Ⓐ Ⓓ	59. Ⓐ Ⓓ	78. Ⓐ Ⓓ
3. Ⓐ Ⓓ	22. Ⓐ Ⓓ	41. Ⓐ Ⓓ	60. Ⓐ Ⓓ	79. Ⓐ Ⓓ
4. Ⓐ Ⓓ	23. Ⓐ Ⓓ	42. Ⓐ Ⓓ	61. Ⓐ Ⓓ	80. Ⓐ Ⓓ
5. Ⓐ Ⓓ	24. Ⓐ Ⓓ	43. Ⓐ Ⓓ	62. Ⓐ Ⓓ	81. Ⓐ Ⓓ
6. Ⓐ Ⓓ	25. Ⓐ Ⓓ	44. Ⓐ Ⓓ	63. Ⓐ Ⓓ	82. Ⓐ Ⓓ
7. Ⓐ Ⓓ	26. Ⓐ Ⓓ	45. Ⓐ Ⓓ	64. Ⓐ Ⓓ	83. Ⓐ Ⓓ
8. Ⓐ Ⓓ	27. Ⓐ Ⓓ	46. Ⓐ Ⓓ	65. Ⓐ Ⓓ	84. Ⓐ Ⓓ
9. Ⓐ Ⓓ	28. Ⓐ Ⓓ	47. Ⓐ Ⓓ	66. Ⓐ Ⓓ	85. Ⓐ Ⓓ
10. Ⓐ Ⓓ	29. Ⓐ Ⓓ	48. Ⓐ Ⓓ	67. Ⓐ Ⓓ	86. Ⓐ Ⓓ
11. Ⓐ Ⓓ	30. Ⓐ Ⓓ	49. Ⓐ Ⓓ	68. Ⓐ Ⓓ	87. Ⓐ Ⓓ
12. Ⓐ Ⓓ	31. Ⓐ Ⓓ	50. Ⓐ Ⓓ	69. Ⓐ Ⓓ	88. Ⓐ Ⓓ
13. Ⓐ Ⓓ	32. Ⓐ Ⓓ	51. Ⓐ Ⓓ	70. Ⓐ Ⓓ	89. Ⓐ Ⓓ
14. Ⓐ Ⓓ	33. Ⓐ Ⓓ	52. Ⓐ Ⓓ	71. Ⓐ Ⓓ	90. Ⓐ Ⓓ
15. Ⓐ Ⓓ	34. Ⓐ Ⓓ	53. Ⓐ Ⓓ	72. Ⓐ Ⓓ	91. Ⓐ Ⓓ
16. Ⓐ Ⓓ	35. Ⓐ Ⓓ	54. Ⓐ Ⓓ	73. Ⓐ Ⓓ	92. Ⓐ Ⓓ
17. Ⓐ Ⓓ	36. Ⓐ Ⓓ	55. Ⓐ Ⓓ	74. Ⓐ Ⓓ	93. Ⓐ Ⓓ
18. Ⓐ Ⓓ	37. Ⓐ Ⓓ	56. Ⓐ Ⓓ	75. Ⓐ Ⓓ	94. Ⓐ Ⓓ
19. Ⓐ Ⓓ	38. Ⓐ Ⓓ	57. Ⓐ Ⓓ	76. Ⓐ Ⓓ	95. Ⓐ Ⓓ

Part B—Memory for Addresses

1 Ⓐ Ⓑ Ⓒ Ⓓ Ⓔ
2 Ⓐ Ⓑ Ⓒ Ⓓ Ⓔ
3 Ⓐ Ⓑ Ⓒ Ⓓ Ⓔ
4 Ⓐ Ⓑ Ⓒ Ⓓ Ⓔ
5 Ⓐ Ⓑ Ⓒ Ⓓ Ⓔ
6 Ⓐ Ⓑ Ⓒ Ⓓ Ⓔ
7 Ⓐ Ⓑ Ⓒ Ⓓ Ⓔ
8 Ⓐ Ⓑ Ⓒ Ⓓ Ⓔ
9 Ⓐ Ⓑ Ⓒ Ⓓ Ⓔ
10 Ⓐ Ⓑ Ⓒ Ⓓ Ⓔ
11 Ⓐ Ⓑ Ⓒ Ⓓ Ⓔ
12 Ⓐ Ⓑ Ⓒ Ⓓ Ⓔ
13 Ⓐ Ⓑ Ⓒ Ⓓ Ⓔ
14 Ⓐ Ⓑ Ⓒ Ⓓ Ⓔ
15 Ⓐ Ⓑ Ⓒ Ⓓ Ⓔ
16 Ⓐ Ⓑ Ⓒ Ⓓ Ⓔ
17 Ⓐ Ⓑ Ⓒ Ⓓ Ⓔ
18 Ⓐ Ⓑ Ⓒ Ⓓ Ⓔ
19 Ⓐ Ⓑ Ⓒ Ⓓ Ⓔ
20 Ⓐ Ⓑ Ⓒ Ⓓ Ⓔ
21 Ⓐ Ⓑ Ⓒ Ⓓ Ⓔ
22 Ⓐ Ⓑ Ⓒ Ⓓ Ⓔ

23 Ⓐ Ⓑ Ⓒ Ⓓ Ⓔ
24 Ⓐ Ⓑ Ⓒ Ⓓ Ⓔ
25 Ⓐ Ⓑ Ⓒ Ⓓ Ⓔ
26 Ⓐ Ⓑ Ⓒ Ⓓ Ⓔ
27 Ⓐ Ⓑ Ⓒ Ⓓ Ⓔ
28 Ⓐ Ⓑ Ⓒ Ⓓ Ⓔ
29 Ⓐ Ⓑ Ⓒ Ⓓ Ⓔ
30 Ⓐ Ⓑ Ⓒ Ⓓ Ⓔ
31 Ⓐ Ⓑ Ⓒ Ⓓ Ⓔ
32 Ⓐ Ⓑ Ⓒ Ⓓ Ⓔ
33 Ⓐ Ⓑ Ⓒ Ⓓ Ⓔ
34 Ⓐ Ⓑ Ⓒ Ⓓ Ⓔ
35 Ⓐ Ⓑ Ⓒ Ⓓ Ⓔ
36 Ⓐ Ⓑ Ⓒ Ⓓ Ⓔ
37 Ⓐ Ⓑ Ⓒ Ⓓ Ⓔ
38 Ⓐ Ⓑ Ⓒ Ⓓ Ⓔ
39 Ⓐ Ⓑ Ⓒ Ⓓ Ⓔ
40 Ⓐ Ⓑ Ⓒ Ⓓ Ⓔ
41 Ⓐ Ⓑ Ⓒ Ⓓ Ⓔ
42 Ⓐ Ⓑ Ⓒ Ⓓ Ⓔ
43 Ⓐ Ⓑ Ⓒ Ⓓ Ⓔ
44 Ⓐ Ⓑ Ⓒ Ⓓ Ⓔ

45 Ⓐ Ⓑ Ⓒ Ⓓ Ⓔ
46 Ⓐ Ⓑ Ⓒ Ⓓ Ⓔ
47 Ⓐ Ⓑ Ⓒ Ⓓ Ⓔ
48 Ⓐ Ⓑ Ⓒ Ⓓ Ⓔ
49 Ⓐ Ⓑ Ⓒ Ⓓ Ⓔ
50 Ⓐ Ⓑ Ⓒ Ⓓ Ⓔ
51 Ⓐ Ⓑ Ⓒ Ⓓ Ⓔ
52 Ⓐ Ⓑ Ⓒ Ⓓ Ⓔ
53 Ⓐ Ⓑ Ⓒ Ⓓ Ⓔ
54 Ⓐ Ⓑ Ⓒ Ⓓ Ⓔ
55 Ⓐ Ⓑ Ⓒ Ⓓ Ⓔ
56 Ⓐ Ⓑ Ⓒ Ⓓ Ⓔ
57 Ⓐ Ⓑ Ⓒ Ⓓ Ⓔ
58 Ⓐ Ⓑ Ⓒ Ⓓ Ⓔ
59 Ⓐ Ⓑ Ⓒ Ⓓ Ⓔ
60 Ⓐ Ⓑ Ⓒ Ⓓ Ⓔ
61 Ⓐ Ⓑ Ⓒ Ⓓ Ⓔ
62 Ⓐ Ⓑ Ⓒ Ⓓ Ⓔ
63 Ⓐ Ⓑ Ⓒ Ⓓ Ⓔ
64 Ⓐ Ⓑ Ⓒ Ⓓ Ⓔ
65 Ⓐ Ⓑ Ⓒ Ⓓ Ⓔ
66 Ⓐ Ⓑ Ⓒ Ⓓ Ⓔ

67 Ⓐ Ⓑ Ⓒ Ⓓ Ⓔ
68 Ⓐ Ⓑ Ⓒ Ⓓ Ⓔ
69 Ⓐ Ⓑ Ⓒ Ⓓ Ⓔ
70 Ⓐ Ⓑ Ⓒ Ⓓ Ⓔ
71 Ⓐ Ⓑ Ⓒ Ⓓ Ⓔ
72 Ⓐ Ⓑ Ⓒ Ⓓ Ⓔ
73 Ⓐ Ⓑ Ⓒ Ⓓ Ⓔ
74 Ⓐ Ⓑ Ⓒ Ⓓ Ⓔ
75 Ⓐ Ⓑ Ⓒ Ⓓ Ⓔ
76 Ⓐ Ⓑ Ⓒ Ⓓ Ⓔ
77 Ⓐ Ⓑ Ⓒ Ⓓ Ⓔ
78 Ⓐ Ⓑ Ⓒ Ⓓ Ⓔ
79 Ⓐ Ⓑ Ⓒ Ⓓ Ⓔ
80 Ⓐ Ⓑ Ⓒ Ⓓ Ⓔ
81 Ⓐ Ⓑ Ⓒ Ⓓ Ⓔ
82 Ⓐ Ⓑ Ⓒ Ⓓ Ⓔ
83 Ⓐ Ⓑ Ⓒ Ⓓ Ⓔ
84 Ⓐ Ⓑ Ⓒ Ⓓ Ⓔ
85 Ⓐ Ⓑ Ⓒ Ⓓ Ⓔ
86 Ⓐ Ⓑ Ⓒ Ⓓ Ⓔ
87 Ⓐ Ⓑ Ⓒ Ⓓ Ⓔ
88 Ⓐ Ⓑ Ⓒ Ⓓ Ⓔ

Part C—Number Series

1. Ⓐ Ⓑ Ⓒ Ⓓ Ⓔ
2. Ⓐ Ⓑ Ⓒ Ⓓ Ⓔ
3. Ⓐ Ⓑ Ⓒ Ⓓ Ⓔ
4. Ⓐ Ⓑ Ⓒ Ⓓ Ⓔ
5. Ⓐ Ⓑ Ⓒ Ⓓ Ⓔ
6. Ⓐ Ⓑ Ⓒ Ⓓ Ⓔ

7. Ⓐ Ⓑ Ⓒ Ⓓ Ⓔ
8. Ⓐ Ⓑ Ⓒ Ⓓ Ⓔ
9. Ⓐ Ⓑ Ⓒ Ⓓ Ⓔ
10. Ⓐ Ⓑ Ⓒ Ⓓ Ⓔ
11. Ⓐ Ⓑ Ⓒ Ⓓ Ⓔ
12. Ⓐ Ⓑ Ⓒ Ⓓ Ⓔ

13. Ⓐ Ⓑ Ⓒ Ⓓ Ⓔ
14. Ⓐ Ⓑ Ⓒ Ⓓ Ⓔ
15. Ⓐ Ⓑ Ⓒ Ⓓ Ⓔ
16. Ⓐ Ⓑ Ⓒ Ⓓ Ⓔ
17. Ⓐ Ⓑ Ⓒ Ⓓ Ⓔ
18. Ⓐ Ⓑ Ⓒ Ⓓ Ⓔ

19. Ⓐ Ⓑ Ⓒ Ⓓ Ⓔ
20. Ⓐ Ⓑ Ⓒ Ⓓ Ⓔ
21. Ⓐ Ⓑ Ⓒ Ⓓ Ⓔ
22. Ⓐ Ⓑ Ⓒ Ⓓ Ⓔ
23. Ⓐ Ⓑ Ⓒ Ⓓ Ⓔ
24. Ⓐ Ⓑ Ⓒ Ⓓ Ⓔ

Part D—Following Oral Instructions

1 Ⓐ Ⓑ Ⓒ Ⓓ Ⓔ	23 Ⓐ Ⓑ Ⓒ Ⓓ Ⓔ	45 Ⓐ Ⓑ Ⓒ Ⓓ Ⓔ	67 Ⓐ Ⓑ Ⓒ Ⓓ Ⓔ
2 Ⓐ Ⓑ Ⓒ Ⓓ Ⓔ	24 Ⓐ Ⓑ Ⓒ Ⓓ Ⓔ	46 Ⓐ Ⓑ Ⓒ Ⓓ Ⓔ	68 Ⓐ Ⓑ Ⓒ Ⓓ Ⓔ
3 Ⓐ Ⓑ Ⓒ Ⓓ Ⓔ	25 Ⓐ Ⓑ Ⓒ Ⓓ Ⓔ	47 Ⓐ Ⓑ Ⓒ Ⓓ Ⓔ	69 Ⓐ Ⓑ Ⓒ Ⓓ Ⓔ
4 Ⓐ Ⓑ Ⓒ Ⓓ Ⓔ	26 Ⓐ Ⓑ Ⓒ Ⓓ Ⓔ	48 Ⓐ Ⓑ Ⓒ Ⓓ Ⓔ	70 Ⓐ Ⓑ Ⓒ Ⓓ Ⓔ
5 Ⓐ Ⓑ Ⓒ Ⓓ Ⓔ	27 Ⓐ Ⓑ Ⓒ Ⓓ Ⓔ	49 Ⓐ Ⓑ Ⓒ Ⓓ Ⓔ	71 Ⓐ Ⓑ Ⓒ Ⓓ Ⓔ
6 Ⓐ Ⓑ Ⓒ Ⓓ Ⓔ	28 Ⓐ Ⓑ Ⓒ Ⓓ Ⓔ	50 Ⓐ Ⓑ Ⓒ Ⓓ Ⓔ	72 Ⓐ Ⓑ Ⓒ Ⓓ Ⓔ
7 Ⓐ Ⓑ Ⓒ Ⓓ Ⓔ	29 Ⓐ Ⓑ Ⓒ Ⓓ Ⓔ	51 Ⓐ Ⓑ Ⓒ Ⓓ Ⓔ	73 Ⓐ Ⓑ Ⓒ Ⓓ Ⓔ
8 Ⓐ Ⓑ Ⓒ Ⓓ Ⓔ	30 Ⓐ Ⓑ Ⓒ Ⓓ Ⓔ	52 Ⓐ Ⓑ Ⓒ Ⓓ Ⓔ	74 Ⓐ Ⓑ Ⓒ Ⓓ Ⓔ
9 Ⓐ Ⓑ Ⓒ Ⓓ Ⓔ	31 Ⓐ Ⓑ Ⓒ Ⓓ Ⓔ	53 Ⓐ Ⓑ Ⓒ Ⓓ Ⓔ	75 Ⓐ Ⓑ Ⓒ Ⓓ Ⓔ
10 Ⓐ Ⓑ Ⓒ Ⓓ Ⓔ	32 Ⓐ Ⓑ Ⓒ Ⓓ Ⓔ	54 Ⓐ Ⓑ Ⓒ Ⓓ Ⓔ	76 Ⓐ Ⓑ Ⓒ Ⓓ Ⓔ
11 Ⓐ Ⓑ Ⓒ Ⓓ Ⓔ	33 Ⓐ Ⓑ Ⓒ Ⓓ Ⓔ	55 Ⓐ Ⓑ Ⓒ Ⓓ Ⓔ	77 Ⓐ Ⓑ Ⓒ Ⓓ Ⓔ
12 Ⓐ Ⓑ Ⓒ Ⓓ Ⓔ	34 Ⓐ Ⓑ Ⓒ Ⓓ Ⓔ	56 Ⓐ Ⓑ Ⓒ Ⓓ Ⓔ	78 Ⓐ Ⓑ Ⓒ Ⓓ Ⓔ
13 Ⓐ Ⓑ Ⓒ Ⓓ Ⓔ	35 Ⓐ Ⓑ Ⓒ Ⓓ Ⓔ	57 Ⓐ Ⓑ Ⓒ Ⓓ Ⓔ	79 Ⓐ Ⓑ Ⓒ Ⓓ Ⓔ
14 Ⓐ Ⓑ Ⓒ Ⓓ Ⓔ	36 Ⓐ Ⓑ Ⓒ Ⓓ Ⓔ	58 Ⓐ Ⓑ Ⓒ Ⓓ Ⓔ	80 Ⓐ Ⓑ Ⓒ Ⓓ Ⓔ
15 Ⓐ Ⓑ Ⓒ Ⓓ Ⓔ	37 Ⓐ Ⓑ Ⓒ Ⓓ Ⓔ	59 Ⓐ Ⓑ Ⓒ Ⓓ Ⓔ	81 Ⓐ Ⓑ Ⓒ Ⓓ Ⓔ
16 Ⓐ Ⓑ Ⓒ Ⓓ Ⓔ	38 Ⓐ Ⓑ Ⓒ Ⓓ Ⓔ	60 Ⓐ Ⓑ Ⓒ Ⓓ Ⓔ	82 Ⓐ Ⓑ Ⓒ Ⓓ Ⓔ
17 Ⓐ Ⓑ Ⓒ Ⓓ Ⓔ	39 Ⓐ Ⓑ Ⓒ Ⓓ Ⓔ	61 Ⓐ Ⓑ Ⓒ Ⓓ Ⓔ	83 Ⓐ Ⓑ Ⓒ Ⓓ Ⓔ
18 Ⓐ Ⓑ Ⓒ Ⓓ Ⓔ	40 Ⓐ Ⓑ Ⓒ Ⓓ Ⓔ	62 Ⓐ Ⓑ Ⓒ Ⓓ Ⓔ	84 Ⓐ Ⓑ Ⓒ Ⓓ Ⓔ
19 Ⓐ Ⓑ Ⓒ Ⓓ Ⓔ	41 Ⓐ Ⓑ Ⓒ Ⓓ Ⓔ	63 Ⓐ Ⓑ Ⓒ Ⓓ Ⓔ	85 Ⓐ Ⓑ Ⓒ Ⓓ Ⓔ
20 Ⓐ Ⓑ Ⓒ Ⓓ Ⓔ	42 Ⓐ Ⓑ Ⓒ Ⓓ Ⓔ	64 Ⓐ Ⓑ Ⓒ Ⓓ Ⓔ	86 Ⓐ Ⓑ Ⓒ Ⓓ Ⓔ
21 Ⓐ Ⓑ Ⓒ Ⓓ Ⓔ	43 Ⓐ Ⓑ Ⓒ Ⓓ Ⓔ	65 Ⓐ Ⓑ Ⓒ Ⓓ Ⓔ	87 Ⓐ Ⓑ Ⓒ Ⓓ Ⓔ
22 Ⓐ Ⓑ Ⓒ Ⓓ Ⓔ	44 Ⓐ Ⓑ Ⓒ Ⓓ Ⓔ	66 Ⓐ Ⓑ Ⓒ Ⓓ Ⓔ	88 Ⓐ Ⓑ Ⓒ Ⓓ Ⓔ

TEAR HERE

SCORE SHEET

ADDRESS CHECKING: Your score on the Address Checking part is based upon the number of questions you answered correctly minus the number of questions you answered incorrectly. To determine your score, subtract the number of wrong answers from the number of correct answers.

Number Right   –   Number Wrong   =   Raw Score

_____   –   _____   =   _____

MEMORY FOR ADDRESSES: Your score on the Memory for Addresses part is based upon the number of questions you answered correctly minus one-fourth of the questions you answered incorrectly (number wrong divided by 4). Calculate this now:

Number Wrong ÷ 4 = _____.

Number Right   –   Number Wrong ÷ 4   =   Raw Score

_____   –   _____   =   _____

NUMBER SERIES: Your score on the Number Series part is based only on the number of questions you answered correctly. Wrong answers do not count against you.

Number Right   =   Raw Score

_____   =   _____

FOLLOWING ORAL INSTRUCTIONS: Your score on the Following Oral Instructions part is based only upon the number of questions you marked correctly on the answer sheet. The worksheet is not scored, and wrong answers on the answer sheet do not count against you.

Number Right   =   Raw Score

_____   =   _____

TOTAL SCORE: To find your total raw score, add together the raw scores for each section of the exam.

Address Checking Score   _____

     +

Memory for Addresses Score   _____

     +

Number Series Score   _____

     +

Following Oral Instructions Score   _____

     =

                   _____

Total Raw Score   _____

Self Evaluation Chart

Calculate your raw score for each test as shown above. Then check to see where your score falls on the scale from Poor to Excellent. Lightly shade in the boxes in which your scores fall.

Part	Excellent	Good	Average	Fair	Poor
Address Checking	80–95	65–79	50–64	35–49	1–34
Memory for Addresses	75–88	60–74	45–59	30–44	1–29
Number Series	21–24	18–20	14–17	11–13	1–10
Following Oral Instructions	27–31	23–26	19–22	14–18	1–13

Final Model Exam

Part A—Address Checking

Sample Questions

You will be allowed three minutes to read the directions and answer the five sample questions that follow. On the actual test, however, you will have only six minutes to answer 95 questions, so see how quickly you can compare addresses and still get the correct answer.

DIRECTIONS: Each question consists of two addresses. If the two addresses are alike in EVERY *way, mark A on your answer sheet. If the two addresses are* different in ANY *way, mark D on your answer sheet.*

1...7418 Lehigh Hwy	7418 Lehigh Hwy
2...Santa Barbara CA 93106	Santa Barbra CA 93106
3...6281 SW 134th St	6821 SW 134th St
4...9163 Barbados Blvd	9163 Barbados Blvd
5...6420 Alexandria Ave E	6420 Alexandria Ave S

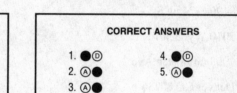

Address Checking

Time: 6 Minutes. 95 Questions.

*DIRECTIONS: For each question, compare the address in the left column with the address in the right column. If the two addresses are ALIKE IN **EVERY** WAY, blacken space A on your answer sheet. If the two addresses are DIFFERENT IN ANY WAY, blacken space D on your answer sheet. Correct answers for this test are on page 287.*

1 ...	1038 Nutgrove St	1038 Nutgrove St
2 ...	4830 Schroeder Ave	4380 Schroeder Ave
3 ...	2343 Martine Ave	2343 Martini Ave
4 ...	Winkelman AZ 85292	Winkelman AZ 85292
5 ...	298 Chatterton Pky	298 Chatterton Pky
6 ...	3798 Hillandale Ave	3798 Hillanddale Ave
7 ...	7683 Fountain Pl	7863 Fountain Pl
8 ...	1862 W 164th St	1864 W 164th St
9 ...	Scarborough NY 10510	Scarbourough NY 10510
10 ...	1734 N Highland Ave	1734 W Highland Ave
11 ...	1385 Queens Blvd	1385 Queens Blvd
12 ...	6742 Mendota Ave	6742 Mendota Ave
13 ...	8496 E 245th St	8496 E 254th St
14 ...	2010 Wyndcliff Rd	2010 Wyndecliff Rd
15 ...	4098 Gramatan Ave	4098 Gramatan Ave
16 ...	Denver CO 80236	Denver CO 80236
17 ...	3778 N Broadway	3778 N Broadway
18 ...	532 Broadhollow Rd	532 Broadhollow Rd
19 ...	1386 Carriage House Ln	1386 Carriage House Ln
20 ...	3284 S 10th St	2384 S 10th St
21 ...	2666 Dunwoodie Rd	266 Dunwoodie Rd
22 ...	Pontiac MI 48054	Pontiac MI 48054
23 ...	1080 Nine Acres Ln	1080 Nine Acres Ln
24 ...	2699 Quaker Church Rd	2669 Quaker Church Rd
25 ...	7232 S 45th Ave	7232 S 45th Ave
26 ...	1588 Grand Boulevard	1588 Grand Boulevard
27 ...	2093 S Waverly Rd	2093 S Waverley Rd
28 ...	Las Vegas NV 89112	Las Vegas NM 89112
29 ...	116 Cottage Pl Gdns	116 Cottage Pl Gdns

30 ...	1203 E Lakeview Ave	1203 E Lakeside Ave
31 ...	3446 E Westchester Ave	3446 E Westchester Ave
32 ...	7482 Horseshoe Hill Rd	7482 Horseshoe Hill Rd
33 ...	Waimanalo HI 96795	Waimanale HI 96795
34	9138 McGuire Ave	9138 MacGuire Ave
35 ...	7438 Meadway	7348 Meadway
36 ...	2510 Maryland Ave NW	2510 Maryland Ave NW
37 ...	1085 S 83rd Rd	1085 S 83rd Rd
38 ...	5232 Maplewood Wy	523 Maplewood Wy
39 ...	Kansas City MO 64108	Kansas City MO 61408
40 ...	1063 Valentine Ln	1063 Valentine Ln
41 ...	1066 Furnace Dock Rd	1606 Furnace Dock Rd
42 ...	2121 Rosedale Rd	2121 Rosedale Rd
43 ...	1396 Orawapum St	1396 Orawampum St
44 ...	3004 Palisade Ave	3004 Palisades Ave
45 ...	1776 Independence St	1776 Independence St
46 ...	Canton OH 44707	Canton OH 44707
47 ...	1515 Geoga Cir	1515 Geogia Cir
48 ...	1583 Central Ave	1583 Central Ave
49 ...	4096 Valley Terr	4096 Valley Terr
50 ...	2075 Boston Post Rd	2075 Boston Post Rd
51 ...	1016 Frost Ln	1016 Frost La
52 ...	2186 Ashford Ave	2186 Ashford Ave
53 ...	Battle Mountain NV 89820	Battle Mountain NV 89820
54 ...	6634 Weber Pl	6634 Webber Pl
55 ...	6832 Halycon Terr	6832 Halcyon Terr
56 ...	198 Gedney Esplnde	198 Gedney Esplnde
57 ...	8954 Horsechestnut Rd	8954 Horsechestnut Rd
58 ...	1926 S 283rd Wy	1926 S 283rd Wy
59 ...	Hartsdale NY 10530	Hartsdale NY 15030
60 ...	1569 Ritchy Pl	1569 Ritchy Pl
61 ...	423 S Columbia Ave	423 S Colombia Ave
62 ...	2466 Linette Ct	2466 Linnette Ct
63 ...	2970 Rockledge Ave	2970 Rockridge Ave
64 ...	5764 Guion Blvd	5764 Guion Blvd

65 ...	6976 SW 5th Ave	6976 SE 5th Ave
66 ...	Milwaukie OR 97222	Milwaukee OR 97222
67 ...	2243 Hudson View Ests	2234 Hudson View Ests
68 ...	7743 S 3rd Ave	7743 S 3rd Ave
69 ...	2869 Romaine Ave	2869 Romaine Ave
70 ...	2943 Windermere Dr	2943 Windemere Dr
71 ...	5117 Balmoral Crsnt	5117 Balmoral Crsnt
72 ...	3797 Wappanocca Ave	3797 Wappannocca Ave
73 ...	Arkabutla MS 38602	Arkabutla MS 38602
74 ...	2275 Greenway Terr	2275 Greenaway Terr
75 ...	7153 Taymil Rd	7153 Taymil Rd
76 ...	3864 W 248th St	3864 W 284th St
77 ...	2032 Central Park S	2023 Central Park S
78 ...	1803 Pinewood Rd	1803 Pineywood Rd
79 ...	New York NY 10023	New York NY 10023
80 ...	1555 E 19th St	1555 E 19th St
81 ...	3402 Comer Cir	3402 Comer Ct
82 ...	.9416 Lakeshore Dr	9416 Lakeshore Dr
83 ...	.1576 Kimball Ave	1576 Kimbell Ave
84 ...	2015 W 51st Ln	2015 W 51st Ln
85 ...	Silver Springs NV 89429	Silver Springs NV 89429
86 ...	2354 N Washington St	2354 N Washington St
87 ...	8528 Convent Pl	8258 Convent Pl
88 ...	1911 Downer Ave	1911 Downer Ave
89 ...	6108 Woodstock Rd	6108 Woodstock St
90 ...	Akron OH 44308	Akron OK 44308
91 ...	4548 College Pt Ave	4548 College Pk Ave
92 ...	8194 Great Oak Ln	8194 Great Oak Ln
93 ...	280 SW Collins Ave	280 SW Collins Ave
94 ...	8276 Abbott Mews	8726 Abbott Mews
95 ...	4717 Deerfield Blvd	4717 Deerfield Blvd

END OF ADDRESS CHECKING

Part B—Memory for Addresses

Sample Questions

The sample questions for this part are based upon the addresses in the five boxes below. Your task is to mark on your answer sheet the letter of the box in which each address belongs. You will have five minutes now to study the locations of the addresses. Then, cover the boxes and try to mark the location of the sample questions. You may look back at the boxes if you cannot yet mark the address locations from memory.

The exam itself provides three practice sessions before the question set that really counts. Practice I and Practice III supply you with the boxes and permit you to refer to them if necessary. Practice II and the Memory for Addresses test itself do not permit you to look at the boxes. The test itself is based on memory.

A	B	C	D	E
3700–4099 Rink Chapel	5200–5399 Rink Elephant	4800–5199 Rink Bluff	4100–4799 Rink Windmill	5400–5599 Rink Quill
4800–5199 Bank River	5400–5599 Bank Package	3700–4099 Bank Juggler	5200–5399 Bank Thistle	4100–4799 Bank Monsoon
5400–5599 Love	3700–4099 Love	4100–4799 Love	4800–5199 Love	5200–5399 Love

1. 5400–5599 Bank

2. 4800–5199 Love

3. 5400–5599 Rink

4. Windmill

5. Elephant

6. 5400–5599 Love

7. 5200–5399 Rink

8. Bluff

9. River

10. 4100–4799 Rink

11. 4800–5199 Bank

12. 3700–4099 Love

13. Juggler

14. Quill

SAMPLE ANSWER SHEET

1. Ⓐ Ⓑ Ⓒ Ⓓ Ⓔ
2. Ⓐ Ⓑ Ⓒ Ⓓ Ⓔ
3. Ⓐ Ⓑ Ⓒ Ⓓ Ⓔ
4. Ⓐ Ⓑ Ⓒ Ⓓ Ⓔ
5. Ⓐ Ⓑ Ⓒ Ⓓ Ⓔ
6. Ⓐ Ⓑ Ⓒ Ⓓ Ⓔ
7. Ⓐ Ⓑ Ⓒ Ⓓ Ⓔ

8. Ⓐ Ⓑ Ⓒ Ⓓ Ⓔ
9. Ⓐ Ⓑ Ⓒ Ⓓ Ⓔ
10. Ⓐ Ⓑ Ⓒ Ⓓ Ⓔ
11. Ⓐ Ⓑ Ⓒ Ⓓ Ⓔ
12. Ⓐ Ⓑ Ⓒ Ⓓ Ⓔ
13. Ⓐ Ⓑ Ⓒ Ⓓ Ⓔ
14. Ⓐ Ⓑ Ⓒ Ⓓ Ⓔ

CORRECT ANSWERS

1. Ⓐ ● Ⓒ Ⓓ Ⓔ
2. Ⓐ Ⓑ Ⓒ ● Ⓔ
3. Ⓐ Ⓑ Ⓒ Ⓓ ●
4. Ⓐ Ⓑ Ⓒ ● Ⓔ
5. Ⓐ ● Ⓒ Ⓓ Ⓔ
6. ● Ⓑ Ⓒ Ⓓ Ⓔ
7. Ⓐ ● Ⓒ Ⓓ Ⓔ

8. Ⓐ Ⓑ ● Ⓓ Ⓔ
9. ● Ⓑ Ⓒ Ⓓ Ⓔ
10. Ⓐ Ⓑ Ⓒ ● Ⓔ
11. ● Ⓑ Ⓒ Ⓓ Ⓔ
12. Ⓐ ● Ⓒ Ⓓ Ⓔ
13. Ⓐ Ⓑ ● Ⓓ Ⓔ
14. Ⓐ Ⓑ Ⓒ Ⓓ ●

Practice for Memory for Addresses

DIRECTIONS: *The five boxes below are labelled A, B, C, D, and E. In each box are three sets of number spans with names and two names that are not associated with numbers. In the next THREE MINUTES, you must try to memorize the box location of each name and number span. The position of a name or number span within its box is not important. You need only remember the letter of the box in which the item is to be found. You will use these names and numbers to answer three sets of practice questions that are NOT scored and one actual test that is scored. Correct answers are on pages 288 and 289.*

A	B	C	D	E
3700–4099 Rink	5200–5399 Rink	4800–5199 Rink	4100–4799 Rink	5400–5599 Rink
Chapel	Elephant	Bluff	Windmill	Quill
4800–5199 Bank	5400–5599 Bank	3700–4099 Bank	5200–5399 Bank	4100–4799 Bank
River	Package	Juggler	Thistle	Monsoon
5400–5599 Love	3700–4099 Love	4100–4799 Love	4800–5199 Love	5200–5399 Love

Practice I

DIRECTIONS: *Use the next THREE MINUTES to mark on the Practice I answer sheet the letter of the box in which each item that follows is to be found. Try to mark each item without looking back at the boxes. If, however, you get stuck, you may refer to the boxes during this practice exercise. If you find that you must look at the boxes, try to memorize as you do so. This test is for practice only. It will not be scored.*

1. 4800–5199 Rink
2. 5200–5399 Love
3. 5400–5599 Bank
4. Bluff
5. Thistle
6. 4100–4799 Love
7. 5200–5399 Bank
8. 3700–4099 Rink
9. Windmill
10. Quill
11. 5400–5599 Love
12. 3700–4099 Bank
13. 5400–5599 Rink
14. River
15. Package
16. 4100–4799 Bank
17. 4100–4799 Rink
18. 4800–5199 Love
19. Chapel

20. Monsoon
21. Thistle
22. 4100–4799 Bank
23. 3700–4099 Rink
24. 5400–5599 Love
25. 3700–4099 Bank
26. 4800–5199 Rink
27. Bluff
28. Elephant
29. 5200–5399 Love
30. 4800–5199 Love
31. 5200–5399 Rink
32. 4800–5199 Bank
33. 5400–5599 Bank
34. Chapel
35. Quill
36. 5400–5599 Rink
37. 4100–4799 Love
38. 5200–5399 Bank

39. 4100–4799 Rink
40. River
41. Package
42. 3700–4099 Love
43. Windmill
44. 3700–4099 Bank
45. 3700–4099 Rink
46. 5200–5399 Love
47. Bluff
48. Thistle
49. 4800–5199 Bank
50. 4100–4799 Rink
51. 4800–5199 Love
52. Juggler
53. Monsoon
54. 4100–4799 Love
55. 5400–5599 Bank
56. 5200–5399 Bank
57. Quill

58. Elephant

59. 5200–5399 Rink

60. 3700–4099 Rink

61. 5400–5599 Love

62. Windmill

63. Thistle

64. 3700–4099 Love

65. 4800–5199 Rink

66. 3700–4099 Bank

67. Chapel

68. Package

69. 4100–4799 Bank

70. 5400–5599 Rink

71. 5200–5399 Love

72. 5200–5399 Bank

73. Bluff

74. River

75. 3700–4099 Bank

76. 3700–4099 Love

77. 3700–4099 Rink

78. 4800–5199 Love

79. 4800–5199 Rink

80. 4800–5199 Bank

81. Package

82. Elephant

83. 4100–4799 Rink

84. 5200–5399 Rink

85. 5200–5399 Love

86. 5400–5599 Bank

87. Quill

88. Bluff

Practice I Answer Sheet

1 Ⓐ Ⓑ Ⓒ Ⓓ Ⓔ
2 Ⓐ Ⓑ Ⓒ Ⓓ Ⓔ
3 Ⓐ Ⓑ Ⓒ Ⓓ Ⓔ
4 Ⓐ Ⓑ Ⓒ Ⓓ Ⓔ
5 Ⓐ Ⓑ Ⓒ Ⓓ Ⓔ
6 Ⓐ Ⓑ Ⓒ Ⓓ Ⓔ
7 Ⓐ Ⓑ Ⓒ Ⓓ Ⓔ
8 Ⓐ Ⓑ Ⓒ Ⓓ Ⓔ
9 Ⓐ Ⓑ Ⓒ Ⓓ Ⓔ
10 Ⓐ Ⓑ Ⓒ Ⓓ Ⓔ
11 Ⓐ Ⓑ Ⓒ Ⓓ Ⓔ
12 Ⓐ Ⓑ Ⓒ Ⓓ Ⓔ
13 Ⓐ Ⓑ Ⓒ Ⓓ Ⓔ
14 Ⓐ Ⓑ Ⓒ Ⓓ Ⓔ
15 Ⓐ Ⓑ Ⓒ Ⓓ Ⓔ
16 Ⓐ Ⓑ Ⓒ Ⓓ Ⓔ
17 Ⓐ Ⓑ Ⓒ Ⓓ Ⓔ
18 Ⓐ Ⓑ Ⓒ Ⓓ Ⓔ
19 Ⓐ Ⓑ Ⓒ Ⓓ Ⓔ
20 Ⓐ Ⓑ Ⓒ Ⓓ Ⓔ
21 Ⓐ Ⓑ Ⓒ Ⓓ Ⓔ
22 Ⓐ Ⓑ Ⓒ Ⓓ Ⓔ

23 Ⓐ Ⓑ Ⓒ Ⓓ Ⓔ
24 Ⓐ Ⓑ Ⓒ Ⓓ Ⓔ
25 Ⓐ Ⓑ Ⓒ Ⓓ Ⓔ
26 Ⓐ Ⓑ Ⓒ Ⓓ Ⓔ
27 Ⓐ Ⓑ Ⓒ Ⓓ Ⓔ
28 Ⓐ Ⓑ Ⓒ Ⓓ Ⓔ
29 Ⓐ Ⓑ Ⓒ Ⓓ Ⓔ
30 Ⓐ Ⓑ Ⓒ Ⓓ Ⓔ
31 Ⓐ Ⓑ Ⓒ Ⓓ Ⓔ
32 Ⓐ Ⓑ Ⓒ Ⓓ Ⓔ
33 Ⓐ Ⓑ Ⓒ Ⓓ Ⓔ
34 Ⓐ Ⓑ Ⓒ Ⓓ Ⓔ
35 Ⓐ Ⓑ Ⓒ Ⓓ Ⓔ
36 Ⓐ Ⓑ Ⓒ Ⓓ Ⓔ
37 Ⓐ Ⓑ Ⓒ Ⓓ Ⓔ
38 Ⓐ Ⓑ Ⓒ Ⓓ Ⓔ
39 Ⓐ Ⓑ Ⓒ Ⓓ Ⓔ
40 Ⓐ Ⓑ Ⓒ Ⓓ Ⓔ
41 Ⓐ Ⓑ Ⓒ Ⓓ Ⓔ
42 Ⓐ Ⓑ Ⓒ Ⓓ Ⓔ
43 Ⓐ Ⓑ Ⓒ Ⓓ Ⓔ
44 Ⓐ Ⓑ Ⓒ Ⓓ Ⓔ

45 Ⓐ Ⓑ Ⓒ Ⓓ Ⓔ
46 Ⓐ Ⓑ Ⓒ Ⓓ Ⓔ
47 Ⓐ Ⓑ Ⓒ Ⓓ Ⓔ
48 Ⓐ Ⓑ Ⓒ Ⓓ Ⓔ
49 Ⓐ Ⓑ Ⓒ Ⓓ Ⓔ
50 Ⓐ Ⓑ Ⓒ Ⓓ Ⓔ
51 Ⓐ Ⓑ Ⓒ Ⓓ Ⓔ
52 Ⓐ Ⓑ Ⓒ Ⓓ Ⓔ
53 Ⓐ Ⓑ Ⓒ Ⓓ Ⓔ
54 Ⓐ Ⓑ Ⓒ Ⓓ Ⓔ
55 Ⓐ Ⓑ Ⓒ Ⓓ Ⓔ
56 Ⓐ Ⓑ Ⓒ Ⓓ Ⓔ
57 Ⓐ Ⓑ Ⓒ Ⓓ Ⓔ
58 Ⓐ Ⓑ Ⓒ Ⓓ Ⓔ
59 Ⓐ Ⓑ Ⓒ Ⓓ Ⓔ
60 Ⓐ Ⓑ Ⓒ Ⓓ Ⓔ
61 Ⓐ Ⓑ Ⓒ Ⓓ Ⓔ
62 Ⓐ Ⓑ Ⓒ Ⓓ Ⓔ
63 Ⓐ Ⓑ Ⓒ Ⓓ Ⓔ
64 Ⓐ Ⓑ Ⓒ Ⓓ Ⓔ
65 Ⓐ Ⓑ Ⓒ Ⓓ Ⓔ
66 Ⓐ Ⓑ Ⓒ Ⓓ Ⓔ

67 Ⓐ Ⓑ Ⓒ Ⓓ Ⓔ
68 Ⓐ Ⓑ Ⓒ Ⓓ Ⓔ
69 Ⓐ Ⓑ Ⓒ Ⓓ Ⓔ
70 Ⓐ Ⓑ Ⓒ Ⓓ Ⓔ
71 Ⓐ Ⓑ Ⓒ Ⓓ Ⓔ
72 Ⓐ Ⓑ Ⓒ Ⓓ Ⓔ
73 Ⓐ Ⓑ Ⓒ Ⓓ Ⓔ
74 Ⓐ Ⓑ Ⓒ Ⓓ Ⓔ
75 Ⓐ Ⓑ Ⓒ Ⓓ Ⓔ
76 Ⓐ Ⓑ Ⓒ Ⓓ Ⓔ
77 Ⓐ Ⓑ Ⓒ Ⓓ Ⓔ
78 Ⓐ Ⓑ Ⓒ Ⓓ Ⓔ
79 Ⓐ Ⓑ Ⓒ Ⓓ Ⓔ
80 Ⓐ Ⓑ Ⓒ Ⓓ Ⓔ
81 Ⓐ Ⓑ Ⓒ Ⓓ Ⓔ
82 Ⓐ Ⓑ Ⓒ Ⓓ Ⓔ
83 Ⓐ Ⓑ Ⓒ Ⓓ Ⓔ
84 Ⓐ Ⓑ Ⓒ Ⓓ Ⓔ
85 Ⓐ Ⓑ Ⓒ Ⓓ Ⓔ
86 Ⓐ Ⓑ Ⓒ Ⓓ Ⓔ
87 Ⓐ Ⓑ Ⓒ Ⓓ Ⓔ
88 Ⓐ Ⓑ Ⓒ Ⓓ Ⓔ

Practice II

DIRECTIONS: The next 88 questions constitute another practice exercise. Mark your answers on the Practice II answer sheet. Again, the time limit is THREE MINUTES. This time, however, you must NOT look at the boxes while answering the questions. You must rely on your memory in marking the box location of each item. This practice test will not be scored.

1. 5400–5599 Rink
2. 5200–5399 Bank
3. 4100–4799 Love
4. 5400–5599 Bank
5. 3700–4099 Rink
6. 5400–5599 Love
7. Thistle
8. Windmill
9. Elephant
10. 4800–5199 Rink
11. 4100–4799 Bank
12. 4800–5199 Bank
13. Quill
14. Package
15. 5200–5399 Love
16. 3700–4099 Love
17. 5200–5399 Rink
18. Chapel
19. Monsoon
20. 3700–4099 Bank
21. 4100–4799 Rink
22. 4800–5199 Love
23. River
24. Juggler
25. Bluff
26. 3700–4099 Love
27. 4100–4799 Rink
28. 3700–4099 Bank
29. Quill
30. Chapel

31. 3700–4099 Rink
32. 5400–5599 Bank
33. 4100–4799 Love
34. Monsoon
35. Thistle
36. 5200–5399 Love
37. 5200–5399 Bank
38. 4800–5199 Rink
39. Bluff
40. Elephant
41. 4800–5199 Bank
42. 4100–4799 Bank
43. 4800–5199 Love
44. Juggler
45. Windmill
46. 5400–5599 Love
47. 5200–5399 Rink
48. 5400–5599 Rink
49. River
50. Package
51. Juggler
52. Monsoon
53. 5200–5399 Love
54. 4100–4799 Rink
55. 3700–4099 Bank
56. 5200–5399 Rink
57. 4800–5199 Bank
58. 5400–5599 Love
59. Windmill
60. Thistle

61. Elephant
62. 4800–5199 Rink
63. 4100–4799 Bank
64. 3700–4099 Love
65. Chapel
66. Package
67. Quill
68. 3700–4099 Rink
69. 5200–5399 Bank
70. 4100–4799 Love
71. Bluff
72. River
73. 4800–5199 Love
74. 5400–5599 Bank
75. 5400–5599 Rink
76. Juggler
77. Quill
78. 5400–5599 Rink
79. 5200–5399 Love
80. 3700–4099 Bank
81. 3700–4099 Rink
82. Windmill
83. Elephant
84. 4800–5199 Rink
85. 4100–4799 Love
86. Juggler
87. 5400–5599 Bank
88. 4800–5199 Love

Practice II Answer Sheet

1 Ⓐ Ⓑ Ⓒ Ⓓ Ⓔ	23 Ⓐ Ⓑ Ⓒ Ⓓ Ⓔ	45 Ⓐ Ⓑ Ⓒ Ⓓ Ⓔ	67 Ⓐ Ⓑ Ⓒ Ⓓ Ⓔ
2 Ⓐ Ⓑ Ⓒ Ⓓ Ⓔ	24 Ⓐ Ⓑ Ⓒ Ⓓ Ⓔ	46 Ⓐ Ⓑ Ⓒ Ⓓ Ⓔ	68 Ⓐ Ⓑ Ⓒ Ⓓ Ⓔ
3 Ⓐ Ⓑ Ⓒ Ⓓ Ⓔ	25 Ⓐ Ⓑ Ⓒ Ⓓ Ⓔ	47 Ⓐ Ⓑ Ⓒ Ⓓ Ⓔ	69 Ⓐ Ⓑ Ⓒ Ⓓ Ⓔ
4 Ⓐ Ⓑ Ⓒ Ⓓ Ⓔ	26 Ⓐ Ⓑ Ⓒ Ⓓ Ⓔ	48 Ⓐ Ⓑ Ⓒ Ⓓ Ⓔ	70 Ⓐ Ⓑ Ⓒ Ⓓ Ⓔ
5 Ⓐ Ⓑ Ⓒ Ⓓ Ⓔ	27 Ⓐ Ⓑ Ⓒ Ⓓ Ⓔ	49 Ⓐ Ⓑ Ⓒ Ⓓ Ⓔ	71 Ⓐ Ⓑ Ⓒ Ⓓ Ⓔ
6 Ⓐ Ⓑ Ⓒ Ⓓ Ⓔ	28 Ⓐ Ⓑ Ⓒ Ⓓ Ⓔ	50 Ⓐ Ⓑ Ⓒ Ⓓ Ⓔ	72 Ⓐ Ⓑ Ⓒ Ⓓ Ⓔ
7 Ⓐ Ⓑ Ⓒ Ⓓ Ⓔ	29 Ⓐ Ⓑ Ⓒ Ⓓ Ⓔ	51 Ⓐ Ⓑ Ⓒ Ⓓ Ⓔ	73 Ⓐ Ⓑ Ⓒ Ⓓ Ⓔ
8 Ⓐ Ⓑ Ⓒ Ⓓ Ⓔ	30 Ⓐ Ⓑ Ⓒ Ⓓ Ⓔ	52 Ⓐ Ⓑ Ⓒ Ⓓ Ⓔ	74 Ⓐ Ⓑ Ⓒ Ⓓ Ⓔ
9 Ⓐ Ⓑ Ⓒ Ⓓ Ⓔ	31 Ⓐ Ⓑ Ⓒ Ⓓ Ⓔ	53 Ⓐ Ⓑ Ⓒ Ⓓ Ⓔ	75 Ⓐ Ⓑ Ⓒ Ⓓ Ⓔ
10 Ⓐ Ⓑ Ⓒ Ⓓ Ⓔ	32 Ⓐ Ⓑ Ⓒ Ⓓ Ⓔ	54 Ⓐ Ⓑ Ⓒ Ⓓ Ⓔ	76 Ⓐ Ⓑ Ⓒ Ⓓ Ⓔ
11 Ⓐ Ⓑ Ⓒ Ⓓ Ⓔ	33 Ⓐ Ⓑ Ⓒ Ⓓ Ⓔ	55 Ⓐ Ⓑ Ⓒ Ⓓ Ⓔ	77 Ⓐ Ⓑ Ⓒ Ⓓ Ⓔ
12 Ⓐ Ⓑ Ⓒ Ⓓ Ⓔ	34 Ⓐ Ⓑ Ⓒ Ⓓ Ⓔ	56 Ⓐ Ⓑ Ⓒ Ⓓ Ⓔ	78 Ⓐ Ⓑ Ⓒ Ⓓ Ⓔ
13 Ⓐ Ⓑ Ⓒ Ⓓ Ⓔ	35 Ⓐ Ⓑ Ⓒ Ⓓ Ⓔ	57 Ⓐ Ⓑ Ⓒ Ⓓ Ⓔ	79 Ⓐ Ⓑ Ⓒ Ⓓ Ⓔ
14 Ⓐ Ⓑ Ⓒ Ⓓ Ⓔ	36 Ⓐ Ⓑ Ⓒ Ⓓ Ⓔ	58 Ⓐ Ⓑ Ⓒ Ⓓ Ⓔ	80 Ⓐ Ⓑ Ⓒ Ⓓ Ⓔ
15 Ⓐ Ⓑ Ⓒ Ⓓ Ⓔ	37 Ⓐ Ⓑ Ⓒ Ⓓ Ⓔ	59 Ⓐ Ⓑ Ⓒ Ⓓ Ⓔ	81 Ⓐ Ⓑ Ⓒ Ⓓ Ⓔ
16 Ⓐ Ⓑ Ⓒ Ⓓ Ⓔ	38 Ⓐ Ⓑ Ⓒ Ⓓ Ⓔ	60 Ⓐ Ⓑ Ⓒ Ⓓ Ⓔ	82 Ⓐ Ⓑ Ⓒ Ⓓ Ⓔ
17 Ⓐ Ⓑ Ⓒ Ⓓ Ⓔ	39 Ⓐ Ⓑ Ⓒ Ⓓ Ⓔ	61 Ⓐ Ⓑ Ⓒ Ⓓ Ⓔ	83 Ⓐ Ⓑ Ⓒ Ⓓ Ⓔ
18 Ⓐ Ⓑ Ⓒ Ⓓ Ⓔ	40 Ⓐ Ⓑ Ⓒ Ⓓ Ⓔ	62 Ⓐ Ⓑ Ⓒ Ⓓ Ⓔ	84 Ⓐ Ⓑ Ⓒ Ⓓ Ⓔ
19 Ⓐ Ⓑ Ⓒ Ⓓ Ⓔ	41 Ⓐ Ⓑ Ⓒ Ⓓ Ⓔ	63 Ⓐ Ⓑ Ⓒ Ⓓ Ⓔ	85 Ⓐ Ⓑ Ⓒ Ⓓ Ⓔ
20 Ⓐ Ⓑ Ⓒ Ⓓ Ⓔ	42 Ⓐ Ⓑ Ⓒ Ⓓ Ⓔ	64 Ⓐ Ⓑ Ⓒ Ⓓ Ⓔ	86 Ⓐ Ⓑ Ⓒ Ⓓ Ⓔ
21 Ⓐ Ⓑ Ⓒ Ⓓ Ⓔ	43 Ⓐ Ⓑ Ⓒ Ⓓ Ⓔ	65 Ⓐ Ⓑ Ⓒ Ⓓ Ⓔ	87 Ⓐ Ⓑ Ⓒ Ⓓ Ⓔ
22 Ⓐ Ⓑ Ⓒ Ⓓ Ⓔ	44 Ⓐ Ⓑ Ⓒ Ⓓ Ⓔ	66 Ⓐ Ⓑ Ⓒ Ⓓ Ⓔ	88 Ⓐ Ⓑ Ⓒ Ⓓ Ⓔ

Practice III

DIRECTIONS: The names and addresses are repeated for you in the boxes below. Each name and each number span is in the same box in which you found it in the original set. You will now be allowed FIVE MINUTES to study the locations again. Do your best to memorize the letter of the box in which each item is located. This is your last chance to see the boxes.

A	B	C	D	E
3700–4099 Rink	5200–5399 Rink	4800–5199 Rink	4100–4799 Rink	5400–5599 Rink
Chapel	Elephant	Bluff	Windmill	Quill
4800–5199 Bank	5400–5599 Bank	3700–4099 Bank	5200–5399 Bank	4100–4799 Bank
River	Package	Juggler	Thistle	Monsoon
5400–5599 Love	3700–4099 Love	4100–4799 Love	4800–5199 Love	5200–5399 Love

DIRECTIONS: This is your last practice test. Mark the location of each of the 88 items on the Practice III answer sheet. You will have FIVE MINUTES to answer these questions. Do NOT look back at the boxes. This practice test will not be scored.

1. 4800–5199 Rink
2. 5400–5599 Love
3. 5200–5399 Love
4. Chapel
5. Quill
6. 3700–4099 Bank
7. 4800–5199 Bank
8. 4100–4799 Rink
9. 5400–5599 Rink
10. Elephant
11. Bluff
12. 4800–5199 Love
13. 4100–4799 Love
14. 5200–5399 Rink
15. Windmill
16. Monsoon
17. 4100–4799 Bank
18. 5200–5399 Rink
19. 3700–4099 Rink
20. 5200–5399 Love
21. 5400–5599 Love

22. 5400–5599 Rink
23. Thistle
24. River
25. Package
26. Bluff
27. 3700–4099 Bank
28. 4800–5199 Bank
29. 4100–4799 Rink
30. 4100–4799 Love
31. 4800–5199 Love
32. Chapel
33. 5200–5399 Rink
34. Quill
35. 4100–4799 Bank
36. 3700–4099 Love
37. 3700–4099 Rink
38. Thistle
39. Windmill
40. 5200–5399 Love
41. 4100–4799 Rink
42. 5400–5599 Bank

43. 5200–5399 Bank
44. Juggler
45. Chapel
46. 4100–4799 Love
47. 3700–4099 Bank
48. 4800–5199 Love
49. Monsoon
50. Elephant
51. 4800–5199 Bank
52. 4800–5199 Rink
53. 5400–5599 Rink
54. 5400–5599 Love
55. River
56. Bluff
57. Package
58. 5200–5399 Bank
59. 3700–4099 Rink
60. 5200–5399 Love
61. 5400–5599 Rink
62. Thistle
63. Windmill

64. River

65. 3700–4099 Bank

66. 5400–5599 Love

67. 4100–4799 Rink

68. 5200–5399 Bank

69. Quill

70. Bluff

71. 5200–5399 Rink

72. 4100–4799 Love

73. 3700–4099 Love

74. Chapel

75. Monsoon

76. 4800–5199 Rink

77. 4800–5199 Bank

78. 4100–4799 Bank

79. Juggler

80. Package

81. 4800–5199 Love

82. 5200–5399 Love

83. 5400–5599 Bank

84. Elephant

85. 3700–4099 Rink

86. 5400–5599 Rink

87. 4100–4799 Love

88. Bluff

Practice III Answer Sheet

1 Ⓐ Ⓑ Ⓒ Ⓓ Ⓔ
2 Ⓐ Ⓑ Ⓒ Ⓓ Ⓔ
3 Ⓐ Ⓑ Ⓒ Ⓓ Ⓔ
4 Ⓐ Ⓑ Ⓒ Ⓓ Ⓔ
5 Ⓐ Ⓑ Ⓒ Ⓓ Ⓔ
6 Ⓐ Ⓑ Ⓒ Ⓓ Ⓔ
7 Ⓐ Ⓑ Ⓒ Ⓓ Ⓔ
8 Ⓐ Ⓑ Ⓒ Ⓓ Ⓔ
9 Ⓐ Ⓑ Ⓒ Ⓓ Ⓔ
10 Ⓐ Ⓑ Ⓒ Ⓓ Ⓔ
11 Ⓐ Ⓑ Ⓒ Ⓓ Ⓔ
12 Ⓐ Ⓑ Ⓒ Ⓓ Ⓔ
13 Ⓐ Ⓑ Ⓒ Ⓓ Ⓔ
14 Ⓐ Ⓑ Ⓒ Ⓓ Ⓔ
15 Ⓐ Ⓑ Ⓒ Ⓓ Ⓔ
16 Ⓐ Ⓑ Ⓒ Ⓓ Ⓔ
17 Ⓐ Ⓑ Ⓒ Ⓓ Ⓔ
18 Ⓐ Ⓑ Ⓒ Ⓓ Ⓔ
19 Ⓐ Ⓑ Ⓒ Ⓓ Ⓔ
20 Ⓐ Ⓑ Ⓒ Ⓓ Ⓔ
21 Ⓐ Ⓑ Ⓒ Ⓓ Ⓔ
22 Ⓐ Ⓑ Ⓒ Ⓓ Ⓔ

23 Ⓐ Ⓑ Ⓒ Ⓓ Ⓔ
24 Ⓐ Ⓑ Ⓒ Ⓓ Ⓔ
25 Ⓐ Ⓑ Ⓒ Ⓓ Ⓔ
26 Ⓐ Ⓑ Ⓒ Ⓓ Ⓔ
27 Ⓐ Ⓑ Ⓒ Ⓓ Ⓔ
28 Ⓐ Ⓑ Ⓒ Ⓓ Ⓔ
29 Ⓐ Ⓑ Ⓒ Ⓓ Ⓔ
30 Ⓐ Ⓑ Ⓒ Ⓓ Ⓔ
31 Ⓐ Ⓑ Ⓒ Ⓓ Ⓔ
32 Ⓐ Ⓑ Ⓒ Ⓓ Ⓔ
33 Ⓐ Ⓑ Ⓒ Ⓓ Ⓔ
34 Ⓐ Ⓑ Ⓒ Ⓓ Ⓔ
35 Ⓐ Ⓑ Ⓒ Ⓓ Ⓔ
36 Ⓐ Ⓑ Ⓒ Ⓓ Ⓔ
37 Ⓐ Ⓑ Ⓒ Ⓓ Ⓔ
38 Ⓐ Ⓑ Ⓒ Ⓓ Ⓔ
39 Ⓐ Ⓑ Ⓒ Ⓓ Ⓔ
40 Ⓐ Ⓑ Ⓒ Ⓓ Ⓔ
41 Ⓐ Ⓑ Ⓒ Ⓓ Ⓔ
42 Ⓐ Ⓑ Ⓒ Ⓓ Ⓔ
43 Ⓐ Ⓑ Ⓒ Ⓓ Ⓔ
44 Ⓐ Ⓑ Ⓒ Ⓓ Ⓔ

45 Ⓐ Ⓑ Ⓒ Ⓓ Ⓔ
46 Ⓐ Ⓑ Ⓒ Ⓓ Ⓔ
47 Ⓐ Ⓑ Ⓒ Ⓓ Ⓔ
48 Ⓐ Ⓑ Ⓒ Ⓓ Ⓔ
49 Ⓐ Ⓑ Ⓒ Ⓓ Ⓔ
50 Ⓐ Ⓑ Ⓒ Ⓓ Ⓔ
51 Ⓐ Ⓑ Ⓒ Ⓓ Ⓔ
52 Ⓐ Ⓑ Ⓒ Ⓓ Ⓔ
53 Ⓐ Ⓑ Ⓒ Ⓓ Ⓔ
54 Ⓐ Ⓑ Ⓒ Ⓓ Ⓔ
55 Ⓐ Ⓑ Ⓒ Ⓓ Ⓔ
56 Ⓐ Ⓑ Ⓒ Ⓓ Ⓔ
57 Ⓐ Ⓑ Ⓒ Ⓓ Ⓔ
58 Ⓐ Ⓑ Ⓒ Ⓓ Ⓔ
59 Ⓐ Ⓑ Ⓒ Ⓓ Ⓔ
60 Ⓐ Ⓑ Ⓒ Ⓓ Ⓔ
61 Ⓐ Ⓑ Ⓒ Ⓓ Ⓔ
62 Ⓐ Ⓑ Ⓒ Ⓓ Ⓔ
63 Ⓐ Ⓑ Ⓒ Ⓓ Ⓔ
64 Ⓐ Ⓑ Ⓒ Ⓓ Ⓔ
65 Ⓐ Ⓑ Ⓒ Ⓓ Ⓔ
66 Ⓐ Ⓑ Ⓒ Ⓓ Ⓔ

67 Ⓐ Ⓑ Ⓒ Ⓓ Ⓔ
68 Ⓐ Ⓑ Ⓒ Ⓓ Ⓔ
69 Ⓐ Ⓑ Ⓒ Ⓓ Ⓔ
70 Ⓐ Ⓑ Ⓒ Ⓓ Ⓔ
71 Ⓐ Ⓑ Ⓒ Ⓓ Ⓔ
72 Ⓐ Ⓑ Ⓒ Ⓓ Ⓔ
73 Ⓐ Ⓑ Ⓒ Ⓓ Ⓔ
74 Ⓐ Ⓑ Ⓒ Ⓓ Ⓔ
75 Ⓐ Ⓑ Ⓒ Ⓓ Ⓔ
76 Ⓐ Ⓑ Ⓒ Ⓓ Ⓔ
77 Ⓐ Ⓑ Ⓒ Ⓓ Ⓔ
78 Ⓐ Ⓑ Ⓒ Ⓓ Ⓔ
79 Ⓐ Ⓑ Ⓒ Ⓓ Ⓔ
80 Ⓐ Ⓑ Ⓒ Ⓓ Ⓔ
81 Ⓐ Ⓑ Ⓒ Ⓓ Ⓔ
82 Ⓐ Ⓑ Ⓒ Ⓓ Ⓔ
83 Ⓐ Ⓑ Ⓒ Ⓓ Ⓔ
84 Ⓐ Ⓑ Ⓒ Ⓓ Ⓔ
85 Ⓐ Ⓑ Ⓒ Ⓓ Ⓔ
86 Ⓐ Ⓑ Ⓒ Ⓓ Ⓔ
87 Ⓐ Ⓑ Ⓒ Ⓓ Ⓔ
88 Ⓐ Ⓑ Ⓒ Ⓓ Ⓔ

Memory for Addresses

Time: 5 Minutes. 88 Questions.

DIRECTIONS: Mark your answers on the answer sheet in the section headed "MEMORY FOR ADDRESSES." This test will be scored. You are NOT permitted to look at the boxes. Work from memory, as quickly and as accurately as you can. Correct answers are on page 289.

1. 3700–4099 Love
2. 4800–5199 Rink
3. 3700–4099 Bank
4. Quill
5. Windmill
6. 5200–5399 Bank
7. 5400–5599 Rink
8. 5400–5599 Love
9. Elephant
10. Juggler
11. 4800–5199 Bank
12. 5200–5399 Rink
13. 5200–5399 Love
14. Monsoon
15. Thistle
16. 4100–4799 Love
17. 4100–4799 Rink
18. 4100–4799 Bank
19. Bluff
20. River
21. Chapel
22. 5400–5599 Bank
23. 5400–5599 Love
24. Package
25. Quill
26. 5400–5599 Rink
27. 4800–5199 Rink
28. 4800–5199 Bank
29. 5200–5399 Love
30. Thistle

31. Chapel
32. Bluff
33. 3700–4099 Bank
34. 4100–4799 Bank
35. 4100–4799 Rink
36. 4100–4799 Love
37. Windmill
38. Monsoon
39. Juggler
40. 4800–5199 Love
41. 3700–4099 Rink
42. 5200–5399 Bank
43. 5200–5399 Love
44. 4100–4799 Bank
45. 4800–5199 Rink
46. Juggler
47. Package
48. 5200–5399 Rink
49. 4100–4799 Love
50. 4800–5199 Bank
51. Quill
52. Thistle
53. 5400–5599 Bank
54. 5200–5399 Bank
55. 5400–5599 Rink
56. 3700–4099 Rink
57. Windmill
58. Bluff
59. Elephant
60. 5400–5599 Love

61. 4800–5199 Love
62. 3700–4099 Bank
63. 4100–4799 Rink
64. 3700–4099 Love
65. Monsoon
66. River
67. Chapel
68. 4100–4799 Love
69. 4800–5199 Bank
70. 5400–5599 Rink
71. 3700–4099 Rink
72. 5400–5599 Bank
73. 4100–4799 Love
74. Quill
75. Windmill
76. 5200–5399 Love
77. 4100–4799 Bank
78. 5400–5599 Rink
79. Bluff
80. Chapel
81. 4800–5199 Bank
82. 3700–4099 Love
83. 4800–5199 Love
84. 3700–4099 Bank
85. Juggler
86. Elephant
87. River
88. 4800–5199 Rink

END OF MEMORY FOR ADDRESSES

Part C—Number Series

Sample Questions

The following sample questions show you the type of questions that will be used in Part C. You will have three minutes to answer the sample questions and to study the explanations.

DIRECTIONS: Each number series question consists of a series of numbers that follows some definite order. The numbers progress from left to right according to some rule. One pair of numbers to the right of the series comprises the next two numbers in the series. Study each series to try to find a pattern to the series and to figure out the rule that governs the progression. Choose the answer pair that continues the series according to the pattern established and mark its letter on your answer sheet.

1. 21 24 29 32 37 40 45..........(A) 50 55 (B) 48 51 (C) 50 53 (D) 48 53 (E) 48 55

   Write the direction and degree of change between the numbers of the series. The pattern that emerges is: +3, +5; +3, +5; +3, +5. Continue the series: 45 + 3 = 48 + 5 = 53. (**D**) is the answer.

2. 51 51 30 47 47 30 43..........(A) 43 43 (B) 30 30 (C) 43 30 (D) 30 39 (E) 43 39

   If you look carefully, you realize that 30 is inserted after every two numbers. Ignoring 30 for a moment, the pattern for the remaining numbers is: repeat the number, –4; repeat the number, –4; repeat the number, –4. To continue the series, you must repeat the number 43; then, since the number 30 appears after each set of two numbers, you must insert the number 30. (**C**) is the correct answer. If the series were to continue, the next few numbers would be 39 39 30 35….

3. 8 16 9 18 11 22 15..............(A) 30 23 (B) 12 25 (C) 25 13 (D) 12 44 (E) 30 20

   At first glance this problem looks impossible. You may need to try more than one approach before you can figure out the pattern. Do not allow yourself to be bound by the fact that most of the progressions advance by + or –. The pattern is ×2, –7;×2, –7; ×2, –7. Continue the series: 15× 2 = 30 – 7 = 23. The answer is (**A**).

4. 32 25 86 32 25 86 32..........(A) 32 25 (B) 32 86 (C) 86 25 (D) 26 87 (E) 25 86

   This series follows no mathematical rule. The sequence 32 25 86 simply repeats itself over and over. The answer is (**E**), continuation of the sequence.

5. 75 65 56 48 41 35 30..........(A) 27 23 (B) 26 23 (C) 29 28 (D) 25 20 (E) 26 22

   The pattern is: –10, –9, –8, –7, –6, –5. Continue with: 30 – 4 = 26 – 3 = 23. (**B**) is the answer.

SAMPLE ANSWER SHEET	CORRECT ANSWERS
1. Ⓐ Ⓑ Ⓒ Ⓓ Ⓔ	1. Ⓐ Ⓑ Ⓒ ● Ⓔ
2. Ⓐ Ⓑ Ⓒ Ⓓ Ⓔ	2. Ⓐ Ⓑ ● Ⓓ Ⓔ
3. Ⓐ Ⓑ Ⓒ Ⓓ Ⓔ	3. ● Ⓑ Ⓒ Ⓓ Ⓔ
4. Ⓐ Ⓑ Ⓒ Ⓓ Ⓔ	4. Ⓐ Ⓑ Ⓒ Ⓓ ●
5. Ⓐ Ⓑ Ⓒ Ⓓ Ⓔ	5. Ⓐ ● Ⓒ Ⓓ Ⓔ

Number Series

Time: 20 Minutes. 24 Questions.

DIRECTIONS: Each number series question consists of a series of numbers that follows some definite order. The numbers progress from left to right according to some rule. One lettered pair of numbers comprises the next two numbers in the series. Study each series to try to find a pattern to the series and to figure out the rule that governs the progression. Choose the answer pair that continues the series according to the pattern established and mark its letter on your answer sheet. Correct answers are on page 289.

1. 5 7 30 9 11 30 13 ....(A) 15 16   (B) 15 17   (C) 14 17   (D) 15 30   (E) 30 17

2. 5 7 11 13 17 19 23 ....(A) 27 29   (B) 25 29   (C) 25 27   (D) 27 31   (E) 29 31

3. 9 15 10 17 12 19 15 21 19 ......(A) 23 24   (B) 25 23   (C) 17 23   (D) 23 31   (E) 21 24

4. 34 37 30 33 26 29 22 ....(A) 17 8   (B) 18 11   (C) 25 28   (D) 25 20   (E) 25 18

5. 10 16 12 14 14 12 16 ....(A) 14 12   (B) 10 18   (C) 10 14   (D) 14 18   (E) 14 16

6. 11 12 18 11 13 19 11 14 ....(A) 18 11   (B) 16 11   (C) 20 11   (D) 11 21   (E) 17 11

7. 20 9 8 19 10 9 18 11 10 ...(A) 19 11   (B) 17 10   (C) 19 12   (D) 17 12   (E) 19 10

8. 28 27 26 31 30 29 34 ....(A) 36 32   (B) 32 31   (C) 33 32   (D) 33 36   (E) 35 36

9. 12 24 15 30 21 42 33 ....(A) 66 57   (B) 44 56   (C) 28 43   (D) 47 69   (E) 24 48

10. 46 76 51 70 56 64 61 ....(A) 61 68   (B) 69 71   (C) 58 65   (D) 66 71   (E) 58 66

11. 37 28 28 19 19 10 10 ....(A) 9 9   (B) 1 1   (C) 10 9   (D) 10 1   (E) 9 1

12. 1 2 3 6 4 5 6 15 7 ....(A) 8 15   (B) 7 8   (C) 8 9   (D) 9 17   (E) 9 24

13. 55 51 12 56 52 12 57 ....(A) 57 12   (B) 12 53   (C) 58 12   (D) 53 12   (E) 12 57

14. 75 75 8 50 50 9 25 ....(A) 25 25   (B) 25 10   (C) 10 25   (D) 25 12   (E) 10 10

15. 1 2 3 4 5 5 4 ....(A) 3 2   (B) 5 4   (C) 4 5   (D) 5 6   (E) 4 4

16. 3 6 9 4 7 10 5 ....(A) 8 9   (B) 9 6   (C) 8 11   (D) 9 12   (E) 11 8

17. 5 7 9 18 20 22 44 ....(A) 60 66   (B) 66 80   (C) 66 68   (D) 88 90   (E) 46 48

18. 94 82 72 64 58 54 ....(A) 52 50   (B) 54 52   (C) 50 46   (D) 52 52   (E) 54 50

19. 85 85 86 85 86 87 85 ....(A) 85 86   (B) 86 87   (C) 87 89   (D) 87 86   (E) 84 83

20. 99 89 79 69 59 49 39 ....(A) 29 19   (B) 39 29   (C) 38 37   (D) 39 38   (E) 19 9

21. 33 42 41 39 48 47 45 ....(A) 42 41   (B) 44 42   (C) 54 53   (D) 54 52   (E) 54 63

22. 85 89 89 84 88 88 83 ....(A) 83 87   (B) 83 83   (C) 87 87   (D) 87 82   (E) 87 83

23. 1 2 3 3 4 5 5 6 7 ....(A) 7 7   (B) 8 8   (C) 8 9   (D) 7 6   (E) 7 8

24. 5 10 15 15 20 15 25 ....(A) 30 35   (B) 15 30   (C) 15 15   (D) 30 15   (E) 30 30

END OF NUMBER SERIES

Part D—Following Oral Instructions

Directions and Sample Questions

LISTENING TO INSTRUCTIONS: When you are ready to try these sample questions, give the following instructions to a friend and have the friend read them aloud to you at the rate of 80 words per minute. Do not read them to yourself. Your friend will need a watch with a second hand. Listen carefully and do exactly what your friend tells you to do with the worksheet and answer sheet. Your friend will tell you some things to do with each item on the worksheet. After each set of instructions, your friend will give you time to mark your answer by darkening a circle on the sample answer sheet. Since B and D sound very much alike, your friend will say "B as in baker" when he or she means B and "D as in dog" when he or she means D.

> **Before proceeding further, tear out the worksheet on page 279. Then hand this book to your friend.**

TO THE PERSON WHO IS TO READ THE INSTRUCTIONS: The instructions are to be read at the rate of 80 words per minute. Do not read aloud the material which is in parentheses. Do not repeat any instructions.

Read Aloud to the Candidate

Look at line 1 on your worksheet. (Pause slightly.) Draw a line under all the odd numbers between 5 and 14 that cannot be divided by 3. (Pause 10 seconds.) Now, on your answer sheet, darken the space for the letter D as in dog next to the number or numbers that you have underlined. (Pause 10 seconds.)

Look at line 2 on your worksheet. (Pause slightly.) In each circle there is a time when the mail must leave. In the circle for the earliest time, write on the line the last two figures of the time. (Pause 5 seconds.) Now, on your answer sheet, darken the space for the number-letter combination that is in the circle you just wrote in. (Pause 5 seconds.)

Look at line 2 again. (Pause slightly.) Find the circle with the latest time and write on the line the last two figures of the time. (Pause 5 seconds.) Now, on your answer sheet, darken the space for the number-letter combination that is in the circle you just wrote in. (Pause 5 seconds.)

Look at line 3 on your worksheet. (Pause slightly.) Draw two lines under every number between 7 and 15 that is odd. (Pause 10 seconds.) Now, on your answer sheet, for every number that you drew two lines under, darken space B as in baker. (Pause 10 seconds.)

Sample Worksheet

DIRECTIONS: Listening carefully to each set of instructions, mark each item on this worksheet as directed. Then complete each question by marking the sample answer sheet below as directed. For each answer you will darken the answer for a number-letter combination. Should you fall behind and miss an instruction, don't become excited. Let that one go and listen for the next one. If, when you start to darken a space for a number, you find that you have already darkened another space for that number, either erase the first mark and darken the space for the new combination or let the first mark stay and do not darken a space for the new combination. Write with a pencil that has a clean eraser. When you finish, you should have no more than one space darkened for each number.

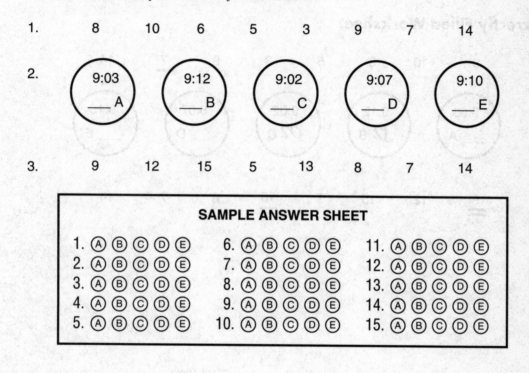

1. 8   10   6   5   3   9   7   14

2. 9:03 ___A   9:12 ___B   9:02 ___C   9:07 ___D   9:10 ___E

3. 9   12   15   5   13   8   7   14

SAMPLE ANSWER SHEET

1. Ⓐ Ⓑ Ⓒ Ⓓ Ⓔ   6. Ⓐ Ⓑ Ⓒ Ⓓ Ⓔ   11. Ⓐ Ⓑ Ⓒ Ⓓ Ⓔ
2. Ⓐ Ⓑ Ⓒ Ⓓ Ⓔ   7. Ⓐ Ⓑ Ⓒ Ⓓ Ⓔ   12. Ⓐ Ⓑ Ⓒ Ⓓ Ⓔ
3. Ⓐ Ⓑ Ⓒ Ⓓ Ⓔ   8. Ⓐ Ⓑ Ⓒ Ⓓ Ⓔ   13. Ⓐ Ⓑ Ⓒ Ⓓ Ⓔ
4. Ⓐ Ⓑ Ⓒ Ⓓ Ⓔ   9. Ⓐ Ⓑ Ⓒ Ⓓ Ⓔ   14. Ⓐ Ⓑ Ⓒ Ⓓ Ⓔ
5. Ⓐ Ⓑ Ⓒ Ⓓ Ⓔ   10. Ⓐ Ⓑ Ⓒ Ⓓ Ⓔ   15. Ⓐ Ⓑ Ⓒ Ⓓ Ⓔ

TEAR HERE

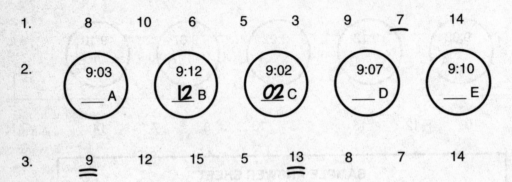

CORRECT ANSWERS TO SAMPLE QUESTIONS

1. (A) (B) (C) (D) (E) 6. (A) (B) (C) (D) (E) 11. (A) (B) (C) (D) (E)
2. (A) (B) ● (D) (E) 7. (A) (B) (C) ● (E) 12. (A) ● (C) (D) (E)
3. (A) (B) (C) (D) (E) 8. (A) (B) (C) (D) (E) 13. (A) ● (C) (D) (E)
4. (A) (B) (C) (D) (E) 9. (A) ● (C) (D) (E) 14. (A) (B) (C) (D) (E)
5. (A) (B) (C) (D) (E) 10. (A) (B) (C) (D) (E) 15. (A) (B) (C) (D) (E)

Correctly Filled Worksheet

1. 8 10 6 5 3 9 <u>7</u> 14

2.
| 9:03 ___A | 9:12 <u>12</u> B | 9:02 <u>02</u> C | 9:07 ___D | 9:10 ___E |

3. <u>9</u> 12 15 5 <u>13</u> 8 7 14

Following Oral Instructions

Time: 25 Minutes.

Listening to Instructions

DIRECTIONS: When you are ready to try this test of the Model Exam, give the following instructions to a friend and have the friend read them aloud to you at the rate of 80 words per minute. Do NOT read them to yourself. Your friend will need a watch with a second hand. Listen carefully and do exactly what your friend tells you to do with the worksheet and with the answer sheet. Your friend will tell you some things to do with each item on the worksheet. After each set of instructions, your friend will give you time to mark your answer by darkening a circle on the answer sheet. Since B and D sound very much alike, your friend will say "B as in baker" when he or she means B and "D as in dog" when he or she means D.

> **Before proceeding further, tear out the worksheet on page 285 of this test. Then hand this book to your friend.**

TO THE PERSON WHO IS TO READ THE INSTRUCTIONS: The instructions are to be read at the rate of 80 words per minute. Do not read aloud the material that is in parentheses. Once you have begun the test itself, do not repeat any instructions. The next three paragraphs consist of approximately 120 words. Read these three paragraphs aloud to the candidate in about one and one-half minutes. You may reread these paragraphs as often as necessary to establish an 80-words-per-minute reading speed.

Read Aloud to the Candidate

On the job you will have to listen to instructions and then do what you have been told to do. In this test, I will read instructions to you. Try to understand them as I read them; I cannot repeat them. Once we begin, you may not ask any questions until the end of the test.

On the job you won't have to deal with pictures, numbers, and letters like those in the test, but you will have to listen to instructions and follow them. We are using this test to see how well you can follow instructions.

You are to mark your test booklet according to the instructions that I'll read to you. After each set of instructions, I'll give you time to record your answers on the separate answer sheet.

The actual test begins now.

Look at line 1 on your worksheet. (Pause slightly.) Draw a line under the sixth number in line 1. (Pause 2 seconds.) Now, on your answer sheet, darken space E for the number under which you just drew a line. (Pause 5 seconds.)

Look at line 1 again. (Pause slightly.) Draw two lines under the third number on the line. (Pause 2 seconds.) Now, on your answer sheet, darken space B as in baker for the number under which you drew two lines. (Pause 5 seconds.)

Look at line 2 on your worksheet. (Pause slightly.) Find the letter that is fifth in the alphabet and circle it. (Pause 2 seconds.) Now darken that letter for number 77 on your answer sheet. (Pause 5 seconds.)

Look at line 3 on your worksheet. (Pause slightly.) Write the number 17 in the third box. (Pause 2 seconds.) Now, on your answer sheet, darken the number-letter combination that is in the box you just wrote in. (Pause 5 seconds.)

Look at line 3 again. (Pause slightly.) In the fourth box, write the number of hours in a day. (Pause 2 seconds.) Now, on your answer sheet, darken the number-letter combination that is in the box you just wrote in. (Pause 5 seconds.)

Look at line 4 on your worksheet. (Pause slightly.) Write D as in dog in the circle right next to the second-lowest number. (Pause 5 seconds.) Now, on your answer sheet, darken the space for the number-letter combination in the circle you just wrote in. (Pause 5 seconds.)

Look at line 4 again. (Pause slightly.) Write the letter C on the line in the middle circle. (Pause 2 seconds.) Now, on your answer sheet, darken the space for the number-letter combination in the circle you just wrote in. (Pause 5 seconds.)

Look at line 5 on your worksheet. Each box represents a letter carrier and the amount of money that he or she collected on the route in one day. (Pause slightly.) Find the carrier who collected the smallest amount of money that day and circle his or her letter. (Pause 2 seconds.) On your answer sheet, darken the number-letter combination in the box in which you circled a letter. (Pause 5 seconds.)

Look at line 6 on your worksheet. (Pause slightly.) Write the first letter of the third means of transportation on the second line. (Pause 8 seconds.) Write the last letter of the first means of transportation on the first line. (Pause 8 seconds.) Write the middle letter of the middle means of transportation on the last line. (Pause 8 seconds.) Now, on your answer sheet, darken the number-letter combinations on the three lines. (Pause 15 seconds.)

Look at line 7 on your worksheet. (Pause slightly.) Reading right to left, find the first number that is higher than the number 39 and draw a box around the number. (Pause 5 seconds.) Now, on your answer sheet, darken D as in dog for the number around which you just drew a box. (Pause 5 seconds.)

Look at line 8 on your worksheet. (Pause slightly.) Find, on line 8, the letter that appears first in the alphabet and underline that letter. (Pause 5 seconds.) Now, on your answer sheet, darken that letter for space number 1. (Pause 5 seconds.)

Look at line 9 on your worksheet. (Pause slightly.) In the figure with the least number of points, write the letter A. (Pause 2 seconds.) In the figure with the greatest number of points, write the letter E. (Pause 2 seconds.) Now, on your answer sheet, darken the number-letter combinations in the two figures you just wrote in. (Pause 10 seconds.)

Look at line 10 on your worksheet. (Pause slightly.) If the third number in line 10 should, in normal counting, appear before the fourth number in line 10, write the letter B as in baker above the third number; if not, write the letter A above the fourth number. (Pause 5 seconds.) Now, on your answer sheet, darken the number-letter combination of the number you just wrote in. (Pause 5 seconds.)

Look at line 11 on your worksheet. (Pause slightly.) Write the letter A in the second box. (Pause 2 seconds.) Now, on your answer sheet, darken the number-letter combination in the box you just wrote in. (Pause 5 seconds.)

Look at line 11 again. (Pause slightly.) If the number in the smallest box is greater than the number in the first box, write the letter C in the largest box (pause 5 seconds); if not, write the letter D as in dog in the largest box. (Pause 2 seconds.) Now, on your answer sheet, darken the number-letter combination in the box you just wrote in. (Pause 5 seconds.)

Look at line 12 on your worksheet. (Pause slightly.) Draw one line under each number that falls between 75 and 90 and is even. (Pause 8 seconds.) Now, on your answer sheet, blacken space D as in dog for each number that you drew one line under. (Pause 10 seconds.)

Look at line 12 again. (Pause slightly.) Draw two lines under each number that falls between 75 and 90 and is odd. (Pause 8 seconds.) Now, on your answer sheet, darken space E for each number under which you drew two lines. (Pause 5 seconds.)

Look at line 13 on your worksheet. (Pause slightly.) Write the letter A in the left-hand circle. (Pause 2 seconds.) Now, on your answer sheet, darken the space for the number-letter combination in the figure you just wrote in. (Pause 5 seconds.)

Look at line 13 again. (Pause slightly.) Write the letter B as in baker in the right-hand square. (Pause 2 seconds.) Now, on your answer sheet, darken the space for the number-letter combination in the figure in which you just wrote. (Pause 5 seconds.)

Look at line 14 on your worksheet. (Pause slightly.) Write the answer to this question at the end of line 14: $22 \times 2 =$. (Pause 2 seconds.) Find the answer that you wrote among the numbers on line 14 (pause 2 seconds) and darken that number-letter combination on your answer sheet. (Pause 5 seconds.)

Look at line 15 on your worksheet. (Pause slightly.) If 3 is less than 5 and more than 7, write the letter E next to number 89 (pause 5 seconds); if not, write the letter E next to number 61. (Pause 2 seconds.) Now, on your answer sheet, darken the number-letter combination of the line you just wrote on. (Pause 5 seconds.)

Look at line 16 on your worksheet. (Pause slightly.) Count the number of V's on line 16 and write the number at the end of the line. (Pause 2 seconds.) Now, add 11 to that number and, on your answer sheet, darken space D as in dog for the number of V's plus 11. (Pause 10 seconds.)

Look at line 17 on your worksheet. (Pause slightly.) Each time represents the scheduled arrival time of a mail truck. Write the letter A on the line beside the earliest scheduled time. (Pause 2 seconds.) Write the letter C next to the latest scheduled time. (Pause 2 seconds.) Now, on your answer sheet, darken the number-letter combinations of the last two digits of the times beside which you wrote letters. (Pause 10 seconds.)

Look at line 18 on your worksheet. (Pause slightly.) If in one day there are more hours before noon than after noon, write the number 47 in the second circle (pause 2 seconds); if not, write the number 38 in the first circle. (Pause 2 seconds.) Now, on your answer sheet, blacken the space for the number-letter combination in the circle in which you just wrote. (Pause 5 seconds.)

Look at line 18 again. (Pause slightly.) Write the number 69 in the second circle from the right. (Pause 2 seconds.) Now, on your answer sheet, darken the space for the number-letter combination in the circle in which you just wrote. (Pause 5 seconds.)

Look at line 19 on your worksheet. (Pause slightly.) Write the smallest of these numbers in the first box: 84, 35, 73. (Pause 5 seconds.) Now, on your answer sheet, darken the space for the number-letter combination in the figure in which you just wrote. (Pause 5 seconds.)

Following Oral Instructions

Worksheet

DIRECTIONS: Listening carefully to each set of instructions, mark each item on this worksheet as directed. Then complete each question by marking the answer sheet as directed. For each answer you will darken the answer for a number-letter combination. Should you fall behind and miss an instruction, don't become excited. Let that one go and listen for the next one. If, when you start to darken a space for a number, you find that you have already darkened another space for that number, either erase the first mark and darken the space for the new combination or let the first mark stay and do not darken a space for the new combination. Write with a pencil that has a clean eraser. When you finish, you should have no more than one space darkened for each number. Correct answers are on page 292.

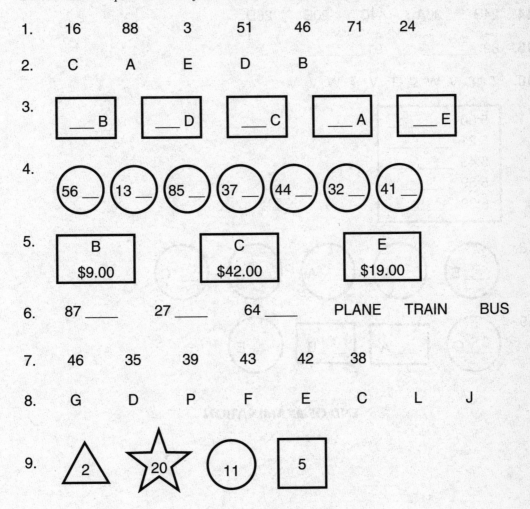

1. 16   88   3   51   46   71   24

2. C   A   E   D   B

3. ___B   ___D   ___C   ___A   ___E

4. 56___   13___   85___   37___   44___   32___   41___

5. B $9.00   C $42.00   E $19.00

6. 87 ____   27 ____   64 ____   PLANE   TRAIN   BUS

7. 46   35   39   43   42   38

8. G   D   P   F   E   C   L   J

9. 2   20   11   5

TEAR HERE

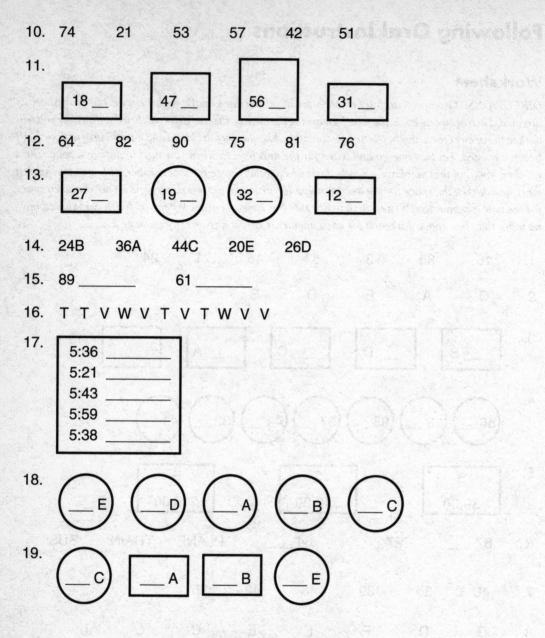

10.   74   21   53   57   42   51

11.

    [18 __]   [47 __]   [56 __]   [31 __]

12.   64   82   90   75   81   76

13.

    [27 __]   (19 __)   (32 __)   [12 __]

14.   24B   36A   44C   20E   26D

15.   89 _____   61 _____

16.   T T V W V T V T W V V

17.
    5:36 _____
    5:21 _____
    5:43 _____
    5:59 _____
    5:38 _____

18.   (__ E)   (__ D)   (__ A)   (__ B)   (__ C)

19.   (__ C)   [__ A]   [__ B]   (__ E)

END OF EXAMINATION

Correct Answers for Final Model Exam

Part A—Address Checking

1. A	13. D	25. A	37. A	49. A	61. D	73. A	85. A
2. D	14. D	26. A	38. D	50. A	62. D	74. D	86. A
3. D	15. A	27. D	39. D	51. D	63. D	75. A	87. D
4. A	16. A	28. D	40. A	52. A	64. A	76. D	88. A
5. A	17. A	29. A	41. D	53. A	65. D	77. D	89. D
6. D	18. A	30. D	42. A	54. D	66. D	78. D	90. D
7. D	19. A	31. A	43. D	55. D	67. D	79. A	91. D
8. D	20. D	32. A	44. D	56. A	68. A	80. A	92. A
9. D	21. D	33. D	45. A	57. A	69. A	81. D	93. A
10. D	22. A	34. D	46. A	58. A	70. D	82. A	94. D
11. A	23. A	35. D	47. D	59. D	71. A	83. D	95. A
12. A	24. D	36. A	48. A	60. A	72. D	84. A	

Analyzing Your Errors

Type of Error	Tally	Total Number
Number of addresses that were alike and you incorrectly marked "different"		
Number of addresses that were different and you incorrectly marked "alike"		
Number of addresses in which you missed a difference in NUMBERS		
Number of addresses in which you missed a difference in ABBREVIATIONS		
Number of addresses in which you missed a difference in NAMES		

Part B—Memory for Addresses

Practice I

1. C	12. C	23. A	34. A	45. A	56. D	67. A	78. D
2. E	13. E	24. A	35. E	46. E	57. E	68. B	79. C
3. B	14. A	25. C	36. E	47. C	58. B	69. E	80. A
4. C	15. B	26. C	37. C	48. D	59. B	70. E	81. B
5. D	16. E	27. C	38. D	49. A	60. A	71. E	82. B
6. C	17. D	28. B	39. D	50. D	61. A	72. D	83. D
7. D	18. D	29. E	40. A	51. D	62. D	73. C	84. B
8. A	19. A	30. D	41. B	52. C	63. D	74. A	85. E
9. D	20. E	31. B	42. B	53. E	64. B	75. C	86. B
10. E	21. D	32. A	43. D	54. C	65. C	76. B	87. E
11. A	22. E	33. B	44. C	55. B	66. C	77. A	88. C

Practice II

1. E	12. A	23. A	34. E	45. D	56. B	67. E	78. E
2. D	13. E	24. C	35. D	46. A	57. A	68. A	79. E
3. C	14. B	25. C	36. E	47. B	58. A	69. D	80. C
4. B	15. E	26. B	37. D	48. E	59. D	70. C	81. A
5. A	16. B	27. D	38. C	49. A	60. D	71. C	82. D
6. A	17. B	28. C	39. C	50. B	61. B	72. A	83. B
7. D	18. A	29. E	40. B	51. C	62. C	73. D	84. B
8. D	19. E	30. A	41. A	52. E	63. E	74. B	85. C
9. B	20. C	31. A	42. E	53. E	64. B	75. E	86. C
10. C	21. D	32. B	43. D	54. D	65. A	76. C	87. B
11. E	22. D	33. C	44. C	55. C	66. B	77. E	88. D

Practice III

1. C	12. D	23. D	34. E	45. A	56. C	67. D	78. E
2. A	13. C	24. A	35. E	46. C	57. B	68. D	79. C
3. E	14. B	25. B	36. B	47. C	58. D	69. E	80. B
4. A	15. D	26. C	37. A	48. D	59. A	70. C	81. D
5. E	16. E	27. C	38. D	49. E	60. E	71. B	82. E
6. C	17. E	28. A	39. D	50. B	61. E	72. C	83. B
7. A	18. B	29. D	40. E	51. A	62. D	73. B	84. B
8. D	19. A	30. C	41. D	52. C	63. D	74. A	85. A
9. E	20. E	31. D	42. B	53. E	64. A	75. E	86. E
10. B	21. A	32. A	43. D	54. A	65. C	76. C	87. C
11. C	22. E	33. B	44. C	55. A	66. A	77. A	88. C

Memory for Addresses

1. B	12. B	23. A	34. E	45. C	56. A	67. A	78. E
2. C	13. E	24. B	35. D	46. C	57. D	68. C	79. C
3. C	14. E	25. E	36. C	47. B	58. C	69. A	80. A
4. E	15. D	26. E	37. D	48. B	59. B	70. E	81. A
5. D	16. C	27. C	38. E	49. C	60. A	71. A	82. B
6. D	17. D	28. A	39. C	50. A	61. D	72. B	83. D
7. E	18. E	29. E	40. D	51. E	62. C	73. C	84. C
8. A	19. C	30. D	41. A	52. D	63. D	74. E	85. C
9. B	20. A	31. A	42. D	53. B	64. B	75. D	86. B
10. C	21. A	32. C	43. E	54. D	65. E	76. E	87. A
11. A	22. B	33. C	44. E	55. E	66. A	77. E	88. C

Part C—Number Series

1. D	4. E	7. D	10. E	13. D	16. C	19. B	22. C
2. B	5. B	8. C	11. B	14. B	17. E	20. A	23. E
3. A	6. C	9. A	12. C	15. A	18. D	21. C	24. D

Explanations

1. **(D)** The series increases by +2. The number <u>30</u> appears after each two numbers in the series.

2. **(B)** The pattern is: +2, +4; +2, +4; +2, +4; etc.

3. **(A)** There are two alternating series that advance according to different rules. The first series begins with <u>9</u>. The rule for this series is +1, +2, +3, +4, +5. The alternating series begins with <u>15</u> and advances in steady increments of +2.

4. **(E)** There are two alternating series, one series beginning with <u>34</u> and the other with <u>37</u>. Both series decrease by subtracting 4 each time.

5. **(B)** The two series are moving in opposite directions. The first series begins with <u>10</u> and increases by +2. The alternating series begins with <u>16</u> and decreases by –2.

6. **(C)** You may be able to figure this one by reading it rhythmically. If not, consider that there are two series, one beginning with <u>12</u>, the other with <u>18</u>. Both series advance by +1. The number <u>11</u> separates each progression of the two series.

7. **(D)** There are two series alternating at the rate of 1 to 2. The first series decreases by –1: 20 19 18 <u>17</u>. The other series goes one step backward and two steps forward, or –1, +2. Read: $9\,^{-1}\,8\,^{+2}\,10\,^{-1}\,9\,^{+2}\,11\,^{-1}\,10\,^{+2}\,\underline{12}$.

8. **(C)** The pattern is –1, –1, +5, and repeat; –1, –1, +5, and repeat again.

9. **(A)** The pattern is: ×2, –9; ×2, –9; . . .

10. **(E)** There are two alternating series. The first series increases by +5. The alternating series decreases at the rate of –6.

11. **(B)** The pattern is –9 and repeat the number; –9 and repeat the number; –9 and repeat the number.

12. **(C)** The series is: 1 2 3 4 5 6 7 8 . . . . After each three numbers in the series we find the sum of those three numbers. So: 1 + 2 + 3 = 6; 4 + 5 + 6 = 15; 7 + <u>8</u> + <u>9</u> = 24; 10 . . . .

13. **(D)** The pattern is –4, +5, and the number <u>12</u>; –4, +5, and the number <u>12</u> . . . .

14. **(B)** There are two series. One series proceeds: repeat the number, –25; repeat the number, –25. The other series simply advances by +1.

15. **(A)** The series proceeds upwards from <u>1</u> to <u>5</u>, then turns around and descends, one number at a time.

16. **(C)** There are two interpretations for this series. You may see +3, +3, –5; +3, +3, –5 . . . . Or, you might see a series of +3, +3 mini-series, each mini-series beginning at a number one higher than the beginning number of the previous mini-series.

17. **(E)** The pattern is: +2, +2, ×2; +2, +2, ×2 . . . .

18. **(D)** The pattern is: –12, –10, –8, –6, –4, –2, –0 . . . .

19. **(B)** Each mini-series begins with <u>85</u>. With each cycle the series progresses to one more number: 85; 85 86; 85 86 87; 85 86 87 88 . . . .

20. **(A)** This is a simple –10 series.

21. **(C)** The pattern is: +9, –1, –2; +9, –1, –2 . . . .

22. (**C**) The pattern is +4, repeat the number, –5; +4, repeat the number, –5; +4 . . . . You might instead have seen two descending series, one beginning with <u>85</u> and descending by –1, the other beginning with <u>89</u> and repeating itself before each descent.

23. (**E**) This is a deceptive series. Actually, the series consists of a series of mini-series, each beginning with the last number of the previous mini-series. If you group the numbers, you can see: 1 2 3; 3 4 5; 5 6 7; <u>7</u> <u>8</u> . . . .

24. (**D**) The series is a +5 series with the number <u>15</u> interposing after each two numbers of the series. If you substitute <u>X</u> for the interposing <u>15</u>, you can see that the series reads: 5 10 X 15 20 X 25 30 X.

Part D—Following Oral Instructions

Correctly Filled Answer Grid

1 Ⓐ Ⓑ ● Ⓓ Ⓔ	23 Ⓐ Ⓑ Ⓒ Ⓓ Ⓔ	45 Ⓐ Ⓑ Ⓒ Ⓓ Ⓔ	67 Ⓐ Ⓑ Ⓒ Ⓓ Ⓔ
2 Ⓐ Ⓑ Ⓒ Ⓓ Ⓔ	24 ● Ⓑ Ⓒ Ⓓ Ⓔ	46 Ⓐ Ⓑ Ⓒ Ⓓ Ⓔ	68 Ⓐ Ⓑ Ⓒ Ⓓ Ⓔ
3 Ⓐ ● Ⓒ Ⓓ Ⓔ	25 Ⓐ Ⓑ Ⓒ Ⓓ Ⓔ	47 ● Ⓑ Ⓒ Ⓓ Ⓔ	69 Ⓐ ● Ⓒ Ⓓ Ⓔ
4 Ⓐ Ⓑ Ⓒ Ⓓ Ⓔ	26 Ⓐ Ⓑ Ⓒ Ⓓ Ⓔ	48 Ⓐ Ⓑ Ⓒ Ⓓ Ⓔ	70 Ⓐ Ⓑ Ⓒ Ⓓ Ⓔ
5 Ⓐ Ⓑ Ⓒ Ⓓ Ⓔ	27 Ⓐ ● Ⓒ Ⓓ Ⓔ	49 Ⓐ Ⓑ Ⓒ Ⓓ Ⓔ	71 Ⓐ Ⓑ Ⓒ Ⓓ ●
6 Ⓐ Ⓑ Ⓒ Ⓓ Ⓔ	28 Ⓐ Ⓑ Ⓒ Ⓓ Ⓔ	50 Ⓐ Ⓑ Ⓒ Ⓓ Ⓔ	72 Ⓐ Ⓑ Ⓒ Ⓓ Ⓔ
7 Ⓐ Ⓑ Ⓒ Ⓓ Ⓔ	29 Ⓐ Ⓑ Ⓒ Ⓓ Ⓔ	51 Ⓐ Ⓑ Ⓒ Ⓓ Ⓔ	73 Ⓐ Ⓑ Ⓒ Ⓓ Ⓔ
8 Ⓐ Ⓑ Ⓒ Ⓓ Ⓔ	30 Ⓐ Ⓑ Ⓒ Ⓓ Ⓔ	52 Ⓐ Ⓑ Ⓒ Ⓓ Ⓔ	74 Ⓐ Ⓑ Ⓒ Ⓓ Ⓔ
9 Ⓐ ● Ⓒ Ⓓ Ⓔ	31 Ⓐ Ⓑ Ⓒ Ⓓ Ⓔ	53 Ⓐ ● Ⓒ Ⓓ Ⓔ	75 Ⓐ Ⓑ Ⓒ Ⓓ Ⓔ
10 Ⓐ Ⓑ Ⓒ Ⓓ Ⓔ	32 Ⓐ Ⓑ Ⓒ ● Ⓔ	54 Ⓐ Ⓑ Ⓒ Ⓓ Ⓔ	76 Ⓐ Ⓑ Ⓒ ● Ⓔ
11 ● Ⓑ Ⓒ Ⓓ Ⓔ	33 Ⓐ Ⓑ Ⓒ Ⓓ Ⓔ	55 Ⓐ Ⓑ Ⓒ Ⓓ Ⓔ	77 Ⓐ Ⓑ Ⓒ Ⓓ ●
12 Ⓐ ● Ⓒ Ⓓ Ⓔ	34 Ⓐ Ⓑ Ⓒ Ⓓ Ⓔ	56 Ⓐ Ⓑ ● Ⓓ Ⓔ	78 Ⓐ Ⓑ Ⓒ Ⓓ Ⓔ
13 Ⓐ Ⓑ Ⓒ Ⓓ Ⓔ	35 ● Ⓑ Ⓒ Ⓓ Ⓔ	57 Ⓐ Ⓑ Ⓒ Ⓓ Ⓔ	79 Ⓐ Ⓑ Ⓒ Ⓓ Ⓔ
14 Ⓐ Ⓑ Ⓒ Ⓓ Ⓔ	36 Ⓐ Ⓑ Ⓒ Ⓓ Ⓔ	58 Ⓐ Ⓑ Ⓒ Ⓓ Ⓔ	80 Ⓐ Ⓑ Ⓒ Ⓓ Ⓔ
15 Ⓐ Ⓑ Ⓒ Ⓓ Ⓔ	37 Ⓐ Ⓑ ● Ⓓ Ⓔ	59 Ⓐ Ⓑ ● Ⓓ Ⓔ	81 Ⓐ Ⓑ Ⓒ Ⓓ ●
16 Ⓐ Ⓑ Ⓒ ● Ⓔ	38 Ⓐ Ⓑ Ⓒ Ⓓ ●	60 Ⓐ Ⓑ Ⓒ Ⓓ Ⓔ	82 Ⓐ Ⓑ Ⓒ ● Ⓔ
17 Ⓐ Ⓑ ● Ⓓ Ⓔ	39 Ⓐ Ⓑ Ⓒ Ⓓ Ⓔ	61 Ⓐ Ⓑ Ⓒ Ⓓ ●	83 Ⓐ Ⓑ Ⓒ Ⓓ Ⓔ
18 Ⓐ Ⓑ Ⓒ Ⓓ Ⓔ	40 Ⓐ Ⓑ Ⓒ Ⓓ Ⓔ	62 Ⓐ Ⓑ Ⓒ Ⓓ Ⓔ	84 Ⓐ Ⓑ Ⓒ Ⓓ Ⓔ
19 ● Ⓑ Ⓒ Ⓓ Ⓔ	41 Ⓐ Ⓑ Ⓒ Ⓓ Ⓔ	63 Ⓐ Ⓑ Ⓒ Ⓓ Ⓔ	85 Ⓐ Ⓑ Ⓒ Ⓓ Ⓔ
20 Ⓐ Ⓑ Ⓒ Ⓓ ●	42 Ⓐ Ⓑ Ⓒ ● Ⓔ	64 ● Ⓑ Ⓒ Ⓓ Ⓔ	86 Ⓐ Ⓑ Ⓒ Ⓓ Ⓔ
21 ● Ⓑ Ⓒ Ⓓ Ⓔ	43 Ⓐ Ⓑ Ⓒ Ⓓ Ⓔ	65 Ⓐ Ⓑ Ⓒ Ⓓ Ⓔ	87 Ⓐ Ⓑ Ⓒ Ⓓ ●
22 Ⓐ Ⓑ Ⓒ Ⓓ Ⓔ	44 Ⓐ Ⓑ ● Ⓓ Ⓔ	66 Ⓐ Ⓑ Ⓒ Ⓓ Ⓔ	88 Ⓐ Ⓑ Ⓒ Ⓓ Ⓔ

Correctly Filled Worksheet

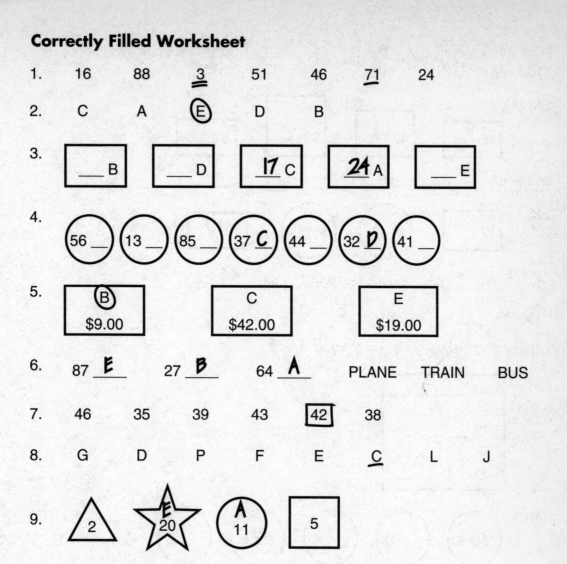

1.   16   88   <u>3</u>   51   46   <u>71</u>   24

2.   C   A   Ⓔ   D   B

3.   [___ B]   [___ D]   [<u>17</u> C]   [<u>24</u> A]   [___ E]

4.   (56 __) (13 __) (85 __) (37 <u>C</u>) (44 __) (32 <u>D</u>) (41 __)

5.   [Ⓑ $9.00]   [C $42.00]   [E $19.00]

6.   87 <u>E</u>   27 B   64 A   PLANE   TRAIN   BUS

7.   46   35   39   43   [42]   38

8.   G   D   P   F   E   <u>C</u>   L   J

9.   △2   ☆E/20   ⓐ11   □5

10. 74   21   *B*
                   53   57   42   51

11.

| 18 __ | | 47 **A** | | 56 **C** | | 31 __ |

12. 64   82   90   75   81   76

13.

| 27 __ | (19 **A**)   (32 __) | 12 **B** |

14. 24B   36A   44C   20E   26D   *44*

15. 89 _____   61 _____ *E* _____

16. T T V W V T V T W V V   *5*

17.

5:36 _____
5:21 ___ **A** ___
5:43 _____
5:59 ___ **C** ___
5:38 _____

18. (*38* E)   (___ D)   (___ A)   (*69* B)   (___ C)

19. (___ C) | *35* A | | ___ B | (___ E)

Progress Charts

Darken the column up to your score for each test of the exam.

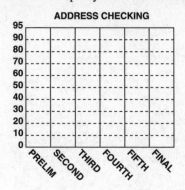

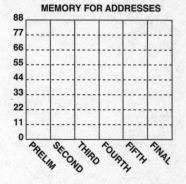

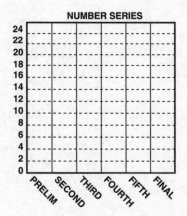

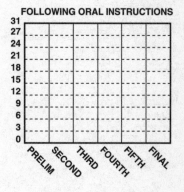

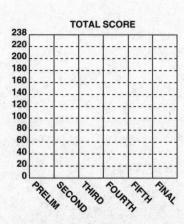